TABLE OF CONTENTS

D1122604

THE BURNING LEGION RETURNS

We who fought in the Third War never deceived ourselves that the war had put an end to the Burning Legion. Kil'jaeden and his vast army were cut off from Azeroth, but not indefinitely. Yet with the threat of all-out war between Horde and Alliance, and the continuing danger of the Scourge, what could we do about the Legion? How could we prepare for a war that might be millennia in the future when so much conflict was already at our doorstep?

Now that the Dark Portal has been reactivated, we must reevaluate our priorities. The world of Draenor did not, after all, perish under the strain of the magical portals Ner'zhul created eighteen years ago. Rather, Draenor has been reduced to the shattered territories of Outland, where, just as rumor had it, the demon Illidan Stormrage is fighting to solidify his power base.

Many of the loved ones we thought had perished with Draenor may in fact have survived the hardships of life on Outland. Sizable tracts of land have been largely untouched by either fel magic or Ner'zhul's reckless sorcery. Better still, the Alliance and Horde have recently gained new allies in the draenei and blood elves, respectively.

Nonetheless, the reactivation of the Dark Portal is a two-edged sword. Illidan and his allies are fighting to keep all the other portals of Outland closed, but his loyalties and capabilities remain an open question. Should even one portal be reopened, the forces of the Legion would pour into Outland. Their almost inevitable triumph over Illidan would set off a chain reaction—countless worlds falling to the Legion—that Azeroth has little hope of withstanding.

In the interests of preventing such a scenario, we have dispatched a number of scouts to bring back information from Outland. Today we understand the current layout and disposition of the enemies waiting beyond the Dark Portal. We have compiled maps, bestiaries, and strategies, all of which are provided herein. Knowledge will be the key to our conquest of Outland.

Make no mistake: the tensions between Horde and Alliance did not arise overnight. They were not the work of a whim, and they cannot be lightly set aside. I think of the lives lost, and I grieve bitterly; I, too, wish to kill. But we cannot afford to be blinded by bloodlust. Remember who first set our people at one another's throats. We cannot permit the Burning Crusade to engulf other worlds.

We must bring it to an end. We must find a way.

WITHIN THESE PAGES

- A Breakdown of Gameplay Changes Integrated Into Burning Crusade
- Strategies and Information About New Abilities and Talents (Expanded Talent Trees With Two New Tiers)
- Updated Crafting Tables With Jewelcrafting, New Recipes, and a New Tier of Mastery
- Full Explanations of the New Races (Blood Elves and Draenei)
- Leveling Guides for Twenty Levels of Unique New Content (Start New Characters and Savor the Blood Elf and Draenei Territory)
- Developed Maps for New Zones in Azeroth and Outland (NPC Locations, Trainers, Crafters, Vendors, Monsters, and Points of Interest)
- Tables, Monster Information, and Anything Else That We Could Fit Between the Covers

A New Dawn

Burning Crusade brings with it a number of major and minor gameplay changes. Not only is there new content to discover and conquer, but higher character levels, flying mounts, interface improvements, and many other more subtle changes.

This chapter's goal is to help everyone understand all of the differences. It makes it easier to refine your characters and get the most out of the new system without taking too much time away from your exploration! After explaining the new terminology and general changes, we'll move into class additions, player versus player combat in Outland, and a zone-by-zone introduction of the newest territory.

Gameplay Changes

No matter what your interests, be they PvP combat, dungeon delving, roleplaying, and so forth, the first thing that you might notice is that the game feels different. There are new options, areas, levels, abilities, Talents, creatures, and more. Read this section to learn about all of this fresh material.

INTERFACE AND STATISTIC CHANGES

Many of the new options and terms nestled in the various menus can be easy to miss. Though less trumpeted than graphical improvements, raid zones, and fresh items, these things make a big impact on how people relate to the game.

New Terminology and Statistics

Before you spend too much time in the new game, it is likely that you will come across some new or updated terms. Critical Rating? Dodge Rating? Haste?

Don't worry; though these terms are new, it won't take you long to figure them out. After you have learned what everything affects, we'll explain how the numbers add up!

New Terminology	
Term	Improves These Stat(s)
Bonus Damage	Bonus Damage to Spell Effects
Bonus Healing	Bonus Healing to Healing Effects

New Terminology	
Term	**Improves These Stat(s)**
Critical Rating	Melee and Ranged Critical Chance
Defense Rating	Block Percentage, Dodge Percentage, Parry Percentage
Dodge Rating	Dodge Percentage
Haste	Attack Speed
Hit Rating	Hit Percentage
Parry Rating	Parry Percentage
Resilience	Decreased Chance of Receiving Critical Hits, Decreased Damage from Critical Hits

By selecting the information displayed in your Character Screen, via the drop-down menu that is in place, you have the power to learn everything about your new and old stats. Highlighting each attribute of your character reveals even more. As before, this information is updated in real-time, so it is very simple to judge the value of various equipment changes. Even the new point system for Criticals, Spell Damage, and other statistics is easy to understand if you use the Character Screen heavily and watch for the appropriate value changes.

GRADED ON A CURVE NOW

As a World of Warcraft player, you've already dealt with the idea of having a growth curve, whether you've known it or not. For instance, you might have gained a level and had your Critical Chance go down. This might have confused you at first, but in time it becomes clear that you need to keep your Agility up to a certain value to maintain a given Critical Chance. If you just rely on gear that is 30 levels out of date, your values fall as your character is falling farther under the par value for Agility.

The new system adds par values for many other types of statistics. Instead of having equipment that adds +1% to Dodge, you get a Dodge Rating from your equipment. Four points of Dodge Rating at level 20 can be pretty darn nice, giving you a very noticeable chance in your Dodge Chance. At level 60, however, it will add far less. This is true for items that raise your Defense, Dodge, Parry, Hit Rate, Critical Rates, Attack Speed, or Resilience.

This may seem like a nerf, but you won't log in to find your characters in worse shape than they were before. The system has been well balanced to provide more flexibility in most equipment, and your characters are going to be just fine. In fact, the system allows for lower-level items to get these effects, and that is an awesome improvement for the early stages of the game.

In the older days of WoW, you wouldn't see many +Hit, +Crit, or other such items until well into the second half of your leveling. Even then, cheesy greens wouldn't be able to give you anything to raise such stats; you needed to wait for the right items of Superior quality. That limited the customization of some characters in the early game.

THE NEW CHARACTER SCREEN

The Character Screen in World of Warcraft has been upgraded, and it is now amazing. Stats that were previously more troublesome for new players to find (e.g. Dodge, Parry, Critical Rate) are shown without any difficulty. Even better, stats that needed to be tested and calculated (e.g. Spell Critical Rates) are shown too!!!

5

Because the system scales on a much finer basis now, items are being added that give characters more options. One has only to play around in the new Blood Elf or Draenei lands to see this. This brings the option for far more customization into the hands of casual players, who aren't always decked out in Superior or Epic gear. Very nice indeed.

Sample Rating Points at Level 60	
Rating Type	**Value in Traditional Statistics**
Weapon Skill Rating	2.5 Rating grants 1 Weapon Skill
Hit Rating	10 Rating grants 1% Hit Chance
Spell Hit Rating	8 Rating grants 1% Spell Hit Chance
Critical Strike Rating	14 Rating grants 1% Critical Chance
Spell Critical Strike Rating	14 Rating grants 1% Spell Critical Strike Chance
Haste	10 Rating for 1% Haste (1% Improvement to Physical Attack Speed)
Spell Haste	10 Rating grants 1% Spell Haste (1% Improvement to Spell Casting Speed)

OFFENSIVE RATINGS

Most of the Ratings control statistics are already very familiar to most players. Weapon Skill, Criticals, Dodge, Parry, and other such statistics have been in use for a very long time.

To help give players an idea of what to expect at level 60, Blizzard provided a number of conversions. These figures provide a baseline (so that you don't go into the field without a general idea of what these points are "worth").

Specifically, Weapon Skill has been dramatically changed in how it functions (not just how it is gained). Weapon Skill Rating adds to Weapon Skill; Weapon Skill itself no longer determines whether a melee character gets Glancing Blows and other forms of damage mitigation against a higher-level opponent. This is a very major change for Warriors and Rogues, and is somewhat significant to any melee user. With regard to creatures above the player's level, Weapon Skill Rating is far less important in the expansion than it was in the old system. Against creatures at the same level or lower than the player, Weapon Skill Rating is just as useful as before because Glancing Blows are not an issue. You now receive Crit Rating bonuses from having a high Weapon Skill, but this is a minor increase rather than something major to rely on. You can get more bang for your buck with Crit Rating improvements than by upping your Weapon Skill Rating.

DEFENSE RATING

Defense has changed too, such that items that add bonuses to Defense are on a Rating that is converted into actual Defense Skill bonuses. As before, Defense Skill controls the percentage chances for a character to Dodge, Parry, Block, be missed, or be Critically Struck.

Weapon Skills follow suit, with their Ratings being converted into actual Weapon Skill improvements. These alter the chance for a character to successfully strike their targets.

Resilience is a new stat that is being added to help mitigate burst damage against characters. While Defense works to reduce general damage (by avoiding attacks more often), it is a stat that does nothing to stop damage that gets through. That is where Resilience comes in.

Not only does Resilience reduce the chance that your character will be hit critically but it also reduces the damage done to your character by a Critical Hit. Note that the damage reduction of Resilience is a percentage that is twice as high as the reduction in chance for an enemy Critical Hit (thus, enough Resilience to lower an enemy's Critical Hit value by 10% would also reduce Critical damage to your character by 20%).

Sample Defense Values at 60	
Rating Type	**Value in Traditional Statistics**
Defense Skill Rating	1.5 Rating grants 1 Defense Skill
Dodge Rating	12 Rating grants 1% Dodge
Parry Rating	20 Rating grants 1% Parry
Block Rating	5 Rating grants 1% Block chance

Sample Resilience Values at 60	
Rating Type	**Value in Traditional Statistics**
Resilience	25 Rating grants 1% Reduction to Critical Hit Damage Received

RESILIENCE

BONUS DAMAGE AND BONUS HEALING

Casters of all classes have seen bonuses to various damage types before. A few items have always given a boost to spell damage and/or healing, so these aren't new concepts at all (or even new terms). What has changed is that these bonuses are found on a wealth of high-level items, to the point where it is now easy to start accumulating a substantial pool of bonuses.

One reflection of this change is the inclusion of new Talents that give characters improvements to their Bonus Damage values. The difference this makes is quite noticeable for casters. It is much easier to seek items that raise casting DPS or healing capabilities without making gigantic sacrifices in survivability. Weapons and armor alike have high numbers to add into Bonus Healing or Damage.

It is also far less common that you will find items with only one type of Bonus Damage. Instead of something adding +Fire Damage, it is likely that you will find items with just a generic Bonus Damage value. For quite some time casters have had to live with itemization that was not entirely ideal, and this change makes up for it. Caster gear now *feels* far more important toward specialization and effectiveness, rather than being kind of a blunt improvement.

INSTANT LOOTING

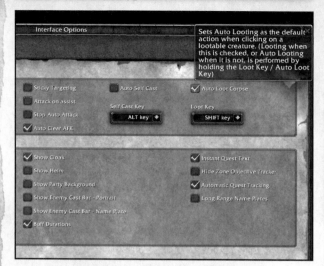

This new Interface Option is wonderful. People who are shift-click addicts no longer have to worry about their looting problem any longer. You can now set a default Instant Loot for your character. This saves a bit of time as you plow through waves of creatures while soloing. And, this doesn't force you to grab everything in sight either (for example, if you enter a group with Free-For-All looting in place). This is because you can use Shift+Click to loot the old piece-by-piece way. Put simply, this option is wonderful and effective.

SPELL UPDATES AFTER TRAINING

Unlike the earlier days of WoW, your spells now automatically update after gaining a new rank. Though you can always access you lower-rank spells (via your spellbook), any of the spells that are already on your quickbar update to the highest rank when a new rank is purchased.

IMPROVED LOOKING FOR GROUP OPTIONS

The new Looking For Group functionality is a sweeping change, allowing players to look for specific dungeon, quest, or fighting groups with only a few moments of selecting options. Using the /lfg option brings up the page, and from there you can start searching. You can also use the new icon on the bottom of the screen to access this (Click on Looking For Group/Looking For More). This system is even refined enough to allow searches for Heroic Dungeon runs, specific Elite Quests, and so forth.

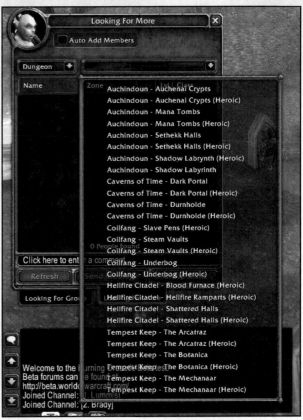

The Looking for Group interface now has primary and secondary drop-down menus that allow players to refine their searches for comrades. This search can be made on the basis of a given dungeon, raid, battleground, or zone. Or, you can search for buddies even for a given quest.

All of these choices, only selected in the primary field, provide a level-appropriate group of options in the second field. In the case of quests, the system even provides a list from your current quest log.

Use the bottom of the screen to enter any comments that would help people to figure out what you are looking for.

At the top of the screen is the Auto Join toggle. This determines whether you are interested in being thrown automatically into groups that are interested in the same goals. If you want to screen for the better pick-up-groups, leave this option off. If you just want a group of any sort to get your quest/dungeon run started, leave it on for convenience.

Once you have entered the information for your first goal, the second set of menus lights up. This allows you to look for multiple groups simultaneously; up to three search flags can be up as you travel around!

The Looking For More tab is at the bottom of the /lfg page. This tool lets you search the active list of interested characters and invite them directly into your group if they meet your qualifications.

If you choose to toggle Automatically Add Members at the top of the page, your group can be filled quickly with any of the available people in the list. With that off, it's much easier to search and find people that you might already know or even have grouped with previously.

Without even leaving the screen to type, you can click on the available buttons to invite characters individually or send the players messages.

WANT A CHALLENGE? TRY HEROIC MODE!

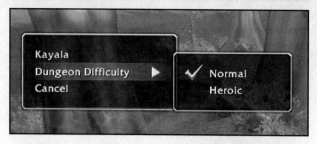

Dungeons are now going to have a mode for capped players. Heroic Mode allows for new rewards, adds a ton of difficulty, and lets you build up toward purchasing epic armor for 5-man groups. This is an awesome change, and it really helps to give non-raiders even more content and challenges to look forward to. This won't be free epic time, but your work will get you the goodies you want in the end. Finally, a fair system for all players concerned.

The idea is that your group leader can use the normal group interface to select Heroic Mode. This means that any Instance Dungeon you enter will be set for a level 70 group. Expect the monsters to be a couple levels above you, and their bosses might even have new tricks up their sleeves.

Be aware that you need to unlock Heroic Dungeons. The keys for each are going to be unique, such that you may need higher Reputation to be able to use them. Being Revered in Honor Hold/Thrallmar might be required for your Heroic Hellfire Citadel runs, just as Revered Reputation with Sha'tar may be required for Tempest Keep Instances.

When you defeat a boss, they drop epic gear for the level 70s, and they also drop a token for each person in the group. These tokens are used to purchase Tier 4 Epic armor for level 70s.

Heroic Mode instances have a raid timer similar to normal raid instances; you can run any Heroic Mode instance only once per day.

RESETTING INSTANCES

There have always been odd ways to change Instances so that players can rerun them without waiting for a full respawn of enemies and bosses. Now, things are much more convenient than they used to be, as Blizzard has added the Reset Instance feature.

To access this feature the leader clicks on their own portrait, and then they select the option to Reset Instance. From there, they will get a query for whether to reset all Instances. Once they select "Yes," the chat box will list all of the Instances that have been reset. After that point, the group can return to any Instance and start from the beginning.

So, when your group finishes an Instance and wants to run it again, all you have to do is head out and use this option before returning. However, note that there is a maximum number of times you can reset an instance per hour.

CRAFTING AND FINDING NEW GEAR

Equipment statistics have changed, and their creation and effects have as well.

Master-tier crafting has been added to the game, opening an entirely new set of pieces for the dedicated crafters of WoW. There are more Superior and Epic pieces than before that can be learned, and just a glance at your trainer's recipes lets you know that these are serious pieces.

Beyond the new recipes for various professions, there is also an entirely new profession to master: Jewelcrafting.

And if that isn't enough, non-crafters can join in the fun with Socketed Items. These are found in Outland, and they are pieces that can be improved by adding various gems to the item.

Another perk for non-crafters is the change in gear quality during the post-60 levels. Even a number of simple green drop items start to look good as you travel through Outland. The equipment curve rises substantially, to help a number of more casual players partially compete with the raiders who have their second- or third-tier sets completed. This won't overcome the equipment gap in a level or two, but it helps to soften the difference.

For those who have been waiting at 300 in their chosen Professions, it is time to move on. Seek the new Grand Master Trainers, and have them teach you the secrets of Master Crafting.

After purchasing this new rank, your crafter will be able to start gaining points again. This new tier, like all of the ones that came before it, stretches for 75 points (capping at 375). In many of the Professions, there are some incredible new options for what you can harvest or create.

Beyond doing more of the same, the Burning Crusade additions attempt to relieve some of the burden on Professions that had a hard time previously. For example, Blacksmiths suffered from having only a few pieces that many players were interested in purchasing.

Now, there are not only good pieces of weapons and armor to sell (even for high-end players) but there are also bind-on-pickup recipes that allow Blacksmiths of the highest skill to create upgradeable equipment for themselves. Epic-quality gear is just on the horizon for dedicated crafters, and these pieces are pretty impressive.

There is also a far better distribution of stats for the items that some Professions make. You used to see some recipes that added +Agility/Spirit and other such odd combinations. Things like this are rarely see anymore (if at all).

MASTER TIER CRAFTING

Alliance Grand Masters

Trade	Location
Alchemy	Honor Hold Tower, Hellfire Peninsula
Blacksmithing	Honor Hold Blacksmith, Hellfire Peninsula
Cooking	Honor Hold Inn, Hellfire Peninsula (Purchase Book)
Enchanting	Honor Hold Tower, Hellfire Peninsula
Engineering	Telredor, Zangarmarsh
First Aid	Temple of Telhamat, Hellfire Peninsula
Fishing	Cenarion Post, Zangarmarsh
Herbalism	Honor Hold Tower, Hellfire Peninsula
Jewelcrafting	Honor Hold Inn, Hellfire Peninsula
Leatherworking	Outside Honor Hold Inn, Hellfire Peninsula
Mining	Honor Hold Blacksmith, Hellfire Peninsula
Skinning	Honor Hold Inn, Hellfire Peninsula
Tailoring	Honor Hold Inn, Hellfire Peninsula

Horde Grand Masters

Trade	Location
Alchemy	Bat Tower of Thrallmar, Hellfire Peninsula
Blacksmithing	Thrallmar Smith, Hellfire Peninsula
Cooking	Thrallmar Inn, Hellfire Peninsula (Purchase Book)
Enchanting	Bat Tower of Thrallmar, Hellfire Peninsula
Engineering	Thrallmar, Hellfire Peninsula
First Aid	Falcon Watch, Hellfire Peninsula

SOCKETED ITEMS

JEWELCRAFTING

Jewelcrafting is an entirely new Profession that has recipes for Rings, Necklaces, some Trinkets, and gems for Socketed Items. Because some of the rare equipment with Sockets can be upgraded to have very high stats and a wonderful degree of customization, Jewelcrafting is going to be in fairly high demand.

For those who desire this new trade, consider raising Mining along with it. Having a Miner to get easy metal and gemstones is going to decrease the expense of leveling Jewelcrafting by an immense margin. A huge number of Jewelcrafting recipes have a need for both metal and stones, so the Auction House is going to be a familiar place to you if you don't have Mining or a supportive guild behind you.

One very interesting thing about the products from this Profession is that some of them are quite group friendly. Some items have on-use effects that buff your character and any party members within range. Consider the Thick Felsteel Necklace: beyond its +36 Stamina, this necklace has a use that buff party members for +20 Stamina for 30 minutes. That buff may not be huge, but a couple hundred Health can make the difference in those close matches.

Socketed Items are found in Outland, and they offer unprecedented item customization. When highlighting and item that has Sockets, you will quickly notice that those open slots are listed in grey and state what form of gems they take.

From there, you can research the gems available for those slots. Use the tables in this guide to get an idea of what you can have. Once you know which gems sound exciting, look up the materials required for Jewelcrafters to do their work and gather/buy these. It's always nice to be able to give crafters what they need (it saves money in the long run). This way, you escape with only a tip most of the time, rather than paying for the time, hassle, and profit of the crafter.

There are several major types of Socketed Gems. Most of these count as having one or two colors, and there are also Meta Gems that can only be used when your items have a certain level of several colors. This is complex enough that it requires some explanation for those who aren't yet familiar with the system.

The four types of Sockets are as follows: Blue, Red, Yellow, and Meta. The first three are the most common types, and they appear as Sockets in a fair number of Outland rewards. You character can use any gems of a corresponding color in those slots. Or, they can use any gem that has a mixed color where one of the two colors matches that slot. The table below expands on this.

Socketed Gem Types

Gem Type	Where Used	Requirements
Blue	Any Blue Sockets	N/A
Red	Any Red Sockets	N/A
Yellow	Any Yellow Sockets	N/A
Green	Any Blue or Yellow Sockets	N/A
Orange	Any Red or Yellow Sockets	N/A
Purple	Any Blue or Red Sockets	N/A
Meta	Head Pieces w/ Meta Slots	Various Points in Multiple Primary Colors (* Explained Below)

Meta Gems and their Sockets are the most complex of these new bonuses. Head pieces are the primary equipment that have Meta Sockets; you won't see chest pieces, legs, and so forth with these. In addition, you won't be able to use these slots even if you do have a Meta Gem unless you meet certain requirements.

The key to having an active Meta Bonus is in having multiple pieces of Socketed gear. The Meta Gem itself determines how many of other colored gems you need. For instance, a Meta Gem might say (2 Red, 1 Yellow). This would mean that the Meta Gem would only function as long as your character has equipment with 2 or more Red Gems and 1 or more Yellow Gems.

One piece of good news is that Green, Orange, and Purple stones count twice! Thus, your character would need 15 Sockets to activate a 5/5/5 Meta Slot if you only used primary colors (5 Blues, 5 Reds, and 5 Yellows). But with Green, Orange, and Purple stones you could get away with fewer.

Example: (3 Greens, 3 Oranges, and 2 Purples would give you enough points in all colors to activate a 5/5/5 Meta Slot. Any 3-3-2 combination of multi-colored gems should succeed in this example.

Samples of Common Gems

Gem Name	Gem Type	Bonuses Conveyed
Bold Blood Garnet	Red	+6 Strength
Luminous Flame Spessarite	Yellow	+7 Healing Bonus, +3 Intellect
Sparkling Azure Moonstone	Blue	+6 Spirit
Mystical Skyfire Diamond	Meta	2% Chance on Spellcast to make next spell Instant

ENCHANTING CHANGE:
DISENCHANT HAS SKILL REQUIREMENTS

It won't be as easy for players to create casual Enchanters for the purpose of disenchanting items without bothering to skill up actual item enchanting. Now, items have certain skill requirements for an Enchanter to be able to break them into their component parts.

To find out what skill is required for breaking a given item, click on Disenchant and bring the mouse to hover over the item that you are considering. This brings up a listing for the required skill.

A NEW GRADE OF EQUIPMENT:
ITEMS POST 60

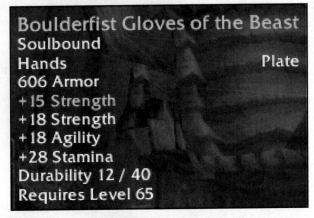

Boulderfist Gloves of the Beast
Soulbound
Hands   Plate
606 Armor
+15 Strength
+18 Strength
+18 Agility
+28 Stamina
Durability 12 / 40
Requires Level 65

When Will My Old Gear Be Obsolete?

Quality of Equipment	When You Might Find Better Gear	Where to Go for a Challenge/Some Loot
Tier .5/Level 60 Rares	60+	Hellfire Peninsula/Hellfire Citadel: Ramparts
Tier 1 Epics	62+	Zangarmarsh/Coilfang
Tier 2 Epics	65+	Nagrand Outdoor Quests
Tier 3 Epics	Late 60s	Karazhan, Netherstorm Instances

Equipment in the post 60 environment is incredible; the scale is entirely different, and it doesn't take long before even casual players are able to find gear that rivals tier 1/tier 2 equipment from before the expansion. Only those who are equipped in the absolute best gear pre-expansion are going to be overly picky about some of the quest items that are found in Outland.

After several days of play, people will be seeing green items that rival things that were epic before. This is the way of things, and it should be understood that what was once the cap has no real meaning now. 90 DPS weaponry is not end-game now. 10,000 Health is not crazy wonderful. You get the idea.

There are so many quests with multiple item choices that it is very easy to gear up for the Outland content just by going through even the safer outdoor quests that you find all over the place. Take a buddy or two with you into Outland and it gets even easier.

So, be careful of letting colors decide whether you are interested in gear. Even if you have blue or purple piece of equipment for a given slot, start training yourself not to immediately pass or Disenchant the greens that you find. When your tank finds a 3000 Armor green shield with tons of Stamina and Block, it should become clear that things are changing quickly.

TRANSPORTATION CHANGES

With so much new territory added to the game, it's important to understand how to get around! Most of the new content has been added as Outland, as a section of 7 outdoor zones, 1 major city (with plenty of smaller towns), and more World Dungeons than you can shake a stick at.

THE DARK PORTAL AND TRAVEL IN OUTLAND

The Dark Portal, located in the southern part of the Blasted Lands, is your key to Outland. This massive gate will be seized by both Alliance and Horde troops, who hold the line against the darkness so that champions from both factions can freely come back and forth between the worlds.

To reach the Dark Portal, keep heading south from Stonard if you are a Horde player and keep going until you pass into Blasted Lands and eventually on to Outland. For Alliance, you can fly from Stormwind directly down to Blasted Lands and make a short run to the Portal.

Some important things to know about Outland: you can get back through the Dark Portal at any time by walking in the opposite direction, there are gateways to all of the major cities (for both factions) in the center of Shattrath City, and there are plenty of Flight Points.

Even in the first zone of Outland, there are multiple Flight Points! Make sure to grab the first one just outside of the Dark Portal. There are separate Flight Points for the Horde and Alliance here, so be sure you are getting the correct flight point.

MEETING STONES

Meeting Stones these days are so much better than they were in the old days. You can use them to teleport grouped members to the Stone's location, and you only need the help of one other group member! This means that Warlocks no longer are forced to rush to sites ahead of time just to wait for two more people to help summon any stragglers. Now, anybody can arrive near the dungeon and summon everyone else as soon as a second member arrives. No wasted time, no wasted effort, and no massive delays if you don't have a Warlock. It doesn't get much easier than this!

FLYING MOUNTS

At level 70, players get the ability to learn how to ride Flying Mounts. These are only usable and available in Outland, and they are the key to safe and fast exploration of any and all outdoor areas. This includes several parcels of land that are entirely unreachable without Flying Mounts! Thus, you can return to Hellfire Peninsula, Terokkar Forest, and all of the other Outland zones and re-explore to see what you missed the first time around. Hard-to-find Herbs, interesting locales, and other surprises wait for those who are able to pay the hefty price for learning this new skill.

Flying Mounts are purchased in Shadowmoon Valley, the final zone that many players seek in Outland. Though the mounts themselves aren't terribly pricey (100 gold for normal Flying Mounts and 200 gold for Swift ones, before discounts), it is quite expensive to master the art of riding them. For training your character to 225 Riding, it costs 800 gold; this allows you to use the standard Flying Mounts. Then, as a necessary progression, you need 5000 gold more to get to 300 Riding. Though money comes in quite easily in Outland, you are still likely to be saving money for a short while at level 70 before you can afford everything.

On PvP servers, Flying Mounts make it much easier to get around regions without being hassled. It is very hard for anyone to get you off of your Mount, as these creatures make your character Immune to a number of crowd control effects. Beyond that, you can avoid damage by flying high enough that grounded characters don't have the range to do anything to you. And, other flying characters can't attack you because those actions aren't allowed while you are mounted.

DRUID FLYING FORM

At level 68, Druids can learn how to shift into a Flying Form! This is a wonderful gift for the class; even though many characters are going to be able to fly a few levels after, it is still wonderful to be able to take to the skies early on and explore the content that is reserved for those who can fly out to seek it. This is also a very inexpensive method of gaining flight!

As with normal flight, this mode is restricted to Outland; you won't be able to dominate Warsong Gulch, fly over Orgrimmar, or otherwise use this new ability to alter the way that earlier content was dealt with.

THE UNDERCITY/SILVERMOON CITY TELEPORTER

For fast transport between the Blood Elven lands and the other sections of Horde territory, use the Teleporter in Undercity and the northern throne room of Silvermoon City. This two-way Teleporter prevents young players from needing to corpse drag themselves all the way across the Plaguelands to reach the comfort of Tirisfal.

Mage Portal Training

There are four new transportation spells added to the Mage repertoire: two teleports and two portals. Horde Mages can use the Undercity/Silvermoon City teleporter to find the Blood Elven Portal trainer nearby and learn how to magic yourself and others to Silvermoon City. The Shattrath City portal trainer, found near the portals to the major cities in the central area (The Terrace of Light), teaches the Shattrath City spells, as do the Portal Trainers in the Aldor/Scryer terraces. Alliance Mages gain the equivalent spells for the Exodar.

MORE FACTIONS THAN EVER

There are many new factions in Outland. Gaining Reputation with these groups is something that crafters and normal players alike are going to enjoy, at least to a fair extend. Many of the Rep systems in Outland are much easier than some of the immensely time-consuming factions that were seen in the earlier game. Read through here to find out what rewards are available and to get a start on what your characters need to achieve their various goals.

HONOR HOLD (ALLIANCE ONLY)

Honor Hold is the first major bastion of Alliance might in Outland. It should be the first stop for any Alliance characters who come through the portal and wish to look for adventure. There are many quests there (ideal for level 60+ characters), and there are two types of rewards for people to consider.

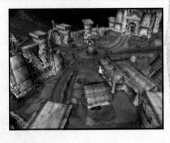

Warrant Officer Tracy Proudwell is a PvP reward NPC; she lets you turn in Marks of Honor Hold for Socketed Gems or one of a few other items. The Honor Hold Favor is wonderful for Reputation grinding, and its boost to experience gained is truly a nifty perk. She is found along the road near the northeast side of Honor Hold.

Only a short distance away, Logistics Officer Ulrike is the Faction NPC for Honor Hold rewards. There are more items there, and you purchase them normally, with gold. Early rewards cover some interesting crafting pieces, including the Elixir of Major Agility and some sweet Enchantments. By the time you reach Exalted there are a few epics items to consider.

Warrant Officer Tracy Proudwell Rewards

Name	Cost	Requirements	Stats
Mighty Blood Garnet	10 Marks of Honor Hold	None	Red Socket Gem (+14 Attack Power)
Stark Blood Garnet	10 Marks of Honor Hold	None	Red Socket Gem (+8 Spell Damage)
Barbed Deep Peridot	10 Marks of Honor Hold	None	Yellow or Blue Socket Gem (+3 STAM, +4 Crit Rating)
Notched Deep Peridot	10 Marks of Honor Hold	None	Yellow or Blue Socket Gem (+3 STAM, +4 Spell Crit Rating)
Band of the Victor	15 Marks of Honor Hold	None	Finger (+25 STAM, Equip for +13 Crit Rating) +1 Red Socket, Unique
Circlet of the Victory	15 Marks of Honor Hold	None	Finger (+25 STAM, Equip for +13 Spell Crit Rating) +1 Red Socket, Unique
Honor Hold Favor	5 Marks of Honor Hold	None	Use in Hellfire Peninsula and Hellfire Citadel to increase Honor Hold Reputation gained from killing monsters by 25% and experience by 5% (lasts 30 Minutes)

Honor Hold Reputation Rewards

Name	Cost	Requirements	Stats
Plans: Felsteel Shield Spike	5 Gold 40 Silver	Exalted, Blocksmithing (360)	Use to attach this crafted Shield Spike (deals 26-38 Damage)
Veteran's Musket	144 Gold	Exalted	Gun (72.0 DPS +11 AGI, Equip for +11 Hit Rating, +22 Attack Power)
Blade of the Archmage	185 Gold 35 Silver	Exalted	Mh Dagger (41.4 DPS +12 STAM, +11 INT, Equip for +21 Spell Crit Rating, +150 to Damage and Healing Bonus), Unique
Honor's Call	178 Gold 81 Silver	Exalted	1h Sword (78.9 DPS +12 STAM, Equip for +16 Defense Rating, +6 Hit Rating), Unique
Honor Hold Tabard	90 Silver	Exalted	A Unique Honor Hold Tabard

Thrallmar (Horde Only)

The forward base of the Horde in Outland is at Thrallmar. These Orcs are extremely loyal to Thrall and to the cause of retaking Outland, so they won't be impressed just because you are a hero back in Orgrimmar. They want fresh blood, eager songs of victory, and a push against the Burning Legion such as rarely been seen before. Triumph against the Hellfire Orcs and the Demons of the area, and perhaps, they will sing of you.

To improve your Reputation with the Orcs of Thrallmar, get to work killing the Hellfire Orcs. Early on, the non-elite Orcs of the area provide more than enough Reputation gain to keep things going quickly. Once these enemies stop giving Reputation gain, move into the early Hellfire Instances and fight those Elites. For the highest advancement of Reputation, you must then shift to the Shattered Halls.

Not far from the Inn of Thrallmar is Battlecryer Blackeye. Speak to this NPC once you have accumulated a modest number of Marks of Thrallmar; these are them used for getting useful Socket Gems or one of a couple rings. For those who wish to grind Thrallmar Reputation more effectively, the Thrallmar Favor is absolutely wonderful. Use this when going into Hellfire Instances for a major boost to your Reputation.

For the actual rewards gained by improving Thrallmar Reputation, speak to Quartermaster Urgronn; this NPC stands just outside of the main barracks in Thrallmar.

Honor Hold Reputation Rewards

Name	Cost	Requirements	Stats
Pattern: Felstalker Belt	10 Gold 80 Silver	Friendly, Leatherworking (350)	Mail Waist (357 Armor +18 AGI, Equip for +50 Attack Power, 7 Mana/5 Seconds) +1 Blue Socket, +1 Red Socket, Felstalker Set
Footman's Waterskin	18 Silver/5	Friendly	Restores 4200 Mana over 30 Seconds
Formula: Enchant Bracer Superior Healing	5 Gold 40 Silver	Friendly, Enchanting (325)	Adds +30 to Healing Bonus Enchantment for Bracers
Dried Mushroom Rations	54 Silver/5	Honored	Restores 3888 Health over 27 Seconds, +10 Stamina for 10 Minutes
Recipe: Elixir of Major Agility	4 Gold 50 Silver	Honored, Alchemy (330)	Use to Add 35 Agility for 1 Hour
Pattern: Felstalker Bracers	14 Gold 40 Silver	Honored, Leatherworking (360)	Mail Wrist (283 Armor +18 AGI, Equip for +38 Attack Power, +4 Mana/5 Seconds) +1 Blue Socket, Felstalker Set
Footman's Longsword	26 Gold 73 Silver	Honored	1h Sword (47.1 DPS +12 STAM, Equip for +9 Hit Rating, +18 Attack Power)
Glyph of Fire Warding	90 Gold	Honored	Permanently Adds +20 Fire Resistance to a Head Item
Sage's Band	10 Gold 33 Silver	Honored	Finger (+12 INT, Equip for +12 Spell Crit Rating, +14 to Damage and Healing Bonus), Unique
Recipe: Transmute Skyfire Diamond	7 Gold 20 Silver	Honored, Alchemy (350)	Teaches your Alchemist how to Transmute a Skyfire Diamond
Pattern: Felstalker Breastplate	14 Gold 40 Silver	Honored, Leatherworking (360)	Mail Chest (646 Armor +26 AGI, Equip for +52 Attack Power, 10 Mana/5 Seconds) +1 Blue Socket, +2 Red Sockets, Felstalker Set
Formula: Enchant Chest Exceptional Stats	5 Gold 40 Silver	Revered, Enchanting (345)	Adds +6 to All Stats Enchantment for Chest
Glyph of Renewal	90 Gold	Revered	Permanently Adds +35 to Healing Bonus and 7 Mana/5 Seconds to a Head Item
Ring of Convalescence	15 Gold 84 Silver	Revered	Finger (+15 INT, Equip for +57 to Healing Bonus, 4 Mana/5 Seconds), Unique
Hellforged Halberd	50 Gold 13 Silver	Revered	Polearm (93.3 DPS +26 AGI, Equip for +19 Hit Rating, +92 Attack Power)

Battlecryer Blackeye's Rewards

Name	Cost	Requirements	Stats
Mighty Blood Garnet	10 Marks of Thrallmar	None	Red Socket Gem (+14 Attack Power)
Stark Blood Garnet	10 Marks of Thrallmar	None	Red Socket Gem (+8 Spell Damage)
Barbed Deep Peridot	10 Marks of Thrallmar	None	Yellow or Blue Socket Gem (+3 STAM, +4 Crit Rating)
Notched Deep Peridot	10 Marks of Thrallmar	None	Yellow or Blue Socket Gem (+3 STAM, +4 Spell Crit Rating)
Band of the Victor	15 Marks of Thrallmar	None	Finger (+25 STAM, Equip for +13 Crit Rating) +1 Red Socket, Unique
Circlet of the Victory	15 Marks of Thrallmar	None	Finger (+25 STAM, Equip for +13 Spell Crit Rating) +1 Red Socket, Unique
Thrallmar Favor	5 Marks of Thrallmar	None	Use in Hellfire Peninsula and Hellfire Citadel to increase Thrallmar Reputation gained from killing monsters by 25% and experience by 5% (lasts 30 Minutes)

Thrallmar Reputation Rewards

Name	Cost	Requirements	Stats
Marksman's Bow	144 Gold	Exalted	Bow (73.7 DPS +11 AGI, Equip for +11 Hit Rating, +22 Attack Power)
Stormcaller	185 Gold 35 Silver	Exalted	Mh Dagger (41.4 DPS +12 STAM, +11 INT, Equip for +21 Spell Crit Rating, +150 to Damage and Healing Bonus), Unique
Warbringer	178 Gold 81 Silver	Exalted	1h Axe (78.9 DPS +12 STAM, Equip for +16 Defense Rating, +6 Hit Rating), Unique
Thrallmar Tabard	90 Silver	Exalted	A Unique Thrallmar Tabard

Thrallmar Reputation Rewards

Name	Cost	Requirements	Stats
Pattern: Felstalker Belt	10 Gold 80 Silver	Friendly, Leatherworking (350)	Mail Waist (357 Armor +18 AGI, Equip for +50 Attack Power, 7 Mana/5 Seconds) +1 Blue Socket, +1 Red Socket, Felstalker Set
Grunt's Waterskin	18 Silver/5	Friendly	Restores 2934 Mana over 30 Seconds
Dried Fruit Rations	54 Silver/5	Honored	Restores 3888 Health over 27 Seconds, +10 Stamina for 10 Minutes
Formula: Enchant Bracer Superior Healing	5 Gold 40 Silver	Friendly, Enchanting (325)	Adds +30 to Healing Bonus Enchantment for Bracers
Recipe: Elixir of Major Agility	4 Gold 50 Silver	Honored, Alchemy (330)	Use to Add 35 Agility for 1 Hour
Formula: Enchant Chest Exceptional Stats	5 Gold 40 Silver	Revered, Enchanting (345)	Adds +6 to All Stats Enchantment for Chest
Pattern: Felstalker Bracers	14 Gold 40 Silver	Honored, Leatherworking (360)	Mail Wrist (283 Armor +18 AGI, Equip for +38 Attack Power, +4 Mana/5 Seconds) +1 Blue Socket, Felstalker Set
Grunt's Waraxe	26 Gold 73 Silver	Honored	1h Axe (47.1 DPS +12 STAM, Equip for +9 Hit Rating, +18 Attack Power)
Glyph of Fire Warding	90 Gold	Honored	Permanently Adds +20 Fire Resistance to a Head Item
Farseer's Band	10 Gold 33 Silver	Honored	Finger (+12 INT, Equip for +12 Spell Crit Rating, +14 to Damage and Healing Bonus), Unique
Recipe: Transmute Skyfire Diamond	7 Gold 20 Silver	Honored, Alchemy (350)	Teaches your Alchemist how to Transmute a Skyfire Diamond
Pattern: Felstalker Breastplate	14 Gold 40 Silver	Honored, Leatherworking (360)	Mail Chest (646 Armor +26 AGI, Equip for +52 Attack Power, 10 Mana/5 Seconds) +1 Blue Socket, +2 Red Sockets, Felstalker Set
Glyph of Renewal	90 Gold	Revered	Permanently Adds +35 to Healing Bonus and 7 Mana/5 Seconds to a Head Item
Ancestral Band	15 Gold 84 Silver	Revered	Finger (+15 INT, Equip for +57 to Healing Bonus, 4 Mana/5 Seconds), Unique
Blackened Spear	50 Gold 13 Silver	Revered	Polearm (93.3 DPS +26 AGI, Equip for +19 Hit Rating, +92 Attack Power)
Plans: Felsteel Shield Spike	5 Gold 40 Silver	Exalted, Blacksmithing (360)	Use to attach this crafted Shield Spike (deals 26-38 Damage)

KURENAI (ALLIANCE ONLY)

The Kurenai are a group of the Broken that have clawed their way back from the brink of slavery. Exerting themselves now, they are helping the Alliance to push back the various nasty forces that cover Outland.

You can find the Kurenai in Zangarmarsh and in Nagrand, but their heaviest concentration of quests and their reward NPC are all found in Telaar, in southern Nagrand. Trade Narasu, west of the inn, has the various goodies that you earn by fighting for the Kurenai. Slaying the foul Ogres and Kilsorrow Orcs of Nagrand is a very fast way to earn a fine Reputation. Then, once the Kurenai are Friendly, turn in the Obsidean Warbeads that you collect from the Ogres for even more Reputation gain.

Kurenai Reputation Rewards

Name	Cost	Requirements	Stats
Pattern: Netherfury Belt	10 Gold 80 Silver	Friendly, Leatherworking (340)	Mail Waist (339 Armor +27 STAM, Equip for +21 to Damage and Healing Bonus, 9 Mana/5 Seconds) +1 Blue Socket, +1 Red Socket, Netherfury Set
Pattern: Reinforced Mining Bag	4 Gold 50 Silver	Honored, Leatherworking (325)	28 Slot Mining Bag

Kurenai Reputation Rewards

Name	Cost	Requirements	Stats
Pattern: Netherfury Leggings	10 Gold 80 Silver	Honored, Leatherworking (340)	Mail Legs (527 Armor +37 STAM, Equip for +29 to Damage and Healing Bonus, 10 Mana/5 Seconds) +2 Blue Sockets, +1 Red Socket, Netherfury Set
Band of Elemental Spirits	15 Gold 84 Silver	Revered	Finger (+15 STAM, +26 INT, +15 SPI), Unique
Kurenai Kilt	19 Gold 62 Silver	Revered	Leather Legs (256 Armor +11 INT, Equip for +18 Spell Crit Rating, +44 to Damage and Healing Bonus), +1 Red Socket, +2 Yellow Sockets
Recipe: Transmute Primal Fire to Earth	7 Gold 20 Silver	Revered	It does exactly what you would expect
Pattern Netherfury Boots	10 Gold 80 Silver	Revered, Leatherworking (350)	Mail Feet (392 Armor +36 STAM, Equip for +21 to Damage and Healing Bonus, 7 Mana/5 Seconds) +1 Blue Socket, +1 Red Socket, Netherfury Set
Cloak of the Ancient Spirits	45 Gold 48 Silver	Exalted	Back (78 Armor +15 STAM, +26 INT, Equip for 6 Mana/5 Seconds)
Arechron's Gift	188 Gold 5 Silver	Exalted	2h Mace (93.3 DPS Equip for +42 Hit Rating, +84 Attack Power)
Far Seer's Helm	74 Gold 30 Silver	Exalted	Mail Head (530 Armor +37 STAM, +25 INT, Equip for +50 Attack Power) +1 Blue Socket, +1 Red Socket, +1 Yellow Socket
Epic Talbuks	90 Gold	Exalted	There are 5 colors of Epic Talbuk Mounts Here

MAG'HAR (HORDE ONLY)

The Mag'har Orcs are a tough breed; they have lived and fought in Outland, and done all that they can to resist the lure of the demonic taint. They aren't overly found of the Alliance (and vice versa), but they'll be glad to make friends with any of the Horde troops that come through the portal.

There are a few initial quests to ingratiate yourself with the Mag'har in Hellfire Peninsula, if you are a Horde character. Their rewards, more quests, and the monsters that raise Mag'har Reputation are primarily in Nagrand. Clear

Sunspring Post of its enemies or fight against the Ogres of Nagrand to raise Reputation. Save the Obsidian Warbeads that you fight from the Ogres, as these too can be used for Mag'har Rep (or Consortium Rep once you reach Friendly with that group).

On the western side of Garadar is Provisioner Nasela; seek her for any of the Reputation rewards that interest you. The equipment is primarily leather or mail, and Warrriors/Paladins have the least to gain there. What might interest anyone, however, is that Epic Talbuks are sold there. The grind to Exalted isn't too bad with these guys, and having a special mount at low cost is certainly interesting to some players!

Mag'har Reputation Rewards

Name	Cost	Requirements	Stats
Pattern: Netherfury Belt	10 Gold 80 Silver	Friendly, Leatherworking (340)	Mail Waist (339 Armor +27 STAM, Equip for +21 to Damage and Healing Bonus, 9 Mana/5 Seconds) +1 Blue Socket, +1 Red Socket, Netherfury Set
Pattern: Reinforced Mining Bag	4 Gold 50 Silver	Honored, Leatherworking (325)	28 Slot Mining Bag
Pattern: Netherfury Leggings	10 Gold 80 Silver	Honored, Leatherworking (340)	Mail Legs (527 Armor +37 STAM, Equip for +29 to Damage and Healing Bonus, 10 Mana/5 Seconds) +2 Blue Sockets, +1 Red Socket, Netherfury Set
Band of Ancestral Spirits	15 Gold 84 Silver	Revered	Finger (+15 STAM, +26 INT, +15 SPI), Unique
Tempest Leggings	19 Gold 62 Silver	Revered	Leather Legs (256 Armor +11 INT, Equip for +18 Spell Crit Rating, +44 to Damage and Healing Bonus), +1 Red Socket, +2 Yellow Sockets
Talbuk Hide Spaulders	15 Gold 4 Silver	Revered	Leather Shoulder (219 Armor +20 AGI, Equip for +15 Hit Rating, +70 Attack Power)
Pattern Netherfury Boots	10 Gold 80 Silver	Revered, Leatherworking (350)	Mail Feet (392 Armor +36 STAM, Equip for +21 to Damage and Healing Bonus, 7 Mana/5 Seconds) +1 Blue Socket, +1 Red Socket, Netherfury Set
Ceremonial Cover	45 Gold 48 Silver	Exalted	Back (78 Armor +15 STAM, +26 INT, Equip for 6 Mana/5 Seconds)
Hellscream's Will	188 Gold 5 Silver	Exalted	2h Axe (93.3 DPS Equip for +42 Hit Rating, +84 Attack Power)
Earthcaller's Headdress	74 Gold 30 Silver	Exalted	Mail Head (530 Armor +37 STAM, +25 INT, Equip for +50 Attack Power) +1 Blue Socket, +1 Red Socket, +1 Yellow Socket
Epic Talbuks	90 Gold	Exalted	There are 5 colors of Epic Talbuk Mounts Here

Cenarion Expedition (Both Factions)

The Cenarion Expedition in Outland has an entirely different Reputation than that of the Cenarion Circle members back in Azeroth. So, you need to start from scratch. Luckily, there are a ton of quests to do for these characters in Zangarmarsh (with a bit in western Hellfire Peninsula as well).

As with all members of the Cenarion Circle, these people are friendly to both the Horde and the Alliance. Dark lines on a map of the world mean nothing to those who care for nature and beauty. Come one and come all, for the greater good of Outland.

If you really want to raise faction with the Expedition, run through the Coilfang Instances consistently. Collecting Unidentified Plant Parts while fighting the native creatures of the area will help too, as those can be turned in to Lauranna Thar'well (at the southern side of the Cenarion Refuge).

Fedryen Swiftspear is the Quartermaster for the Cenarion Expedition. Look for him outside the Inn at the Cenarion Refuge in Zangarmarsh.

Cenarion Expedition Reputation Rewards

Name	Cost	Requirements	Stats
Design: Nightseye Panther	10 Gold 80 Silver	Revered, Jewelcrafting (370)	Trinket (Equip for +1 Stealth Level, +54 Attack Power, Use: +320 Attack Power for 12 Seconds)
Pattern: Heavy Clefthoof Vest	14 Gold 40 Silver	Honored, Leatherworking (360)	Leather Chest (290 Armor +52 STAM, Equip for +28 Defense) +1 Blue Socket, +2 Yellow Sockets, Clefthoof Set
Warden's Arrow	45 Silver	Revered	37 DPS Arrows
Recipe: Major Nature Protection Potion	9 Gold	Exalted, Alchemy (360)	Use to Absorb 2800 to 4000 Nature Damage over 1 Hour
Glyph of Ferocity	90 Gold	Revered	Adds +34 Attack Power and +16 Hit Rating for a Head Slot Item
Watcher's Cowl	11 Gold 46 Silver	Revered	Cloth Head (127 Armor +21 STAM, +36 INT, +14 SPI, Equip for +79 Healing Bonus)
Strength of the Untamed	15 Gold 84 Silver	Revered	Neck (+27 STAM, Equip for +19 Defense Rating, +18 Dodge Rating)
Recipe: Transmute Primal Water to Air	7 Gold 20 Silver	Revered	It does exactly what you would expect
Windcaller's Orb	71 Gold 11 Silver	Exalted	Off-Hand Item (+15 INT, +11 SPI, Equip for +62 Healing Bonus)
Earthwarden	228 Gold 40 Silver	Exalted	2h Mace (102.5 DPS +500 Armor, Equip for +24 Defense Rating, +24 Feral Combat, +525 Attack Power in Cat, Bear, Dire Bear, and Moonkin Forms); Clearly a Paladin Mace

Cenarion Expedition Reputation Rewards

Name	Cost	Requirements	Stats
Pattern: Heavy Netherweave Net	2 Gold 70 Silver	Friendly., Tailoring (325)	Use to capture a target up to 35 Yards away for 3 Seconds.
Pattern: Heavy Clefthoof Boots	12 Gold 60 Silver	Friendly, Leatherworking (355)	Leather Feet (198 Armor +37 STAM, Equip for +24 Defense) +1 Blue Socket, +1 Yellow Socket, Clefthoof Set
Schematic: Green Smoke Flare	5 Gold 40 Silver	Friendly, Engineering (335)	Use to throw a Green Smoke Flare at a location for 5 Minutes
Expedition Flare	72 Silver	Friendly	Use to call a Cenarion Expedition unit to your aid (works only in Zangarmarsh)
Pattern: Heavy Clefthoof Leggings	12 Gold 60 Silver	Honored, Leatherworking (355)	Leather Legs (251 Armor +42 STAM, Equip for +34 Defense) +2 Blue Sockets, +1 Yellow Socket, Clefthoof Set
Plans: Adamantite Sharpening Stone	5 Gold 40 Silver	Honored, Blacksmithing (350)	Use to add +12 Damage and +14 Crit Rating to a weapon for 30 Minutes (Edged Weapons)
Plans: Adamantite Weightstone	5 Gold 40 Silver	Honored, Blacksmithing (350)	Use to add +12 Damage and +14 Crit Rating to a weapon for 30 Minutes (Blunt Weapons)
Scout's Arrows	18 Silver	Honored	26 DPS Arrows
Preserver's Cudgel	27 Gold 32 Silver	Honored	Mh Mace (41.3 DPS +15 STAM, +9 INT, Equip for +57 to Healing Bonus, 4 Mana/5 Seconds)
Warden's Hauberk	13 Gold 76 Silver	Honored	Leather Chest (204 Armor +17 AGI, +25 STAM) +2 Red Sockets, +1 Yellow Socket
Explorer's Walking Stick	34 Gold 3 Silver	Honored	Staff (63.7 DPS +42 STAM, Equip for +54 Attack Power, Slight Run Speed Increase)
Glyph of Nature Warding	90 Gold	Honored	Adds +20 Nature Resistance to a Head Slot Item

Sporeggar (Both Factions)

The cute little fungus-people of Sporeggar are always in need of help. These friendly creatures live in several areas of Zangarmarsh, and they are hunted by many of the Giants that also share that zone. Neither Horde grunts nor Alliance soldiers should be able to resist the lure of helping these cute humanoids.

To ingratiate yourself with Sporeggar, travel to the southwestern part of the zone and look for the quests beside The Spawning Glen. These repeatable quests allow Horde and Alliance characters alike to race toward Friendly with the faction. After that, head up to Sporeggar itself and look at the variety of quests there.

For continued Reputation gain, run the kill quest against the Naga at least once (Now That We're Friends). Then, form large groups to chain-kill Giants in the south for rapid advancement.

As far as rewards go, your characters should collect the bright Glowcap Mushrooms that are found throughout the area, as ground spawns. It does not require Herbalism to pick these! The mushrooms act as currency with the Sporeggar. Alchemists and Cooks are going to be most interested in some of the rewards. To purchase reward items, look in a small building on the western side of Sporeggar.

Sporeggar Reputation Rewards

Name	Cost	Requirements	Stats
Recipe: Sporeling Snack	2 Gold	Cooking (310)	Turns Strange Spores into Sporeling Snacks (+20 STAM/SPI for pets), Lasts 30 Minutes
Recipe: Clam Bar	1 Glowcap Mushroom	Cooking (300)	Food that restores 4320 Health/30 Seconds, After 10 Seconds it adds +20 STAM/SPI for 30 Minutes
Marsh Lichen	2 Glowcap Mushrooms	None	Use to restore 4320 Health/30 Seconds, After 10 Seconds it adds +10 Spirit for 10 Minutes
Tallstalk Mushroom	1 Glowcap Mushroom	Friendly	Use to show the location of Giants on the Minimap, Lasts for 1.Hour
Redcap Toadstool	1 Glowcap Mushroom	Honored	Use to remove 1 Poison Effect, Lowers Nature Resistance by 50 for 1 Minute
Petrified Lichen Guard	15 Glowcap Mushrooms	Honored	Shield (2534 Armor 48 Block +24 STAM, Equip Effect: Afflicts attacker with Deadly Poison when you are struck)
Sporeling's Firestick	20 Glowcap Mushrooms	Revered	Wand (96.9 DPS +12 STAM, +9 INT, Equip for +11 to Damage and Healing Bonus)
Hardened Stone Shard	45 Glowcap Mushrooms	Revered	1h Dagger (55.3 DPS +16 STAM, Equip for +12 Hit Rating, +22 Attack Power), Unique
Recipe: Transmute Primal Earth to Water	25 Glowcap Mushrooms	Revered, Alchemy (350)	It does exactly what you would expect
Muck-Covered Drape	25 Glowcap Mushrooms	Honored	Back (66 Armor +30 STAM, Use to reduce Threat with nearby enemies)
Recipe: Shrouding Potion	30 Glowcap Mushrooms	Exalted, Alchemy (335)	Use to reduce Threat with nearby enemies

Aldor Enchantment Rewards

Name	Cost	Requirements	Stats
Inscription of Discipline	1 Holy Dust	Honored	Adds +15 to Damage and Healing Bonus to a Shoulder Item
Inscription of Faith	1 Holy Dust	Honored	Adds +29 Healing Bonus to a Shoulder Item
Inscription of Vengeance	1 Holy Dust	Honored	Adds +26 Attack Power to a Shoulder Item
Inscription of Warding	1 Holy Dust	Honored	Adds +13 Dodge Rating to a Shoulder Item
Greater Inscription of Discipline	5 Holy Dust	Exalted	Adds +18 to Damage and Healing Bonus to a Shoulder Item
Greater Inscription of Faith	5 Holy Dust	Exalted	Adds +33 Healing Bonus and 4 Mana/5 Seconds to a Shoulder Item
Greater Inscription of Vengeance	5 Holy Dust	Exalted	Adds +30 Attack Power and +10 Crit Rating to a Shoulder Item
Greater Inscription of Warding	5 Holy Dust	Exalted	Adds +15 Dodge Rating and +10 Defense Rating to a Shoulder Item

THE ALDOR (EITHER FACTION)

The Aldor are Draenei who are fully loyal to the Naaru of Shattrath City (the Sha'tar). This loyalty does not extend to the Scryers, who also dwell in Shattrath City; these two factions work toward some common goals, but they do not get along! Peace is kept within the city, but neither side is going to be happy if someone aids the other. Thus, even though Horde or Alliance members can aid the Aldor, it comes at the price of alienating the Scryers.

Seek the upper tier of the Aldor on the western side of Shattrath. There, you can find NPCs who provide various repeatable quests to earn favor with this group. Slaying Demons of the Burning Legion is the most stable way to do this, as there are Insignias and Artifacts to be found and turned in by doing so. Good areas for finding the Burning Legion include western Nagrand and several spots of Netherstorm.

For Aldor Enchantments, turn in the Artifacts in exchange for Reputation and Holy Dust. This Holy Dust is taken to Inscriber Saalyn (at the Aldor bank, on the northern side of the city). This NPC places Enchantments on Shoulder pieces. Nearby is Quartermaster Endarin, who controls the purchasable rewards from the faction.

Aldor Faction Rewards

Name	Cost	Requirements	Stats
Design: Gleaming Golden Draenite	4 Gold 50 Silver	Friendly, Jewelcrafting (305)	Yellow Socket Gem, +6 Spell Crit Rating
Pattern: Shadowguard Belt	7 Gold 20 Silver	Honored, Leatherworking (350)	Leather Waist (146 Armor +27 STAM, +30 Shadow Resistance) +2 Sockets
Pattern: Shadowscale Belt	7 Gold 20 Silver	Honored, Leatherworking (350)	Mail Waist (325 Armor +27 STAM, +30 Shadow Resistance) +2 Blue Sockets
Plans: Shadowbane Bracers	5 Gold 40 Silver	Friendly, Blacksmithing (350)	Plate Wrist (497 Armor +15 STAM, +28 Shadow Resistance) +1 Blue Socket, Shadow Guard Set
Design: Royal Shadow Draenite	4 Gold 50 Silver	Honored, Jewelcrafting (305)	Red or Blue Gem, +7 to Healing Bonus, 1 Mana/5 Seconds
Plans: Shadowbane Gloves	5 Gold 40 Silver	Honored, Blacksmithing (360)	Plate Hands (722 Armor +21 STAM, +30 Shadow Resistance) +1 Blue Socket, +1 Yellow Socket, Shadow Guard Set
Pattern: Mystic Spellthread	5 Gold 40 Silver	Honored, Tailoring (335)	Use to add +25 to Spell Bonus and +15 STAM to a Leg Item
Pattern: Flamescale Boots	7 Gold 20 Silver	Revered, Leatherworking (350)	Mail Feet (397 Armor +27 STAM, +30 Fire Resistance) +2 Blue Sockets
Pattern: Flameheart Boots	7 Gold 20 Silver	Revered, Leatherworking (350)	Leather Feet (178 Armor +27 STAM, +30 Fire Resistance) +2 Blue Sockets
Plans: Firebane Breastplate	7 Gold 20 Silver	Revered, Blacksmithing (365)	Plate Chest (1164 Armor +19 STAM, +40 Fire Resistance) +1 Blue Socket, +1 Red Socket, +1 Yellow Socket, Shadow Guard Set
Pattern: Vindicator's Armor Kit	4 Gold 50 Silver	Revered, Leatherworking (325)	Use to add +8 Defense Rating to a Chest, Leg, Hand, or Feet item that is over Level 60
Anchorite's Robes	16 Gold 18 Silver	Honored	Cloth Chest (156 Armor +16 STAM, +38 INT, +18 SPI, Equip for +29 to Damage and Healing Bonus) +1 Blue Socket, +2 Yellow Sockets

Aldor Faction Rewards

Name	Cost	Requirements	Stats
Auchenai Staff	50 Gold 70 Silver	Revered	Staff (62.8 DPS +46 INT, Equip for +19 Spell Hit Rating, +26 Spell Crit Rating, +121 to Damage and Healing Bonus)
Vindicator's Hauberk	28 Gold	Revered	Plate Chest (1164 Armor +39 STAM, Equip for +46 Defense Rating, +19 Dodge Rating)
Design: Pendant of Shadow's End	10 Gold 80 Silver	Revered, Jewelcrafting (360)	Neck (+31 STAM, +25 Fire Resistance, Use to Absorb 900 to 2700 Shadow Damage for all party members for 5 Minutes)
Lightwarden's Band	2 Gold 55 Silver	Revered	Finger (+18 AGI, +27 STAM, Equip for +38 Attack Power), Unique
Medallion of the Lightbearer	71 Gold	Exalted	Neck (+16 STAM, +28 INT, Equip for 6 Mana/5 Seconds)
Vindicator's Brand	178 Gold	Exalted	1h Sword (78.8 DPS +18 Hit Rating, +38 Attack Power)
Pattern: Runic Spellthread	32 Gold 40 Silver	Exalted, Tailoring (375)	Use to add +27 to Spell Damage Bonus and +18 STAM to a Leg Item
Pattern: Flamescale Leggings	7 Gold 20 Silver	Exalted, Leatherworking (350)	Mail Legs (505 Armor +30 STAM, +40 Fire Resistance) +3 Blue Sockets
Pattern: Flameheart Pants	7 Gold 20 Silver	Exalted, Leatherworking (350)	Leather Legs (227 Armor +30 STAM, +40 Fire Resistance) +3 Blue Sockets
Plans: Flamescale Helm	5 Gold 40 Silver	Exalted, Blacksmithing (355)	Plate Head (930 Armor +19 STAM, +40 Fire Resistance) +1 Blue Socket, +1 Red Socket, +1 Yellow Socket, Shadow Guard Set

Scryer Enchantment Rewards

Name	Cost	Requirements	Stats
Inscription of the Blade	1 Arcane Rune	Honored Reputation	Adds +13 Crit Rating to a Shoulder Item
Inscription of the Knight	1 Arcane Rune	Honored Reputation	Adds +13 Defense Rating to a Shoulder Item
Inscription of the Oracle	1 Arcane Rune	Honored Reputation	Adds +5 Mana per 5 Seconds to a Shoulder Item
Inscription of the Orb	1 Arcane Rune	Honored Reputation	Adds +13 Spell Crit Rating to a Shoulder Item
Greater Inscription of the Blade	5 Arcane Runes	Exalted Reputation	Adds +15 Crit Rating and +20 Attack Power to a Shoulder Item
Greater Inscription of the Knight	5 Arcane Runes	Exalted Reputation	Adds +15 Defense Rating and +10 Dodge Rating to a Shoulder Item
Greater Inscription of the Oracle	5 Arcane Runes	Exalted Reputation	Adds +6 Mana per 5 Seconds and up to 22 Healing to a Shoulder Item
Greater Inscription of the Orb	5 Arcane Runes	Exalted Reputation	Adds +15 Spell Crit Rating and up to 12 Spell Damage Bonus to a Shoulder Item

Scryer Faction Rewards

Name	Cost	Requirements	Stats
Design: Runed Blood Garnet	6 Gold	Friendly, Jewelcrafting 315	Red Socket Gem, +7 Spell Damage
Design: Dazzling Deep Peridot	6 Gold	Honored, Jewelcrafting 325	Yellow or Red Socket Gem, +1 Mana/5 Seconds, +3 Int
Plans: Enchanted Adamantite Belt	6 Gold	Friendly, Blacksmithing (355)	Plate Waist (644 Armor +21 STAM, +30 Arcane Resistance) +1 Blue Socket, +1 Yellow Socket, Enchanted Adamantite Armor Set
Pattern: Enchanted Felscale Gloves	8 Gold	Honored, Leatherworking (350)	Mail Hands (361 Armor +27 STAM, +30 Arcane Resistance) +2 Blue Sockets
Pattern: Enchanted Clefthoof Boots	8 Gold	Honored, Leatherworking (350)	Leather Feet (178 Armor +27 STAM, +30 Arcane Resistance) +2 Blue Sockets
Pattern: Silver Spellthread	6 Gold	Honored, Tailoring (335)	Use to Enchant Leggings with +46 Healing Bonus and +15 STAM
Design: Pendant of Withering	12 Gold	Revered, Jewelcrafting (360)	Necklace (+31 STAM, +25 Nature Resistance, Use to Absorb 900 to 2700 Nature Damage for all Nearby Party Members/10 Charges)
Recipe: Elixir of Major Firepower	6 Gold	Revered, Alchemy (345)	Use to Increase Fire Spell Damage by up to 65 for 1 Hour
Plans: Enchanted Adamantite Boots	6 Gold	Honored, Blacksmithing (355)	Plate Feet (787 Armor +21 STAM, +30 Arcane Resistance) +1 Red Socket, +1 Blue Socket, Enchanted Adamantite Armor Set
Pattern: Enchanted Felscale Boots	8 Gold	Revered, Leatherworking (350)	Mail Feet (397 Armor +27 STAM, +30 Arcane Resistance) +2 Blue Sockets
Pattern: Enchanted Clefthoof Gloves	8 Gold	Revered, Leatherworking (350)	Leather Hands (162 Armor +27 STAM, +30 Arcane Resistance) +2 Blue Sockets
Plans: Enchanted Adamantite Breastplate	6 Gold	Revered, Blacksmithing (360)	Plate Chest (1154 Armor +27 STAM, +40 Arcane Resistance) +2 Blue Sockets, +1 Yellow Socket, Enchanted Adamantite Armor Set
Gauntlets of the Chosen	16 Gold 9 Silver	Revered	Plate Hands (728 Armor +15 AGI, +30 STAM, Equip for +35 Defense Rating)

THE SCRYERS (EITHER FACTION)

This Blood Elven faction is open to members of the Alliance or the Horde, though it's most likely to be chosen by Horde players. As with the Aldor, you must dedicate to one side or the other here. Everything that pushes Scryer Reputation forward will push Aldor Reputation back considerably.

Look in the Scryer's area of Shattrath for small quests and repeatable quests for Reputation. The biggest bread-winners come from hunting Blood Elves in eastern Terrokar or in Netherstorm. The Marks of Kael'thas that drop from these foes are turned in for considerable Rep. In addition, the same targets drop Arcane Tomes; those are turned in for even more Reputation. You also receive Arcane Runes for these turn ins.

Arcane Runes are taken to the Scryers Bank in the city. Look at the back of that building for Inscriber Veredis. This NPC takes Arcane Runes and enchants Shoulder items in return. At Honored, he'll turn a single Arcane Rune into a moderate bonus. At Exalted with Scryers, he'll accept 5 Arcane Runes in exchange for a major enchantment. The table below lists these effects.

Also in the Scryer's Bank is Quartermaster Enuril, the NPC who sells items for those who have proven themselves with the faction. The next table shows what is available from him.

Scryer Faction Rewards

Name	Cost	Requirements	Stats
Retainer's Leggings	22 Gold 61 Silver	Revered	Leather Legs (256 Armor +28 STAM, Equip for +26 Hit Rating, +92 Attack Power)
Seer's Cane	56 Gold 93 Silver	Revered	Staff (62.8 DPS +28 STAM, +46 INT, Equip for +228 Healing Bonus, +10 Mana/5 Seconds)
Scryer's Bloodgem	17 Gold 60 Silver	Revered	Trinket (Equip for +32 Spell Hit Rating, Use for +150 Spell Damage Bonus and +280 Healing Bonus for 15 Seconds)
Pattern: Magister's Armor Kit	5 Gold	Revered, Leatherworking (325)	Patch to Add +3 Mana/5 Seconds to a Chest, Leg, Hand, or Feet Item Over Level 60
Pattern: Golden Spellthread	36 Gold	Exalted, Tailoring (375)	Teaches You to Create Golden Spellthread
Pattern: Enchanted Felscale Leggings	8 Gold	Exalted, Leatherworking (350)	Mail Legs (505 Armor +30 STAM, +40 Arcane Resistance) +3 Blue Sockets
Plans: Enchanted Adamantite Leggings	8 Gold	Exalted, Blacksmithing (365)	Plate Legs (1019 Armor +27 STAM, +40 Arcane Resistance) +2 Blue Sockets, +1 Red Socket, Adamantite Armor Set
Pattern: Enchanted Clefthoof Leggings	8 Gold	Exalted, Leatherworking (350)	Leather Legs (227 Armor +30 STAM, +40 Arcane Resistance) +3 Blue Sockets
Retainer's Blade	198 Gold 71 Silver	Exalted	1h Dagger (78.7 DPS +21 AGI, +21 STAM)
Seer's Signet	79 Gold 1 Silver	Exalted	Finger (+22 STAM, Equip for +11 Spell Crit Rating, +33 to Damage and Healing Bonus), Unique

THE SHA'TAR (BOTH FACTIONS)

Shattrath City is the only place in Outland that has survived war against Illidan and the Burning Legion. The Naaru that peacefully rule this city are known as the Sha'tar. More than willing to befriend Horde or Alliance, Aldor or Scryer, these powerful beings are pivotal in the struggle to save Outland from the forces of evil.

When you reach level 70, look for G'eras in the Terrace of Light (on the western side of the main room). This Naaru sells the rewards for turning in Badges of Justice.

Sha'tar Rewards for Badges of Justice

Name	Cost	Requirements	Stats
Khadgar's Backpack	30 Badges of Justice	None	Off-Hand (Adds +43 to Damage and Healing Bonus)
Talisman of Kalecgos	30 Badges of Justice	None	Off-Hand (Adds +12 INT, +46 to Damage by Arcane Spells/Effects)

Sha'tar Rewards for Badges of Justice

Name	Cost	Requirements	Stats
Mazthoril Honor Shield	40 Badges of Justice	None	Shield (4058 Armor 94 Block +15 STAM, +15 INT, Equip for +19 Spell Crit Rating, +22 to Damage and Healing Bonus)
Searing Sunblade	60 Badges of Justice	None	Off-Hand Dagger (78.5 DPS +21 AGI, +21 STAM)
Flametongue Seal	30 Badges of Justice	None	Off-Hand (Equip for +13 Spell Crit Rating, +44 Damage to Fire Spells/Effects)
Sapphiron's Wing Bone	30 Badges of Justice	None	Off-Hand (Equip for +10 to Spell Hit Rating, +47 Damage to Frost Spells/Effects)
Tears of Heaven	30 Badges of Justice	None	Off-Hand (Equip for +68 to Healing Bonus, 5 Mana/5 Seconds)
Light-Bearer's Faith Shield	40 Badges of Justice	None	Shield (4058 Armor 94 Block +18 STAM, +20 INT, Equip for +53 to Healing Bonus)
Orb of the Soul Eater	30 Badges of Justice	None	Off-Hand (+15 STAM, Equip for +47 Shadow Damage for Spells/Effects)
Azure-Shield of Coldarra	40 Badges of Justice	None	Shield (4058 Armor +28 STAM, Equip for +19 Defense Rating, +30 Block)
Ring of Cryptic Dreams	30 Badges of Justice	None	Finger (+15 STAM, +16 INT, Equip for +18 Crit Rating, +21 to Damage and Healing Bonus), Unique
Band of Halos	30 Badges of Justice	None	Finger (+19 STAM, +19 INT, Equip for +42 to Healing Bonus, 6 Mana/5 Seconds), Unique
Ring of Arathi Warlords	30 Badges of Justice	None	Finger (+21 STAM, Equip for +21 Crit Rating, +44 Attack Power), Unique
Ring of Unyielding Force	30 Badges of Justice	None	Finger (200 Armor, +25 STAM, Equip for +21 Defense Rating), Unique
Manasurge Pendant	30 Badges of Justice	None	Neck (+21 STAM, +20 INT, Equip for +27 to Damage and Healing Bonus)
Necklace of Eternal Hope	30 Badges of Justice	None	Neck (+21 STAM, +21 INT, Equip for +44 to Healing Bonus, 3 Mana/5 Seconds)
Choker of Vile Intent	30 Badges of Justice	None	Neck (+19 AGI, +16 STAM, Equip for +16 Hit Rating, +38 Attack Power)
Necklace of the Juggernaut	30 Badges of Justice	None	Neck (+18 AGI, +30 STAM, Equip for +20 Defense)
Shawl of Shifting Probabilities	30 Badges of Justice	None	Back (81 Armor +16 STAM, +15 INT, Equip for +21 Spell Crit Rating, +18 to Damage and Healing Bonus)
Bishop's Cloak	30 Badges of Justice	None	Back (81 Armor +15 STAM, +16 INT, Equip for +40 to Healing Bonus, 8 Mana/5 Seconds)
Blood Knight War Cloak	30 Badges of Justice	None	Back (81 Armor +20 AGI, +21 STAM, +46 Attack Power)
Farstrider Defender's Cloak	30 Badges of Justice	None	Back (231 Armor, +28 STAM, Equip for +35 Block)
Icon of the Silver Crescent	50 Badges of Justice	None	Trinket (Equip for +40 to Damage and Healing Bonus, Use for +153 to Damage and Healing Bonus for 20 Seconds)
Essence of the Martyr	50 Badges of Justice	None	Trinket (Equip for +75 to Healing Bonus, Use for +288 to Healing Bonus for 20 Seconds)
Bloodlust Brooch	50 Badges of Justice	None	Trinket (Equip for +66 Attack Power, Use for +270 Attack Power for 20 Seconds)
Gnomeregan Auto-Blocker 600	50 Badges of Justice	None	Trinket (Equip for +51 Block, Use for +200 Block for 20 Seconds)

SHA'TAR LOWER CITY (BOTH FACTIONS)

The refugees of Outland gather in Sha'tar, and they too have their own Reputation. These people won't care a bit whether you are loyal to the Aldor or Scryers; they are quite ready to take help wherever it can be found.

ALLERIAN STRONGHOLD (ALLIANCE ONLY)

Just on the eastern side of Terokkar is the Allerian Stronghold, an Alliance fortress in southern Outland. This area has no faction of its own, as it is linked with the major Alliance push based out of Honor Hold, but there are still some independent rewards here. When the Alliance is in control of the PvP goals in Terokkar Forest, characters from that faction are able to gain Spirit Shards when they kill bosses inside of the area's Instance Dungeons. These Spirit Shards are turned in to Spirit Sage Zran, in the northwestern part of town.

Spirit Sage Zran Rewards

Name	Cost	Requirements	Stats
Band of the Exorcist	100 Spirit Shards	None	Ring (+24 STAM, Equip for +10 Hit Rating, +16 Crit Rating, +11 Resilience Rating, +34 Attack Power), Unique
Seal of the Exorcist	100 Spirit Shards	None	Ring (+24 STAM, Equip for +12 Spell Hit Rating, +11 Resilience Rating, +28 to Bonus Damage and Healing), Unique
Exorcist's Plate Helm	30 Spirit Shards	None	Plate Head (827 Armor +25 STR, +30 STAM, Equip for +25 Crit Rating, +11 Resilience Rating) +1 Meta Socket
Exorcist's Lamellar Helm	30 Spirit Shards	None	Plate Head (827 Armor +30 STAM, +16 INT, Equip for +16 Spell Crit Rating, +11 Resilience Rating, +29 to Damage and Healing Bonus) +1 Meta Socket
Exorcist's Scaled Helm	30 Spirit Shards	None	Plate Head (827 Armor +20 STR, +30 STAM, +15 INT, Equip for +18 Crit Rating, +22 to Damage and Healing Bonus) +1 Meta Socket
Exorcist's Chain Helm	30 Spirit Shards	None	Mail Head (463 Armor +20 AGI, +35 STAM, +15 INT, Equip for +10 Crit Rating, +12 Resilience Rating, +20 Attack Power) +1 Meta Socket
Exorcist's Linked Helm	30 Spirit Shards	None	Mail Head (463 Armor +24 STR, +30 STAM, +13 INT, Equip for +22 Crit Rating, +13 Resilience Rating) +1 Meta Socket
Exorcist's Mail Helm	30 Spirit Shards	None	Mail Head (463 Armor +30 STAM, +16 INT, Equip for +24 Spell Crit Rating, +17 Resilience Rating, +29 Damage and Healing Bonus) +1 Meta Socket
Exorcist's Leather Helm	30 Spirit Shards	None	Leather Head (208 Armor +27 AGI, +33 STAM, Equip for +10 Crit Rating, +14 Resilience Rating, +20 Attack Power) +1 Meta Socket
Exorcist's Dragonhide Helm	30 Spirit Shards	None	Leather Head (248 Armor +23 STR, +17 AGI, +30 STAM, Equip for +11 Resilience Rating, +37 to Healing Bonus) +1 Meta Socket
Exorcist's Wyrmhide Helm	30 Spirit Shards	None	Leather Head (248 Armor +35 STAM, +16 INT, Equip for +10 Resilience Rating, +34 to Damage and Healing Bonus) +1 Meta Socket
Exorcist's Silk Hood	30 Spirit Shards	None	Cloth Head (111 Armor +34 STAM, +14 INT, Equip for +25 Spell Crit Rating, +14 Resilience Rating, +29 to Damage and Healing Bonus) +1 Meta Socket
Exorcist's Dreadweave Hood	30 Spirit Shards	None	Cloth Head (111 Armor +34 STAM, +25 INT, Equip for +20 Resilience Rating, +29 to Damage and Healing Bonus) +1 Meta Socket
Swift Wind Diamond	20 Spirit Shards	None	Meta Gem (+20 Attack Power and Minor Run Speed Increase), Requires 2 Yellow/1 Red
Swift Starfire Diamond	20 Spirit Shards	None	Meta Gem (+12 Spell Damage and Minor Run Speed Increase), Requires 2 Yellow/1 Red

STONEBREAKER HOLD (HORDE ONLY)

Stonebreaker Hold is an Orcish camp in Terokkar Forest. This is not a faction unto itself, but there are several things that you can do with the people there. For one, you can turn in groups of 30 Arakkoa Feathers to Malukaz in the southern part of the camp. This nets you some free magical items with each turn in (and Rare items are possible). These Feather are farmed by killing many of the birdlike humanoids in Terokkar at their camps.

Speak to Spirit Sage Gartok, also in the southern part of the camp, to see what other items are available at Stonebreaker. To pay for the Sage's items, you must go into the Instance dungeons of the area while your faction has control of the PvP areas around the Bone Wastes. Killing each boss inside a Terokkar Instance nets each party member a Spirit Shard. Gartok accepts these are payment for his items.

Spirit Sage Gartok Rewards

Name	Cost	Requirements	Stats
Exorcist's Dragonhide Helm	30 Spirit Shards	None	Leather Head (248 Armor +23 STR, +17 AGI, +30 STAM, Equip for +11 Resilience Rating, +37 to Healing Bonus) +1 Meta Socket
Exorcist's Wyrmhide Helm	30 Spirit Shards	None	Leather Head (248 Armor +35 STAM, +16 INT, Equip for +10 Resilience Rating, +34 to Damage and Healing Bonus) +1 Meta Socket
Exorcist's Silk Hood	30 Spirit Shards	None	Cloth Head (111 Armor +34 STAM, +14 INT, Equip for +25 Spell Crit Rating, +14 Resilience Rating, +29 to Damage and Healing Bonus) +1 Meta Socket
Exorcist's Dreadweave Hood	30 Spirit Shards	None	Cloth Head (111 Armor +34 STAM, +25 INT, Equip for +20 Resilience Rating, +29 to Damage and Healing Bonus) +1 Meta Socket
Swift Wind Diamond	20 Spirit Shards	None	Meta Gem (+20 Attack Power and Minor Run Speed Increase), Requires 2 Yellow/1 Red
Swift Starfire Diamond	20 Spirit Shards	None	Meta Gem (+12 Spell Damage and Minor Run Speed Increase), Requires 2 Yellow/1 Red

Spirit Sage Gartok Rewards

Name	Cost	Requirements	Stats
Band of the Exorcist	100 Spirit Shards	None	Ring (+24 STAM, Equip for +10 Hit Rating, +16 Crit Rating, +11 Resilience Rating, +34 Attack Power), Unique
Seal of the Exorcist	100 Spirit Shards	None	Ring (+24 STAM, Equip for +12 Spell Hit Rating, +11 Resilience Rating, +28 to Bonus Damage and Healing), Unique
Exorcist's Plate Helm	30 Spirit Shards	None	Plate Head (827 Armor +25 STR, +30 STAM, Equip for +25 Crit Rating, +11 Resilience Rating) +1 Meta Socket
Exorcist's Lamellar Helm	30 Spirit Shards	None	Plate Head (827 Armor +30 STAM, +16 INT, Equip for +16 Spell Crit Rating, +11 Resilience Rating, +29 to Damage and Healing Bonus) +1 Meta Socket
Exorcist's Scaled Helm	30 Spirit Shards	None	Plate Head (827 Armor +20 STR, +30 STAM, +15 INT, Equip for +18 Crit Rating, +22 to Damage and Healing Bonus) +1 Meta Socket
Exorcist's Chain Helm	30 Spirit Shards	None	Mail Head (463 Armor +20 AGI, +35 STAM, +15 INT, Equip for +10 Crit Rating, +12 Resilience Rating, +20 Attack Power) +1 Meta Socket
Exorcist's Linked Helm	30 Spirit Shards	None	Mail Head (463 Armor +24 STR, +30 STAM, +13 INT, Equip for +22 Crit Rating, +13 Resilience Rating) +1 Meta Socket
Exorcist's Mail Helm	30 Spirit Shards	None	Mail Head (463 Armor +30 STAM, +16 INT, Equip for +24 Spell Crit Rating, +17 Resilience Rating, +29 Damage and Healing Bonus) +1 Meta Socket
Exorcist's Leather Helm	30 Spirit Shards	None	Leather Head (208 Armor +27 AGI, +33 STAM, Equip for +10 Crit Rating, +14 Resilience Rating, +20 Attack Power) +1 Meta Socket

HALAA (DOMINANT PvP FACTION)

Though not a proper faction, there are rewards for the fighting that is done in and around the city of Halaa, in Nagrand. Whether soloing, grouped, or in a raid, you receive a Battle Token for each killing blow made by you or your team. When Halaa itself is under your faction's control, travel to the larger building on the western side of town and look for Chief Researcher Amereldine (Alliance: Chief Researcher Kartos). She accepts Oshu'gun Crystal Powder Samples; these are gained from standard monster fighting throughout the entire region, from just about every creature you might fight.

With a mixture of Battle Tokens and Research Tokens (that she gives you for every 20 Samples you turn in), your character can purchase Halaa rewards. These are grabbed from Quartermaster Jaffrey Noreliqe (Alliance: Quartermaster Davian Vaclav), who is standing just beside the Chief Researcher. The following table lists the rewards for these turn ins.

Halaa Rewards

Name	Cost	Requirements	Stats
Avenger's Waistguard	20 Battle Tokens, 1 Research Token	None	Plate Waist (573 Armor +16 STR, +24 STAM, +11 INT, Equip for +12 Crit Rating, +17 Resilience Rating, and +20 to Damage and Healing Bonus)
Avenger's Legguards	40 Battle Tokens, 2 Research Tokens	None	Plate Legs (891 Armor +22 STR, +33 STAM, Equip for +14 Crit Rating, +22 Resilience Rating, +27 to Damage and Healing Bonus) +1 Yellow Socket
Marksman's Belt	20 Battle Tokens, 1 Research Token	None	Mail Waist (321 Armor +19 AGI, +28 STAM, +12 INT, Equip for +9 Crit Rating, +13 Resilience Rating, +20 Attack Power)
Marksman's Legguards	40 Battle Tokens, 2 Research Tokens	None	Mail Legs (499 Armor +25 AGI, +39 STAM, +13 INT, Equip for +11 Crit Rating, +13 Resilience Rating, +22 Attack Power) +1 Yellow Socket
Hierophant's Sash	20 Battle Tokens, 1 Research Token	None	Cloth Waist (77 Armor +28 STAM, +19 INT, Equip for +19 Resilience Rating, +22 to Damage and Healing Bonus)
Hierophant's Leggings	40 Battle Tokens, 2 Research Tokens	None	Cloth Legs (119 Armor +39 STAM, +17 INT, Equip for +25 Resilience Rating, +29 to Damage and Healing Bonus) +1 Yellow Socket
Shadowstalker's Sash	20 Battle Tokens, 1 Research Token	None	Leather Waist (144 Armor +17 AGI, +24 STAM, Equip for +13 Crit Rating, +16 Resilience Rating, +26 Attack Power)
Shadowstalker's Leggings	40 Battle Tokens, 2 Research Tokens	None	Leather Legs (224 Armor +23 AGI, +33 STAM, Equip for +15 Crit Rating, +17 Resilience Rating, +30 Attack Power) +1 Yellow Socket
Slayer's Waistguard	20 Battle Tokens, 1 Research Token	None	Plate Waist (573 Armor +22 STR, +24 STAM, Equip for +19 Melee Crit Rating, +19 Resilience Rating)
Slayer's Legguards	40 Battle Tokens, 2 Research Tokens	None	Plate Legs (891 Armor +25 STR, +39 STAM, Equip for +17 Crit Rating, +25 Resilience Rating) +1 Yellow Socket
Stormbreaker's Girdle	20 Battle Tokens, 1 Research Token	None	Mail Waist (321 Armor +28 STAM, +19 INT, Equip for +19 Spell Crit Rating, +19 Resilience Rating)
Stormbreaker's Leggings	40 Battle Tokens, 2 Research Tokens	None	Mail Legs (499 Armor +39 STAM, +16 INT, Equip for +14 Spell Crit Rating, +22 Resilience Rating, +27 to Damage and Healing Bonus) +1 Yellow Socket
Dreamstalker Sash	20 Battle Tokens, 1 Research Token	None	Leather Waist (184 Armor +15 STR, +13 AGI, +24 STAM, +15 INT, Equip for +15 Resilience Rating, +31 to Healing Bonus)
Dreamstalker Leggings	40 Battle Tokens, 2 Research Tokens	None	Leather Legs (284 Armor +20 STR, +6 AGI, +30 STAM, +10 INT, Equip for +20 Resilience Rating, +44 to Healing Bonus) +1 Yellow Socket, +1 Red Socket
Halaani Bag	8 Research Tokens	None	An 18 Slot Bag! (It Binds on Pickup)
Sublime Mystic Dawnstone	500 Battle Tokens	None	Yellow Socket Gem, +10 Resilience

THE CONSORTIUM (BOTH FACTIONS)

The Consortium is a band of dimensional travelers with a colored reputation. These merchants are neutral to just about anyone who comes along, and they can certainly be swayed to your side through various profitable deeds. Early quests in Nagrand make it easy to reach Friendly with the Consortium; with very little time, you can hunt crystals near the Aeris Landing camp and grab tusks from the wandering Elekks as well. Once that is done, the only options are to turn in the Obsidian Warbeads that drop from the Ogres of Nagrand or to return to Terokkar Forest and hit the Mana Tombs (where the monsters provide Consortium Reputation when they die).

Later, however, you reach Netherstorm, where there are many more Consortium quests. Save these for the later end of your Consortium work to get an easy boost. That is also the area where you can purchase Reputation rewards from this group. Seek the Stormspire for these (it is in one of the strange domes on the northern side of the zone), especially if you are a Rogue.

Consortium Faction Rewards

Name	Cost	Requirements	Stats
Pattern: Fel Leather Gloves	12 Gold	Friendly, Leatherworking (340)	Leather Hands (169 Armor, Equip for +17 Hit Rating, +24 Crit Rating, +36 Attack Power) +1 Red Socket, +1 Yellow Socket, Fel Skin Set
Pattern: Bag of Jewels	4 Gold	Honored, Tailoring (340)	24 Slot Gem Bag
Pattern: Fel Leather Boots	14 Gold	Honored, Leatherworking (350)	Leather Feet (196 Armor, Equip for +25 Hit Rating, +17 Crit Rating, +36 Attack Power) +1 Red Socket, +1 Yellow Socket, Fel Skin Set
Pattern: Fel Leather Leggings	14 Gold	Revered, Leatherworking (350)	Leather Legs (249 Armor Equip for +25 Hit Rating, +25 Crit Rating, +52 Attack Power) +1 Red Socket, +2 Yellow Sockets, Fel Skin Set
Consortium Blaster	34 Gold 41 Silver	Revered	Gun (66.2 DPS +15 STAM, Equip for +7 Crit Rating, +36 Attack Power)
Nomad's Leggings	23 Gold 2 Silver	Honored	Leather Legs (256 Armor +33 AGI, +49 STAM, Equip for +66 Attack Power)
Haramad's Bargain	79 Gold 1 Silver	Exalted	Neck (+25 STR, +24 AGI)
Guile of Khoraazi	190 Gold 57 Silver	Exalted	1h Dagger (79.1 DPS +24 AGI, Equip for +50 Attack Power)

A QUICK LIST OF NEW ZONES, DUNGEONS, AND RAIDS

New Dungeons (5 Man Content)

Dungeon Name	Level Range	Location
Hellfire Ramparts	60-62	Hellfire Peninsula
The Blood Furnace	61-63	Hellfire Peninsula
The Shattered Halls	70+	Hellfire Peninsula
The Slave Pens	62-64	Zangarmarsh
The Underbog	63-65	Zangarmarsh
The Steamvault	70+	Zangarmarsh
Auchenai Crypts	64-66	Terokkar Forest
Shadow Labyrinth	65-67	Terokkar Forest
Sethekk Halls	67-69	Terokkar Forest
Mana-Tombs	70+	Terokkar Forest
The Mechanar	69-72	Netherstorm
The Botanica	70+	Netherstorm
The Arcatraz	70+	Netherstorm
Durnholde Keep	66-70	Caverns of Time (Tanaris)
Black Morass	68-70	Caverns of Time (Tanaris)

New Zones

Azeroth

Zone Name	Level Range	Location	Notes
Eversong Woods	1-13	Top of Eastern Kingdoms (Above the Plaguelands and Ghostlands)	
Ghostlands	10-21	Top of Eastern Kingdoms (Above Eastern Plaguelands)	
Silvermoon City	Any	Center of Eversong Woods	Capital City of Blood Elves
Azuremyst Isle	1-13	Island Off of Kalimdor	
Bloodmyst Isle	10-21	Island Off of Kalimdor	
The Exodar	Any	Western Side of Azuremyst Isle	Capital City of Draenei

Outland

Zone Name	Level Range	Location	Notes
Hellfire Peninsula	58-63	First Zone of Outland, Outside the Dark Portal	Reputation With Thrallmar and Mag'Har for Horde/Honor Hold for Alliance
Zangarmarsh	60-64	West of Hellfire Peninsula	Reputation for Both Factions with Sporeggar and the Cenarion Refuge
Terokkar Forest	62-65	South of Hellfire Peninsula	Location of Shattrath City
Shattrath City	58+	Western Side of Terokkar Forest	Ruled by the Sha'tar
Nagrand	64-67	Southwestern Part of Outland	Telaar Faction for Alliance/Garadar for Horde; Halaa is a PvP Location for Both Factions; Aeris is a Consortium Location
Blade's Edge Mountains	65-68	North of Zangarmarsh	Home of Sylvanaar (Alliance), Thunderlord Stronghold (Horde), and the Gronn'bor Shrine (Both Factions)
Shadowmoon Valley	67-70	Southeastern Side of Outland	Home of Wildhammer Stronghold (Alliance), Shadowmoon Village (Horde), and Altar of Sha'tar (Both Factions)
Netherstorm	67-70	Northern End of Outland	Home of the Neutral Cities: Area 52 and The Stormspire

New Raids (25 Man Dungeons, 10 Man for Karazhan)

Raid Name	Level Range	Location
Magtheridon's Lair	70+	Hellfire Peninsula
Serpentshrine Cavern	70+	Zangarmarsh
Gruul's Lair	70+	Blade's Edge Mountains
Tempest Keep	70+	Netherstorm
Black Temple	70+	Shadowmoon Valley
Battle of Mount Hyjal	70+	Caverns of Time (Tanaris)
Karazhan	70+	Deadwind Pass (Between Duskwood and Swamp of Sorrows)

New Battlegrounds/PvP Areas

Name	Location	Rewards
Arena	Multiple/Battleground NPCs	Full Reward System
Eye of the Storm	Netherstorm/Battleground NPCs	Marks/Full Reward System
Hellfire Peninsula PvP	Central Hellfire Peninsula	Marks/5% Damage Bonus to Leading Faction
Zangarmarsh PvP	South-Central Zangarmarsh	5% Damage Bonus to Leading Faction
Terokkar Forest PvP	The Bone Wastes	5% Damage/XP Bonus, Ability to Gather Spirit Shards for Leading Faction
Nagrand PvP	Halaa	5% Damage Bonus/Ability to Turn in PvP and PvE Items for Halaa Rewards for Leading Faction

PvP in Outland

World PvP is a much greater focus in the expansion. Though there is new Battleground content (Eye of the Storm and the new Arena System), there is even more to find with the PvP for several of the outdoor areas. Hellfire Peninsula, Zangarmarsh, Terokkar Forest, and Nagrand each have prominent outdoor PvP features, including a number of rewards that are in place for those who participate.

This section explains what PvP is found in Outland (and the expansion in general); it also explains some of the new combat dynamics that are involved in PvP during the post 60 levels.

FLIGHT CHANGES THINGS

During outdoor PvP, the addition of Flying Mounts makes for some new tactics. Characters are able to stay out of fights as they wish, or enter battle late without the risk of having someone jump on their backs at any moment. This allows the DPS classes and healers to pick their best moments and enter existing skirmishes near their desired targets.

Ganking gets taken to an all new level as well. The bad news is that someone can safely observe your character from a high altitude, then wait for you to try to quest or grind a few monsters before they come to attack. That is a major pain when you are just interested in relaxing and having a good time (luckily, it's not an issue for PvE servers, and if you like sudden PvP it isn't an issue anyway, right?).

The good news is that no low-level characters are going to come to Outland for very long, so that person flapping above you isn't that many levels out of your league, at worst. Grab a partner as soon as possible if a level 70 person has singled you out, and together the two of you might be able to avoid too much harassment.

SEIZING TERRITORY

Seizing territory is done in a very different way in the new content that Blizzard is introducing. Primarily gone are the days of finding flags and clicking on them to take something (with the vulnerability that one shot against your character can spoil the whole affair).

Instead, Blizzard's more recent PvP additions are based on controlling an area through force of numbers. The more PvP-flagged characters that are up on one side, the stronger their control of the area. Whichever side is stronger in this way will be able to take the land after a certain amount of time.

A progress bar appears for this, with the Alliance having control if the bar moves to the left side, and the Horde gaining control if it moves to the right. By killing off any of the enemies who arrive while you are trying to seize an area, you ensure that the bar goes where you want.

Some of the tricks that you might think of to control areas have already been defeated by Blizzard, to keep the fight fair for both sides. For instance, a Rogue or Druid cannot stay in Stealth to help in seizing an area. Nor can a Night Elf with Shadow Meld accomplish this. These characters do not count toward PvP control.

THE OLD HONOR SYSTEM IS DEAD; LONG LIVE THE NEW HONOR SYSTEM

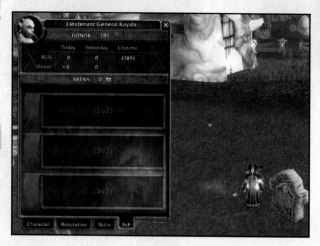

There are now Arena rewards, Eye of the Storm rewards, and new items for higher-level characters throughout the world. In addition to this, players are going to be purchasing these through the new Honor system. Because this system is already incorporated into the live servers before The Burning Crusade, it is likely that you are already familiar with the changes it makes to PvP.

The old Honor system was based on reaching certain ranks by playing consistently (and heavily) over a consecutive number of weeks. It was exciting, but also sometimes tedious or outright tiring if you wanted to achieve the highest ranks and their powerful epic gear.

Now, your characters do not need to play heavily during a given week to accumulate what is needed. Instead, combinations of Marks from the various Battlegrounds are used with Honor to purchase items. This means that is takes a fair bit of time to build up to major purchases, but that it can be done over any period that you like, without fear of Honor Decay! Thank the beautiful fates; it's a much healthier system for all of us who love going after PvP rewards.

Some rewards, such as PvP mounts, require that you collect Marks from multiple Battlegrounds. To make things easier, Blizzard changed the stacking values for all of the Battleground Marks; gone are the stacks of 20! You can now hold huge stacks of Marks without even taking a second slot in your inventory.

HELLFIRE PENINSULA

In the first zone of Outland, fighting takes place in a relatively tight area. Because there are modest faction rewards just for PvPing here, the action is often volatile in Hellfire. The Horde and Alliance have special NPCs in Thrallmar and Honor Hold (respectively) that give items to characters in exchange for turning in their PvP Marks. Because one such reward offers a temporary buff to Experience and Reputation gained, people are quite happy to rush out and join the PvP groups for a time, even if they aren't heavily into PvP in general.

Hellfire Superiority is a buff that adds 5% more damage from all attacks that characters in the leading faction make. You maintain this buff by controlling all three of the towers in the region of Hellfire Peninsula. These towers are named (The Stadium, Broken Hill, and The Overlook). Though it is quite hard to maintain such control, your allies in the region are quite happy when it happens; not only is this buff valid for everyone in the region but it also applies to characters in Hellfire Peninsula Instances.

ZANGARMARSH

Zangarmarsh has a fairly complex system of combat. The Twinspire Graveyard at the center is what controls the buff for the area. Twinspire Blessing conveys a 5% damage bonus to the side that controls the zone, and grants faster corpse runs while doing Coil Fang Reservoir. The way it works is that each side vies for the two Beacons in the region. When one side controls both of them, the Field Scout for that faction starts to hand out Battle Standards. By looking on the zone map, you can clearly see where your Field Scout is standing. The Horde Scout is to the west, and the Alliance Scout is to the east. Both Field

Scouts are Elite, so it is not entirely easy to make a direct run against your enemy's Scout without a substantial party.

When someone takes a Battle Standard from the Field Scout and moves it to the Twinspire Graveyard, they can seize the Graveyard, turning control of it over to their faction. The buff is granted to the side at that time, and it lasts until the other faction wrests control from them.

Battle Standards function in much the same way as carrying a Flag in Warsong Gulch; you cannot Mount or use abilities that make you immune to damage while carrying them. You won't have to maintain control of both Beacons for the buff to stay on your team; it's all about the Graveyard.

Zangarmarsh doesn't have quite as much PvP. This is due to the temporary aspect of the rewards. While Hellfire and Nagrand offer extra benefits for activity in PvP, Zangarmarsh does not. Maintaining the buff and having a good time are the only major perks to participation in this area.

TEROKKAR FOREST

Terokkar Forest has a very interesting system of PvP; the 5 PvP goals of the area are on a single timer, and normally these goals aren't available. When the timer runs out, whichever side was in control loses their buff and all of the sites turn grey. It is then a free-for-all to see which faction can first grab all of the goals (through the standard capturing process). Once this happens, the buff goes up for those on the winning side, and this lasts until the timer again expires.

The faction that is currently in charge of the area gains the Blessing of Auchindoun. This conveys a buff with +5% to Experience Gain and Damage Dealt. It also allows the capture of Spirit Shards.

Not only is the buff here better than in the other open PvP areas, but the ability to capture Spirit Shards is very nice for getting some interesting rewards. The Alliance and Horde each have an NPC in their Terokkar bases that accept Spirit Shards. The rewards focus heavily on several cool Socketed items.

To get Spirit Shards, wait until your faction has Blessing of Auchidoun and head into the Terokkar Instances. All of them are affected by the buff and cause defeated bosses in the various dungeons to drop Spirit Shards when they die. Each member of the victorious party gets a Spirit Shard!

NAGRAND

Nagrand has one of the coolest world PvP systems to date. There is a central camp, called Halaa; this town is captured by either faction in the same way as all of the other world PvP goals in Outland. Thus, only those who come across the bridges while PvP flagged will count toward ownership of the town.

Halaa is protected by up to 15 guards. These are loyal to the current team in control, and all of them have very high Health. You won't be able to quickly rush the town and trash them with a small group. Instead, it is easier (and far more fun) to use the four Wyvern Camps that surround the cliffs beyond Halaa. These allow attackers to launch bombing runs on Halaa, taking out both its NPC defenders and any characters that get in the way! Note that starting such a run flags your character for PvP whether you like it or not, so there aren't any blue wall options here.

Halaa guards are on a very long timer, taking about an hour to respawn. This prevents the sieges from being an especially frustrating affair (and frankly, it's quite a blast to have the town turn back and forth heavily throughout the day).

The bombs that are dropped from the Wyverns have an initial blast and then deal damage-over-time as a percentage of the target's Health. The DOT ticks are the most important part of taking out the guards, because each tick knocks off thousands of Health. One technique is to have a single character collect a few of the guards and bring them out onto a bridge. Once the guards are close together, those making bombing runs can deliver even more punishment. And, if any of the enemies inside town come out to help, your forces can ambush them on the bridge.

The buff provided by control of Halaa is Strength of the Halaani (+5% Damage Dealt). Beyond that buff, the controlling side can safely move through Halaa, which reduces the travel time in the area considerably.

If you have a considerable amount of Oshu'gun Crystal Powder Samples from PvE fighting in the area, talk to the NPCs in Halaa while it is under your team's control. These can be turned in for experience. They are also an essential part of the reward system for Halaa; turn in the Samples and PvP Marks from the fighting here for a couple of good armor pieces and the potential for some 18-slot bags.

THE ARENA SYSTEM

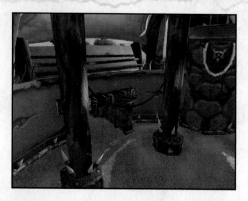

Arena fighting is almost the opposite of the old way that Battlegrounds were used. Instead of trying to run as many fights as possible, this system dramatically encourages that you sign up for only a few matches and do everything in your power to excel at them. Forming small groups (2v2, 3v3, 5v5); you take your character into a situation where the fighting will be at its most challenging.

Expect people to break out their timers quite heavily (though long-term abilities, such as Warrior's Retaliation or a Paladin's Lay on Hands are greyed out). Short-term abilities are used all the time, and anything that gives you an edge in the fight is worth using. Arena matches are rated, and your win-loss ratio is quite important.

To play Rated Matches in the Arena, you form teams and create your own tabard. Characters under level 70 can practice in the Arena, but rated matches are available only after reaching cap at level 70. If you plan on working toward Arena rewards, it is very wise to practice with your friends. Arena fighting feels fairly different from outdoor PvP and the other Battleground environments, so it takes some getting used to.

EYE OF THE STORM

- Once the game begins, don't jump straight down from the starting location; it is a long way down. Use the floating rocks to make your way safely to the ground
- As long as your team has more people at a tower than your opponents, your team will begin to capture or keep that tower
- The amount of Victory Points you receive goes up drastically with the number of towers you control (Thus, having 4 Towers is well over twice as useful as having 2 Towers)
- The area of influence around a Tower is big enough that a group could gain control of the tower without ever being seen; defenders should patrol or use Hunters to find enemies who may be doing this
- The Human tower is the easiest to defend because there is only one path leading up to it
- Flying Mounts are not allowed in Eye of the Storm

Eye of the Storm is a more traditional Battleground, and it has opened in Netherstorm. This BG is a combination of Warsong Gulch and Arathi Basin. Each team is trying to reach a point goal, but they do it through both a Capture the Flag effort and through controlling terrain. You can reach this Battleground quickly by looking for a new Battlemasters for it; they appear in the same areas as the other Battlemasters throughout the world, and queuing functions just as it normally does.

There are four areas to be seized on the map, and this is done by having a consistent number of characters near the desired sites. These provide points over time, and the heaviest focus is on holding three of the sites. A team that can hold three points for the match will win consistently, even if their efforts for the flag are a near or full failure.

As with Arathi Basin, your team needs to be able to flow and stay dynamic throughout each engagement. A predictable team will lose sites to sudden hits with greater numbers, then find little resistance when they go to take it back (discovering instead that a different point is falling even before they fully take back the site they are zerging). Keep a consistent flow of information running; this allows attack forces on your team to know the best places and times to strike.

Even if your team is going to almost ignore the flag in its win strategy, take at least some effort to stymie the enemy's pursuit of it. If you don't have anyone working on the flag, the enemy team can toss a single person out to just rake in the points. Leaving a single person on flag capturing is enough to ensure that the enemy needs to pull two or three members from capturing territory just to have a similar rate of point income. This leaves enough of an opening that your main force should be able to capitalize on it and keep that third point under control.

TWO SURPRISING ALLIES

As the ceasefire between the Horde and Alliance continues to erode, both sides have begun enlisting aid for the coming war. Though goals may differ, no one wants to be the single empire against a united front. The Horde and Alliance alike are eager to find new forces that will grant them an edge they need to be victorious.

Blood Elves

A TALE TARNISHED WITH BLOOD

Countless centuries ago, ships landed on the shores of Lordaeron. The exiled High Elves, led by Dath'Remar Sunstrider tried to make a new home for themselves. Made mortal by the loss of contact with the Well of Eternity, many of the High Elves fell to starvation or illness in their trek across Tirisfal Glades. Insanity claimed many more before the cause was found. An evil influence within Tirisfal Glades itself was eroding what little was left of the High Elves.

Leaving Tirisfal Glades, the High Elves met the Trolls of Zul'Aman. The meeting went poorly and the Trolls vowed to exterminate the High Elves from lands the Trolls saw as theirs. The war continued while the refugee Elves looked for a land to call home. They came to forests so similar to their lost home in Kalimdor that there was no question where they would settle.

The kingdom of Quel'Thalas was founded when the last of the Amani Trolls were pushed out of the region. Using their greatest arcane arts and a vial of water stolen from the Well of Eternity, the High Elves crafted the Sunwell. This bastion of magic energy infused all High Elves with strength and vigor. So powerful was the Sunwell that spring would forever reign in Eversong Forest. The defenses would bring the High Elves four thousand years of peace.

It was during a terrible war with the Amani Trolls that the forces of Quel'Thalas sought aid from the human nation of Arathor. Though the Trolls vastly outnumbered the Elves, the combined forces of Quel'Thalas and Arathor, whom the Elves taught magic, ground the Amani empire into dust. In the wake of this wonderful victory, the alliance between Quel'Thalas and Arathor was celebrated by the founding of Dalaran. This nation of wizards would be home to both Elves and Humans looking to learn the arcane ways.

The Second War brought strife to Quel'Thalas once again. With the help of the Horde, the Amani Trolls torched the borderlands of the Elven nation and slaughtered any and all High Elves they could find. In response to this absurd destruction of life, the Elves committed their entire nation to the war effort.

The Horde was defeated by the combined forces of the Alliance. With the threat over and the Human nations bickering amongst themselves, the Elves withdrew from the Alliance to continue their isolationistic existence. The years drew on and the once warm friendships grew cold.

Perhaps it was the cooling of alliances that brought the downfall of Quel'Thalas. During the Third War, the undead armies overran the Elven nation and closed on the precious Sunwell. Betrayal created the opening and the Sunwell was shattered. The royal family was killed save for Prince Kael'thas Sunstrider, who was studying in Dalaran at the time.

The Elves survived the nightmarish attack of the Scourge, but the survivors

found that life wasn't any easier than death. The High Elves quickly grew ill and lethargic. The power of the Sunwell had suffused their race for so long, that living without it brought symptoms of withdrawal.

The Prince was filled with a thirst for vengeance upon his return. Quel'Thalas was almost entirely obliterated and those of his people who weren't dead soon would be if an answer to the addiction wasn't found. To honor those who died to the Scourge, Kael'thas named his people the "Blood Elves." Taking his strongest warriors, he joined the campaign against the Scourge while Halduron Brightwing was left to defend the homeland.

Prejudice and suspicion led to the Blood Elves being given the most difficult missions possible. Though powerful and angry, the Blood Elves eventually accepted the assistance of the Naga, under Lady Vashj. Grand Marshal Garithos, who had been watching Kael'thas closely for some time, considered the alliance with the Naga high treason. His army descended on the smaller force of Blood Elves and imprisoned them in Dalaran.

The timing of Lady Vashj and her Naga were all that kept the Prince and his elves from execution. The freed Blood Elves fled with the Naga through the portal to Outland.

Kael'thas found the one thing that had eluded him in Azeroth. The hunger of the Elves could be

brought to an end by a powerful demon named Illidan Stormrage. Most of the Elves stayed in Outland, but Rommath was sent back with a message of hope.

Since that time, the Blood Elves have worked to live with their addiction through strict mental discipline. They have begun rebuilding Silvermoon for the day when Kael'thas will return.

LIVING A NEW LIFE

Though their power diminished by the absence of the Sunwell, the Blood Elves have found ways to continue living. The constant hunger for magic has become a way to weed out the ranks of the Elves. The weak become the "Wretched" while the strongest work to rebuild that nation. Meeting a Blood Elf on the field of battle is to meet one of the most disciplined of an entire race.

Rogue

The Blood Elves have learned the art and power of subtlety and shadows. Though the only class of Blood Elves that doesn't use magic actively, they are not to be underestimated. The dedication and discipline of a Blood Elven rogue is nearly mystical in itself.

Mage, Warlock, Hunter

The Elves have used magic for longer than some races have used fire. It isn't a wonder that they excel in the arcane arts. Their contact with the Burning Legion has shown them the power of demons and their inherent love of nature has given the magically inclined more avenues of learning than the traditional wizard.

Paladin, Priest

Through trickery and magical enslavement, the Blood Elves have harnessed the power of the Light. Even the most holy magics of the Naaru are wielded by Elves determined to bring the resurrection of their kingdom. While taken unwillingly, the powers wielded by these Elves is no less potent than the most devout follower of the Light.

THE LEGACY OF THE SUNWELL

The destruction of the Sunwell changed the Blood Elves in as strong a way as the creation of the Sunwell changed the High Elves. Through generations of living with magic flowing in and about them, the Elves have become quite adept at its use. The lack of the Sunwell's energies has only driven them to become stronger.

Mana Tap

Classes	All
Target	Enemies with mana
Range	30 yards
Casting Time	Instant
Cooldown	30 seconds
Effect	Drains 50 mana+(1 per level) from your target and charges you with Arcane energy for 10 minutes. This effect stacks up to 3 times.

Through their mastery of magic energies, Blood Elves can pull mana from any opponent possessing it. This can be quite useful when facing powerful casting enemies. While the cooldown keeps a single Blood Elf from being able to completely drain a target, nothing stops that same Blood Elf from bringing friends.

As your Arcane Torrent's power is based on the number of Mana Tap charges you have accumulated, use Mana Tap at every opportunity. Once you have stacked all three Mana Tap charges, use it occasionally to renew the duration on the stack. This makes sure you have the most potent Arcane Torrent when you need it.

Arcane Torrent

A Blood Elf with mana coursing around him or her is quite dangerous. They have not only mastered pulling it from targets, they can also release it in quite a devastating way.

Classes	Rogue
Target	None
Range	Self
Casting Time	Instant
Cooldown	2 minutes
Effect	Silences all enemies within 8 yards for 2 seconds. In addition, you gain 10 energy for each Mana Tap currently affecting you.

Blood Elf Rogues can release an Arcane Torrent that silences all enemies within 8 yards and restores energy. This ability is best used after an enemy has started casting, but before they finish. That way they have wasted all the time they spent casting their spell, and now they are silenced for two seconds. Another excellent time to use it is right after a finishing move as it restores your energy and allows you to start the next combo set a few seconds earlier.

Classes	Mage, Paladin, Hunter, Priest, Warlock
Target	None
Range	Self
Casting Time	Instant
Cooldown	2 minutes
Effect	Silences all enemies within 8 yards for 2 seconds. In addition, you gain 10+(2 per level)+(2 per 10 levels) mana for each Mana Tap currently affecting you.

Mana-using Blood Elves use Arcane Torrent to silence enemies and restore their own mana. Use Arcane Torrent when an enemy is attempting to cast a spell near you. This interrupts their spell as well as silencing them for two seconds. If you aren't near enemies, release your Arcane Torrent to restore your mana should it ever drop to low levels while you are still in danger.

ARCANE AFFINITY

Classes	All
Target	None
Range	None
Casting Time	Passive
Cooldown	None
Effect	Enchanting skill increased by 10.

Being enchanted by the Sunwell themselves, the Blood Elves have a unique affinity for Enchanting. They can intuitively sense the magical ties within an item and manipulate them.

The greatest power of this ability is allowing Blood Elves to learn recipes at a lower level than their counterparts. While your skill can only progress as quickly as you can collect the materials for it, the auction house can make this limitation moot.

MAGIC RESISTANCE

Classes	All
Target	None
Range	None
Casting Time	Passive
Cooldown	None
Effect	All magical resists increased by 5.

Being infused with magic every minute of every day for years has given the Blood Elves a resistance to magic. While it isn't as strong as some of the other races resistances, Blood Elves are slightly resistant to *every* type of magic.

The benefit of increased magic resistance is the lower damage from magic-based attacks. Magic resistance increases your chance to resist partial damage from magical attacks as well as your chance to fully resist the effects. Being resistant to all schools of magic, these effects include both damage and crowd control abilities.

DRAENEI

THE CHASE

Thousands of years ago, on a world called Argus, the Eredar lived. Masters of their world, they used intelligence and magical affinity to craft a society brighter than the stars themselves. Very little seemed beyond the reach of these people and Argus shone like a beacon across the cosmos.

No beacon goes unseen. Sargeras, the Destroyer of Worlds, saw the accomplishments of the Eredar. They would fit nicely into his plans. Bent on destroying all life, Sargeras saw in the Eredar the power to lead his army of demons.

Contact was made between Sargeras and three of the Eredar's leaders. He offered what all demons offer: power and knowledge in exchange for loyalty. Sargeras didn't want just their loyalty though. He wanted the entire Eredar race. Kil'Jaeden and Archimonde were tempted by the offer while Velen was hesitant. They were given time to think it over.

Velen had cultivated the gift of foresight. He called upon the gift and was bestowed with a vision of the future. He saw the truth of Sargeras' words. The Eredar who accepted his offer would gain almost limitless power and knowledge. The price, Velen saw, would be terrible. The Eredar would be transformed into creatures of evil.

The vision continued and Velen saw the Burning Legion and the purpose for which it was created. He watched as the Legion destroyed civilization after civilization. He awoke from the vision terribly disturbed. Though he warned the others of his vision, Kil'Jaeden and Archimonde ignored Velen. The power that Sargeras offered was too great a temptation.

When next Sargeras contacted the three, Kil'Jaedan and Archimonde swore their allegiance. Velen fled as the others were transformed into creatures of unspeakable evil. To stand against such power would have been suicide.

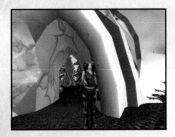

Once again, Velen attempted to call upon his foresight. His despair disturbed his concentration, but it was enough to call a strange creature before him. It explained that his prayer had been heard. Velen listened closely as the creature called itself a Naaru. The Naaru were a race of energy beings that had pledged themselves to stopping the Burning Crusade.

In time, the Naaru explained, Velen and others like him could become a force of great good. For now, they must flee. The Naaru offered to help Velen, and any Eredar who thought as him, flee Argus.

Velen made haste to gather the Eredar who had refused to join Sargeras. With the help of the Naaru, the refugees narrowly escaped the Burning Legion. Velen and the others chose to call them selves the Draenei; meaning "exiled ones."

Kil'jaeden's forces were minutes from the launch pads when the Draenei lifted off. Velen's betrayal would not go unpunished, he vowed. Kil'jaeden gathered his forces and promised to chase Velen until the latter paid for his treachery.

Thousands of years and dozens of worlds would pass as Kil'jaeden hunted the Draenei. Each time the Draenei found a new home, the Burning Legion would be upon them. The Draenei mapped much of the cosmos in the flight, but the hatred of Kil'jaeden knew no bounds.

The Naaru began to teach the Draenei, blessing them with powers and knowledge of the Light. The Naaru spoke of others in the universe that would stand against the Burning Legion. One day, the Naaru would join the forces together and create an army capable of stopping the Legion forever. This hope became a central tenant of life for the Draenei and they vowed to train for the day when they would help vanquish the great evil.

The Draenei landed on the world of Draenor. Over the many attempts at rebuilding, they had become quite good at hiding themselves from Kil'jaeden's forces mystically. They weren't alone on this world. The Orcs of the southern grasslands were peaceful enough and preferred to keep to themselves.

The good neighbors engaged in limited trade, but the peace didn't last long. Kil'jaeden had found the Draenei once again. Rather than rushing in, he took his time and observed first. In the Orcs he saw the instrument of his vengeance.

Through Ner'zhul and Gul'dan, Kil'jaeden corrupted the Orcs into bloodthirsty killers armed with terrible magics that would do more than kill the

Draenei; they would warp them into lesser forms of themselves. Almost annihilated by the Orcs or by the magics they wielded, the Draenei were sent fleeing once again.

Vale Moth

PALADIN, PRIEST

The Naaru may have saved the Draenei, but there was a price. The Draenei chose to become warriors of the Light and promised to fight against the Burning Legion. Their strength wasn't enough. That had been seen. The Naaru taught them to call upon the powers of the Light.

THE POWER OF THE NAARU

The Draenei have learned a great deal from the Naaru, but the changes don't start there. Being in the presence of sentient beings of pure energy and intentions, coupled with the constant fight to survive against the Burning Legion, has put a great deal of stress on the Draenei. Through conviction and a power deep inside the people, the Draenei have changed to meet these challenges.

GIFT OF THE NAARU

Classes	All
Target	Self or friendly
Range	40 yards
Casting Time	1.5 seconds
Cooldown	3 minutes
Effect	Heals 35+(15 per level) health over 15 seconds.

The Naaru have taught the Draenei a great deal. With the blessing and tutelage of these great allies, every Draenei has learned rudimentary healing magic.

This ability is quite powerful for every character in every situation. Melee classes (tanks in particular) should use this ability before entering combat against a tough opponent. The healing provided isn't enough to make a healer unneeded in more difficult fights, but it allows you to build some aggro or deal some damage before your healer needs to worry.

Casters can use the ability on themselves (when soloing generally) in similar situations to melee classes, but its power is truly realized in group settings. At the cost of *zero* mana and very little time, you can throw a heal over time on the group tank or another party member in trouble. This keeps the healer from being over-taxed.

As Gift of the Naaru can stack with itself, you need not worry about 'wasting' it by casting it on a target that is already under the effects of another gift.

The battle was so close that the enemy was able to board the Draenei ship, the Exodar, before it could lift off. The fight continued onboard while the ship fled Draenor. The battle took its toll and the Draenei were forced to make an emergency landing on the closest habitable world. Sabotaged systems failed and the Exodar plummeted to the surface of Azeroth, killing even more of the surviving Draenei.

KNOWING YOURSELF

The Draenei have spent many lifetimes perfecting themselves. Their once brilliant civilization was a place of learning and what the Draenei didn't discover themselves, they learned from others. Perhaps it was this ability to absorb knowledge that Sargeras saw in them.

WARRIOR, MAGE

Whether devoted to war or magic, the keen focus of the Draenei makes them quite adept. The endless days aboard the Exodar and the battles on Draenor have only served to hone these arts that have existed since Argus.

SHAMAN, HUNTER

Though their time on Draenor wasn't long, the Draenei learned much from the Orcs. Their beliefs in the elements and nature, at first, seemed rather barbaric to the Draenei. Slowly, some of the Draenei accepted the beliefs and learned to wield the same powers as the Orcs.

INSPIRING PRESENCE

Classes	Shaman, Priest, Mage
Target	Party Members
Range	30 yards
Casting Time	Passive
Cooldown	None
Effect	Increases chance to hit with spells by 1% for you and all party members within 30 yards.

Standing beside a Draenei in combat is quite motivating. These people have not only survived against the Burning Legion for hundreds of years, but they have explored much of the cosmos and still chosen to continue the fight against this menace.

All party members in range get the increase in hit chance for spells. While only one Inspiring Presence can be active at once (multiple Draenei cannot stack the same presence), both Heroic Presence and Inspiring Presence can be active at the same time.

While the ability is passive and affects the entire group, little strategy is involved in smaller group configurations. In raid situations, consider placing Draenei Shaman, Mages, or Priests in groups with your attacking casters to gain the most benefit from this ability.

HEROIC PRESENCE

Classes	Warrior, Paladin, Hunter
Target	Party Members
Range	30 yards
Casting Time	Passive
Cooldown	None
Effect	Increases chance to hit by 1% for you and all party members within 30 yards.

The noble Draenei neither back down nor run away from a fight. The driving courage of these people makes fighting with them an almost spiritual experience. Having explored much of the cosmos and still considering other races equals says a great deal of their character.

All party members in range get the increase in hit chance. While only one Heroic Presence can be active at once (multiple Draenei cannot stack the same presence), both Heroic Presence and Inspiring Presence can be active at the same time.

The only strategy in smaller groups involves Hunters or healing Paladins. These Draenei should make sure that the melee group members at the front lines are within range to receive the bonus. Raid groups should have a Draenei Warrior, Paladin, or Hunter in every group that will be dealing physical damage to make full use of the amazing ability.

GEMCUTTING

Classes	All
Target	None
Range	None
Casting Time	Passive
Cooldown	None
Effect	Jewelcrafting skill increased by 5.

The Draenei have used crystals and gems as power sources, jewelry, information storage, and healing for centuries. Every Draenei has a Jewelcrafter in their family and as such have picked up an affinity for working with pretty rocks.

The greatest power of this ability is allowing Draenei to learn recipes at a lower level than their counterparts. While your skill can only progress as quickly as you can collect the materials for it, the auction house can make this limitation moot.

SHADOW RESISTANCE

Classes	All
Target	None
Range	None
Casting Time	Passive
Cooldown	None
Effect	Shadow Resistance increased by 10.

The Draenei have so dedicated themselves to the Light and the teachings of the Naaru that every member of their civilization has become a beacon of hope that dispels darkness from around them. This infusing of the Light grants them a slight resistance to Shadow magic.

The benefit of increased Shadow Resistance is the lower damage from Shadow-based attacks. Shadow Resistance increases your chance to resist partial damage from Shadow attacks as well as your chance to fully resist the effects. Being resistant to Shadow magic is quite useful as damage and fear effects are often Shadow-based.

TRAINING THE NEWCOMERS

This chapter takes players, both new and old, through the creation of advancement of the new races. Rather than doing what we did with the master guides, and give you a modest walkthrough of the starting zones, we've gone much farther. This time, the walkthroughs cover the full path from creation to around level 20. Quel'Thalas and Ghostlands are covered first, then we'll start over and give you a tour of Azuremyst and Bloodmyst Isles with the Draenei.

Before starting, take a look at some of the methods used to call out information in this chapter. Throughout the writeups, **bold** text will signal the name of a quest. *Italic* text lets you know that something is used by a quest.

Then, the map legend divides each zone into larger areas (denoted by capital letters) and specific points of interest (shown with numbers). Read the map legends to find out where various monsters and NPCs are located. For fast perusal, notice that a • indicates a hostile creature. A * identifies a neutral creature that won't attack you automatically.

BLOOD ELVES

The two new zones added for the starting Blood Elves are Eversong Woods and Ghostlands. Inside Eversong Woods is the partially razed capital city of the Blood Elves, known as Silvermoon City. These lands are stuffed with quests and content, far more than the starting areas we've already covered in earlier guides. It is very comfortable to level from 1 to 20 on quests alone, without needing to stop for grinding or to use quests from other zones.

EVERSONG WOODS MAP LEGEND

Eversong Woods Legend

A Sunstrider Isle		E The Fountain				L West Sanctum	
• Feral Tender	3	• Feral Tender	3	Garridel	Mage Trainer	* Crazed Dragonhawk	7-8
* Mana Wyrm	1	Scroll of Scourge Magic	Quest Item	Geron	Weapon Merchant	• Darnassian Intruder	7 Drops Quest Item
* Springpaw Cub	1	* Tender	2-3	Hannovia	Hunter Trainer	• Darnassian Scout	7
* Springpaw Lynx	2-3	F Burning Crystal		Innkeeper Delaniel	Innkeeper/Quest Target	Ley-Keeper Velania	Quest Giver
* Tender	2-3	* Mana Wyrm	1	Kanaria	First Aid Trainer	• Mana Stalker	5
B The Sunspire		Solanian's Journal	Quest Item	Kyrenna	Cheese Vendor	• Mana Wraith	6-7
Jesthenis Sunstriker	Paladin Trainer	G Shrine of Dath'Remar		Landraelanis	Tradesman	• Springpaw Stalker	5-6
Julia Sunstriker	Mage Trainer	Plaque	Quest Item	Magister Jaronis	Quest Giver	M The Dead Scar	
Matron Arena	Priest Trainer	H Falthrien Academy		Mailbox		• Angershade	7-8
Pathstalker Kariel	Rogue Trainer	• Arcane Wraith	3-4	Noellene	Paladin Trainer	• Darkwraith	9-10
Ranger Sallina	Hunter Trainer	• Felendren the Banished	5 Quest Target	Novice Ranger		• Plagueborn Pillager	5-6
Shara Sunwing	General Supplies	• Tainted Arcane Wraith	4	Ponaris	Priest Trainer	• Rotlimb Cannibal	6-7
Summoner Teli'Larien	Warlock Trainer	I Ruins of Silvermoon		Quarelestra	Cooking Trainer	• Rotlimb Marauder	8-9
Sunstriker Guardian	65	• Arcane Patroller	5-6	Sergeant Kan'ren		N Stillwhisper Pond	
Well Watcher Solanian	Quest Giver	Unstable Mana Crystals (In Crates)	Quest Target	Sheri	General Goods Vendor	Instructor Antheol	Quest Giver
Yasmine Teli'Larien	Demon Trainer	• Wretched Urchin	4-5	Silvermoon Guardian	24	Silvermoon Apprentice	8
C Armory		J Falconwing Square		Sleyin	Weapon Vendor	O Skinner's Camp	
Arcanist Ithanas	Quest Giver	Aeldon Sunbrand	Quest Giver	Tannaria	Rogue Trainer	Kinamisa	Leatherworking Supplies
Faraden Thelryn	Armorsmith	Aleinia	Jewelcrafter	Telenus	Pet Trainer	Mathreyn	Skinning Trainer
Raelis Dawnstar	Weaponsmith	Anathos	Stable Master	Vara	Cloth and Leather Merchant	Sathein	Leatherworking Trainer
D The Pond		Celoenus	Warlock Trainer	Wanted Poster	Quest Giver	P Fairbreeze Village	
• Feral Tender	3	Daestra	Demon Trainer	K North Sanctum		Anvil	
Solanian's Scrying Orb	Quest Item	Duelist Larenis	Weapon Master	Apprentice Veya		Ardeyn Riverwind	Quest Giver
* Tender	2-3	Farsil	Armor and Shield Merchant	Ley-Keeper Caidanis	Quest Giver	Cooking Fires	
				Prospector Anvilward	Quest Target		

Eversong Woods Legend

Dragonhawk Hatchlings		2
Eversong Ranger		12
Forge		
Halis Dawnstrider		General Goods
Magistrix Landra Dawnstrider		Quest Giver
Mailbox		
Marniel Amberlight		Innkeeper, Quest Giver
Ranger Degolien		Quest Giver
Ranger Sareyn		Quest Giver
Sathiel		Trade Goods Vendor
Silvermoon Guardian		24-25
Velan Brightoak		Quest Giver

Q   Sunsail Anchorage

•	Aldaron the Reckless	8 Quest Target
	Captain Kelisendra	Quest Giver
	Eversong Ranger	12
	Sailor Melinan	Drink Vendor
	Sin'dorei Armament Boxes	Quest Target
	Velendris Whitemorn	Quest Giver
•	Wretched Hooligan	6-7
•	Wretched Thug	7-8

R   Golden Strand

	Barrels of Captain Kelisendra's Cargo	Quest Target

•	Grimscale Murloc	7-8
•	Grimscale Oracle	7-8
•	Mmmmrrrggglll	9

S   East Sanctum

•	Angershade	7-8
	Apprentice Mirveda	Quest Giver
•	Rotlimb Marauder	8-9
	Tainted Soil	Quest Target

T   The Scorched Grove

★	Crazed Dragonhawk	7-8
•	Old Whitebark	10 Quest Target
	Runestone	Quest Target
•	Withered Green Keeper	9-10

U   Farstrider Retreat

Arathel Sunforge	Journeyman Blacksmith, Quest Giver
Areyn	General Goods Vendor
Lieutenant Dawnrunner	Quest Giver
Magister Duskwither	Quest Target
Paelarin	Bowyer
Silvermoon Guardian	25
Zalene Firstlight	Food and Drink Vendor

V   Tor'Watha

•	Amani Axethrower	9-10
•	Amani Berserker	10
•	Amani Shadowpriest	8-10
	Spearcrafter Otembe	10 Quest Target
	Ven'jashi	Quest Giver

W   Zeb'Watha

•	Amani Axethrower	9-10
•	Amani Berserker	10
•	Amani Shadowpriest	8-10
	Chieftain Zul'Marosh	11 Quest Target

X   Duskwither Grounds And Spire

	Apprentice Loralthalis	Quest Giver
•	Ether Fiend	9-10
•	Mana Serpent	9-10
	Power Sources	Quest Target

Y   The Fallen Courier

Apothecary Thedra	Quest Giver
Courier Dawnstrider	Quest Giver

1	Outrunner Alarion	Quest Giver
2	Master Kelerun Bloodmourn	Blood Knight
3	Slain Outrunner	Quest Target
4	Thaelis the Hungerer	6 Quest Target
5	Silanna	
6	Apprentice Meledor	Quest Giver
7	Apprentice Ralen	Quest Target
8	Ranger Jaela	Quest Giver
9	Skymistress Gloaming	Flight Merchant
10	Entrance to Silver Moon City	
11	Perascamin	Mount Trainer
12	Winaestra	Mount Merchant
13	Saltheril's Haven	
14	Larianna Riverwind	Quest Giver
15	Runewarden Deryan	Quest Giver
16	Eastern Runestone	Quest Target
17	Groundskeeper Wyllithen	Quest Giver

EVERSONG WOODS

Eversong Woods is the home of the Blood Elven capital, Silvermoon City. Though still in the process of reclaiming this land, the Blood Elves possess relative safety here due to their recent efforts. Flights from Silvermoon have resumed, and the new union with the Horde makes it possible for the Blood Elves to spread out across Azeroth without the odds being stacked as heavily against them. That said, the Dead Scar is one of the greatest reminders that the doom and peril of the Scourge stands ready to push into Quel'Thalas during even the faintest moment of weakness.

SUNSTRIDER ISLE

Sunstrider Isle is a quiet place on the northwestern end of Eversong Woods. Characters begin here, with a series of quests that help to clear the isle of a few problems. As you first start to get your bearings, look for Magistrix Erona, who should be standing somewhat nearby. Erona has a golden exclamation point, meaning that the Magistrix has a quest for you! Speak to Erona and accept the quest, **Reclaiming Sunstrider Isle**.

Reclaiming Sunstrider Isle	
Faction	Horde
Location	Sunstrider Isle
Quest Giver	Magistrix Erona
Quest Completion	Magistrix Erona
Reward	Green Chain Boots (Mail Feet, 46 Armor), Wyrm Sash (Cloth Waist 6 Armor), Chain to Unfortunate Measures

Erona wants you to kill eight of the *Mana Wyrms* near the Burning Crystals of the area. These enemies practically infest the place, so finding them is a trifle. Luckily, these enemies are quite weak and won't last for more than a minute or two. Even without many abilities, your character should have a very easy time fighting through the Wyrms. Return to Erona when you are finished.

With the first quest done, Erona asks you to begin a new task, **Unfortunate Measures.**

Unfortunate Measures	
Faction	Horde
Location	Sunstrider Isle
Quest Giver	Magistrix Erona
Quest Completion	Magistrix Erona
Reward	Green Chain Vest (Mail Chest 67 Armor), Lynxskin Gloves (Leather Hands, 21 Armor), or Sunrise Bracers (Cloth Wrist, 4 Armor), Chain to Report to Lanthan Perilon

Look for the Springpaw Lynxes and Cubs in the area. These enemies are spread out, but they are also very common. Attack them and collect the *Lynx Collars* that drop with high frequency. When you have eight of the Collars, return to Erona and complete the quest.

No matter which your class, has chosen, there is a small quest to seek your trainer in the nearby building. This is a good time to do that because you are able to train for new abilities upon reaching level two. Read the text of the quest to find out where your trainer is located.

Instead of this tiny quest ending blandly with your trainers, it actually chains into a real quest, with more interesting consequences. Regardless of the trainer you use, the person will give you **Well Watcher Solanian** to accept. Go to the top of Sunspire, the central building, and look for Solanian out

on the ledge above the main area. Solanian gives you the task of finding **Solanian's Belongings**. You are also asked to check on **The Shrine of Dath'Remar**. Also, talk to Erona again for the next step in that chain, **Report to Lanthan Perilon**.

Find Lanthan by following the road roughly southwest. Look for Lanthan by a large tree, and talk to him to get the quest, **Aggression**.

With these quests ready to go, you might notice that there are two other Blood Elves in the area who have taken interest in your activities. There are more golden exclamation points out there, and this is as good a time as any to collect them all. Search the areas nearby for Arcanist Helion and Arcanist Ithanas. The two of them have the quests, **Thirst Unending** and **A Fistful of Slivers**.

You should now have a group of five quests that can be done in a single run: **Solanian's Belongings, The Shrine of Dath'Remar, Aggression, Thirst Unending**, and **A Fistful of Slivers**. Set out and get some leveling done!

Aggression

Faction	Horde
Location	Sunstrider Isle
Quest Giver	Lanthan Perilon
Quest Completion	Lanthan Perilon
Reward	Sunstrider Axe (MH Axe, 2.0 DPS), Sunstrider Dagger (1h Dagger, 2.1 DPS), Sunstrider Mace (MH Mace, 2.0 DPS), Sunstrider Staff (Staff, 2.6 DPS), Sunstrider Sword (MH Sword, 2.0 DPS)

Thirst Unending

Faction	Horde
Location	Sunstrider Isle
Quest Giver	Arcanist Helion
Quest Completion	Arcanist Helion
Reward	Green Chain Gauntlets (Mail Hands, 42 Armor), Vigorous Bracers (Leather Wrists, 15 Armor), and Striding Pants (Cloth Legs, 9 Armor)

Solanian's Belongings

Faction	Horde
Location	Sunstrider Isle
Quest Giver	Well Watcher Solanian
Quest Completion	Well Watcher Solanian
Reward	Sunspire Cord (Leather Waist, 19 Armor), Well Watcher Gloves (Cloth Hands, 6 Armor)

The Shrine of Dath'Remar

Faction	Horde
Location	Sunstrider Isle
Quest Giver	Well Watcher Solanian
Quest Completion	Well Watcher Solanian
Reward	Experience

A Fistful of Slivers	
Faction	Horde
Location	Sunstrider Isle
Quest Giver	Arcanist Ithanas
Quest Completion	Arcanist Ithanas
Reward	Daylight Cloak (Back, 5 Armor)

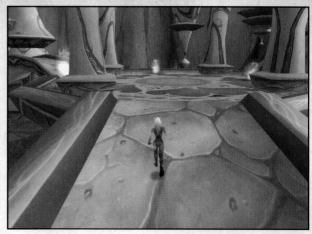

There are three items that Well Watcher Solanian wants you to retrieve: *Solanian's Scrying Orb*, *Scroll of Scourge Magic*, and *Solanian's Journal*. These are found at three separate sites in the isle, so there isn't a good reason to race to retrieve all of them at once. Instead, you want to pick these up while getting some of the other quests in your log finished.

The *Orb* is at the pond (southwest from Sunspire). Kill the Tenders while you are there to satisfy the requirements for **Aggression**. After finishing your work at the pond, walk north toward the fountain. You will find the *Scroll* there. Then, get the *Journal* by one of the Burning Crystals in the area. When you see creatures with mana while doing your fighting, be certain to Mana Tap them!

For **Aggression**, kill 7 *Tenders* and 7 *Feral Tenders*. This is a weapon quest for young characters, so that you won't have to wield the starting equipment for very long. Tarry by the pond to finish off enough of these enemies.

Mana Tap six creatures to satisfy the goal of **Thirst Unending**. Because there is a 30-second cooldown on Mana Tap, you would have to spend a few minutes doing this if you tried to do it by itself. Instead, Mana Tap enemies as you go through the area.

Learning About Mana Tap and Arcane Torrent

Notice how your character can build up to three charges of Mana Tap in preparation for a stronger Arcane Torrent. Being able to give yourself a boost of Mana or Energy is a big deal for any fight that might go the wrong way. In addition, Arcane Torrent gives Blood Elves the ability to Silence nearby enemies. Because there is a two-minute cooldown on Arcane Torrent, you might as well build up a few charges for each use and get the most out of it! Besides, Mana Tap is free, so you don't have to invest Energy or Mana to steal from enemies in the first place.

Speaking of good targets to Mana Tap, there are Mana Wyrms at many of the sites you are passing. These drop the *Arcane Slivers* that you need for **A Fistful of Slivers**. Kill the Mana Wyrms after Mana Tapping them, and use the creatures as targets of opportunity while exploring.

One point of interest is that you get a +5 Stamina/Spirit buff when you complete this quest for Arcanist Ithanas. That will be useful during the final push against the denizens of the Academy (not far in your future).

When all of the other quests are completed, walk to the northwestern part of the isle and look for the Shrine of Dath'Remar. Read the *Plaque* there to complete your quest.

Go back to Sunspire and hand in all five of your completed quests. This gets you a burst of experience, and takes you up to the point where you can train for your level 4 class abilities. Sell any unneeded items that were picked up along the way and collect the last quest from Lanthan Perilon. He wishes you to eliminate **Felendren the Banished**, at the Falthrien Academy.

Felendren the Banished	
Faction	Horde
Location	Sunstrider Isle
Quest Giver	Lanthan Perilon
Quest Completion	Lanthan Perilon
Reward	Sunstrider Bow (Bow, 3.9 DPS), Sunstrider Shield (Shield 55 Armor 1 Block)

Walk to the southwest, the direct route to the Falthrien Academy. Do this while you still have the buffs from turning in A Fistful of Slivers. Your mission is to kill 8 *Arcane Wraiths* and 2 *Tainted Arcane Wraiths* and take *Felendren's Head* before returning.

Like a number of the places in the Blood Elven lands, this Academy is bursting with magic. Held aloft by the forces of the ether, the building is a beautiful sight. Climb carefully up the walkways and into the higher tiers, dealing with the various Wraiths that guard the way. Not many of them come at the same time, so long as you pull them back and away from the open areas.

Loot the corpses for a group drop in this area, the Tainted Arcane Sliver. Use this item to start the quest, **Tainted Arcane Sliver**. This item drops from the Tainted Arcane Wraiths, unsurprisingly.

Felendren is at the top of the Academy. Destroy this fool for his mockery of what the Academy should stand for. Go back to the Sunspire once you have his head. If you still need to kill a few of the Wraiths, stay for that, but enough of them are found on the way up that this is usually moot.

THE JOURNEY SOUTH

This quest leads you away from your humble beginnings. Get it and take care of any parting business at the Sunspire before leaving. Talk to Outrunner Alarion on the road leaving south and away from Sunstrider Isle (toward the Ruins of Silvermoon). She offers you **Slain by the Wretched** in return.

Tainted Arcane Sliver	
Faction	Horde
Location	Sunstrider Isle
Quest Giver	Group Drop Item
Quest Completion	Arcanist Helion
Reward	Experience and Modest Money

Aiding the Outrunners	
Faction	Horde
Location	Sunstrider Isle
Quest Giver	Lanthan Perilon
Quest Completion	Outrunner Alarion
Reward	Chain to Slain by the Wretched

Slain by the Wretched

Faction	Horde
Location	Dawning Lane
Quest Giver	Outrunner Alarion
Quest Completion	Slain Outrunner
Reward	Chain to Package Recovery

Look for the Slain Outrunner in Dawning Lane. Take the main route through the street into the city, and you will find the Slain Outrunner lying right there, not far in. After completing the quest, you start **Package Recovery**.

Take the package back to Outrunner Alarion. She'll give you a new quest, **Completing the Delivery**.

Package Recovery

Faction	Horde
Location	Dawning Lane
Quest Giver	Slain Outrunner
Quest Completion	Outrunner Alarion
Reward	Chain to Completing the Delivery

Completing the Delivery

Faction	Horde
Location	Dawning Lane
Quest Giver	Outrunner Alarion
Quest Completion	Innkeeper Delaniel
Reward	Refreshing Spring Water (5) or Shiny Red Apples (5)

The Inn is on the SE side of the ruins, in a section called Falconwing Square. Complete this quest by going over to Innkeeper Delaniel, bind there so that you can Hearthstone back to it in the future, and look around for the various trainers and vendors in the area. You can learn First Aid and Cooking, sell, repair your equipment, and so forth. There is a recipe for Lynx Steak at the Inn, for those aspiring toward culinary greatness.

Talk to Magister Jaronis to get the **Major Malfunction** quest after you are finished with any immediate errands. Look for Aeldon Sunbrand as well, who has the collection quest **Unstable Mana Crystals**. Finally, look near the eastern side of Falconwing Square for a Wanted Poster. This starts **Wanted: Thaelis the Hungerer**.

With this group of quests initiated, it's time to search through the ruins.

Major Malfunction

Faction	Horde
Location	Falconwing Square
Quest Giver	Magister Jaronis
Quest Completion	Magister Jaronis
Reward	Green Chain Belt (Mail Waist 38 Armor), Light Silk Robe (Cloth Chest 10 Armor), or Soft Leather Vest (Leather Chest 33 Armor), Chain to Delivery to the North Sanctum

Unstable Mana Crystals

Faction	Horde
Location	Falconwing Square
Quest Giver	Aeldon Sunbrand
Quest Completion	Aeldon Sunbrand
Reward	Experience

Wanted: Thaelis the Hungerer	
Faction	Horde
Location	Falconwing Square
Quest Giver	Wanted Poster (East Side of Falconwing Square)
Quest Completion	Sergeant Kan'ren
Reward	Experience

Collect 6 *Arcane Cores* from the Arcane Patrollers that roam the city. These enemies are all over the city, but the best concentration of them is by the roads. You find them frequently there, sometimes with a couple close to each other. They have a very high drop rate, so it only takes six to get what you need.

While going after the Arcane Patrollers, collect six *Unstable Mana Crystals*. Look for crates that contain these. They are all over the place too, but the best area is near Thaelis' building, on the eastern side of the ruins. These crates have a faint glow to them, and that helps you to spot them even at range.

There is a large building that is still intact, and a number of monsters guard the place. Clear a spot for some safe fighting and get your health back to full before pulling Thaelis. He comes with one or two people, so pull carefully if you are nervous. Once you have his head, return to Falconwing Square and turn everything in.

Talk to Jaronis again. With his previous deed finished, he'll ask you to leave the ruins and check on the areas outside the walls. His **Delivery to the North Sanctum** sends you to a small area that is relatively quiet and close by. Also, grab **Darnassian Intrusions** from Aeldon Sunbrand. These are the only quests for the moment.

SPREADING OUT AND EXPLORING THE WILDERNESS

Delivery to the North Sanctum	
Faction	Horde
Location	Falconwing Square
Quest Giver	Magister Jaronis
Quest Completion	Ley-Keeper Caidanis
Reward	Chain to Malfunction at the West Sanctum

Darnassian Intrusions	
Faction	Horde
Location	Falconwing Square
Quest Giver	Aeldon Sunbrand
Quest Completion	Ley-Keeper Velania
Reward	Chain to Arcane Instability

Leave via the southern gate and head to the North Sanctum. All that you need to do there is switch **Delivery to the North Sanctum** over to **Malfunction at the West Sanctum** by talking to Ley-Keeper Caidanis. From there, continue on to the West Sanctum, off on its own island one a short distance away.

Malfunction at the West Sanctum	
Faction	Horde
Location	North Sanctum
Quest Giver	Ley-Keeper Caidanis
Quest Completion	Ley-Keeper Velania
Reward	Experience

Now that you have two targets at the West Sanctum, look for Ley-Keeper Velania. She stands to the east of the Sanctum, run out of her area by the Mana Wraiths and Mana Stalkers that now infest the valley. Agree to help her out by killing 5 of each. As an added bonus the void creatures give power-boffs for magic users when they die

Arcane Instability	
Faction	Horde
Location	West Sanctum
Quest Giver	Ley-Keeper Velania
Quest Completion	Ley-Keeper Velania
Reward	Ley-Keeper's Blade (1H Sword, 2.4 DPS) or Velania's Walking Stick (Staff 3.2 DPS)

When you turn in the Incriminating Documents, Aeldon realizes their significance. To stop the flowing of dangerous information, he charges you with eliminating the insidious source, **The Dwarven Spy**.

While doing this, keep an eye out for the Darnassians that are prowling around. The Darnassian Scouts should be dispatched whenever you see them; go after them as aggressively as possible. If you are lucky, the Darnassians will drop **Incriminating Documents** to begin a quest of the same name.

The Dwarven Spy	
Faction	Horde
Location	Falconwing Square
Quest Giver	Aeldon Sunbrand
Quest Completion	Aeldon Sunbrand
Reward	Bloodhawk Claymore (2H Sword, 3.6 DPS) or Long Knife (1H Sword, 2.9 DPS)

Mostly, the Darnassians stay up on the hills to avoid the Mana Wraiths. If you can't find the Incriminating Documents at first, search along the ridgeline that surrounds the West Sanctum until you find the right target.

Go back to the North Sanctum and talk to Prospector Anvilward. Convince him (using the text option that appears) to come inside and have a private chat with you. Far too late to save himself, the Dwarf recognizes that he is in grave danger. Lay into him with your best attacks, and watch this threat to Eversong go up in smoke (or fall to steel; your preference really). Return to Aeldon and tell him that the problem has been eliminated.

Incriminating Documents	
Faction	Horde
Location	West Sanctum
Quest Giver	Incriminating Documents
Quest Completion	Aeldon Sunbrand
Reward	Chain to The Dwarven Spy

THE DEAD SCAR AND SOME NAUGHTY APPRENTICES

There are now a few assorted quests to gather, as your character moves down toward Fairbreeze Village. On the way are a few off-the-beaten-path chores that are pretty fun. Get **Fairbreeze Village** from Aeldon, at Falconwing Square. That is an introduction quest that is meant to get you where you are supposed to be.

After activating these by right-clicking on them, you can take the papers back to Aeldon, at Falconwing Square. Wait until you have finished with your business at the West Sanctum though, since there won't be any need to come back this far for any return trips.

Training From Time to Time

Players that have leveled characters before will be familiar with training. Even if you aren't as seasoned you should remember the class trainers are located in Falconwing Square and in the eastern part of Silvermoon City.

Soaked Pages

Faction	Horde
Location	Eversong Woods
Quest Giver	Apprentice Meledor
Quest Completion	Apprentice Meledor
Reward	Chains to Taking the Fall

Looking on the map, Fairbreeze Village is not too long a trip to the south. Start walking down the road out of Silvermoon City but stop at the main bridge. Apprentice Meledor starts a chain there that should not be missed (the payoff at the end is wonderful, not in gold or experience, but in sheer amusement).

Taking the Fall

Faction	Horde
Location	Eversong Woods
Quest Giver	Apprentice Meledor
Quest Completion	Instructor Antheol
Reward	Chain to Swift Discipline

Take Antheol's Elemental Grimoire to Instructor Antheol at Stillwhisper Pond. This is to the southeast of Silvermoon. Getting there means you have to cross the Dead Scar, a place where you will soon return to fight. Once you reach Stillwhisper Pond, talk to Instructor Antheol and give him his Grimoire back. Nonplussed over the role his Apprentices played in the affair, Antheol hands you the role of **Swift Discipline**. This is where it all gets good!

Fairbreeze Village

Faction	Horde
Location	Falconwing Square
Quest Giver	Aeldon Sunbrand
Quest Completion	Ranger Degolien
Reward	More Quests

Swift Discipline

Faction	Horde
Location	Stillwhisper Pond
Quest Giver	Instructor Antheol
Quest Completion	Instructor Antheol
Reward	Magister's Pouch (4 Slot Bag)

To retrieve *Antheol's Elemental Grimoire*, dive into the cool water behind the Apprentice and swim underneath the bridge. Still visible in the dirt at the bottom is the journal you are looking for. Right-click on it and swim back to the top. Talk to Meledor again, and he'll give you **Taking the Fall** this time.

Use *Antheol's Disciplinary Rod* on his two students. One of them you've already met, back at the bridge (Apprentice Meledor). The other is northeast up the road from Meledor (Apprentice Ralen). Using the Rod on the two of them causes an interesting effect to occur, as Ralen sadly laments.

When you return to Instructor Antheol, he'll reward you with a four-slot bag, called the Magister's Pouch. It's not much of a bag, but it might do if you don't have a few spare silver to fill out your allotment of six-slot bags.

Return to the Dead Scar and walk to the north, where the Dead Scar passes right through the center of Silvermoon City. The cursed event looks like it ripped right through everything, stopping for neither person nor building. It's no wonder that the Scourge litter the place now. By the city walls is a group of Rangers, led by Ranger Jaela (Jaela and her band are also needed for the priest-specific quest). Offer to help her clear **The Dead Scar**.

The Dead Scar	
Faction	Horde
Location	The Dead Scar
Quest Giver	Ranger Jaela
Quest Completion	Ranger Jaela
Reward	Black Leather Vest (Leather Chest 37), Gatewatcher's Chain Gloves (Mail Hands 46 Armor), or Guard's Leggings (Cloth Legs 10 Armor)

Kill 8 Plagueborn Pillagers in the areas either north or south of the Ranger. Plagueborn Pillagers are the Skeletons of this part of the Dead Scar, and most are close by. If you stray too far to the south along the Scar, you will soon find tougher Undead that are not needed for the quest.

ON TO FAIRBREEZE VILLAGE

Now it's perfectly fine to move southwest and enter Fairbreeze Village. It's just past another fork in the road and is only somewhat west of the Dead Scar. Within are a full range of quests to start.

Don't forget to repair, restock any supplies that are lagging, and rebind at the Inn here.

Complete Aeldon's quest to contact **Fairbreeze Village** by talking to Ranger Degolien. Degolien, who is on the second floor of the Fairbreeze Inn, tells you about the **Situation at Sunsail Anchorage**, which is an area to the west, where Wretched Thugs and Hooligans are taking over. Before hurrying out to do that, talk to Velan Brightoak as well. Velan needs some **Pelt Collection** done, and asks for you to find six *Springpaw Pelts* from the local Lynxes (Springpaw Stalkers). Because these creatures are only seen here or there, it's wise to get this quest right up front and get it done as a matter of opportunity (instead of hunting the creatures on their own). Just attack the Springpaws as you see them, and the quest will pretty much finish itself.

Questing for Lord Saltheril

There is a somewhat involved chain that has you go to several places on the map and pick up a few items in the chain. If you are interested in this, talk to Magistrix Landra Dawnstrider while you are still in town. You learn that there is a place called **Saltheril's Haven**, just to the west of town. There, Lord Saltheril is busy partying away while the other Blood Elves fight the good fight.

Go there and talk to Lord Saltheril next. **The Party Never Ends** is the Lord's claim, but for that to stay true a few items are needed. You must collect Suntouched Special Reserve, Springpaw Appetizers, and a Bundle of Fireworks. Doing all of this will get you an award of experience and the ability to talk to the party goers (some of them are trainers). You can also loot and interact with some of the very items that you brought to the party.

When you bring these back, you get a profit of a few silver, so don't worry about the out-of-pocket expenses. You can also use the Invitation that is given to you to pick up goodies from the tables; there are multiple spawns of these.

Saltheril's Haven

Faction	Horde
Location	Fairbreeze Village
Quest Giver	Magistrix Landra Dawnstrider
Quest Completion	Lord Saltheril
Reward	Access to Party Items/Interaction With Party Goers

The Party Never Ends

Faction	Horde
Location	Saltheril's Haven
Quest Giver	Lord Saltheril
Quest Completion	Lord Saltheril
Reward	Saltheril's Haven Party Invitation

Situation at Sunsail Anchorage

Faction	Horde
Location	Fairbreeze Village
Quest Giver	Ranger Degolien
Quest Completion	Ranger Degolien
Reward	Experience

This quest should be done while adventuring. So, while doing other quests throughout Eversong Woods, keep an eye out for the following vendors.

For the *Suntouched Special Reserve*, trade with Vinemaster Suntouched in the Silvermoon City Inn, near the Royal Exchange. This is inside the actual capital of Silvermoon City, so look on that map instead of the Eversong Woods one. This item costs 3 silver, without any discounts for reputation.

Springpaw Appetizers only cost 1 silver and are purchased from Zalene First-light at the Farstrider Retreat. This is on the eastern side of the map and is the location for some of the anti-Troll questing later in the region.

A *Bundle of Fireworks* can be had for 1 silver and 50 copper. These are found directly at Fairbreeze Village, so you can pick them up at any time. Buy them from Halis Dawnstrider.

Pelt Collection

Faction	Horde
Location	Fairbreeze Village
Quest Giver	Velan Brightoak
Quest Completion	Velan Brightoak
Reward	Springpaw Hide Leggings (Leather Legs 36 Armor), Fur Lined Chain Shirt (Mail Chest 81 Armor), or Springpaw Hide Cloak (Back 7 Armor)

Now that you are on the lookout for easy *Pelts*, head west until you approach Sunsail Anchorage. Just before you reach the main area, where the Wretched Thugs and Hooligans patrol, you should spot Captain Kelisendra. The Captain's group has a few extra quests for you, while you are in the area. Start these now, in addition to fighting the *5 Wretched Thugs* and *5 Wretched Hooligans* for Ranger Degolien.

Captain Kelisendra gives you **Grimscale Pirates!** Velendris Whitemorn starts **Lost Armaments**. The Captain's quest takes you up north along the coast, to hit the Murloc camps. Velendris' quest chain has you attacking the Anchorage directly. For a few reasons, start with the Anchorage quests.

It's wise to start with the Lost Armaments quest because there may not be enough of the boxes in the area to collect 8 Sin'dorei Armaments in a single run. When other people are in the area, you might need to wait a few minutes for a respawn of these boxes.

So, make your run, then divert farther west if competition causes you to cool your heels a little. Run the **Grimscale Pirates!** quest in the meanwhile, and there should be plenty of new boxes by the time you get back.

Lost Armaments	
Faction	Horde
Location	Sunsail Anchorage
Quest Giver	Velendris Whitemorn
Quest Completion	Velendris Whitemorn
Reward	Rusty Sin'dorei Sword (MH Sword 3.0 DPS), or Rusty Mace (1H Mace 2.6 DPS)

Wretched Ringleader	
Faction	Horde
Location	Sunsail Anchorage
Quest Giver	Velendris Whitemorn
Quest Completion	Velendris Whitemorn
Reward	Sunsail Bracers (Mail Wrist 39 Armor), Longshoreman's Bindings (Leather Wrist 20 Armor), or Silk Wristbands (Cloth Wrist 7 Armor)

Once you have this quest, walk in the main entrance of the building above the Anchorage and start to fight your way to the top. Avoid walking through the center of the rooms unless you want extra aggro from all of the enemies at once; though these are soft targets, the adds might not be healthy for you.

Aldaron is at the top of the tower, and it is possible to pull him by himself if you are careful. The leader has a two-handed sword for some decent DPS, and he casts fire spells on top of that not a lot of subtlety here to this guy. Mana Tap Aldaron early on, and Silence him with Arcane Torrent once he tries to use fire on you. In doing so, the fight should be a piece of cake. Snag *Aldaron's Head* and give it to Velendris at your convenience.

With the Anchorage in good shape, move north to fight the Murlocs (if you haven't done so already).

Move into the lower area of the Anchorage and fight against the Thugs and Hooligans. These foes are low level and spread out when you fight down on the docks. As you head up toward the building above the docks, their numbers begin to increase slightly, so more care is needed if you are alone or are poorly equipped.

While fighting against the enemies there, look for the boxes that are spread over the Anchorage. The highest concentration of them is in and around the main building, but the boxes stretch along the entire length of the docks. These contain the *Sin'dorei Armaments* that Velendris desires. Once you have killed the enemies you need and collected 8 Sin'dorei Armaments, return to Velendris to get the next step, **Wretched Ringleader**.

Grimscale Pirates!	
Faction	Horde
Location	Sunsail Anchorage
Quest Giver	Captain Kelisendra
Quest Completion	Captain Kelisendra
Reward	Experience

Look for six sets of *Captain Kelisendra's Cargo* by fighting the Murlocs in the Golden Strand, along the western coast. Not only do the little guys hold the *Cargo* directly, but there are barrels that have additional sets as well. This won't take terribly long, but be certain to fight enough that you get the Drop Quest Item, *Captain Kelisendra's Lost Rudders*. Also, look for the larger Murloc, Mmmmrrrggglll, as he is fun to fight.

Defending Fairbreeze Village	
Faction	Horde
Location	Fairbreeze Village
Quest Giver	Ranger Sareyn
Quest Completion	Ranger Sareyn
Reward	Experience

Captain Kelisendra's Lost Rudders	
Faction	Horde
Location	Golden Strand
Quest Giver	Captain Kelisendra's Lost Rudders
Quest Completion	Captain Kelisendra
Reward	Experience

You get these as a random group drop off of the Murlocs. It usually doesn't take too many kills to discover, and it's easy experience when you return to item to Captain Kelisendra.

This completes the quests in and around the Anchorage. After turning in both quests to Kelisendra and finishing with Velendris, you should return to Fairbreeze Village and talk to Degolien again for your reward. If you've found all six *Sprinpaw Pelts* already, turn those in as well (though you'd have to be fairly lucky to have that done so soon).

Marniel Amberlight, the Innkeeper, sends you out to meet **Ranger Sareyn**. After greeting the Ranger, who is on the eastern road out of Fairbreeze, you receive **Defending Fairbreeze Village**. Also, ask Magistrix Landra Dawnstrider about **The Wayward Apprentice** before leaving town.

The Wayward Apprentice	
Faction	Horde
Location	Fairbreeze Village
Quest Giver	Magistrix Landra Dawnstrider
Quest Completion	Apprentice Mirveda
Reward	Chain to Corrupted Soil

The East Sanctum has the targets that you need for **Defending Fairbreeze Village**. So, follow your map and run over to East Sanctum. When you get there, look on the eastern side of the Dead Scar; behind the Sanctum itself is Apprentice Mirveda, who asks you to help her research the **Corrupted Soil**.

Ranger Sareyn	
Faction	Horde
Location	Fairbreeze Village
Quest Giver	Marniel Amberlight
Quest Completion	Ranger Sareyn
Reward	Chain to Defending Fairbreeze Village

As soon as you start the quest, three enemies attack Apprentice Mirveda. Two of the enemies are Angerwraiths, and the third is Gharsul the Remorseless. If you didn't have Mirveda's help in the fight, things might be pretty dangerous indeed. Let her hold aggro for at least one of the enemies, as she is up to the challenge. Blast through the Angerwraiths, as they are very fast to drop. Then, focus on Gharsul, who is named but not Elite.

When the fight ends, Mirveda asks you to take her **Research Notes** back to Magistrix Landra Dawnstrider.

Corrupted Soil

Faction	Horde
Location	East Sanctum
Quest Giver	Apprentice Mirveda
Quest Completion	Apprentice Mirveda
Reward	Chain to Unexpected Results

While grabbing the glowing green *Tainted Soil Samples* for Mirveda, you end up killing the *4 Rotlimb Marauders* and *4 Darkwraiths* that you wanted to fight anyway. If you end up short on *Darkwraiths*, the harder ones to find, then travel south later to pick up any stragglers.

After turning in **Corrupted Soil**, wait for Mirveda to finish testing what you brought. Be certain to have full health when you talk to her again and receive **Unexpected Results**.

Research Notes

Faction	Horde
Location	East Sanctum
Quest Giver	Apprentice Mirveda
Quest Completion	Magistrix Landra Dawnstrider
Reward	Experience

Take Mirveda's *Research Notes* back to Fairbreeze village and hand them over to Landra. This is already on your way, because there are some tasks at Fairbreeze that lead you to the southwest anyway, and those are perfectly fitting at this stage.

Once you are in Fairbreeze again, ask Ardeyn Riverwind about **The Scorched Grave**. You learn that Larianna Riverwind is near that area, at the bottom

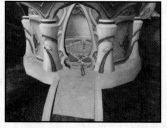

of Eversong Woods. With the problems there, it is likely that your assistance is needed as soon as possible.

Unexpected Results

Faction	Horde
Location	East Sanctum
Quest Giver	Apprentice Mirveda
Quest Completion	Apprentice Mirveda
Reward	Chain to Research Notes

The Scorched Grave

Faction	Horde
Location	Fairbreeze Village
Quest Giver	Ardeyn Riverwind
Quest Completion	Larianna Riverwind
Reward	Chain to A Somber Task

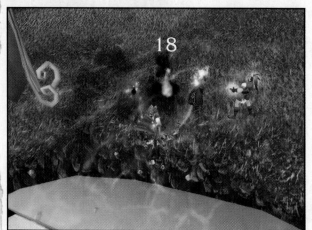

Travel to the south, to the map location marked with Larianna Riverwind. Talk with her and receive **A Somber Task**.

Whitebark's Memory

Faction	Horde
Location	The Scorched Grove
Quest Giver	Larianna Riverwind
Quest Completion	Whitebark's Spirit
Reward	Experience

Bury Old Whitebark's Pendant at the blue Runestone that dominates the eastern part of the Scorched Grove. This summons Whitebark's Spirit, which will be aggressive at first. Start the fight at range to capitalize on the slow advancement that the Spirit makes. Not that you probably need to run and keep hitting it at range, but it is an option if you want to have fun. When the Spirit is almost defeated, it will turn Friendly and talk to you, completing the quest.

Instead of heading back, move farther to the east and look for the next Runestone on your map. This is the location of Runewarden Deryan, who is involved in **Powering Our Defenses**. He notes that two of the three Runestones in the area have been trashed by the recent wars. However, one of the Runestones might be activated again, he hopes. This final Runestone is to the east, and it won't take you long to reach it.

A Somber Task

Faction	Horde
Location	The Scorched Grove
Quest Giver	Larianna Riverwind
Quest Completion	Larianna Riverwind
Reward	Experience

Kill 10 of the *Withered Green Keepers* that control The Scorched Grave. You can't swing a stick without hitting one; of course, that stick is probably one of their discarded limbs, so they might take it quite personally. Either way, look for a larger tree while doing this, a tougher elemental by the name of Old Whitebark. This one drops a quest item (*Old Whitebark's Pendant*). Right click on that to start a quest of the same name.

Powering Our Defenses

Faction	Horde
Location	Eversong Woods
Quest Giver	Runewarden Deryan
Quest Completion	Runewarden Deryan
Reward	Experience

Old Whitebark's Pendant

Faction	Horde
Location	The Scorched Grove
Quest Giver	Old Whitebark's Pendant
Quest Completion	Larianna Riverwind
Reward	Chain to Whitebark's Memory.

Return the item to Larianna Riverwind once you have destroyed all 10 of the required *Withered Green Keepers*. Hand in both quests, and receive **Whitebark's Memory**.

Attempt to *Energize the Runestone*, but keep your wits about you; Energized Wraiths attack in two waves. Though they have low health, you must face three of them at a time. After the first three drop, use any food or water that you have to restore yourself; otherwise, the next wave will hit before you are ready to deal with them. Once the task is complete, return to Runewarden Deryan.

ROLLING OVER TO EAST SIDE

Stop back at Fairbreeze Village for any chores that need doing, and start Ranger Degolien's next quest, **Farstrider Retreat**. You are now high enough in level and equipment to be able to handle the monsters on the eastern side of the map. Travel northeast, across the river that feeds Stillwhisper Pond, and look for the large Farstrider building.

The Spearcrafter's Hammer	
Faction	Horde
Location	Farstrider Retreat
Quest Giver	Arathel Sunforge
Quest Completion	Arathel Sunforge
Reward	Farstrider Sword (2H Sword 5.8 DPS), Smooth Metal Staff (Staff 5.7 DPS), or Ranger's Pocketknife (1H Dagger 4.3 DPS)

Take the path up into the hills, to the region northwest of Tor'Watha on your map. These outlying areas are where you can find the *Amani Berserkers* and *Axe Throwers* that are needed for your quest. At the center of the first camp with actual buildings is *Spearcrafter Otembe*, another important target for you. Knock down all of these foes and speak with Ven'jashi, who is trapped in a cage not far from where Otembe lives. This conversation sparks the quest, **Zul'Marosh**.

Though Tor'Watha extends south for a great distance, you won't find any quest targets in the lower areas. All of the foes you need are up in the hills at the very beginning of the Tor'Watha area, as shown on the map.

Farstrider Retreat	
Faction	Horde
Location	Fairbreeze Village
Quest Giver	Ranger Degolien
Quest Completion	Lieutenant Dawnrunner
Reward	Experience

Go inside the enclave and meet its residents. Lieutenant Dawnrunner is combatting the **Amani Encroachment**. Arathel Sunforge, the blacksmith of the Retreat, also wants you to combat the Trolls. We wants you to find and return **The Spearcrafter's Hammer**, which is in the hands of Spearcrafter Otembe.

Zul'Marosh	
Faction	Horde
Location	Tor'Watha
Quest Giver	Ven'jashi
Quest Completion	Ven'jashi
Reward	Ven'jashi's Bow (Bow 6.7 DPS), Hoodoo Wand (Wand 8.1 DPS)

Before returning to the Farstrider Retreat, come down from the hills and cross the Lake Elrendar. Zeb'Watha is on the other side, and that is where Chieftain Zul'Marosh lives. The largest building of the area is his hut, and you should see the big guy on the second floor of it even while standing outside the hut.

Amani Encroachment	
Faction	Horde
Location	Farstrider Retreat
Quest Giver	Lieutenant Dawnrunner
Quest Completion	Lieutenant Dawnrunner
Reward	Experience

Fight your way in, clearing the lower floor. On top is a platform with three guards and the Chieftain. Keep an eye out for the patrolling guard who comes all the way up to the top. If you see that guy, nail him sooner rather than later.

Pull both of the peripheral guards ahead of time, to avoid complications. Then, attack the final guard and the Chieftain simultaneously. Go after the guard first, for the fast victory, then turn on Zul'Marosh. Mana Tap him and use Arcane Torrent for a boost.

Once he dies, you can return *Zul'Marosh's Head* to Ven'jashi, and take the *Amani Invasion Plans* that drop to Lieutenant Dawnrunner, back at the Farstrider Retreat. You have two other quests to turn in there anyway!

Amani Invasion

Faction	Horde
Location	Zeb'Watha
Quest Giver	Amani Invasion Plans
Quest Completion	Lieutenant Dawnrunner
Reward	Chain to Warning Fairbreeze Village

Lieutenant Dawnrunner is concerned enough about the Amani's plans that it seems sensible to tell the good folks in Fairbreeze Village. The good news is that this can wait until you are down in that neck of the woods for other things. Instead, your next target is the Duskwither Spire. Purchase the *Springpaw Appetizers* from Zalene Firstlight if you are doing **The Party Never Ends**. After that, travel north and take the path out to the Duskwither Spire.

Warning Fairbreeze Village

Faction	Horde
Location	Farstrider Retreat
Quest Giver	Lieutenant Dawnrunner
Quest Completion	Ranger Degolien
Reward	Blackened Chain Girdle (Mail Waist 61 Armor), Ranger's Vest (Leather Chest 55 Armor), or Satin Lined Boots (Cloth Feet 14 Armor)

The north road from Farstrider Retreat has an eastern branch. Take that and look for Apprentice Loralthalis, a sad student of the arcane who regrets the current state of the Spire. To cheer her up, you can take on the job of **Deactivating the Spire** and find out **Where's Wyllithen?**

Deactivating the Spire

Faction	Horde
Location	Duskwither Spire
Quest Giver	Apprentice Loralthalis
Quest Completion	Apprentice Loralthalis
Reward	Chain To Word From The Spire

Where's Wyllithen

Faction	Horde
Location	Duskwither Spire
Quest Giver	Apprentice Loralthalis
Quest Completion	Groundskeeper Wyllithen
Reward	Chain to Cleaning Up The Grounds

Stay on the northern path and follow it down in the gardens of the Spire. Ignore the Translocation Orb you pass on the way (for now), and look to see if you can spot old Willie. Surrounded by enemies, Groundskeeper Wyllithen is spitting mad with the chaos these things are causing. He wants *6 Mana Serpents* and just as many *Ether Fiends* put down immediately. That is his way of **Cleaning the Grounds**.

Cleaning Up The Grounds	
Faction	Horde
Location	Duskwither Grounds
Quest Giver	Groundskeeper Wyllithen
Quest Completion	Groundskeeper Wyllithen
Reward	Experience

Word From The Spire	
Faction	Horde
Location	Duskwither Grounds
Quest Giver	Apprentice Loralthalis
Quest Completion	Magister Duskwither
Reward	Fallen Apprentice's Robe (Cloth Chest 19 Armor, +1 Stam, +1 Int)

Fighting those targets as you go, return to the Translocation Orb and use it to enter the Spire. Take down all three power sources using the Jewel that Loralthalis gave you.

The inside of Duskwither Spire has modest fighting against the mystic creatures of the area, but they never come in too large a group. Thus, it is very safe to solo here. There are three floors to clear, and each has one of the *Power Sources* that you are trying to disable. On top, with the last *Power Source*, is another Translocation Orb that will spit you back outside.

Let Loralthalis know that all is well, and he'll have you send **Word From The Spire** to Magister Duskwither, back at the Farstrider Retreat. Hit that on the way for your just reward, and consider a stop at the capital as well. If you haven't already gotten the Flight Point from Skymistress Gloaming, do so now. Then head inside for class training, learning new weapon skills from the Weapon Master, and other such tasks. If you want to keep up with **The Party Never Ends**, look for the *Suntouched Special Reserve* at the Silvermoon City Inn.

SILVERMOON CITY MAP LEGEND

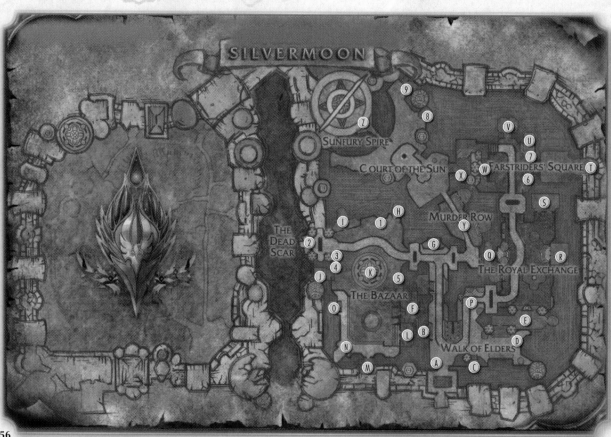

A Front Gate

Arcane Guardian	65
Gatewatcher Aendor	
Harassed Citizen	
Silvermoon City Guardian	65
Silvermoon Guardian	22

B Wayfarer's Rest   Shortcut Between Bazaar/Walk of Elders

Cooking Stove	
Innkeeper Jovia	Innkeeper
Mailbox	
Quelis	Cooking Supplier
Rarthein	
Sylann	Cook

C Registrar of Guilds

Kredis	Tabard Vendor
Tandrine	Guild Master

D Skinner's Corner

Lynalis	Expert Leatherworker
Talmar	Journeyman Leatherworker
Tyn	Skinner
Zaralda	Leatherworking Supplier

E Jewelers

Amin	Journeyman Jewelcrafter
Blood Elf Magister	
Gelanthis	Jewelcrafting Supplier
Kalinda	Master Jewelcrafter
Telia	Expert Jewelcrafter
Toban	Artisan Jewelcrafter
Worker Mo'rrisroe	Silvermoon Builder's Association

F Velanni's Arcane Goods

Velanni	Arcane Goods Vendor
Zathanna	Wand Vendor

G Elder's Park

Conjurer Tyren	
Harene Plainwalker	Druid Trainer
Silvermoon City Guardian	65

H Silvermoon Finery

Andra	Clothier
Rathin	Bag Vendor
Zyandrel	Cloth Armor Merchant

I Keelen's Trustworthy Tailoring

Deynna	Tailoring Supplier
Galana	Journeyman Tailor
Leper Gnome Laborer	
Sheets	Expert Tailor

Sirigna'no	Sheets' Minion

J Blades by Rehein/Feledis' Axes

Rahein	Blade Vendor
Reledis	Axe Vendor

K The Auctionhouse

Darise	Auctioneer
Feynna	Auctioneer
Jenath	Auctioneer
Vynna	Auctioneer

L The Bank of Silvermoon

Ceera	Banker
Elana	Banker
Hatheon	Banker
Silvermoon City Guardian	65

M Shields of Silver/Plate and Mail Protection

Keeli	Mail Armor Merchant
Tynna	Plate Armor Merchant
Winthren	Shield Merchant

N The Rabble

Lyria Skystrider	
Melaya Tassler	
Priest Ennas	
Silvermoon Citizen	
Silvermoon Magister	
Terric Brightwind	
Vaeron Kormar	

O General Goods

Rarthein	
Sathren Azuredawn	General Goods
Zalle	Reagent Vendor

P Tradesmen on the Corner

Alestus	First Aid Trainer
Drathen	Fishing Trainer
Olirea	Fishing Supplier

Q Silvermoon City Inn   Shortcut Between Murder Row/Royal Exchange

Blood Knight Adept	
Blood Knight Stillblade	
Innkeeper Velandra	Innkeeper
Vinemaster Suntouched	Wine and Spirits Merchant

R The Royal Exchange

Caidari	Auctioneer
Itthilan	Auctioneer
Silvermoon City Guardian	65
Tandron	Auctioneer

S Royal Exchange Bank

Daenice	Banker
Mailbox	
Novia	Banker
Periel	Banker
Silvermoon City Guardian	65

T Farstrider Square

Bipp Glizzitor	Arena Master
Champion Vranesh	
Duyash the Cruel	Eye of the Storm Battlemaster
Gurok	Alterac Valley Battlemaster
Ileda	Weapon Master (Bow/Dagger/Polearm/1H Sword/2H Sword/Thrown)
Initiate Colin	
Initiate Emeline	
Ithelis	Paladin Trainer
Karen Wentworth	Arathi Basin Battlemaster
Knight-Lord Bloodvalor	
Krukk	Warsong Gulch Battlemaster
Osselan	Paladin Trainer
Silvermoon City Guardian	65
Wylaris	Paladin Trainer

U Entrance to Lady Liadrin's Area

Blood Elf Magister	
Blood Knight Adept	
Lady Liadrin	Blood Knight Matriarch (Boss)
Magister Astalor Bloodsworn	

V Hunter's Guild

Halthenis	Pet Trainer
Oninarth	Hunter Trainer
Shalenn	Stable Master
Silvermoon Ranger	
Tana	Hunter Trainer
Zandine	Hunter Trainer

W The Forge

Anvil	
Belil	Mining Trainer
Bemarrin	Expert Blacksmith
Eriden	Blacksmithing Supplier
Forge	
Mirvedon	Journeyman Blacksmith
Zelan	Mining Supplies

X Engineer's Corner

Anvil	
Danwe	Expert Engineer
Gloresse	Journeyman Engineer
Yatheon	Engineering Supplier

Y Murderer's Row

Alamma	Warlock Trainer
Blood Elf Warlock	
Darlia	Poison Supplier
Elara	Rogue Trainer
Instructor Cel	
Keyanomir	
Mailbox	
Nerisen	Rogue Trainer
Nimrida	Keyanomir's Minion
Talionia	Warlock Trainer
Torian	Demon Trainer
Trainee Alcor	
Trainee Firea	
Zanien	Warlock Trainer
Zelanis	Rogue Trainer

Z Sunfury Spire

Aldrae	Priest Trainer
Aurosalia	
Belestra	Priest Trainer
Elrodan	
Inethven	Mage Trainer
Lor'themar Theron	Regent Lord of Quel'Thalas (Boss)
Lotheolan	Priest Trainer
Narinth	Portal Trainer
Quithas	Mage Trainer
Silvermoon City Guardian	65
Teleporter to Undercity	
Zaedana	Mage Trainer

1 Bithrus	**Fireworks Vendor**
2 West Gate	
3 Welethelon	**Blunt Weapon Merchant**
4 Noraelath	**Leather Armor Merchant**
5 Parnis	**Tradesman**
6 Mathaleron	**Gunsmith**
7 Celana	**Bowyer**
8 Enchants Enhanced	**Enchanting Training and Supplies**
9 Silvermoon Alchemy	**Herbalism and Alchemy Training and Supplies**

Return to Fairbreeze, turn in **Word From The Spire** and **Warning Fairbreeze Village**, and pick up the final ingredient for **The Party Never Ends**, if you like. This is the *Bundle of Fireworks*, from Halis Dawnstrider. Take those items over to Saltheril's Haven and turn in that considerable quest to keep the party going.

Very little is left to accomplish in Eversong Woods. You can fought long and hard, and now it's time to move on. Magistrix Landra Dawnstrider, in Fairbreeze, lets you know that a courier has been lost on the way to the Ghostlands. Accept the quest **Missing in the Ghostlands**, then leave the village.

THE GHOSTLANDS CALL

Look on the eastern side of the Dead Scar, just on the border between the two zones. Courier Dawnstrider has been ambushed by the Scourge, and he now clings barely to life. With some luck, a Forsaken by the name of Apothecary Thedra is there to tend the Courier. Talk with both of these people, in turn, to get **The Fallen Courier** quest.

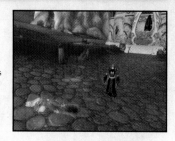

Keep going south, into Ghostlands. To "save" the Courier from his fate, kill the beasts of the area until you can collect *4 Plagued Blood Samples*. Any of the beasts from that area can drop the Blood you need, and their levels are comparable to what you've already been fighting and defeating.

Hasten back to the Apothecary when you are done. Hand her the Blood and talk to Courier Dawnstrider after his partial recovery. He'll transfer his duties over to you. Thus, you now have a **Delivery to Tranquillien** to take care of.

Missing in the Ghostlands

Faction	Horde
Location	Fairbreeze Village
Quest Giver	Magistrix Landra Dawnstrider
Quest Completion	Courier Dawnstrider
Reward	Chain to The Fallen Courier

The Fallen Courier

Faction	Horde
Location	Southern Tip of Eversong Woods
Quest Giver	Apothecary Thedra
Quest Completion	Apothecary Thedra
Reward	Chain to Delivery to Tranquillien

Delivery to Tranquillien

Faction	Horde
Location	Southern Tip of Eversong Woods
Quest Giver	Courier Dawnstrider
Quest Completion	Arcanist Vandril
Reward	Courier's Wraps (Cloth Wrist 8 Armor, +1 Int), Tranquillien Scout's Bracers (Leather Wrist 24 Armor, +1 AGI), or Bronze Mail Bracers (Mail Wrist 47 Armor, +1 STR) AND Courier's Bag (6 Slot Bag)

GHOSTLANDS MAP LEGEND

Ghostlands Legend

A Tranquillien (East Side)

Anvil	
Apothecary Renzithen	Quest Giver
Arcanist Vandril	Quest Giver
Blacksmith Frances	Blacksmithing Supplies (Repairer)
Eralan	Poison Vendor, Rogue Quest Giver
Forge	
Ghostlands Guardian	26-30
Innkeeper Kalarin	Innkeeper
Magistrix Aminel	Repeatable Quest Giver
Mailbox	
Master Chef Mouldier	Cooking Trainer and Supplier, Quest Giver
Paniar	Stable Master
Provisioner Vredigar	Factional Goods Vendor
Quartermaster Lymel	General Goods
Rathis Tomber	Quest Giver
Terellia	Trade Goods Vendor
Wanted Poster	Quest Giver

B Tranquillien (West Side)

Advisor Valwyn	Quest Giver
Dame Auriferous	Quest Giver
Deathstalker Maltendis	Quest Giver
Deathstalker Rathiel	Quest Giver
Ghostlands Guardian	26-30
High Executor Mavren	Quest Giver
Magister Darenis	Quest Giver
Ranger Lethvalin	Quest Giver
Skymaster Sunwing	Flight Merchant, Quest Target

C Suncrown Village

• Anok'suten	11 Elite Quest Target
Dying Blood Elf	Quest Giver
• Nerubis Guard	9-10 Quest Target

D An'daroth

• Sentinel Leader	11 Quest Target
• Sentinel Spy	10-11 Quest Target

E Goldenmist Village

• Quel'dorei Ghost	10-11 Quest Target
• Quel'dorei Wraith	11 Quest Target
Rune of Summoning	

F The Plagued Coast

• Withered Grimscale	12-13
• Zombified Grimscale	12-13

G Shalandis Isle

• Darnassian Druid	13-14
• Darnassian Huntress	14-15
Night Elf Plans	An'daroth Quest Target
Night Elf Plans	An'owyn Quest Target
Scrying on the Sin'dorei	Quest Target

H Sanctum of the Moon

• Arcane Devourer	11-12
• Mana Shifter	12

I The Dead Scar

• Dreadbone Sentinel	17-18
• Dreadbone Skeleton	10
• Gangled Cannibal	12-13 Quest Target
• Luzran	21 Elite
• Phantasmal Watcher	12
• Risen Creeper	9-10
• Risen Hungerer	13-14 Quest Target
• Risen Stalker	16-17

J Windrunner Village

• Knucklerot	21 Elite (Patrols to the East)
• Phantasmal Seeker	12-13
• Stonewing Slayer	13-14

EVERSONG WOODS

GOLDENMIST VILLAGE

SUNCROWN VILLAGE

DAWNSTAR SPIRE

WINDRUNNER VILLAGE

SANCTUM OF THE MOON

TRANQUILLIEN

FARSTRIDER ENCLAVE

SANCTUM OF THE SUN

WINDRUNNER SPIRE

ZUL'AMAN

DEATHOLME

EASTERN PLAGUELANDS

Ghostlands Legend

K Underlight Mines
Apprentice Shatharia		Quest Giver
• Blackpaw Gnoll	14	Quest Target
• Blackpaw Scavenger	12-13	Quest Target
• Blackpaw Shaman	12-14	Quest Target

L Amani Catacombs
Mummified Remains		Quest Target
• Mummified Headhunter	16-17	
Ranger Lilatha		Quest Giver
• Shadowpine Oracle	15-16	

M Valanna's Camp
Lieutenant Tomathren	
Ranger Valanna	Quest Giver

N Isle of Tribulations
Brazier		
• Nerubis Guard	9-10	Quest Target

O Lake Elrendar
• Aquantion	13	Quest Target
Glistening Mud		Quest Target
• Ravening Apparition	11-12	Quest Target
• Vengeful Apparition	12	Quest Target

P Zeb'Sora
• Shadowpine Ripper	10-11	
• Shadowpine Witch	11-12	

Q Dawnstar Spire
• Arcane Reaver	15-16	
Dusty Journal		Quest Target

R Farstrider Enclave
Apothecary Venustus	Quest Giver
Captain Helios	Quest Giver
Farstrider Dusking	
Farstrider Sedina	Quest Giver
Farstrider Solanna	Quest Giver
Heron Skygaze	Food and Drink Vendor
Narina	Bowyer
Ranger Krenn'an	Quest Giver
Ranger Vynna	Quest Giver
Wanted Poster	Quest Giver

S Zeb'Tela
• Shadowpine Headhunter	17-18	
• Shadowpine Shadowcaster	17-18	

T An'telas
Magister Sylastor	Quest Giver
Night Elf Moon Crystal	
Tranquillien Scout	16

U Sanctum of the Sun
Arcanist Janeda	Quest Giver
Ghostlands Guardian	30
Magister Idonis	Quest Giver

Magister Kaendris	Quest Giver
Magister Quallestis	

V Zeb'Nowa
Fresh Fish Rack		Quest Target
• Ghostclaw Lynx	15-16	
• Kel'gash the Wicked	20 Elite	Quest Target
Raw Meat Rack		Quest Target
• Shadowpine Catlord	18-19	
• Shadowpine Hexxer	17-19	
Smoked Meat Rack		Quest Target

W Windrunner Spire
• Deatholme Acolyte	14-15	Quest Target
• Fallen Ranger	15	Quest Target

X An'owyn
Scrying Crystal		Quest Giver
• Sentinel Infiltrator	15-16	

Y Deatholme
• Deatholme Necromancer	18-19	
• Dreadbone Skeleton	18-19	
• Eye of Dar'Khan	19-20	Quest Target
• Nerubis Centurion	18-19	Quest Target
• Wailer	18-19	Quest Target

Z Dark Temples
Apprentice Varnis	Quest Target (At Eastern Temple)

• Borgoth the Bloodletter		Quest Target (spawn at either Temple)
• Deatholme Necromancer	18-19	
• Dreadbone Skeleton	18-19	
• Eye of Dar'Khan	19-20	Quest Target
Ranger Vedoran		Quest Target (At Southern Temple)

1 Keltus Darkleaf Rogue Quest Giver

2 Tomber's Cart

3 Geranis Whitemorn Quest Giver

4 Apprentice Vor'el Quest Giver

5 Howling Ziggurat

6 Bleeding Ziggurat

7 Mirdoran the Fallen 20 Quest Target

8 Jurion the Deceiver Apothecary and 20 Quest Target Enith

9 Masophet the Black 20 Quest Target (Can Spawn in 2 Places)

10 Dar'Khan Drathir 21 Elite Quest Target

WALKTHROUGH FOR GHOSTLANDS

Greatly affected by the ravages of the plague, Ghostlands are currently dark and dangerous. Lurking within the shadows of the mist and trees are many animals that have been changed by the influence of the Scourge. Here too the Dead Scar runs horribly through the wilderness, a highway for the legions of unthinking monsters that serve The Lich King's will.

TRANQUILLIEN REPUTATION

The people who have chosen to make a stand here are quite independent, and as such will view your character on his or her own merits. If you do enough of the quests in the region, people here will not only offer you discounts, they will sell you special merchandise!

ATTACKING THE DARKNESS

Despite these perils, it's time to advance. You have a job to do, and Tranquillien isn't that far away. Look on the provided map until you see the area of Tranquillien. This isn't more than a minute or so to the south from where you enter the region, and the hills surrounding it protect from attack on most sides. Use the road that leads in from the north and examine the town.

Split in the center by the road, the town is naturally divided into two halves. On the west side is the Flight Merchant, Skymaster Sunwing. Get the Flight Point from this person immediately, then look on the eastern side of town for the Inn. That is the only building there, as everything else is merely a glorified stand. Rebind at the Inn, then get down to business. Talk to Arcanist Vandril to learn more about the town and turn in **Delivery to Tranquillien**.

In return for helping the town, Arcanist Vandril recommends you to High Executor Mavren so that you can see more of the town's workings. Because **The Forsaken** are partially in charge here, it's best to get in good with them. High Executor Mavren is the guy to talk to for this.

The Forsaken	
Faction	Horde
Location	Tranquillien
Quest Giver	Arcanist Vandril
Quest Completion	High Executor Mavren
Reward	Chain to Return to Arcanist Vandril

Mavren is inside the building on the west side of town, and the group in there is always arguing over one thing or another. Mavren has you **Return to Arcanist Vandril** to begin your exciting quests for Tranquillien.

Return to Arcanist Vandril	
Faction	Horde
Location	Tranquillien
Quest Giver	High Executor Mavren
Quest Completion	Arcanist Vandril
Reward	Chain to Suncrown Village

Vandril does indeed have fun tasks for you. The first of these is to seek **Suncrown Village** and hunt ten of the *Nerubis Guards* that patrol the region. These Undead are quite foul to look upon, but they and their leader must be destroyed.

LEARNING TO FLY

As with all areas adjacent to starting zones, there is a chain to learn about the Flight Merchants. This starts in Tranquillien, when you talk with Quartermaster Lymel. Don't rush off to do this until you have other chores in Silvermoon City; this lets you kill two birds with one Hearthstone. Wait until your character needs to train again, perhaps at level 14.

Bind at the Inn in Tranquillien first. Then, take the flight that has just opened and go to Silvermoon City. Talk to Sathren Azuredawn there. On our map, Sathren is found by the "O" callout and is a General Goods Vendor. This step chains into **Skymistress Gloaming**.

Skymistress Gloaming

Faction	Horde
Location	Silvermoon City
Quest Giver	Sathren Azuredawn
Quest Completion	Skymistress Gloaming
Reward	Chain to Return to Quartermaster Lymel

Goods From Silvermoon City

Faction	Horde
Location	Tranquillien
Quest Giver	Quartermaster Lymel
Quest Completion	Skymaster Sunwing
Reward	Chain to Fly to Silvermoon City

Move to speak with **Skymistress Gloaming**, just outside the gates of Silvermoon City. Talk to her to complete the quest and start the next step, but do not take her flight. Instead, use your Hearthstone to skip straight back to town.

Talk to the Skymaster and get the flight route for this area. Then, complete the quest by speaking to Skymaster Sunwing about the Quartermaster's Goods. This opens the quest to **Fly to Silvermoon City**.

Return to Quartermaster Lymel

Faction	Horde
Location	Silvermoon City
Quest Giver	Skymistress Gloaming
Quest Completion	Quartermaster Lymel
Reward	Experience

Fly to Silvermoon City

Faction	Horde
Location	Tranquillien
Quest Giver	Skymaster Sunwing
Quest Completion	Sathren Azuredawn
Reward	Chain to Skymistress Gloaming

Port back to Tranquillien and turn in the quest for a good experience boost. This is the end of the chain.

Suncrown Village

Faction	Horde
Location	Tranquillien
Quest Giver	Arcanist Vandril
Quest Completion	Arcanist Vandril
Reward	Chain to Goldenmist Village

While approaching Suncrown Village, keep an eye out for the Dying Blood Elf. This NPC is lying on the road just west of the village. The Blood Elf gives you a charge of slaying **Anok'suten**, the Nerubis leader. Look on top of the southern building in the town to find *Anok'suten*. If he isn't there, be cautious, as he'll be patrolling the streets. Pull as many of the nearby Nerubis as possible ahead of time, to keep the area clear, then attack *Anok'Suten* directly. It might even be worthwhile to grab a friend for assisstance. Put all damage on any Nerubis that add to the fight, then slap as many DOTs, Sunder Armors, and other such effects onto *Anok'suten*. Though Elite, this leader is low in level, so it's likely that you can solo the fight even without a great deal of practice.

Anok'suten	
Faction	Horde
Location	Suncrown Village
Quest Giver	Dying Blood Elf
Quest Completion	Arcanist Vandril
Reward	Fortified Oven Mitts (Mail Hands 72 Armor, +1 STR), Stung (1H Sword 6.0 DPS, +1 STR), Vandril's Hand Me Down Pants (Cloth Legs 18 Armor, +1 SPI), or Tranquillien Breeches (Leather Legs, +1 AGI, +1 STAM)

Goldenmist Village	
Faction	Horde
Location	Tranquillien
Quest Giver	Arcanist Vandril
Quest Completion	Arcanist Vandril
Reward	Goldenmist Special Brew (Adds 70 Maximum Health for 1 Hour), Quel'Thalas (Bow 7.0 DPS, +1 AGI), Chain to Windrunner Village

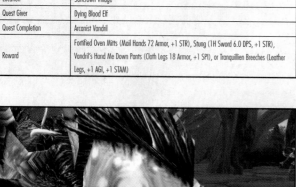

Investigate An'daroth	
Faction	Horde
Location	Tranquillien
Quest Giver	Dame Auriferous
Quest Completion	Dame Auriferous
Reward	Lesser Healing Potions (2), Chain to Into Occupied Territory

When this is done, rest and polish off any remaining Nerubis guards to complete your primary quest here. Run back to town and turn in **Anok'suten** and **Suncrown Village**.

Arcanist Vandril receives both sets of good news and sends you right back out, this time to **Goldenmist Village**. Spirits of the fallen remain there, and many of them must be destroyed before the place can hope to be reclaimed. In addition, look into the western building and talk to Dame Auriferous. She wants you to **Investigate An'daroth**, which is close to Goldenmist Village.

You have to cross the Dead Scar to reach the northwest, but you don't have to stay in it for very long, nor do you have to walk through the lower sections of that awful place. With each step to the south, the Dead Scar becomes stronger, carrying a greater influence on Ghostlands. For now, you can just run happily across it. This is good, because the Scourge in the lower section of the Dead Scar are much higher in level and can be quite aggressive. There is also an Elite Abomination that patrols up and down a fair length of the Dead Scar, and you won't want to run into him yet.

Investigate An'daroth is the first quest on your route. Use our map instead of the in-game one to find the area, as An'daroth is not that easy to see. The place is only a collection of stones normally. At the moment, however, it also has a wide range of *Sentinel Spies* and their Sentinel Leader! Go about the task of informing these arrogant Night Elves that their hopes of completing their mission, and indeed their lives, are over. Slay *12 Sentinel Spies* to get the idea across.

Because the Sentinel Spies and their Leader move around somewhat, pull at range if you are having any trouble with them. None of the enemies stealth, fortunately, so you are free to back away while fighting if anything unwanted draws near.

With that done, move to the west. Climb over the hills there and down into the valley beyond. When you arrive in **Goldenmist Village**, kill eight *Quel'dorei Ghosts* and just as many *Quel'dorei Wraiths*. The Wraiths are easier to get because they come out from the buildings of the village and patrol. There are many of them, and they like to aggro on people's backs when you aren't careful. Finding enough Ghosts is the real trick; look inside the buildings and on the upper levels to collect more of them.

Tricksy Spirits

The Quel'dorei spirits are tough to hit in the second half of their health bar. If you are a class with physical damage, especially if you are a Warrior, save some strength for the later part of the encounter. Put any DOTs on the Quel'dorei enemies early on, and get them debuffed before they fade into their evasive state.

Also, be ready to have them debuff you as well. The Ghostly Touch these guys lay on characters causes a -5 debuff to Stamina and Spirit.

A CLEAN SWEEP OF THE WEST

Talk to Arcanist Vandril and Dame Auriferous again, then seek Tomber, Apothecary Renzithen, Master Chef Mouldier (ick), and Deathstalker Rathiel. This accumulates a nice spread of quests, all within a moderate range of each other. When you are done in town, you should have **Windrunner Village**, **Tomber's Supplies**, **The Plagued Coast**, **Culinary Crunch**, and **Down the Dead Scar**.

Tomber's Supplies	
Faction	Horde
Location	Tranquillien
Quest Giver	Rathis Tomber
Quest Completion	Rathis Tomber
Reward	Tomber Becomes a Merchant

The Plagued Coast	
Faction	Horde
Location	Tranquillien
Quest Giver	Apothecary Renzithen
Quest Completion	Apothecary Renzithen
Reward	Swim Speed Potions (2) and Renzithen's Dusty Cloak (Back 12 Armor, +1 STAM)

Return to town and collect several quests this time. You have advanced enough in strength and reputation in town that there should be more that people are willing to trust you.

Into Occupied Territory

Faction	Horde
Location	Tranquillien
Quest Giver	Dame Auriferous
Quest Completion	Dame Auriferous
Reward	Experience

Down the Dead Scar

Faction	Horde
Location	Tranquillien
Quest Giver	Deathstalker Rathiel
Quest Completion	Deathstalker Rathiel
Reward	Experience

Next, look at our map again to find **Tomber's Supplies**. His cart is located just bit south from An'daroth. You'll know when you are getting close because of the Ghouls that are kicking back in the surrounding area. Kill one of those Undead to make room for your approach, then collect what you need from the cart. Simple!

BACK IN BUSINESS

Once you complete his quest, Tomber becomes a full merchant for you. Not only does he sell a variety of Trade Supplies, but he has a few rare goods as well. Sometimes you will see limited rare items such as Scrolls for various attributes, Copper Ore, and other useful goodies.

Culinary Crunch

Faction	Horde
Location	Tranquillien
Quest Giver	Master Chef Mouldier
Quest Completion	Master Chef Mouldier
Reward	Crunchy Spider Surprise (5), Recipe Crunchy Spider Surprise

The Plagued Coast is off to the west. Keep going until you see the cute Murlocs playing on the happy beaches of Ghostlands. It looks just like it did in the travel brochures. Collect *6 Plagued Murloc Spines* from the Murlocs there. Many of them have ranged weapons, but you are lucky in that the Murlocs are fairly spread out. Avoid the huts to save yourself from fighting a few Murlocs at a time, and instead fight the loners on the beach and in the water.

Windrunner Village

Faction	Horde
Location	Tranquillien
Quest Giver	Arcanist Vandril
Quest Completion	Arcanist Vandril
Reward	Experience

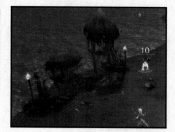

Rogues and casters have to grit their teeth through this. The Murlocs have a 5-minute debuff called Decayed Agility. They can also slap people with Fevered Fatigue, which hits Intellect and Spirit.

After getting enough of the *Plagued Murloc Spines*, swim to the nearby island; it should be within your immediate sight. This place is known as Shalandis Isle, and a ship of Night Elves has anchored near there. Even more audacious, the Darnassians have set up a camp. Clearly they are planning on staying for some time, so you should discover what they are doing coming **Into Occupied Territory**.

Because both the Darnassian Huntresses and Druids have ranged attacks, you won't want to be coy with them. Instead, hit them directly and use burst damage. This is especially important against the Druids, who would love to engage you in a long, drawn-out fight where their healing can make a big difference. Save your attacks that Stun or otherwise interrupt casting (Blood Elves can Silence on cue) and use those to prevent successful heals.

Two sets of the plans that you need are here on the island. Search inside the tents for the *Night Elf Plans for An'daroth and An'owyn*. Next, climb up the gangway onto the pretty ship by the western edge of Shalandis Isle. Clear your way to the top of the deck and steal the document *Scrying on the Sin'dorei*.

With that much intelligence gathered, you've done your part. Hop down off the ship, and turn to the south. Not only are there Spindleweb Lurkers to collect down there, for **Culinary Crunch**, but **Windrunner Village** is also in that neck of the woods. After a short swim, you can work on both.

Clear the area near Windrunner Village of as many Spindleweb Lurkers as possible. They are targets of opportunity, and you don't need to get all of

their nice *Crunchy Spiders Legs* at once. When their numbers are diminished, walk into town and fight the Stonewing Slayers and Phantasmal Seekers.

Gather *6 Phantasmal Substances* and *4 Gargoyle Fragments*. The *Gargoyle Fragments* don't drop off of every Stonewing Slayer, but you have to cut through a lot of those Gargoyles to get deeper into the town anyway. The *Phantasmal Substances* fall at a one-per-kill drop rate, so you only need six of those Seekers to get everything you want. For a great cluster of the Phantasmal Seekers, climb up to the second floor of the southeast building.

STAY PARANOID

While fighting on the eastern side of Windrunner Village, or when you are out hunting the Spindleweb Lurkers, be alert. Knucklerot, another Elite patroller, comes to the outskirts of Windrunner Village. If he aggros on your back, it's probably going to end poorly. Run and pray if that happens, or perhaps elbow any buddies you have in the stomach and hope it winds them!

With backpack bursting, you have just finished two more quests. Stop at the Dead Scar on your way back to town. Most of the northern Scar is filled with Risen Hungerers and Gangled Cannibals. If the enemies are too tough, you've gone too far south. And only at the VERY top of the Scar is there anything weaker to fight. Kill *10 Risen Hungerers* and *10 Gangled Cannibals*.

Go into Tranquillien and turn in all of the quests that you've completed.

Repairing in Tranquillien

You might notice that there are not many people who can repair equipment in Tranquillien. On the eastern side of the town, nestled behind most of the vendors and such, is Blacksmith Frances. Ask the Blacksmith to repair anything that has been damaged during your recent fighting.

Accept **Salvaging The Past** from Magister Darenis and **Trouble at the Underlight Mines** from Deathstalker Maltendis. Take **Deliver the Plans to An'telas** as well, from Dame Auriferous, though you won't get around to this step in the chain for some time. These are saved for the last quests on this part of the western side because they are close together and because one of them is somewhat challenging. **Trouble at the Underlight Mines** requires you to go into a valley where aggro can be fierce. With the extra experience you've gained, it's probably doable. If not, this is a good time to pick up a companion to assist in the fighting.

Salvaging The Past

Faction	Horde
Location	Tranquillien
Quest Giver	Magister Darenis
Quest Completion	Magister Darenis
Reward	Experience

Travel west from town and seek the Sanctum of the Moon. **Salvaging the Past** requires you to collect *8 Crystalized Mana Essences* from Arcane Devourers and Mana Shifters. These are the only two types of enemies around the Sanctum of the Moon. Both of them are fun targets for Blood Elves, and you can Mana Tap to your heart's content. After **Salvaging the Past** is completed, move south and stay above the Underlight Mines until you see Apprentice Shatharia, who stands on the eastern side of the hill. Shatharia cannot stand a chance against the horde of Gnolls that have taken over the valley, and will beg for you to collect the **Underlight Ore Samples** in her stead. This can be done while slaying the Blackpaw Gnolls, Scavengers, and Shamans for **Trouble at the Underlight Mines**.

Trouble at the Underlight Mines

Faction	Horde
Location	Tranquillien
Quest Giver	Deathstalker Maltendis
Quest Completion	Deathstalker Maltendis
Reward	Experience

Underlight Ore Samples

Faction	Horde
Location	Underlight Mines
Quest Giver	Apprentice Shatharia
Quest Completion	Magister Quallestis
Reward	Experience

Because the Gnolls wander, have a wide aggro radius, and like to bring friends, you could choose to be quite cautious in pulling them. Use Snares to keep runners from getting into other groups of Gnolls (e.g., Ice Bolt is your friend).

When fighting a pack, drop the Shamans first. Their high DPS and ranged capabilities make them the hardest to move around and control. They also have low health and won't survive for long. Use Arcane Torrent to Silence the Shamans if they become troublesome or petulant.

Collect 6 *Underlight Ore* samples from the Gnolls. These samples must eventually go to Magister Quallestis, at the Sanctum of the Sun. If you want to get there quickly, take the back route from Tranquillien next time you are in town. A path through the hills, between Tranquillien and the Sanctum, can be seen by the faint torchlight that lines the path.

When you do go, pick up **The Sanctum of the Sun** from Magister Darenis of Tranquillien. This is an introduction quest, so it doesn't have to do done, but there is no reason to skip it since you pass through Tranquillien anyway.

The Sanctum of the Sun

Faction	Horde
Location	Tranquillien
Quest Giver	Magister Darenis
Quest Completion	Magister Idonis
Reward	Experience

Help Ranger Valanna

Faction	Horde
Location	Tranquillien
Quest Giver	Ranger Lethvalin
Quest Completion	Ranger Valanna
Reward	Chain to Dealing With Zeb'Sora

Investigate the Amani Catacombs

Faction	Horde
Location	Tranquillien
Quest Giver	Advisor Valwyn
Quest Completion	Advisor Valwyn
Reward	Experience

TIME TO EXPLORE THE EAST

You have cleared a huge amount of content in the west, and done it quite quickly at that! Now, it is time to push eastward and see more of what that region has to offer. Make one more trip to Tranquillien and stock up on supplies. You might be some time in the bush, so a training run to the capital could be in order as well. Either way, ask Ranger Lethvalin what is going on. The response: **Help Ranger Valanna!** It sounds like two of the Rangers have gone a bit missing, and you must find them to see if they are in trouble. Advisor Valwyn also has a quest for that region. **Investigate the Amani Catacombs** passes close to the Rangers' previous position. While there, you'll be able to collect **Troll Juju** for Deathstalker Maltendis as well.

Troll Juju	
Faction	Horde
Location	Tranquillien
Quest Giver	Deathstalker Maltendis
Quest Completion	Deathstalker Maltendis
Reward	Rotting Handwraps (Cloth Hand 19 Armor, +2 STAM, +2 INT), Undertaker's Gloves (Leather Hands 45 Armor, +2 AGI, +2 STAM), Maltendis' Handguards (Mail Hands 99 Armor, +2 STAM, +2 INT)

Collect the *8 Troll Juju* that you need during the fighting (Oracles and Headhunters alike drop the *Juju*), and right-click on the bodies that line the walls. Torching these will show that you are investigating in style. However, **Investigate the Amani Catacombs** won't be complete until you search the room at the far end of the upper corridor. This room has several enemies, but it also has a prisoner. When you have checked to ensure that **Troll Juju** is also completed, free Ranger Lilatha and receive the quest to help her to safety.

Corpse Bonfire

Everyone in a group receives credit when one member torches some remains in the Amani Catacombs. Because of this and the fact that the Torch has a cooldown, **Investigate the Amani Catacombs** is extremely group friendly. If you see other characters in the area, and they are competing with you for bodies, just ask them to join you. Everyone gets the quest done faster, and you won't have to wait for bodies to respawn.

Hit the Amani Catacombs first, as they are on the way. Stay on the northern side of the mountains, while leaving Tranquillien, and slip into the pass through the hills once you see the Trolls wandering about. There are two entrances to the Catacombs, and it doesn't matter which you take.

Inside, there are Mummified Headhunters and Shadowpine Oracles. The Oracles are very easy to dispatch, despite their casting abilities. Instead, it is the Undead that cause you the most problems. Mummified Headhunters deal plenty of damage on their own, plus they burst into a toxic gas when they die. Either loot immediately or come back and loot groups of them later, once the gas has dispersed. When fighting a few enemies at a time, retreat once the first Headhunter dies. This keeps you from standing around in the goo!

Escape From The Catacombs	
Faction	Horde
Location	Amani Catacombs
Quest Giver	Ranger Lilatha
Quest Completion	Captain Helios
Reward	Troll Kickers (Mail Feet 109 Armor, +3 STR), Troll Kickers (Cloth Feet 21 Armor, +1 STAM, +1 INT, Increases damage and healing by 2), Troll Kickers (Leather Feet 50 Armor, +3 AGI)

This is an escort quest. Take Ranger Lilatha out of the Catacombs and get her over to the Farstrider Enclave. Captain Helios is there, and he'll reward you for your success. In addition, there are many quests based out of the Farstrider Enclave!

For now, accept **Spirits of the Drowned** from Ranger Krenn'an and **Bearers of the Plague** from Farstrider Sedina. The *Ghostclaw Lynxes* are your targets of opportunity now. You only need to kill 10 of them, and that can be done as you go about other tasks. Keep your best eye out for them while passing by the Farstrider Enclave or along the eastern side of the map, near the various Troll areas.

Because Zeb'Sora is just across the lake, swim there now and start slashing, blasting, and mashing the Trolls. The Witches and Rippers there drop *Troll Ears* for Ranger Valanna, but their drop rate is not terribly high. It'll take a number of kills to finish this group off, but the Trolls are so soft that it's rather relaxing.

Swim back when you are done, and fight any stray *Ravening Apparitions* or *Vengeful Apparitions* that you see; they will be your primary targets in such a moment. Talk to Ranger Valanna again, and she'll order you to **Report to Captain Helios**. You certainly know where he is, and on your next trip there that will be a free turn-in.

Spirits of the Drowned

Faction	Horde
Location	Farstrider Enclave
Quest Giver	Ranger Krenn'an
Quest Completion	Ranger Krenn'an
Reward	Experience

Travel north, along the western side of Lake Elrendar. Meet Ranger Valanna. This completes the quest, **Help Ranger Valanna**, and gets you the quest **Dealing With Zeb'Sora**.

Report to Captain Helios

Faction	Horde
Location	Lake Elrendar
Quest Giver	Ranger Valanna
Quest Completion	Captain Helios
Reward	Farstrider's Tunic (Leather Chest 62 Armor, +1 AGI, +1 STAM), Troll Handler Gloves (Cloth Hands 14 Armor, +1 INT, +1 SPI), or Farstrider's Shield (Shield 239 Armor 4 Block, +1 STAM)

Bearers of the Plague

Faction	Horde
Location	Farstrider
Quest Giver	Farstrider Sedina
Quest Completion	Farstrider Sedina
Reward	Chains to Curbing the Plague

Before reporting back to the Farstrider Enclave, swim to the tiny island southeast of Valanna's position; it's marked with a "3" on our map. Stand fast when you see the spirit of Geranis Whitemorn, and trust that he means you no harm. Talk to him and accept the quest **Forgotten Rituals**.

Dealing With Zeb'Sora

Faction	Horde
Location	Lake Elrendar
Quest Giver	Ranger Valanna
Quest Completion	Ranger Valanna
Reward	Chain to Report to Captain Helios

Forgotten Rituals

Faction	Horde
Location	Lake Elrendar
Quest Giver	Geranis Whitemorn
Quest Completion	Geranis Whitemorn
Reward	Vanquishing Aquantion

Vanquishing Aquantion	
Faction	Horde
Location	Lake Elrendar
Quest Giver	Geranis Whitemorn
Quest Completion	Geranis Whitemorn
Reward	Experience

Curbing the Plague	
Faction	Horde
Location	Farstrider Enclave
Quest Giver	Farstrider Sedina
Quest Completion	Farstrider Sedina
Reward	Ranger's Sash (Cloth Waist 16 Armor, +2 STAM, +2 INT), Farstrider's Belt (Leather Waist 39 Armor, +2 AGI, +2 STAM), or Rusted Chain Girdle (Mail Belt 81 Armor, +2 STR, +2 STAM) AND Survival Knife (1H Dagger 7.7 DPS +1 AGI)

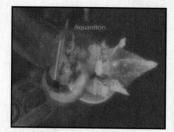

Now you get to finish killing the various *Apparitions* of the lake while searching for *8 Wavefront Medallions*. Dig into the Glistening Mud at the bottom of the Lake while fighting. Remember to come up for air after every *Medallion* or two, and pull Apparitions to the top with ranged weapons if it makes you nervous to fight underwater.

When you are finished collecting these items for Geranis, return to him and hand them in. He'll teach you how to summon the elemental named *Aquantion*. Swim north, just a short distance, and look for the altar at the bottom of the Lake. Clear any Apparitions that are close by, then use the altar for your ritual. Attack the Water Elemental as soon as it appears, and swim to the top while engaging *Aquantion*. This prevents you from drowning if you take too long during the battle.

When Aquantion collapses lifeless into the deep, swim again to Geranis and turn in his quest. Continue from there out to the Farstrider Enclave again. **Report to Captain Helios** for a reward and see if you can finish **Bearers of the Plague** now. Having taken out a number of the Lynxes as targets of opportunity, there shouldn't be too many left to grab. Look south of the Enclave to find any that you need, then switch that quest into its next step, **Curbing the Plague**. That portion of the chain has you kill *8 Spindleweb Lurkers* and *10 Vampiric Mistbats*. Because the Lurkers are on the other side of the map, you won't complete this quest until later, when you have a few more reasons to head in that direction. The Mistbats, however, are close to the Enclave and can be fought now, while you are passing through the area constantly.

Talk to Captain Helios again to start **Shadowpine Weaponry**, and listen to Farstrider Solanna's suggestion to start the **Attack on Zeb'Tela**. Both of these quests should be within your grasp, though the chains lead into some difficult fighting. This should be clear when you use the Wanted Poster at the southern entrance to the Farstrider Enclave. That Poster starts the quest, **Bring Me Kel'Gash's Head!** You won't have to fight Kel'Gash quite yet, but

that Elite Troll is coming up. This might be a good time to find a partner or two, unless you are happy to do most of these quests now and return later to finish the last bits off.

Shadowpine Weaponry	
Faction	Horde
Location	Farstrider Enclave
Quest Giver	Captain Helios
Quest Completion	Captain Helios
Reward	Experience

Attack on Zeb'Tela	
Faction	Horde
Location	Farstrider Enclave
Quest Giver	Farstrider Solanna
Quest Completion	Farstrider Solanna
Reward	Chains to Assault on Zeb'Nowa

Bring Me Kel'Gash's Head!	
Faction	Horde
Location	Farstrider Enclave
Quest Giver	Wanted Poster
Quest Completion	Captain Helios
Reward	Well Crafted Long Bow (Bow 10.9 DPS), Well Crafted Sword (MH Sword 10.2 DPS, +3 STR), or Well Crafted Staff (Staff 13.0 DPS, Increases Damage and Healing by up to 4)

It's likely that you will finish the kill quest before you have the two sets of weapons needed from Zeb'Tela. Stay until both aspects are completed, then return to the Farstrider Enclave. Zeb'Nowa has the other weapons that you need, but there are two additional quests that you can get for that area. Turn in Attack on Zeb'Tela; this chains into the **Assault on Zeb'Nowa**. Also, talk to Apothecary Venustus, on the second floor of the Enclave. Chillingly, the Apothecary has some great ideas about how to deal with the Trolls. Accept **A Little Dash of Seasoning** before moving to the southeast.

Shadowpine Weaponry requires you to collect 3 weapons from each of the four Troll types found in the next two villages. Zeb'Tela has *Shadowpine Shadowcasters* and *Headhunters*; these drop *Shadowcaster Maces* and *Head-hunter Axes*. You need to kill the Trolls there for **Attack on Zeb'Tela** anyway and can collect the weapons while you finish that quest.

Assault on Zeb'Nowa	
Faction	Horde
Location	Farstrider Enclave
Quest Giver	Farstrider Solanna
Quest Completion	Farstrider Solanna
Reward	Sentry Bracers (Mail Wrist 72 Armor, +2 STR, +2 STAM), Supple Cotton Bracers (Cloth Wrist 14 Armor, +1 STAM, +1 INT, Increases Damage and Healing by up to 2), and Farstrider's Bracers (Leather Wrist 33 Armor, +2 AGI, +2 STAM)

A Little Dash of Seasoning	
Faction	Horde
Location	Farstrider Enclave
Quest Giver	Apothecary Venustus
Quest Completion	Apothecary Venustus
Reward	Experience

While visiting this eastern Troll camp, keep your interrupt abilities at their best. The *Shadowcasters* use Mark of Shadow to increase the amount of damage taken from Shadow by a fair margin (20 points). Because of this, it's very useful to Silence casters with Arcane Torrent or to use abilities like Kick, Gouge, Hammer of Justice, and such to disable the casters before they finish their spells.

Fighting the *Hexxers* and *Catlords* is once again useful for two quests, as you work on the kill quest and the collection of weapons. From these two drop *Hexxer Staves* and *Catlord Claws*. Because the enemies in Zeb'Nowa are higher in level, you can expect the aggro to be some-what fierce in this village. Draw

enemies out from longer range, and fight where you know the area is clear. Don't approach the huts of Zeb'Nowa from the sides either, as the enemies aggro once they see you passing either their doors or windows.

While the numbers are stacking up for your first two quests, search for the three meat sources that need to be poisoned for **A Little Dash of Seasoning**. Zeb'Nowa is a big place, so it takes some work to find everything.

The *Hexxers* aren't skilled casters at range; they prefer to run up and smack you. What makes them troublesome is that they have mastered the art of Polymorph to Chicken. It is extremely likely that they will turn you into a chicken. This only lasts for a few moments, but it makes running away from *Hexxers* a bit edgy.

Once you have killed enough of the Trolls to complete your assault and get your weapons, it's time for extra credit. Three quests here should be completed, but Kel'Gash still has his head. If you have a partner or two, or if you have done some extra leveling and think that you can take a level 20 Elite by yourself, look on the southern end of Zeb'Nowa. There is a small path, still guarded by Trolls, that leads into a narrow valley. A single building back there has two floors, and the balcony above is where you see Kel'Gash hanging about.

Tainting the Meat in Zeb'Nowa

Goal	Location
Raw Meat Rack	Outside Between Two Huts, South Side; Near the Road
Smoked Meat Rack	Almost at the Bottom of Zeb'Nowa; Also Outside Between Two Huts
Fresh Fish Rack	Inside Large Building, North Side (First Floor)

As for the *Catlords*, they are more a challenge of combined resources. Acting like Survival Hunters, they like to close as well, bringing their pet Lynxes with them. Attack the *Catlords* first, then switch to their kitties. This gets the combined damage of the pair down quickly enough that they shouldn't be too nasty.

Clear all of the wandering Trolls from the area near the building, and kill everything on the lower floor and balcony. You can't afford to have an add during this fight, unless you are so powerful that the entire strategy is moot. While clearing, build up three charges with your Mana Tap.

Next, after healing and regaining mana, attack Kel'Gash with your best opener. Ambush him as a Rogue, hit him with your best Fireball, etc. From there, it's a rush to stay ahead of Kel'Gash's damage curve.

This Elite Troll is a caster, so your Arcane Torrent is best used late in one of the big guy's casting phases. Be sure to hold on just long enough that you receive the full use of the free Mana/Energy from hitting Arcane Torrent. As always with casters, other interrupts are essential to survival. Stun this creep as often as possible before his lightning completes.

At some point in the encounter, you are probably going to get Cursed with a Shrink ability. This takes 6 points off of your Strength and Stamina; it's bad

Faster Recovery

Zeb'Nowa is the type of place where casual resting is a bit risky. Wandering Catlords have the potential to bump into you at almost any time, and that sure can spoil your day if you are at one-third Health.

Remember to practice First Aid; get into the better tiers of bandages as soon as possible. This makes it much easier to maintain a higher degree of Health.

For casters, drink that water whenever you can. If you are a Mage or bump into them often enough, get a few big stacks and use them like you mean it. Tip and thank Mages that are nice enough to help you out like this, because it makes a huge difference in leveling speed and general survivability of all casters.

for everyone, but especially cruel to Paladins and Rogues who are soloing the encounter. There isn't much that you can do to avoid this, so anticipate it and be ready to use a Healing Potion to keep your Health at a safe range in the later stage of the fight.

Once you happily collect *Kel'Gash's Head*, return to the Farstrider Enclave and turn in all four of your quests. This gets you a few nice items and quite a dose of experience as well!

As soon as the Night Elves are down, talk to Magister Sylastor again and promise to **Deactivate An'owyn**. Your trip will be a short one, but the rewards are quite fair.

GETTING CLOSE TO THE END

Start wrapping up the other loose ends and side quests of the Ghostlands. Dame Auriferous still has her chain for dealing with the Night Elves of Darnassus. Though you discovered the plans some time ago, you weren't in the right neighborhood to follow up on the issue. The next step, **Deliver The Plans to An'telas**, is now a good choice for your hero. Pick this up from Auriferous, in Tranquillien (if you don't have it already).

Deactivate An'owyn	
Faction	Horde
Location	An'telas
Quest Giver	Magister Sylastor
Quest Completion	Magister Sylastor
Reward	Sylastor's Cloak (Back 15 Armor, +2 STAM), Divining Crystal (Off-Hand +1 INT, Improves Spell Hit Rating by 1), or An'telas Scale Shirt (Mail Chest 151 Armor, +3 STR, +2 INT)

Travel south toward An'owyn. Walk past the road and over to the mountains at the base of the map. Slay a few of the Sentinels there, and you should find the *Crystal Controlling Orb* on one of their bodies. This is a random drop, but it is often fairly quick to achieve.

With that, you can *Deactivate the Scrying Crystal* at the center of the camp! That done, you should return to the Magister and let him know of your success.

Pick up another burst of quests from Tranquillien when this is done: **Retaking Windrunner Spire** from High Executor Mavren and both **Rotting Hearts** and **Spinal Dust** from Magistrix Aminel. If you don't already know where Magistrix Aminel is, climb to the second floor of the Tranquillien Inn and look for her on the left side. These should all be available now, and each takes you to the west, so it's a good loop to get done in a single sweep.

Deliver The Plans to An'telas	
Faction	Horde
Location	Tranquillien
Quest Giver	Dame Auriferous
Quest Completion	Magister Sylastor
Reward	Chain to Deactivate An'owyn

Look at the mountains northeast from the Sanctum of the Sun. In a tiny cubby of the land, there is a Night Elf site that has been taken over by Magister Sylastor and his companions. Give him the plans and hear what he has to say.

Even as you talk, two more of the Darnassian riders approach. Stay near the Magister's guards, to keep yourself safe while fighting these enemies. Focus on a single target with burst damage to ensure that you get experience credit when the foe goes down, then assist with the other. With NPC allies there to help, there is no substantial danger, so you can afford to put all Energy/Mana into damage rather than crowd control or improved survival.

Retaking Windrunner Spire	
Faction	Horde
Location	Tranquillien
Quest Giver	High Executor Mavren
Quest Completion	High Executor Mavren
Reward	Experience

Rotting Hearts

Faction	Horde
Location	Tranquillien
Quest Giver	Magistrix Aminel
Quest Completion	Magistrix Aminel
Reward	Scourgebane Draught (+30 Attack Power Vs. Undead for 30 Minutes)

Of the three Scourge targets that you are hunting here, the Death-cage Sorcerers are the worst; they are able to aggro from long range, and their attacks are ice based. For Rogues, this can be troublesome if you don't see them until after they aggro. It is wise to scan the field ahead of time, pick out the Sorcerers, then use Stealth to get the drop on them.

The Fun Never Stops

Rotting Hearts and Spinal Dust can be collected before you get the quests for these items; they can also be found after you complete the quests for Magistrix Aminel. Turning these in to the Magistrix continues to get you Scourgebane Draughts and Infusions. Create a stockpile of these items if you plan on doing a lot of soloing against the Undead during your later fighting in Ghostlands.

Spinal Dust

Faction	Horde
Location	Tranquillien
Quest Giver	Magistrix Aminel
Quest Completion	Magistrix Aminel
Reward	Scourgebane Infusion (Increases Spell Damage Vs. Undead by up to 15 for 30 Minutes)

You pass through the Dead Scar first, so collecting the *Rotting Hearts* and *Spinal Dust* might be better to get first, though it's purely a matter of interest. You need 10 of each item, so it's going to take a while to get everything.

Once you finish the quests, or if you tire of the Scourge momentarily and want a break and resume your westward journey. Windrunner Spire is by the coast, and it is a beautiful structure, despite the vermin that call it home currently. Your task is to cleanse the place, eradicating 8 Deatholme Acolytes and 10 Fallen Rangers.

If you have trouble fighting casters, be especially wary of this quest. Both the Acolytes and the Rangers are casters, and a few of them patrol. Don't engage in any fights before looking past your foe to see what might wander over in the near future. Mana Tap and Arcane Torrent are very useful here; save your Torrent for any fights where you suddenly find yourself in a pinch.

During the looting, it is likely that you will find **The Lady's Necklace**. This useful item is used to start a quest of the same name.

Endlessly Roaming

Luzran is still happily running about the Dead Scar in his unending patrol. While fighting the Risen Stalkers, Dreadbone Sentinels, and Deathcage Sorcerers, stay by the eastern edge of the Dead Scar to give yourself a better sight of Luzran's route. Once you spot him, follow his trail visually and keep your character's orientation in that general direction so that he won't surprise you on the way back.

The Lady's Necklace

Faction	Horde
Location	Windrunner Spire
Quest Giver	The Lady's Necklace
Quest Completion	High Executor Mavren
Reward	Chain to Journey to Undercity

When you turn in Retaking Windrunner Spire, give Mavren this item as well. The immediate experience reward is a friendly boost, and he'll also ask that you **Journey to Undercity** and give the Necklace to Lady Sylvanas. You can do this now, if you want. However, there is going to be another quest that takes you to Lady Sylvanas before much time has passed. For efficiency, wait until you are done with the Ghostlands. Otherwise, go now and have fun! Either way, use the Teleporter to Undercity at the back of the Sunfury Spire to get you where you need to go.

The Traitor's Shadow

Faction	Horde
Location	Farstrider Enclave
Quest Giver	Ranger Vynna
Quest Completion	Dar'Khan
Reward	Chain to Hints of the Pest

Journey to Undercity

Faction	Horde
Location	Tranquillien
Quest Giver	High Executor Mavren
Quest Completion	Lady Sylvanas
Reward	Experience

While running about, kill *10 Greater Spindlewebs* and *10 Ghostclaw Ravagers*. As for primary quest chains, you are also ready to go into the coolest one of the Ghostlands. Begin **The Traitor's Shadow**, over at the Farstrider Enclave.

Travel to Dawnstar Spire and look for the *Dusty Journal* on the second floor of the building there. You must fight through a number of Arcane Reavers; some of them are patrolling, so it's best to advance slowly, especially if you are alone.

Use bandages or food to keep Health as high as possible, and stick to the walls of the buildings so that you aren't in danger of having proximity aggro from multiple directions. Having a single Arcane Reaver attack isn't too bad, despite their high damage, but being Stunned (via knockdown) by two creatures is quite brutal.

A small kill quest that you should pick up during your growing expeditions through the southern parts of the map is **Clearing the Way**. Apprentice Vor'el provides this, and he is found at the Andilien Estate. Look at our map, in the area south of Tranquillien to find this.

Climb to the second story of the spire and out onto the ledge beyond. The *Dusty Journal* is there! Read it and accept the next step in the chain: **Hints of the Past**.

Clearing the Way

Faction	Horde
Location	Andilien Estate
Quest Giver	Apprentice Vor'el
Quest Completion	Apprentice Vor'el
Reward	Experience

Hints of the Past

Faction	Horde
Location	Dawnstar Spire
Quest Giver	Dusty Journal
Quest Completion	Ranger Vynna
Reward	Chain to Report to Magister Kaendris

Return to the Farstrider Enclave and talk to Ranger Vynna. You are quickly sent on from there to **Report to Magister Kaendris** at the Sanctum of the Sun.

The *Stone of Flame* and the *Stone of Light* are placed in the same spots within the Ziggurats, so your strategy will be identical for each. Collect both items before heading back to the Sanctum of the Sun.

Report to Magister Kaendris	
Faction	Horde
Location	Farstrider Enclave
Quest Giver	Ranger Vynna
Quest Completion	Magister Kaendris
Reward	Red Silk Trousers (Cloth Legs 25 Armor, +2 STAM, +3 INT), Black Leather Jerkin (Leather Chest 71 Armor, +3 AGI, +2 STAM), or Tranquillien Scale Leggings (Mail Legs 132 Armor, +3 STAM, +2 INT), and Chain to The Twin Ziggurats

This might seem like the end of the chain, considering that you get a nice choice of armor rewards here. That is far from the reality of things, however, as Magister Kaendris is only getting warmed up. This step chains into **The Twin Ziggurats**, which is a very fun quest.

The Twin Ziggurats	
Faction	Horde
Location	Sanctum of the Sun
Quest Giver	Magister Kaendris
Quest Completion	Magister Kaendris
Reward	Sunwell Blade (1H Sword 10.0 DPS, +3 STAM, Use on Dar'Khan Drathir to Deal 500 Damage + Silence), or Sunwell Orb (Off-Hand +3 INT, Use on Dar'Khan Drathir to Deal 500 Damage + Silence)

Both of the Ziggurats are marked clearly on the map, so finding them is a piece of cake. Stonewing Trackers guard the exterior of the buildings, and they can hit fairly hard. If you pull at range there won't be any chance for multiple Trackers to come at the same time, and that should be safe enough for easy entrance.

Inside, there are several Deatholme Darkmages. Fighting even a single Darkmage while standing out in the open is just foolish; they deal damage in heavy doses. Rather than risk a ranged duel or a charge that might aggro the rest of the Ziggurat, creep into the room from either side until one of the Darkmages proximity aggros. In response, slip back around the corner. This breaks line of sight and forces the Darkmage to run all the way to you. You thus avoid the dangers of multiple casters attacking you, and the issue of ranged damage is negated as well!

BRINGING DESTRUCTION TO THE SCOURGE

With all in place, those at the Sanctum of the Sun are ready to make **War on Deatholme**. You too should gather your forces while accepting this quest. These final actions against the creatures of Deatholme and the surrounding area can be quite challenging. Though soloable for players with the right patience, equipment, and skill, it is far easier and just as rewarding to get a group of three or so characters and roll through the rest of the Ghostlands. Stop at Tranquillien as well, and receive the Wanted Poster quest for **Knucklerot and Luzran**. The Wanted Poster is just outside the Tranquillien Inn.

War on Deatholme	
Faction	Horde
Location	Sanctum of the Sun
Quest Giver	Magister Idonis
Quest Completion	Magister Idonis
Reward	Chain to Dar'Khan's Lieutenants and A Restorative Draught

Wanted: Knucklerot and Luzran	
Faction	Horde
Location	Tranquillien
Quest Giver	Wanted Poster
Quest Completion	Deathstalker Rathiel
Reward	Invoker's Signet (Ring +3 Int, +2 Spell Critical Rating), Slayer's Band (Ring +3 STAM, +2 Critical Rating)

For those forming a group, it's good to start getting everyone together during **War on Deatholme**. This is a quest that can be finished very quickly in a group. Beyond that, this is the easiest Deatholme quest to solo; you don't have to go inside or near any of the buildings, and that minimizes the risks to your soloist. While the group is forming, you can start on the quest and get extra experience without having to sit on your hindquarters.

There are three types of enemies needed for the quest (out of the five enemy types found in the open area of Deatholme). Search for *Eyes of Dar'Khan*, *Nerubis Centurions*, and *Wailers*. Stay away from Deatholme Necromancers and their Dreadbone Skeleton pets, as these are not needed.

Eyes of Dar'Khan are the dark, Wraith-type enemies that you see quite commonly wandering about. They are one used as both patrollers in Deatholme and as static guards for buildings. Their meanest aspect is that they love to use an instant Curse of Agony. Because it's hard to avoid this Curse, you might as well take out the Eyes last when there is a group of mixed enemies.

Nerubis Centurions are the most melee capable of the enemies outside of the ziggurats and towers of Deatholme. These enemies are seen by the edges of the area, along the inner walls. Though they have a Deadly Poison DOT that they enjoy applying to their victims, it doesn't land as commonly as the Curse of Agony from the *Eyes of Dar'Khan*. For this reason, it's good to hit Centurions first in the hope that they won't get to use their DOT in time.

Wailers are Banshee-type creatures. Instead of using DOTs like many of their allies, they try to debuff targets with Wailing Dead, a general attribute-lowering attack. This has a short duration, and at least it's better than having them constantly Silence you (as many of their higher-level relatives would try). Still, this lowers all attributes by 9%.

When You Have Enough Levels or People

You can silence Luzran and Knucklerot at any time; they aren't part of the chain, and the reward for bringing justice to them is quite impressive! Having a solid ring at this stage of your character's development is sweet.

So, when you have gotten enough people to join your quest or when you have gotten up to level 20 or so, look for these foes. Luzran, as said, patrols the western part of the Dead Scar. He walks up and down relentlessly.

Knucklerot is much trickier to find, as his route between Windrunner Village and the Dead Scar goes over more uneven terrain. If you have buddies, get people to spread out and scout for the bad guy. Turn on Undead Tracking, if anyone has the ability at their disposal.

Once you spot an Abomination, estimate the path that it is taking. Because these fiends walk slowly, you have the time to run ahead of them and clear all of the possible adds out of the way. Finish that, rest, and organize people to get as many ranged attacks as possible. Have your most solid character stay in a defensive style of play throughout the fight, and try to keep aggro on them. Paladins are quite dependable for these fights.

Because Abominations are often slow kills, invest in anything that lessens armor, lands high-efficiency DOTs, or keeps character Health higher.

Once you finish, it's time for rings!

Of all the generic enemies in Deatholme, it is the Necromancers and their Skeleton pets that do the most damage to a solo character. The Skeletons hit hard enough on their own, and the Necromancers are no slouches on Shadow attacks themselves. Always use corners and cover to force the Necromancers out of casting range, and take them out before worrying about their pets. Though these targets are avoidable in the outdoor areas, you are going to fight several of them when going after the Lieutenants and leader of the area.

With all right in the world, back up to the Sanctum of the Sun and turn in your quests. Accept **Dar'Khan's Lieutenants**, **The Traitor's Destruction**, and **A Restorative Draught** at this time. Make a short run to Tranquillien to advance **A Restorative Draught** into **Captives of Deatholme** and to turn in the Wanted Poster quest if you were able to take down both *Luzran* and *Knucklerot* already.

A Restorative Draught	
Faction	Horde
Location	Sanctum of the Sun
Quest Giver	Arcanist Janeda
Quest Completion	Apothecary Renzithen
Reward	Chain to Captives at Deatholme

Dar'Khan's Lieutenants	
Faction	Horde
Location	Sanctum of the Sun
Quest Giver	Magister Idonis
Quest Completion	Magister Idonis
Reward	Reforged Quel'dorei Crest (Shield 411 Armor 7 Block, +2 STR, +2 STAM), Ley-Keeper's Wand (Wand 15.0 DPS), Ghostclaw Leggings (Leather Legs 68 Armor, +4 AGI, +4 STAM)

Captives of Deatholme	
Faction	Horde
Location	Tranquillien
Quest Giver	Apothecary Renzithen
Quest Completion	
Reward	Experience

The Traitor's Destruction	
Faction	Horde
Location	Sanctum of the Sun
Quest Giver	Magister Kaendris
Quest Completion	Magister Kaendris
Reward	Staff of the Sun (Staff 18.3 DPS, +10 INT, +4 SPI), Farstrider's Longbow (Bow 14.4 DPS), Dawnblade (1H Dagger 13.7 DPS, +5 STAM), or Sin'dorei Warblade (2H Sword 18.2 DPS, +10 STR, +4 STAM)

Be certain that everyone keeps their quest reward from **The Twin Ziggurats** at the ready. You will soon be going after the leader of Deatholme, and both items from the earlier quest have a special ability that nails Dar'Khan for impressive damage. Even a soloer has a considerable chance of stopping this Elite caster if they use the class wisely in conjunction with the reward items.

Return to Deatholme and use to map to locate the Captives and the Lieutenants that you need. In the north, always in the same crypt, are *Jurion the Deceiver* and the innocent *Apothecary Enith*. Slay Jurion after clearing the way into the building, then rescue the Apothecary. Jurion is a named Wraith, but he doesn't have much more potential for carnage than one of the Eyes.

Next, walk along the road to the open-air structure in the northeastern part of the area. Wailers are frequent in that section, and at the center of the building is *Mirdoran the Fallen*. Ambush him, and notice that you are getting a faint amount of Argent Dawn Reputation from this work. That is kind of a nice perk! Fight Mirdoran inside the building, by over at a wall. This limits the number of wandering things that could trouble you.

The next two Lieutenants can be in a couple of spots. *Borgoth the Bloodletter* is always in one of the temples. There is one temple on the eastern side of Deatholme, up on a hill; the other temple is directly by the south wall of Deatholme. You need to get inside both of these anyway, because the other two Captives are inside those buildings. Search for *Apprentice Varnis* and *Ranger Vedoran*, and save them both.

When you do find *Borgoth the Bloodletter*, he'll always be standing behind the two altars in the lower level of each temple. Monsters love to patrol into these buildings from the outside, so wait for a moment at the top of the building and look to see if anyone is coming. If they are, wait for them and attack the patrollers before going downstairs.

Eyes are in the cubbies within the lower floor, so you won't want to take up a lot of space down there either. Pull Borgoth back to you, and destroy this non-Elite Abomination. His damage is impressive for a non-Elite, so you want a fast fight if there are no healers. Use damaging attacks and keep the action rapid rather than efficient. You can always rest afterward, since you avoided the patroller issue.

With **Captives of Deatholme** completed, you now want to finish off the last Lieutenant. *Masophet the Black* is inside one of the ziggurats on the south side of Deatholme. Look inside either of them. If you have a Rogue present, let them stealth behind the two Eye guards outside the building, then poke their head around the corner to see if Masophet is there. Done carefully, you don't need to fight at all to check while in Stealth.

When you do find this target, clear the fight against both Eyes at the entrance while standing around the side of the building (to save yourself from road wanderers). Then, have one person look inside and proximity aggro one of the casters. Slip back around the wall and fight the Necromancer and his pet. Repeat this on the other side. Carefully do this a third time to get the last Necromancer out of the way, then take on Masophet directly.

If any of the pulled Necromancers gets too close to him on the way out, he'll come earlier. If that happens, you'll get a fairly big fight, with two of the casters, their pets, and Masophet. Use crowd control on Masophet, eliminate the casters, then do the same on the Skeletons until Masophet breaks out of Poly (or whatever you are using). Turn the damage on him then, and clear the encounter.

There is only one quest left to worry about. To ensure **The Traitor's Destruction**, carefully approach the Tower of the Damned in the center of Deatholme. Eyes and Wailers patrol outside and inside the building. If you are soloing, hug the walls to avoid aggroing a wanderer and one of the Necromancers in the lower levels. This would bring three things at once, and you might be hard pressed to win such a fight without using potions or timed abilities.

The final room at the bottom has two more Necromancers and Dar'Khan himself. Pulling Dar'Khan directly does not cause the Necromancers to add, so you can ignore them entirely. That said, you can also pull the Necromancers one by one and clear the room beforehand (if it would make you more comfortable). As usual, the key is not to screw up and get too close to your targets until the pulls are done.

Whatever you are pulling, use the walls for cover to force the targets up the stairs and into your ambush. Once Dar'Khan enters the fray, use the weapons that you received from The Twin Ziggurats. Dar'Khan won't lost as long with that free damage hitting him in the face!

Use Arcane Torrent to Silence Dar'Khan as well, promising at least a couple of easy seconds and one spell interrupted in the process. Rely also on any Stuns or interrupts that your group can provide; these do a great deal to mitigate Dar'Khan's best actions.

Extract yourself from the Tower of the Damned, or even Hearth back to Tranquillien if you like. Turn in the quests there and at the Sanctum of the Sun. Fine work!

SEEING THE WORLD

Your actions have helped to save the Ghostlands, at least for now. However, with the Plaguelands so close, it would be near insanity to leave it at that. Listen to Magister Kaendris and take a flight to the capital so that you can meet Lor'Themar Theron, the leader of Quel'Thalas. This time, you arrive at in Silvermoon City as a **Hero of the Sin'dorei**.

Lady Sylvanas is in the lower chambers of Undercity, just as she was before if you delivered **The Lady's Necklace** to her. Look for her in the Royal Quarter and greet her as an emissary of your people. Stick around as Sylvanas doesn't grant completion immediately. Returning the good will of the Blood Elves, she suggests that you also travel to Orgrimmar, to **Meet the Warchief**.

Meeting the Warchief

Faction	Horde
Location	Royal Quarter, Undercity
Quest Giver	Lady Sylvanas Windrunner
Quest Completion	Thrall
Reward	Chain to Allegiance to the Horde

Hero of the Sin'dorei

Faction	Horde
Location	Sanctum of the Sun
Quest Giver	Magister Kaendris
Quest Completion	Lor'Themar Theron
Reward	Chain to Envoy of the Horde

Exit Undercity and climb the hill toward the flight tower across from the city's entrance. Check to make sure you are taking the correct flight (the lower dock is the one you want for Orgrimmar, but it's always good to double check). Then, enter Orgrimmar after your flight arrives. Head to the back of the city and have an audience with Thrall, then return home to share the offer of **Allegiance to the Horde**.

Allegiance to the Horde

Faction	Horde
Location	Orgrimmar
Quest Giver	Thrall
Quest Completion	Lor'Themar Theron
Reward	Experience

The chain ends with Lor'Themar, when you bring him up to speed about the current status of Horde relations. You receive a nice boost to your Silvermoon City Reputation, and the experience award is quite fair.

This ends you passage through the Blood Elven lands. It is now your character's duty to enter the other

Once you arrive in Silvermoon City, walk to the back of the Sunfury Spire. There, Lor'Themar Theron will give you a most honorable distinction. As an **Envoy to the Horde**, you will be able to travel to Undercity and see the sights in style. Use the teleporter on the right side of the Spire for a much faster (and safer) trip.

besieged regions of Kalimdor and Azeroth. If you continue to show the tenacity and devotion that you have here, it won't be long at all before you too pass through the Dark Portal, to aid your people in their fight for Outland.

Envoy to the Horde

Faction	Horde
Location	Silvermoon City
Quest Giver	Lor'Themar Theron
Quest Completion	Lady Sylvanas Windrunner
Reward	Chain to Meeting the Warchief

In the meanwhile, try some of the questing in southern Barrens or Hillsbrad. Branch out, and start to work with the other Horde races. They may not look as pretty as your kin, but do not doubt their honor, strength, or courage. They won't let you down!

Draenei

The Exodar crashed on a small cluster of islands. The primary two are Azuremyst Isle and Bloodmyst Isle. While parts of the Exodar were scattered across the islands, the largest portion has become the hub of the Draenei civilization on Azuremyst Isle. The quests throughout these two zones teach you quite a bit about the Draenei and yourself. Be prepared to adventure in these islands until level 20 if you want to use them to their fullest.

AZUREMYST ISLE MAP LEGEND

Azuremyst Isle Legend

A	**Ammen Vale**		Jel	Cloth & Leather Merchant	•	Mutated Owlkin	3-4
	Draenei Survivor	Quest Target	Aurelon	Paladin Trainer		Emitter Spare Part	Quest Target
★	Vale Moth	1	Zalduun	Priest Trainer	**D**	**Shadow Ridge**	
★	Volatile Mutation	1-2	Valaatu	Mage Trainer	•	Blood Elf Scout	4-5
★	Root Lasher		Firmanvaar	Shaman Trainer	•	Surveyor Candress	5 Quest Target
			Kore	Warrior Trainer	**E**	**Ammen Fields**	
B	**Crash Site**		Keilnei	Hunter Trainer	★	Volatile Mutation	1-2
	Proenitus	Quest Giver	Ryosh	General Supplies	•	Mutated Root Lasher	3
	Botanist Taerix	Quest Giver	Mura	Weaponsmith		Corrupted Flower	Quest Target
	Apprentice Vishael		Vindicator Aldar	Quest Giver	**F**	**The Sacred Grove**	
	Apprentice Tedon		Technician Zhanaa	Quest Giver		Spirit of the Vale	70
	Aurok	Armorsmith Quest Giver	**C**	**Nestlewood Thicket**		Spirit of Water	3
	Jaeleil	Quest Giver	★	Nestlewood Owlkin	3-4		

Spirit of Fire		3
Spirit of Air		3
• Restless Spirit of Earth		4

G Azuremyst Isle East

★ Skittering Crawler	7-8
★ Moongraze Stag	6-7
• Timberstrider Fledgling	6-7
• Timberstrider	7-8
• Root Trapper	5-6
Azure Snapdragon Bulb	Quest Target

H Azure Watch

Tullas	Paladin Trainer
Caregiver Chellan	Innkeeper
Guvan	Priest Trainer
Esbina	Stable Master
Semid	Mage Trainer
Ruada	Warrior Trainer
Cryptographer Aurren	Quest Giver
Arugoo of the Stillpine	Quest Giver
Totem of Akida	Quest Giver
Buruk	Pet Trainer
Acteon	Hunter Trainer
Kioni	Cloth & Leather Merchant
Nabek	Weapons & Armor Merchant
Ziz	Tradesman
Otonambusi	General Goods Vendor
Anchorite Fateema	First Aid Trainer
Daedal	Journeyman Alchemist
Artificer Daelo	Journey Engineer
Heur	Herbalist
Exarch Menelaous	Quest Giver
Tuluun	Shaman Trainer
Technician Dyvuun	Quest Target
Dulvi	Mining Trainer
Azuremyst Peacekeeper	23
Mailbox	
Forge	
Anvil	

I Odesyus' Landing

Logan Daniel	General Goods Vendor
Blacksmith Calypso	Blacksmithing Trainer & Supplies
Erin Kelly	Journeyman Tailor
"Cookie" McWeaksauce	Cooking Trainer & Supplies
Admiral Odesyus	Quest Giver

Priestess Kyleen Il'dinare	Quest Giver
Archaeologist Adamant Ironheart	Quest Giver
Engineer "Spark" Overgrind	Quest Target
Alliance Axeman	10
★ Skittering Crawler	5-7

J Geezle's Camp

• Venture Co. Gemologist	6-7
• Venture Co. Saboteur	7
Nautical Compass	Quest Target
Nautical Maps	Quest Target

K Wrathscale Point

★ Skittering Crawler	5-7
• Wrathscale Myrmidon	7-8
• Wrathscale Naga	7-8
• Wrathscale Siren	7-8
Ancient Relic	Quest Target

L Tide's Hollow

• Wrathscale Myrmidon	7-8
• Wrathscale Naga	7-8
• Wrathscale Siren	7-8
• Warlord Sriss'tiz	10 Quest Target

M Moonwing Den

• Aberrant Owlbeast	9-10
• Deranged Owlbeast	8-9
• Raving Owlbeast	9-10

N Silvermyst Isle

★ Barbed Crawler	8-9
• Siltfin Murloc	9-10
• Siltfin Oracle	9-10
• Siltfin Hunter	9-10

O Bristlelimb Village

Totem of Vark	Quest Giver
• Stillpine Captive	6-9
• Bristlelimb Ursa	7-8
• Bristlelimb Windcaller	6-7
• Bristlelimb Furbolg	6-7

P Azuremyst Isle Central

★ Moongraze Buck	7-8
• Infected Nightsaber Runt	7-8
• Timberstrider	6-8

Q Azuremyst Isle West

• Moongraze Buck	7-8
• Nightstalker	8-9

• Root Thresher		7-8
• Greater Timberstrider		7-9

R Silting Shore

• Blood Elf Bandit	7 Drops Quest Item
• Siltfin Murloc	9-10
• Siltfin Oracle	9-10
• Siltfin Hunter	9-10
• Murgurgula	13 Drops Quest Item

S Menagerie Wreckage

• Ravager Specimen	9-10
• Death Ravager	11 Quest Target

Stillpine Hold

T Parkat Steelfur	**General Goods**
Moordo	Journeyman Leatherworker
Gurf	Skinner
Kurz the Revelator	
Stillpine the Younger	
High Chief Stillpine	
Stillpine Hunter	10
Stillpine Defender	9-10
Crazed Wildkin	9-10
Chieftain Oomooroo	11
The Kurken	12
The Blood Crystal	Quest Target

U Docks

Huntress Kella Nightbow	
Shalannius	Druid Trainer
Boat to Auberdine	

1	Megelon	Quest Giver
2	Tolaan	Quest Giver
3	Aeun	Quest Giver
4	Dyktynna	Fishing Trainer & Supplies
5	Totem of Tikti	Quest Giver
6	Cowlen	Quest Giver
7	Magwin	Quest Giver
8	Totem of Coo	Quest Giver
9	Totem of Yor	Quest Giver
10	Temper	Quest Giver
11	Ammen Vale Guard	65

WALKTHROUGH FOR AZUREMYST ISLE

The quiet tranquility of Azuremyst Isle was shattered when the burning and fragmenting hulk of the Exodar plummeted to Azeroth. Much of the wildlife was killed when the flaming pieces of metal and crystal hit the ground. Even more were mutated and corrupted when the systems that were vital to the Exodar's functions proved toxic to the plants and wildlife of Azeroth.

AMMEN VALE

Your pod crashed in the small valley of Ammen Vale. While you are not alone, there are only a few other Draenei who have landed here. With much of the technology from the Exodar in ruins, you'll have to rely on your own abilities to survive and help others.

Megelon is standing just down the path from your pod. Above him floats a yellow "!" NPCs with quests you can obtain have these. If the "!" is grey, you are not yet high enough level for the quest. Speak with Megelon by right-clicking on him. He's not in the greatest shape, but he directs you to follow the path to a larger spot of wreckage called the Crash Site and speak with Proenitus (**You Survived!**). Follow his instructions and head southwest to find other survivors.

You Survived!	
Faction	Alliance
Location	Ammen Vale
Quest Giver	Megelon
Quest Completion	Proenitus
Reward	Chains to Replenish the Healing Crystals

Proenitus has a yellow "?" floating above him. This shows that you have a completed quest that Proenitus will reward you for. NPCs with grey "?" above them are waiting for you to complete a quest before they can reward you. Proenitus also shows on your mini-map as a yellow dot. This makes it very easy to obtain rewards for work done.

Proenitus needs your help **Replenishing the Healing Crystals**. He's found the blood of some of the local wildlife to be a suitable replacement, but needs you to hunt them. Head north and hunt the *Vale Moths* to collect the blood. Once an enemy is dead, its body will have gold sparkles rising off it to show that there is loot to be collected. Right-click on the body to open the loot window and then left-click on each item to put it in your inventory. To speed your looting, hold shift when you right-click the corpse to automatically put

all the loot in your backpack or initiate the auto-loot function from the interface menu as a shortcut. The *Vials of Moth Blood* (like many quest items) are items that drop from the Vale Moths and must be looted to be collected.

Replenish the Healing Crystals	
Faction	Alliance
Location	Crash Site
Quest Giver	Proenitus
Quest Completion	Proenitus
Reward	Choice of Salvaged Leather Belt (Leather Waist, 19 Armor), Slightly Rusted Bracers (Mail Wrist, 29 Armor), or Worn Slippers (Cloth Feet, 7 Armor).

Return to Proenitus for your reward. With the blood gathered, he asks you to bring it to Zalduun (**Urgent Delivery**). Zalduun is in the largest part of the Crash Site tending the wounded. He's so grateful to you that he wants you to help him **Rescue the Survivors!** He gives you a *Healing Crystal* and sends you to find the scattered wounded, while he tends to the ones here. Speak with your trainer before using the southwest exit. Mura is there and will buy any excess items you've accumulated. Proenitus (back outside) also asks you to speak with **Botanist Taerix** on the west side of the crash site.

Urgent Delivery	
Faction	Alliance
Location	Crash Site
Quest Giver	Proenitus
Quest Completion	Zalduun
Reward	Chains to Rescue the Survivors

Rescue the Survivors!

Faction	Alliance
Location	Crash Site
Quest Giver	Zalduun
Quest Completion	Zalduun
Reward	Empty Draenei Supply Pouch (4 Slot Bag).

Botanist Taerix

Faction	Alliance
Location	Crash Site
Quest Giver	Proenitus
Quest Completion	Botanist Taerix
Reward	Chains to Volatile Mutations

The Spoils of War

Your backpack is nearly full. First, take the time to look through it and see if there is any usable equipment for you. Second, become familiar with any recover items (potions, food, drink, etc.) you've accumulated. Everything else that can be sold to vendors should be.

With new abilities learned and your inventory cleared, head out and around to the west side of the Crash Site. Botanist Taerix also needs help. Before she starts to cure the wildlife, you need to prune back the **Volatile Mutations**. Head west and kill eight of the mutations before returning to Taerix.

Volatile Mutations

Faction	Alliance
Location	Crash Site
Quest Giver	Botanist Taerix
Quest Completion	Botanist Taerix
Reward	Chains to What Must Be Done…

Taerix's team needs samples of the plants and wildlife to help find a way to cure the contamination. Apprentice Vishael asks you to do some **Botanical Legwork** while Taerix tells you **What Must Be Done…** You can hunt the *Mutated Root Lashers* while looking for survivors and *Corrupted Flowers*, so accept the quests.

What Must Be Done…

Faction	Alliance
Location	Crash Site
Quest Giver	Botanist Taerix
Quest Completion	Botanist Taerix
Reward	Chains to Healing the Lake

Botanical Legwork

Faction	Alliance
Location	Crash Site
Quest Giver	Apprentice Vishael
Quest Completion	Apprentice Vishael
Reward	Chains to Experience

The Draenei that need your assistance are the ones that can't make it to the Crash Site. Look around the wreckage of pods for the *Draenei Survivors*. To heal the survivors, select them by left-clicking on the body and then open your inventory. Right-click on the *Healing Crystal* to activate it. An alternate way to use items in your inventory is to drag them onto one of your quickbars and push the appropriate hotkey. Once the survivors can move on their own, they'll go to the Crash Site for better care.

The *Corrupted Flowers* are in the Ammen Fields to the west, but they don't drop from enemies. They are a ground spawn and you need to right-click on them when the cursor turns into a gold gear to collect them (a grey gear means you are not close enough). Wait for a loot window to open and left-click on the flower to put it in your inventory. With *Mutated Root Lashers* and survivors here also, you can accomplish all three quests at once!

Inoculation

Faction	Alliance
Location	Crash Site
Quest Giver	Vindicator Aldar
Quest Completion	Vindicator Aldar
Reward	3 Minor Healing Potions (Use Restores 70 to 90 health) and the choice of 3 Elixir of Minor Defense (Use Increases armor by 50 for 1 hour) or 3 Elixir of Lion's Strength (Use Increases Strength by 4 for 1 hour).

Traveling the Bloody Way

As you are traveling from point A to point B, kill everything your level or lower that gets near you. The enemies in Ammen Vale are fairly weak and the additional experience and usable equipment make it worth your time. Don't deviate too much from your path (unless you really enjoy the slaughter), but the extra kills give practice and loot.

With some good work done, return to the Crash Site. Botanist Taerix has more work for you now that the samples have been collected (**Healing the Lake**). Inside, Zalduun gives you a small bag as a reward. As your backpack fills up quite quickly, even a bag this small is very useful. To equip it, open your inventory and drag the bag onto one of the slots to the left of your backpack. The bag locks into place and items can now be store inside it. Zalduun is finished with you for now, but there are others who need help outside the southern exit.

Technician Zhanaa is working to restore a communications device, but needs you to collect some **Spare Parts** while Vindicator Aldar asks you to do some **Inoculation**. Sell any excess items before moving south to Silverline Lake.

Spare Parts

Faction	Alliance
Location	Crash Site
Quest Giver	Technician Zhanaa
Quest Completion	Technician Zhanaa
Reward	Choice of Beaten Chain Leggings (Mail Legs, 58 Armor), Rough Leather Leggings (Leather Legs, 29 Armor), or Hand Sewn Pants (Cloth Legs, 9 Armor)

Healing the Lake

Faction	Alliance
Location	Crash Site
Quest Giver	Botanist Taerix
Quest Completion	Botanist Taerix
Reward	Experience

The *Irradiated Power Crystal* polluting the lake is quite large. Dive into the water and disperse the *Neutralizing Agent* on it. With the source dealt with, you need to deal with the affected. Northeast of the lake is Nestlewood Thicket. You have much to do. Use the *Inoculating Crystal* on the *Nestlewood Owlkin*. The Mutated Owlkin have become aggressive and will attack you on sight. Be prepared to defend yourself. Follow the winding path through the hills and look for the *Emitter Spare Parts*. Finish the remainder of your quests before heading back to the Crash Site for your well-deserved rewards. That was a lot!

Taerix thanks you for your work and asks you to speak with **Vindicator Aldar**. Head to the south edge of the Crash Site and speak with Aldar about a couple things. Aldar asks you to find **The Missing Scout** near Shadow Ridge.

Tolaan is near the entrance to Shadow Ridge and in dire need of medical attention. He waves you off and insists that you instead deal with **The Blood Elves**. Travel up the paths slaying the *Blood Elf Scouts*.

The Blood Elves

Faction	Alliance
Location	Shadow Ridge
Quest Giver	Tolaan
Quest Completion	Tolaan
Reward	Choice of Weathered Cloth Armor (Cloth Chest, 9 Armor), Weathered Leather Vest (Leather Chest, 31 Armor), or Weathered Mail Tunic (Mail Chest, 63 Armor)

Use ranged attacks to pull the enemies away from each other to avoid larger fights. When you've slain all 10 of the scouts, return to Tolaan. With the scouts dead, Tolaan asks you to deal with the **Blood Elf Spy**.

Vindicator Aldar

Faction	Alliance
Location	Crash Site
Quest Giver	Botanist Taerix
Quest Completion	Vindicator Aldar
Reward	Experience

Blood Elf Spy

Faction	Alliance
Location	Shadow Ridge
Quest Giver	Tolaan
Quest Completion	Vindicator Aldar
Reward	Choice of Exodar Bastard Sword (Two-hand Sword, 2.7 DPS), or Exodar Dagger (One-hand Dagger, 1.9 DPS), Exodar Maul (Main-hand Mace, 2.1 DPS), Exodar Shortsword (Main-hand Sword, 2.1 DPS), Exodar Crossbow (Crossbow, 4.0 DPS), or Exodar Staff (Two-hand Staff, 2.7 DPS)

The Missing Scout

Faction	Alliance
Location	Crash Site
Quest Giver	Vindicator Aldar
Quest Completion	Tolaan
Reward	Chains to The Blood Elves

Make your way back up the paths to the very top of the camp. *Candress* stands with a body guard, so it is impossible to fight only her. When you start the fight, kill *Candress* first. She does more damage then her partner and is weaker. With Candress dead, loot the **Blood Elf Plans** from her body and return to Vindicator Aldar.

The *Blood Elf Plans* are a quest-starting item. With it in your inventory, right-click on it to bring up the quest. Click "Accept" to add the quest to your log.

Blood Elf Plans

Faction	Alliance
Location	Shadow Ridge
Quest Giver	Blood Elf Plans
Quest Completion	Vindicator Aldar
Reward	Experience

Travel to Azure Watch

Faction	Alliance
Location	Crash Site
Quest Giver	Technician Zhanaa
Quest Completion	Technician Dyvuun
Reward	Experience

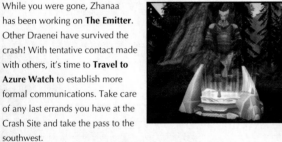

While you were gone, Zhanaa has been working on **The Emitter**. Other Draenei have survived the crash! With tentative contact made with others, it's time to **Travel to Azure Watch** to establish more formal communications. Take care of any last errands you have at the Crash Site and take the pass to the southwest.

THE PATH TO AZURE WATCH

On the road to Azure Watch is Aeun. He was attacked by some of the mutated creatures in the area and can't take the **Request for Emergency Supplies** to Azure Watch in his condition. Accept the quest and continue west across the river.

The Emitter

Faction	Alliance
Location	Crash Site
Quest Giver	Vindicator Aldar
Quest Completion	Technician Zhanaa
Reward	Chains to Travel to Azure Watch

Request for Emergency Supplies

Faction	Alliance
Location	Azuremyst Isle
Quest Giver	Aeun
Quest Completion	Caregiver Chellan
Reward	Choice of 5 Brilliant Smallfish (Use Restores 61 health over 18 sec. Must remain seated while eating) or 5 Refreshing Spring Water (Use Restores 151 mana over 18 sec. Must remain seated while drinking)

Take a short break from your journey and speak to Diktynna. She can teach you to fish and has work for you. Help her catch some **Red Snapper – Very Tasty!** and she'll give you a fishing pole. Use her fishing net on the nearby schools of red snapper and be ready for a fight as Angry Murlocs are after the same fish you are.

Angry Murlocs also have a decent chance to drop a 6 slot bag. Return to her and Diktynna asks you to **Find Acteon!** As Acteon is at Azure Watch, you're in luck! Follow the road west.

Red Snapper – Very Tasty!

Faction	Alliance
Location	Azuremyst Isle
Quest Giver	Diktynna
Quest Completion	Diktynna
Reward	Fishing Pole and Shiny Bauble (Use When applied to your fishing pole, increases Fishing by 25 for 10 min.)

Find Acteon!

Faction	Alliance
Location	Azuremyst Isle
Quest Giver	Diktynna
Quest Completion	Acteon
Reward	Chains to The Great Moongraze Hunt

AZURE WATCH

Without missing a beat, Acteon gives you more work to do. He asks you to join **The Great Moongraze Hunt**, but speak with everyone in town before you head out. Anchorite Fateema speaks about the **Medicinal Purpose** of hunting lashers, while a number of Draenei here can teach you various professions or class abilities.

The Great Moongraze Hunt

Faction	Alliance
Location	Azure Watch
Quest Giver	Acteon
Quest Completion	Acteon
Reward	5 Roasted Moongraze Tenderloin (Use Restores 61 health over 18 sec. Must remain seated while eating. If you spend at least 10 seconds eating you will become well fed and gain 2 Stamina and Spirit for 15 min.), Recipe Roasted Moongraze Tenderloin, and choice of Moongraze Fur Cloak (Back, 8 Armor) or Moongraze Hide Boots (Leather Feet, 31 Armor)

Medicinal Purpose

Faction	Alliance
Location	Azure Watch
Quest Giver	Anchorite Fateema
Quest Completion	Anchorite Fateema
Reward	Chains to An Alternative Alternative

Speak with Caregiver Chellan and "Make this inn your home." This will allow you to use your Hearthstone to return here from across great distances. With errands done, head west to hunt the *Moongraze Stags* and *Root Trappers*. Both sides of the road hold your targets. The enemies here are tougher than in Ammen Vale. The timber striders and root trappers are aggressive and will attack you on sight. Keep your health and mana above half by resting, eating, or drinking between fights. This gives you the staying power to pull through a difficult encounter if things go poorly.

Return to Azure Watch once you have collected the lasher roots. You'll be going back out shortly, so don't worry about collecting all the meat. Fateema's ointment is ineffective, but Daedal has **An Alternative Alternative.** He needs 5 *Azure Snapdragon Bulbs* for his concoction. They grow near the trees north of the road to Ammen Vale.

An Alternative Alternative

Faction	Alliance
Location	Azure Watch
Quest Giver	Daedal
Quest Completion	Daedal
Reward	Chains to The Prophecy of Velen

Bring the bulbs back to Daedal and he will tell you of **The Prophecy of Velen**. He charges you with traveling south to find the kin of the wounded creature, but first you need to finish **The Great Moongraze Hunt**. Exit to the northwest of Azure Watch and climb the hill to look for the *Moongraze Bucks*. Return when you have the hides you need.

The Prophecy of Velen

Faction	Alliance
Location	Azure Watch
Quest Giver	Daedal
Quest Completion	Admiral Odesyus
Reward	Experience

ODESYUS' LANDING

Follow the south road until you find a hastily constructed fort bearing odd blue banners. Though the people are strange, they will not attack you. Introduce yourself to their commander Admiral Odesyus. He is very appreciative of your efforts to help his crewmember. Most of the camp doesn't trust you yet, but Admiral Odesyus tells you how to make **A Small Start** toward earning that trust.

A Small Start

Faction	Alliance
Location	Odesyus' Landing
Quest Giver	Admiral Odesyus
Quest Completion	Admiral Odesyus
Reward	Opens a number of quests

Follow the shoreline east in search of the goblins and their allies. Search the camp near the ruins first. The *Nautical Compass* is sitting on one of the crates. The *Nautical Map*, however, is in the primary camp is more difficult to obtain.

The Venture Company Saboteurs and Gemologists stick together like Draenei and, unless you are careful, will overwhelm you when one of them is in trouble. Use ranged attacks to pull the enemies away from the camp one at a time and make your way slowly to the center of the camp. With both pieces in hand, return to Odesyus.

With Admiral Odesyus' trust on your side, the rest of his crew is willing to speak with you about their difficulties. Look around and grab **Cookie's Jumbo Gumbo**, **Precious and Fragile Things Need Special Handling**, and **Reclaiming the Ruins**. Follow the shoreline west toward Wrathscale Point and hunt the *Skittering Crawlers* for **Cookie's Jumbo Gumbo** on the way.

Cookie's Jumbo Gumbo	
Faction	Alliance
Location	Odesyus' Landing
Quest Giver	"Cookie" McWeaksauce
Quest Completion	"Cookie" McWeaksauce
Reward	10 Cookie's Jumbo Gumbo (Use Restores 61 health over 18 sec. Must remain seated while eating. If you spend at least 10 seconds eating you will become well fed and gain 2 Stamina and Spirit for 15 min.)

Reclaiming the Ruins	
Faction	Alliance
Location	Odesyus' Landing
Quest Giver	Priestess Kyleen Il'dinare
Quest Completion	Priestess Kyleen Il'dinare
Reward	Experience

While **Reclaiming the Ruins**, by killing the Wrathscale, keep your eyes out for the *Ancient Relics*. These **Precious and Fragile Things Need Special Handling**. The Wrathscale are very aggressive and fairly dangerous. Pull each one away from any others as a fight against two will be your doom. Some of the Naga and relics are found underwater. When you dive below the surface, a breath meter will show in the center of the screen. Do not let this run out as you take damage very quickly when it does. The Naga also carry a **Rune Covered Tablet**. Priestess Kyleen Il'dinare will want to see this when you return to the landing.

The *Wrathscale Myrmidon* and *Siren* can be found on the beach, but the *Naga* are found in the ruins. As the Ancient Relics are found all over, it's a win-win situation. Continue killing and collecting until your quests are completed before traveling back to the landing. You probably haven't collected all the *Skittering Crawler Meat* you need, so do a bit of hunting before you enter Odesyus' Landing.

Precious and Fragile Things Need Special Handling	
Faction	Alliance
Location	Odesyus' Landing
Quest Giver	Archaeologist Adamant Ironheart
Quest Completion	Archaeologist Adamant Ironheart
Reward	Experience

Rune Covered Tablet	
Faction	Alliance
Location	Wrathscale Point
Quest Giver	Rune Covered Tablet
Quest Completion	Priestess Kyleen Il'dinare
Reward	Chains to Warlord Sriss'tiz

The people of the landing are warming up to you, but there is still a long way to go before they can call you friend. Priestess Kyleen Il'dinare asks you to kill **Warlord Sriss'tiz**. Return to Wrathscale point and continue east until you find Tides' Hollow.

Warlord Sriss'tiz	
Faction	Alliance
Location	Odesyus' Landing
Quest Giver	Priestess Kyleen Il'dinare
Quest Completion	Priestess Kyleen Il'dinare
Reward	Choice of Battle Tested Blade (Main-hand Sword, 4.3 DPS) or Naga Scale Boots (Mail Feet, 70 Armor)

With nowhere to run, the cave can be very dangerous. If there are other Draenei close by, ask to join them, but don't fret if no help is found. The cave can be taken alone. Follow the downward slope to the left. Be ready to call upon the Gift of the Naaru if more than one enemy attacks you. The Naga are quite strong and can fell even the proudest of warriors.

At the bottom of the down slope, head west into some ruins. **Warlord Sriss'tiz** is in sight, but do not engage him yet. Clear the guards from around him to ensure that you only fight him when the time comes. Without an army of Naga behind him, Sriss'tiz is just a bully. The Gift of the Naaru should be more than enough to tip the balance in your favor and make the fight as difficult as any other. Slay him and bring word of the deed back to Odesyus' Landing.

The relationship between your people and the strangers has been aided greatly by your actions. Now it is time to return to your people. Travel north to Azure Watch with the news of new friends.

THE PATH TO STILLPINE HOLD

Aurren is **Learning the Language** of the Furbolg and wants you to as well. Use the *Stillpine Furbolg Language Primer* he gives you and speak with the Totem of Akida. The Stillpine Ancestor Akida will appear before you and show you the way to the **Totem of Coo**. Follow him up the hill and speak with the totem. Skirt the north edge of the hill and kill a couple Infected Nightsaber Runts until you find the *Faintly Glowing Crystal*. Open you inventory and use the item to start the quest **Strange Findings**. You don't need to follow the spirit if you know where you're going.

Learning the Language	
Faction	Alliance
Location	Azure Watch
Quest Giver	Cryptographer Aurren
Quest Completion	Totem of Akida
Reward	Chains to Totem of Coo

Totem of Coo	
Faction	Alliance
Location	Azure Watch
Quest Giver	Totem of Akida
Quest Completion	Totem of Coo
Reward	Chains to Totem of Tikti

Strange Findings

Faction	Alliance
Location	Azuremyst Isle
Quest Giver	Faintly Glowing Crystal
Quest Completion	Exarch Menelaous
Reward	Chains to Nightsaber Clean Up, Isle 2…

Understanding Stillpine Ancestor Yor is much easier than the others so far. He grants you an amazing power and leads you to the final totem. He gives you the form of a cat, invisibility, and increased speed. He becomes difficult to see once you are transformed, so select him before hand and follow his name through the world of shadows to the **Totem of Vark** that shows you **The Prophecy of Akida.**

Totem of Tikti

Faction	Alliance
Location	Azuremyst Isle
Quest Giver	Totem of Coo
Quest Completion	Totem of Tikit
Reward	Chains to Totem of Yor

The Prophecy of Akida

Faction	Alliance
Location	Azuremyst Isle
Quest Giver	Totem of Vark
Quest Completion	Arugoo of the Stillpine
Reward	Choice of Stillpine Defender (Shield, 239 Armor, 4 Block, +1 STA), Stillpine Shocker (Wand, 8.6 DPS, +1 INT), or Arugoo's Crossbow of Destruction (Crossbow, 7.3 DPS, +1 AGI)

Totem of Yor

Faction	Alliance
Location	Azuremyst Isle
Quest Giver	Totem of Tikti
Quest Completion	Totem of Yor
Reward	Chains to Totem of Vark

Totem of Vark

Faction	Alliance
Location	Azuremyst Isle
Quest Giver	Totem of Yor
Quest Completion	Totem of Vark
Reward	Chains to The Prophecy of Akida

The totem of Coo stands on the top of the hill amongst the ruins. Speak with it to receive aid getting to the **Totem of Tikti**. The Stillpine Ancestor Coo gives you the ability to survive falls and walk on water. Jump off the cliff to the east and make your way across the river to the Totem of Tikti.

As you speak with each totem, the symbols of the Stillpine language make more sense to you. The Totem of Tikti is far from your final destination and sends you down the river to look along the bottom for the **Totem of Yor.** The Stillpine Ancestor Tikti allows you to swim at great speeds and breathe underwater.

The Totem of Vark has much to say now that you fully grasp the language of the Stillpine. It shows you a war between the Stillpine and the Bristlelimb and charges you with freeing the captive Stillpine Furbolg. They are in cages throughout the camp and the keys are kept by the Bristlelimb Furbolg. Kill them one at a time and set a captive free as soon as you have a key and an opening. Using the cage with a *Bristlelimb Key* in your inventory will open the cage. The keys are automatically put into your key ring, so don't panic if they don't show up in your bag. When all captives are freed, use your Hearthstone for a quick return to Azure Watch. Arugoo is very happy to see you and hear of your deeds. He asks you to visit **Stillpine Hold** to the north.

Before you head out, speak with Exarch Menelaous and give him the *Faintly Glowing Shard.* While he believes he knows what caused the problem, the damage is done and the tainted must be killed before they can spread. He asks for a **Nightsaber Clean Up, Isle 2…**

Stillpine Hold	
Faction	Alliance
Location	Azure Watch
Quest Giver	Arugoo of the Stillpine
Quest Completion	Speak with High Chief Stillpine at Stillpine Hold
Reward	Chains to Searching Stillpine Hold

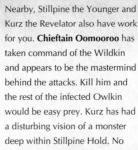

Nearby, Stillpine the Younger and Kurz the Revelator also have work for you. **Chieftain Oomooroo** has taken command of the Wildkin and appears to be the mastermind behind the attacks. Kill him and the rest of the infected Owlkin would be easy prey. Kurz has had a disturbing vision of a monster deep within Stillpine Hold. No Furbolg is safe as long as **The Kurken is Lurkin'**. Fortify yourself and sell excess loot before descending into the darkness.

Searching Stillpine Hold	
Faction	Alliance
Location	Stillpine Hold
Quest Giver	High Chief Stillpine
Quest Completion	Blood Crystal
Reward	Chains to Blood Crystals

Nightsaber Clean Up, Isle 2...	
Faction	Alliance
Location	Azure Watch
Quest Giver	Exarch Menelaous
Quest Completion	Exarch Menelaous
Reward	Choice of Huntsman's Bracers (Leather Wrist, 18 Armor), Reinforced Mail Boots (Mail Feet, 56 Armor), or Slightly Worn Bracer (Cloth Wrist, 6 Armor)

Chieftain Oomooroo	
Faction	Alliance
Location	Stillpine Hold
Quest Giver	Stillpine the Younger
Quest Completion	Stillpine the Younger
Reward	Sturdy Belt (Leather Waist, 29 Armor) or Fortified Wristguards (Mail Wrist, 45 Armor)

While Stillpine Hold is your ultimate goal, there are many *Infected Nightsaber Runts* in the woods on the way. Avoid the road and kill the runts (and anything else that looks tasty) to complete your quest. It will be a while before you turn it in, but killing the targets while you travel makes it much faster.

STILLPINE HOLD

The Stillpine Furbolg have been forced out of their home by aggressive Owlkin. Warriors stand behind fortifications and corpses litter the entrance to the hold. Speak with High Chief Stillpine about **Searching Stillpine Hold**. He knows something's wrong, but none of his warriors are strong enough to get inside the hold.

The Kurken is Lurkin'

Faction	Alliance
Location	Stillpine Hold
Quest Giver	Kurz the Revelator
Quest Completion	Kurz the Revelator
Reward	Chains to The Kurken's Hide

The Owlkin move slowly and are vulnerable to long-ange attacks. If you have these, use them as the Owlkin have high health and do a good bit of damage. Avoid fighting more than one at a time and joining with others makes this area much easier. Take the right path up to the second level.

Fight your way along the left side of this level until you find the bridge going northwest. *Oomooroo* is just across the bridge and to the left. Pull him to the bridge to avoid getting more monsters than you can handle. At low health, Oomooroo enrages and inflicts even more damage. Use potions if you need to keep your health high and finish your opponent.

Continue killing the *Crazed Wildkin* along the path to the northeast until the path ends. Down a short cliff is a pool of water and the *Kurken*. Drop down away from the Kurken and prepare yourself. Like Oomooroo, the Kurken has

high health and deals a good bit of damage. Pull and kill the two wandering Owlkin before you engage the Kurken. Having either of them attack your back during the fight with the *Kurken* is death.

With the area clear, rest to full health and mana. If you're alone, be ready to use Gift of the Naaru when your health falls to half. Pound away at the Kurken and be ready to use more potions. Even the Kurken will eventually fall and victory is yours.

Rest to full again before wading into the water and examining the *Blood Crystal*. It looks like a piece of the Exodar, but it's dissolving into the water supply. Two enemies attack when you get too close to the crystal. Kill them one at a time to minimize the damage you take. With an understanding about the **Blood Crystals**, take the only path up and out of the cave.

Blood Crystals

Faction	Alliance
Location	Stillpine Hold
Quest Giver	Blood Crystal
Quest Completion	High Chief Stillpine
Reward	Experience

Don't waste time exiting the cave as several Owlkin will likely be right on your heels. A fight of five to one isn't in your favor, but the Stillpine are very close. Keep running and let the Furbolg stop the Owlkin. Turn in all your quests. Kurz gives you **The Kurken's Hide** as a reward for your valiant efforts. Take it to the west side of the camp and have a piece of armor made for you. High Chief Stillpine tells you to **Warn Your People**, but there is still much to do up here.

Collect **Beasts of the Apocalypse** and **Murlocs…Why Here? Why Now?** These quests involve hunting in the northern part of Azuremyst Isle and should be done before you head south again.

The Kurken's Hide

Faction	Alliance
Location	Stillpine Hold
Quest Giver	Kurz the Revelator
Quest Completion	Moordo
Reward	Kurkenstoks (Cloth Feet, 13 Armor, +1 STA) or Kurken Hide Jerkin (Leather Chest, 55 Armor, +1 AGI)

Warn Your People	
Faction	Alliance
Location	Stillpine Hold
Quest Giver	High Chief Stillpine
Quest Completion	Exarch Menelaous
Reward	Experience

Murlocs...Why Here? Why Now?	
Faction	Alliance
Location	Stillpine Hold
Quest Giver	Gurf
Quest Completion	Gurf
Reward	Experience

Beasts of the Apocalypse	
Faction	Alliance
Location	Stillpine Hold
Quest Giver	Moordo
Quest Completion	Moordo
Reward	Ravager Hide Leggings (Leather Legs, 48 Armor, +1 AGI) or Ravager Chitin Tunic (Mail Chest, 108 Armor, +1 STR) or Thick Ravager Belt (Cloth Waist, 11 Armor, +1 INT)

When you've sold your loot and are ready to leave, head east toward the Menagerie Wreckage. The Ravagers in the area do a good bit of damage and will sense you from a good range. They also use a Rend ability that causes damage over time. Don't try to bandage while you are taking damage as the next tick will interrupt your bandaging and leave you with the recently bandaged debuff. Kill them one at a time and collect the *Ravager Hides*. Move north through the wreckage as you kill them.

When you've acquired enough hides, take the road north and west toward the Silting Shore. Skinners, Miners, and Herbalists should avoid walking on the road as resources in this area are plentiful.

The Silting Shore has several dangers for you. Murloc guard the *Sacks of Stillpine Grain*. Several of the Murloc used ranged attacks or spells. This makes them very difficult to pull away from others and battles with two or more are likely unless you're very careful. Use your longest range attack and then back up. As long as you stay out of their range, they will try to get closer. When they stray away from their friends run toward them and finish the job. You'll take damage before the fight even begins, but it's better than fighting an entire camp.

Siltfin Oracle

Becoming More Talented

Every level (starting at level 10), you gain a Talent Point. These can be used to increase your abilities or learn new ones. Open your talent window (defaulted to 'n'). There are three panels in the window. Look at each talent carefully before choosing as once you spend your points, it takes gold to relearn them. There is more about the benefits of each talent in the Class section.

Menelaous believes you are **Coming of Age**. He asks you to travel to the Exodar and speak with the pack handler. If your inventory has been filling up recently, take the time to buy a bag or two from the General Goods merchant. While the cost seems substantial at first, it will be made up quickly by selling the extra loot you bring back each time.

Coming of Age	
Faction	Alliance
Location	Azure Watch
Quest Giver	Exarch Menelaous
Quest Completion	Torallius the Pack Handler
Reward	Experience

The Exodar Legend

A	Flightpoint	
	Stephanos	Hippogryph Master
	Exodar Peacekeeper	65
	Miglik Blotstrom	Arena Master
B	**Mailbox**	
	Exodar Peacekeeper	65
	Exodar Proselyte	30
	Mailbox	
C	**Elekk Herd**	
	Torallius the Pack Handler	Quest Giver
	Exodar Peacekeeper	65
	Elekk	10
D	**Inn**	
	Caregiver Breel	Innkeeper
	Arthaid	Stable Master
	Mailbox	
E	**Cooking**	
	Mumman	Cook
	Phea	Cooking Supplier

F	Jewelcrafting	
	Farii	Master Jewelcrafter
	Arred	Jewelcrafting Supplier
	Padaar	Expert Jewelcrafter
	Elaando	Artisan Jewelcrafter
	Driaan	Journeyman Jewelcrafter
G	**First Aid**	
	Nus	First Aid Trainer
	Duumehi	
	Ereuso	
H	**Fishing**	
	Erett	Fishing Trainer
	Dekin	Fishing Supplier
I	**Enchanting**	
	Kudrii	Journeyman Enchanter
	Egomis	Enchanting Supplier
	Nahogg	Expert Enchanter
J	**General Goods**	
	Onnis	General Goods Vendor
	Cuzi	Bag Vendor

K	Auction House	
	Eoch	Auctioneer
	Iressa	Auctioneer
	Fanin	Auctioneer
	Mailbox	
L	**Anchorites Sanctum**	
	Fallat	Priest Trainer
	Izmir	Priest Trainer
	Caedmos	Priest Trainer
M	**Alchemy & Herbalism**	
	Cemmorhan	Herbalist
	Deriz	Journeyman Alchemist
	Lucc	Expert Alchemist
	Altaa	Alchemy Supplier
N	**Vindicator's Sanctum**	
	Jol	Paladin Trainer
	Baatun	Paladin Trainer
	Kavaan	Paladin Trainer
O	**Hall of Mystics**	
	Oss	Wand Vendor

Lunaraa	Portal Trainer	Feera	Engineering Supplier	X	Tailoring
Bati	Mage Trainer	Ockil	Expert Engineer		Kayaart	Journeyman Tailor
Harnan	Mage Trainer	**T**	**Mining & Smithing**		Neii	Tailoring Supplier
Edirah	Mage Trainer	Muaat	Mining Trainer		Refik	Expert Tailor
Musal	Arcane Goods Vendor	Merran	Mining Supplies	**1**	Primary Entrance

P Guild Master & Tabards

Issca	Tabard Vendor
Funaam	Guild Master

Q Hunters' Sanctum

Vord	Hunter Trainer
Deremiis	Hunter Trainer
Killac	Hunter Trainer
Muhaa	Gunsmith
Ganaar	Pet Trainer
Avelii	Bowyer

R Ring of Arms

Kazi	Warrior Trainer
Behomat	Warrior Trainer
Ahonan	Warrior Trainer
Handiir	Weapon Master (Dagger)
Fingin	Poison Supplier

S Engineering

Ghermas	Journeyman Engineer

Arras	Blacksmithing Supplier
Miall	Expert Blacksmith
Edrem	Journeyman Blacksmith
Forge	
Anvil	

U Plate Armor & Shields

Yil	Mail Armor Merchant (Top Floor)
Gotaan	Plate Armor Merchant
Treall	Shield Merchant

V Bladed Weapons

Mahri	Leather Armor Merchant (Top Floor)
Gornii	Cloth Armor Merchant (Top Floor)
Ven	Blade Vendor

W Leatherworking & Skinning

Remere	Skinner
Haferet	Leatherworking Supplier
Akham	Expert Leatherworker
Feruul	Journeyman Leatherworker

2	Sulaa	Shaman Trainer
3	Bildine	Reagent Vendor
4	Hobahken	Shaman Trainer
5	Foreman Dunaer	
6	Farseer Nobundo	Shaman Trainer
7	Gurrag	Shaman Trainer
8	Nurguni	Tradesman
9	Jihi	Warsong Gulch Battlemaster
10	Mahul	Alterac Valley Battlemaster
11	Tolo	Arathi Basin Battlemaster
12	Prophet Velen	Quest Giver
13	Back Exit	
14	Ellomin	Blunt Weapon Merchant
15	O'ros	

What's left of the Exodar stands as testament to the strength of the Draenei. Not even crashing into a planet can stop them!

It's *So* Big!

Ironforge is a rather impressive town, but its dwarfed compared with the Exodar. Exploring all of it would take quite a bit of effort, but you're not the first to get lost in this city. The guards are accustomed to newcomers needing directions and they give them freely. To find things in a hurry, ask a guard and they will plot it on your minimap.

There are a great many people you may want to talk with in the Exodar. Every craft and professions is represented as is every class. Take the time to choose your professions (if you haven't already) and set your Hearthstone to the inn here.

Speak with Torallius the Pack Handler outside, but don't get **Elekks are Serious Business** just yet. You have other business to attend to. Speak with Hippogryph Master Stephanos on your way out to collect the flight point (this will be important later). Take the road south and west from the Exodar to the docks. To the south is Silvermyst Isle and your destination. Follow the coastline and swim to the island.

Hiding near a log is Magwin. She's a younger elf and fairly frightened. Speak with her. Her story is **A Cry for Help** that can't be ignored.

A Cry For Help	
Faction	Alliance
Location	Silvermyst Isle
Quest Giver	Magwin
Quest Completion	Cowlen
Reward	Cowlen's Bracer's of Kinship (Cloth Wrist, 8 Armor, + 1 STA)

As soon as you accept the quest, Magwin will start walking south. This is an escort quest. You have to follow Magwin and keep her safe from harm until she reaches her destination. Don't stray too far from her and don't worry about being attacked. She'll stop to help you fight but continue on her journey as soon as the immediate threat is gone.

Cowlen is her final goal and he is very relieved to see his daughter. Get your reward from him and listen to his story. **All that Remains** now is to avenge the death of his wife and bring her remains back to him.

killing until you have them. With the deed done, return to Cowlen for your reward before using your Hearthstone to return to the Exodar.

Now it's time to take the Elekk ride to Kessel's Crossing. Speak with Torallius and accept **Elekks are Serious Business**. You can't control the Elekk in the least, so just sit back and enjoy the ride.

All That Remains	
Faction	Alliance
Location	Silvermyst Isle
Quest Giver	Cowlen
Quest Completion	Cowlen
Reward	Experience

Head back into the Moonwing Den and begin slaying the Owlkin. The *Remains of Cowlen's Family* can be dropped by any of the beasts, so keep

Elekks are Serious Business	
Faction	Alliance
Location	The Exodar
Quest Giver	Torallius the Pack Handler
Quest Completion	Vorkhan the Elekk Herder
Reward	Experience

BLOODMYST ISLE MAP LEGEND

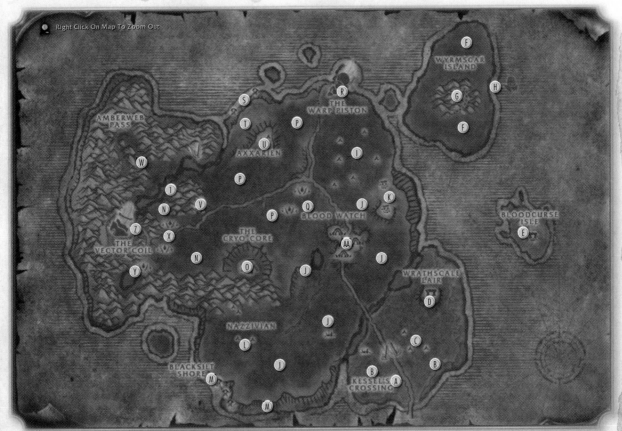

A Kessel's Landing

Aonar	Quest Giver
Vorkhan the Elekk Herder	Quest Giver
Kessel Elekk Lord	Quest Giver

B Bloodmyst Isle South

Brown Bear	9
Bloodmyst Hatchling	10-11
Blue Flutterer	9-10
Sand Pear	Quest Item

C Bristlelimb Enclave

Princess Stillpine	Quest Giver
• Bristlelimb Warrior	10-11
• Bristlelimb Shaman	10-11
• High Chief Bristlelimb	13 Drops Quest Item

D Wrathscale Lair

• Wrathscale Shorestalker	12-13
• Wrathscale Screamer	12-13
• Lord Xiz	13 Quest Target

E Bloodcurse Isle

• Bloodcursed Naga	15-16

F Wyrmscar Island

Prince Toreth	Quest Giver
• Veridian Broodling	17-18
• Veridian Whelp	16-17

G Talon Stand

• Veridian Broodling	17-18
• Veridian Whelp	16-17
• Razormaw	20 Elite Quest Target

H Bloodcursed Reef

Captain Edward Hanes	Quest Giver
• Bloodcursed Naga	15-16
✶ Bloodcursed Voyager	16-17

I Ragefeather Ridge

• Irradiated Wildkin	13-15
• Infected Wildkin	13-14
• Contaminated Wildkin	14-15

J Bloodmyst Isle Central

• Mutated Lasher	11-12
• Corrupted Treant	11-13
• Grizzled Brown Bear	12-13
Blood Mushroom	Quest Item
Aquatic Stinkhorn	Quest Item

K Ruins of Loreth'Aran

• Wrathscale Sorceress	13-14
• Wrathscale Marauder	13-14
Draenei Cartographer	Quest Giver
Ruinous Polyspore	Quest Item

L Nazzivian

• Nazzivus Felsworn	14
• Nazzivus Satyr	12
• Nazzivus Rogue	13-14
• Tzerak	14
Fel Cone Fungus	Quest Item
Nazzivus Monument Glyph	Quest Item

M Blacksilt Shore

• Blacksilt Forager	11-12
• Blacksilt Tidecaller	11-12
• Blacksilt Scout	12-13

N Bloodmyst Isle West

• Enraged Ravager	17
• Corrupted Stomper	16-17
• Mutated Tangler	17-18

O The Cryo-Core

Galaen's Corpse	Quest Giver
Galaen's Journal	Quest Giver
• Sunhawk Reclaimer	16-17

P Bloodmyst Isle North

• Mutated Constrictor	14-15
• Elder Brown Bear	15-16
• Royal Blue Flutterer	16

Q Bladewood

• Sunhawk Spy	13-14

R The Warp Piston

• Void Anomaly	15-16

S Coastline

• Blacksilt Shorestriker	15-16
• Blacksilt Warrior	16-17
• Blacksilt Seer	16-17
Clopper Wizbang	Quest Giver
Clopper's Equipment	Quest Item

T Bloodmyst Isle Waterfall

• Mutated Constrictor	14-15
• Elder Brown Bear	15-16
• Royal Blue Flutterer	16
• Deathclaw	17 Quest Target

U Axxarien

• Axxarien Shadowstalker	15-16
• Axxarien Hellcaller	15-17
• Axxarien Trickster	16
Zevrax	18 Quest Target
Corrupted Crystal	Quest Item

V Vindicator's Rest

Scout Loryi	Quest Giver
Scout Jorli	Quest Giver
Demolitionist Legoso	Quest Giver
Vindicator Corin	Quest Giver

W Amberweb Pass

• Myst Spinner	16-17
• Myst Leecher	17-18
• Webbed Creature	15
• Zarakh	19 Quest Target

X Sunhawk Camps

• Sunhawk Pyromancer	17-18
• Sunhawk Defender	16-17
• Matis the Cruel	18 Elite Quest Target

Y The Portal

• Sunhawk Pyromancer	17-18
• Sunhawk Defender	16-17
• Void Critter	4
• Void Anomaly	3
• Sunhawk Portal Controller	17-18 Elite

Z The Vector Coil

• Sunhawk Agent	18-19 Elite
• Sunhawk Saboteur	17-18 Elite
• Sironas	20 Elite Quest Target
AA	Blood Watch
Morae	Herbalism Trainer
Achelus	Quest Giver
Beega	Bowyer
Fazu	Tradesman
Harbinger Mikolaas	Quest Giver
Exarch Admetius	Quest Giver
Interrogator Elysia	Quest Giver
Anchorite Paetheus	Quest Giver
Messenger Hermesius	Quest Giver
Prospector Nachlan	Quest Giver
Vindicator Boros	Quest Giver
Vindicator Aesom	Quest Giver
Vindicator Kuros	Quest Giver
Stillpine Ambassador Frasaboo	Quest Target
Laando	Hippogryph Master
Jessera of Mac'Aree	Quest Giver
Tracker Lyceon	Quest Giver
Vindicator Aalesia	Quest Giver
Meriaad	General Goods
Astur	Stable Master
Caregiver Topher Loaal	Innkeeper
Wanted Poster	Quest Giver
Mailbox	
Forge	
Anvil	
Blade of Argus	14
Blood Watch Peacekeeper	31

1 Tel'athion's Camp

WALKTHROUGH FOR BLOODMYST ISLE

While the bulk of the Exodar landed on Azuremyst Isle, many of the more toxic systems landed on what is now Bloodmyst Isle. The Draenei have had the unfortunate experience of watching the land become corrupted before their very eyes.

Declaration of Power	
Faction	Alliance
Location	Kessel's Crossing
Quest Giver	Kessel
Quest Completion	Kessel
Reward	Choice of Kessel's Cinch Wrap (Cloth Waist, 16 Armor, +2 STA, +2 INT), Kessel's Sweat Stained Elekk Leash (Leather Waist, 39 Armor, +3 STA), and Kessel's Sturdy Riding Handle (Mail Waist, 81 Armor, +3 STA)

KESSEL'S CROSSING

There isn't much to Kessel's Crossing. It's just a few Draenei, some Elekk, and a lot of work to do. Speak with Kessel first and grab **The Kessel Run**. This is a timed quest, so don't delay. Begin heading south back into Azuremyst Isle as soon as you mount the Elekk.

The Kessel Run	
Faction	Alliance
Location	Kessel's Crossing
Quest Giver	Kessel
Quest Completion	Kessel
Reward	Chains to Declaration of Power

Take the west (right) fork in the road and swing around the mountains to Stillpine Hold. The Elekk allows you to move at incredible speeds. Avoid running right through enemies and they'll never be able to catch you. Warn High Chief Stillpine of the coming invasion and take the road south.

Quick stops at Azure Watch and Odesyus' Landing complete the quest, but you're on the wrong side of the island now! You have plenty of time before you lose the help of the Elekk, so cruise back to Kessel in style.

Kessel is pleased with your performance and gives you a more challenging task. The Naga have been getting uppity and Kessel wants you to make a **Declaration of Power** to show them who's the boss. Grab **Alien Predators** and **A Favorite Treat** before you head out.

A Favorite Treat	
Faction	Alliance
Location	Kessel's Crossing
Quest Giver	Aonar
Quest Completion	Aonar
Reward	Choice of Elekk Handler's Leathers (Leather Chest, 58 Armor, +1 AGI, +1 STA), Farmhand's Vest (Cloth Chest, 21 Armor, +1 STA, +1 INT), or Elekk Rider's Mail (Mail Chest, 115 Armor, +1 STR, +1 STA) and 20 Sand Pear Pie (Use Restores 243 health over 21 sec. Must remain seated while eating.)

Alien Predators	
Faction	Alliance
Location	Kessel's Crossing
Quest Giver	Aonar
Quest Completion	Aonar
Reward	Choice of 2 Stone Sledgehammer (Two-hand Mace, 7.7 DPS, +1 STR, +1 STA) or Elekk Handler's Blade (Main-hand Sword, 6.0 DPS, +1 STR) or Old Elekk Prod (One-hand Mace, 5.8 DPS, +1 STA) or Surplus Bastard Sword (Two-hand Sword, 7.8 DPS, +1 STR, +1 AGI)

These Furbolg are stronger than most of the enemies you've fought before. They hit harder and take more damage to bring down. Use ranged attacks against the enemies without mana (they have to close the distance before they can hurt you) and have abilities that interrupt casting ready for the shamans.

The Bristlelimb Shamans also cast a Searing Totem. This can't be interrupted and the totem will use fire attacks against you constantly. Finish the shaman and then destroy the totem. Don't destroy the totem first as the shaman can cast another one instantly.

Saving Princess Stillpine is easier said than done. Her cage is locked and only *High Chief Bristlelimb's Key* can open it. The chief is a coward and won't

show his face unless absolutely necessary. Kill the Furbolg on your way northeast. They won't be killing the princess any time soon and you have other things to take care of.

Head into the woods to the east. The *Sand Pears* can be found on the ground near the trees, while the *Bloodmyst Hatchlings* can be found trying to kill you. All the enemies in this area are aggressive. This isn't new, but there is one difference from previous areas: the Bloodmyst Hatchlings will run away in fear when they get low in health. They need to be killed before they find help, so keep a damaging attack held in reserve to finish them off.

An alternative is using movement-impairing abilities such as Hamstring or Frost Bolt. These keep the enemy from running very far before you finish the job.

The appearance of Furbolg between the trees heralds a change in plans. You aren't done with any of your quests and don't have one for the Furbolg. In the center of the easternmost camp stands a large cage with Princess Stillpine in it. She has a quest mark above her head, so kill your way to her.

Saving Princess Stillpine	
Faction	Alliance
Location	Bristlelimb Enclave
Quest Giver	Princess Stillpine
Quest Completion	Ambassador Frasaboo at Blood Watch
Reward	Choice of Stillpine Shocker (Wand, 9.4 DPS) or The Thumper (Main-hand Mace, 6.9 DPS, +1 STR)

Head to the northeast corner of this smaller island. Naga patrol around a small hill topped with ruins. Watch the patrols and pull single targets when the patrols are away. Once you have a clear spot, pull the patrols to get them out of the way so you can start making your way to the ramp on the west side.

The Naga are your level or higher and are quite damaging. Be ready to rest more often as you shouldn't start a fight with less than 75% health and never fight two at once. If the fighting is more difficult that you want to engage in, take some time to kill the Fur-bolg and other life around Kessel's Crossing. A level and gear upgrades can make the difference.

Make your way to the top of the ramp and clear the immediate area. *Lord Xiz* patrols inside the ruins. Watch his movement patterns and pull any Naga near him. You don't want to fight him with another enemy. If you pull both, turn and run for it. Fighting two is certain death. Run and return to try again.

When you have the area clear of nearby enemies, pull Lord Xiz. Have potions and Gift of the Naaru ready. He hits like an Elekk and is almost as pretty. If you cleared the area quickly, you can snare him and retreat to heal or use ranged attacks. Be careful about retreating into other enemies, though.

Once he's dead, stand over his corpse and plant the banner in his body. With this quest done, descend and return to the woods. Watch for *Bloodmyst Hatchlings* and *Sand Pears* to finish those quests.

Fight your way into the northern Furbolg camp. Continue killing the Furbolg until *High Chief Bristlelimb* yells "Face the wrath of Bristlelimb!" This will

show up as red text (unless you've altered your interface) in the chat window. This signals the spawn of High Chief Bristlelimb in the northern camp.

Take the time to clear some of the Furbolg from around him before you pull him. Have a potion ready as he also hits fairly hard, but he isn't as dangerous as Lord Xiz. Pry the *High Chief's Key* from his dead hands and return to Princess Stillpine.

Release the princess and make your way back to Kessel's Crossing. If you haven't finished **A Favorite Treat** and **Alien Predators**, linger in the woods a bit longer before you head in.

Kessel is quite pleased with your progress and asks you to **Report to Exarch Admetius**. There isn't anything left for you at Kessel's Crossing. Follow the road north to Blood Watch and the front lines of the restoration effort.

Report to Exarch Admetius	
Faction	Alliance
Location	Kessel's Crossing
Quest Giver	Kessel
Quest Completion	Exarch Admetius
Reward	Experience

BLOOD WATCH

There are quite a few people in Blood Watch and many of them want to speak with you. Ignore most of them for now and turn in your quest to Exarch Admetius. Speak with Caregiver Topher Loaal about **Beds, Bandages, and Beyond**. This is a quest chain that shows you how to using the hippogryphs for faster travel.

Speak with Laando at the northeast part of camp on the highest ride. He'll explain about transport **On the Wings of a Hippogryph**. With the screen open, select the landing you want to be taken to (in this case, the Exodar). The hippogryph takes you to your destination faster than an Elekk.

Beds, Bandages, and Beyond	
Faction	Alliance
Location	Blood Watch
Quest Giver	Caregiver Topher Loaal
Quest Completion	Laando
Reward	Chains to On the Wings of a Hippogryph

After your **Return to Topher Loaal**, there is much to do in Blood Watch. Reset your Hearthstone by speaking with Topher. Move around and collect all the quests. This is the largest group of quests you've gotten at once. There is plenty to do and plenty of time to do it in.

Return to Topher Loaal	
Faction	Alliance
Location	The Exodar
Quest Giver	Stephanos
Quest Completion	Caregiver Topher Loaal
Reward	Experience

On the Wings of a Hippogryph	
Faction	Alliance
Location	Blood Watch
Quest Giver	Laando
Quest Completion	Nurguni
Reward	Chains to Hippogryph Master Stephanos

Make a quick trip into the Exodar to speak with Nurguni and train. Nurguni takes the supply order and gives you everything that can fit on a hippogryph. She'll send the heavier items by wagon, but sends you to **Hippogryph Master Stephanos**.

There are a few quests that can be done in town. **What Argus Means to Me** sends you to speak with Vindicator Boros. With all the killing you've already done, you may have the **Irradiated Crystal Shards** Tracker Lyceon is asking for.

Hippogryph Master Stephanos	
Faction	Alliance
Location	The Exodar
Quest Giver	Nurguni
Quest Completion	Stephanos
Reward	Chains to Return to Topher Loaal

What Argus Means to Me	
Faction	Alliance
Location	Blood Watch
Quest Giver	Exarch Admetius
Quest Completion	Vindicator Boros
Reward	Chains to Blood Watch

Irradiated Crystal Shards	
Faction	Alliance
Location	Blood Watch
Quest Giver	Tracker Lyceon
Quest Completion	Tracker Lyceon
Reward	Choice of Crystal of Vitality (Use Increases Stamina by 5. Lasts 30 mins.) or Crystal of Insight (Use Increases Intellect by 5. Lasts 30 mins.) or Crystal of Ferocity (Use Increases Attack Power by 10. Lasts 30 mins.)

Victims of Corruption	
Faction	Alliance
Location	Blood Watch
Quest Giver	Morae
Quest Completion	Morae
Reward	Experience

Turning in **Irradiated Crystal Shards** causes a blue "?" to appear above Tracker Lyceon. This shows he has a repeatable quest available. Speak with him again and **More Irradiated Crystal Shards** is an option you can choose, but it doesn't let you accept the quest. From now on, any time you bring him 10 *Irradiated Crystal Shards*, he will give you the reward for the quest. He doesn't give you money or experience after the first time, but the buffs from the items are quite nice.

South of Blood Watch

Check the General Goods merchant and see if you can afford another bag if you don't have all slots used. The questing in Bloodmyst will fill your bags quickly, and it's time to head out. The first quests you'll be doing are **Learning from the Crystals**, **Victims of Corruption**, **Catch and Release**, **Mac'Aree Mushroom Menagerie**, and **Know Thine Enemy**.

Catch and Release		
Faction	Alliance	
Location	Blood Watch	
Quest Giver	Morae	
Quest Completion	Morae	
Reward	Choice of Protective Field Gloves (Mail Hands, 72 Armor, +1 STA) or Researcher's Gloves (Leather Hands, 39 Armor) or Scholar's Gloves (Cloth Hands, 15 Armor, +1 INT, +1 SPI)	

Learning from the Crystals	
Faction	Alliance
Location	Blood Watch
Quest Giver	Harbinger Mikolaas
Quest Completion	Harbinger Mikolaas
Reward	Choice of Crystal-Flecked Pants (Cloth Legs, 20 Armor, +2 INT) or Crystal-Studded Legguards (Mail Legs, 107 Armor, +1 STR, +1 STA), or Shard-Covered Leggings (Leather Legs, 54 Armor, +2 AGI)

Mac'Aree Mushroom Menagerie	
Faction	Alliance
Location	Blood Watch
Quest Giver	Jessera of Mac'Aree
Quest Completion	Jessera of Mac'Aree
Reward	Choice of Jessera's Fungus Lined Cuffs (Cloth Wrist, 11 Armor, +1 INT) or Jessera's Fungus Lined Bands (Leather Wrist, 28 Armor, +1 STA) or Jessera's Fungus Lined Bracers (Mail Wrist, 57 Armor, +1 STA)

When you're in range of the *Blacksilt Scout,* use the *Murloc Tagger.* The scout will walk around a moment longer before vanishing. Continue along the shoreline tagging scouts and killing everything else until the quest is complete. If there aren't any scouts (or not enough), kill everything in the area and wait a short while. This will force some scouts to respawn.

Your next target is Nazzivian. Approach the northern most portion of Nazzivian from the west side. This should be a short walk as you've been following the coastline looking for murlocs. Keep an eye out for the *Fel Cone Fungus* that grows around the satyrs tainted energies. It's harder to see than the other mushrooms as it's dull in color and short.

Fight your way into the ruins. The satyrs won't run, but some use ranged spells, and all of them are mean. They will attack you in groups if you're careless in your pulling. Watch your text window as you fight your way toward the monument. If you see Tzerak say anything, then watch your back. This demon is tougher than the satyr, travels with friends, and wanders the length of the camp.

Grab the *Nazzivus Monument Glyph* and use your Hearthstone to get back to Blood Watch in a hurry. Don't worry if you haven't completed **Victims of Corruption** or **Mac'Aree Mushroom Menagerie**. There will be more time in the future.

Know Thine Enemy	
Faction	Alliance
Location	Blood Watch
Quest Giver	Vindicator Aalesia
Quest Completion	Vindicator Aalesia
Reward	Chains to Containing the Threat

Strike out in a southerly direction. Don't bother following the road as you have quests for nearly every enemy out here but take care moving about as the enemies wander a great deal and are aggressive. Even when resting or fighting, watch for other enemies that are getting too close. Move your fight away from potential adds if necessary.

The Corrupted Treants wander this area are drop the *Crystallized Bark* you need. Watch for them as you cut your way toward the river. The *Blood Mushroom* also grows in this area. Its glowing top makes it easier to see by those looking. Crossing the river is a painless affair. The red water won't hurt you, but the *Aquatic Stinkhorn* might draw your attention.

Look for the wreckage patrolled by Bloodmyst Hatchlings. You've fought these before. Make your way to the red crystal at the center of the wreckage and use your *Crystal Mining Pick* to get the sample you need.

The next quest on the list is a bit different. Make your way to Blacksilt Shore. The scouts you need are purple in color, but you don't need to kill them; in fact, you can't kill them if you want to complete the quest. Put the *Murloc Tagger* on a quickbar slot and kill the other murlocs to clear a path to the scouts.

WEST OF BLOOD WATCH

Take care of your in-town errands (selling, repairing, and turning in quests). Make sure to grab **Blood Watch** and **The Second Sample** before leaving camp to the west.

The Second Sample	
Faction	Alliance
Location	Blood Watch
Quest Giver	Harbinger Mikolaas
Quest Completion	Harbinger Mikolaas
Reward	Leads to The Final Sample

Blood Watch	
Faction	Alliance
Location	Blood Watch
Quest Giver	Vindicator Boros
Quest Completion	Vindicator Boros
Reward	Choice of Fist of Argus (Main-hand Mace, 8.2 DPS, +1 STA, +1 INT) or Blade of Argus (Main-hand Sword, 8.1 DPS, +1 AGI +1 STA) or Hand of Argus Crossbow (Crossbow, 9.1 DPS, +1 AGI, +1 STA)

The Missing Survey Team	
Faction	Alliance
Location	Blood Watch
Quest Giver	Harbinger Mikolaas
Quest Completion	Draenei Cartographer
Reward	Chains to Salvaging the Data

Watch for *Corrupted Treats* as you make your way toward Bladewood. The *Sunhawk Spies* won't appreciate your approach, so be ready for any hiding near the trees or in the bushes. They have Demoralizing Shout, which reduces attack power, and Mark of the Sunhawk, which increases the damage you take. Use ranged attacks when possible as they have no way of countering these. Casters should be wary as the spies can also interrupt spellcasts. Use spells with shorter cast times to avoid this.

Make your way to the westernmost of the three camps. At the center of the magical device is a short red crystal. Use your *Crystal Mining Pick* on this to obtain the crystal sample. You have to be very close to get the sample, so clear the camp before approaching. Finish killing Sunhawk Spies on your way back to Blood Watch. Not all quest groups are long and involved.

EAST OF BLOOD WATCH

Turn in your quests, repair your gear, sell your excess loot, and pick up any quests you didn't have before. The next quests are **Victims of Corruption, Mac'Aree Mushroom Menagerie**, and **The Missing Survey Team**.

Exit Blood Watch to the east and pick off a few more treants (if you haven't finished the quest) on your way to the Ruins of Loreth'Aman. The Naga patrol the ruins. Watch the patrols to avoid fighting more than one at a time. The female Naga are casters and use Frost Bolt, while the males are melee opponents. Don't try to run from the casters as the movement-slowing ability of Frost Bolt will spell your doom.

Climb the hill to the ruins and find what's left of the survey team. The Draenei Cartographer is quite dead, but there is still hope. **Salvaging the Data** will keep them from dying in vain. Kill the Naga in the area until you find the *Survey Data Crystal* and keep an eye out for the *Ruinous Polyspore* while you're here. As its name implies, it grows near the ruins.

Salvaging the Data	
Faction	Alliance
Location	Ruins of Loreth'Aran
Quest Giver	Draenei Cartographer
Quest Completion	Harbinger Mikolaas
Reward	Surveyor's Mantle (Cloak, 12 Armor, +1 STA)

With three quests done, make your way back to Blood Watch and prepare for a much longer quest group. Repair, sell anything you can, and stock up on recover items if you need them.

NORTHERN BLOODMYST

Before heading out, take a trip to the Exodar to train. When you return to Blood Watch, check your quest log. Make sure you have **WANTED: Deathclaw**, **Culling the Aggression**, **Constrictor Vines**, **The Bear Necessities**, **The Final Sample**, **Containing the Threat**, and **Explorers' League, Is That Something for Gnomes?**

Constrictor Vines

Faction	Alliance
Location	Blood Watch
Quest Giver	Tracker Lyceon
Quest Completion	Tracker Lyceon
Reward	Experience

The Bear Necessities

Faction	Alliance
Location	Blood Watch
Quest Giver	Tracker Lyceon
Quest Completion	Tracker Lyceon
Reward	Experience

The Final Sample

Faction	Alliance
Location	Blood Watch
Quest Giver	Harbinger Mikolaas
Quest Completion	Harbinger Mikolaas
Reward	Experience

WANTED: Deathclaw

Faction	Alliance
Location	Blood Watch
Quest Giver	Wanted Poster
Quest Completion	Tracker Lyceon
Reward	Choice of Carved Crystalline Orb (Off-hand, +2 STA, +2 INT) or Peacekeeper's Buckler (Shield, 361 Armor, 6 Block, +2 STR, +2 STA)

Culling the Aggression

Faction	Alliance
Location	Blood Watch
Quest Giver	Tracker Lyceon
Quest Completion	Tracker Lyceon
Reward	Choice of Cincture of Woven Reeds (Cloth Waist, 19 Armor, +3 STA, +4 INT) or Ornately Tooled Belt (Leather Waist, 44 Armor, +3 STA, Equip +8 Attack Power) or Segmented Girdle (Mail Waist, 94 Armor, +4 STR, +3 STA)

Containing the Threat

Faction	Alliance
Location	Blood Watch
Quest Giver	Vindicator Aalesia
Quest Completion	Vindicator Aalesia
Reward	Choice of Huntsman's Crossbow (Crossbow, 9.5 DPS, +1 AGI) or Lightspark (Wand, 12.8 DPS, +1 INT)

Explorers' League, Is That Something for Gnomes!	
Faction	Alliance
Location	Blood Watch
Quest Giver	Prospector Nachlan
Quest Completion	Clopper Wizbang
Reward	Experience

Artifacts of the Blacksilt	
Faction	Alliance
Location	Blacksilt Shore
Quest Giver	Clopper Wizbang
Quest Completion	Clopper Wizbang
Reward	Weathered Treasure Map (This Item Begins a Quest)

Pilfered Equipment	
Faction	Alliance
Location	Blacksilt Shore
Quest Giver	Clopper Wizbang
Quest Completion	Clopper Wizbang
Reward	Experience

This seems like quite a bit…and it is! Follow the road north out of Blood Watch. When the road splits, follow the northern fork toward the Warp Piston. Wander off the left side of the road and start killing the Elder Brown Bears for the *Elder Brown Bear Flanks*, the Mutated Constrictors for the *Thorny Constrictor Vines*, and the *Royal Blue Flutterers* for being there.

The Mutated Constrictors can cast Entangling Roots and can't be run from. The Elder Brown Bears and Royal Blue Flutterers both do decent melee damage and are best fought at range when possible. All the enemies in this area are aggressive and move around a great deal. Keep watch around you at all times and be ready to move a fight if more enemies are wandering too close.

Now you have quests to kill *everything*! Take your time to get used to the area. The Blacksilt Seers are casters and drop the *Crude Murloc Idols*, while the Blacksilt Shorestrikers and Warriors are melee enemies and drop the *Crude Murloc Knives*.

The murlocs function much better in the water than you do, so fight them on land whenever possible. To pull the Blacksilt Seers to land, shoot them and run away until they follow you onto firmer ground. You need a good bit of room behind you for this to work, but it's possible.

Kill your way along the shoreline west. Look in each of the camps for *Clopper's Equipment*; it's in a small crate and easy to miss if you aren't looking. When the shoreline meets the river, follow the river to the waterfall and get ready for a tough fight.

Continue moving north until you reach The Coastline. Keep killing everything as you move west. On the beach is a large turtle skeleton. As you get closer to it, make your way down to the beach. Kill the murlocs that are wandering about the skeleton and peak inside to find *Clopper Wizbang*.

The crazy little man has been living inside the turtle shell! He'll buy excess loot from you and he has a couple quests for you. Offer to help him collect **Artifacts of the Blacksilt** and find his **Pilfered Equipment**.

Deathclaw lives down here. Kill the enemies near Deathclaw in preparation. She doesn't have as much health as you might think, but she hits very hard. Have a potion ready and lay on the damage as quickly as possible.

With *Deathclaw's Paw* in your possession, return to killing everything around you. Alternate between killing murlocs on the shoreline to killing bears, plants, and moths inland. Switch between the two any time one has been cleared completely.

When both **Pilfered Equipment** and **Artifacts of the Blacksilt** are complete, return to Clopper. Sell your excess loot as you still have a while before you return to town. Use the *Weathered Treasure Map*. It's a map, but **A Map to Where?**

A Map to Where?	
Faction	Alliance
Location	Blacksilt Shore
Quest Giver	Weathered Treasure Map
Quest Completion	Battered Ancient Book
Reward	Leads to Deciphering the Book

The map is pretty vague, so we'll stick with what we know first. Follow the cliff east and south as you continue killing bears, plants, and moths for your quests. Before long, you begin climbing toward Axxarien and satyrs begin appearing.

The *Axxarien Shadowstalkers* have a mean damage-over-time curse, while the *Axxarien Hellcallers* can blanket an entire area in a rain of fire. Have abilities that interrupt their spellcasting ready. The fights up here will be tough, so recruit help from others if you need it.

Slowly kill your way into the east side of Axxarien. The *Corrupted Crystals* are scattered throughout the camp, but make sure each one is clear of enemies before you approach. None of the satyrs stealth, but they tend to hide in the huts, so be watchful.

At the north edge of Axxarien stands a monument guarded by *Zevrax*. Without any special abilities (aside from those the other satyrs have), he's a straightforward fight. Throw damage at him until he stops twitching. Nearby is a short red crystal that looks familiar. Use your *Crystal Mining Pick* to acquire the sample before moving on.

Finish killing satyrs and collecting crystals as you move south. Kill any bears, plants, and moths that get in your path to Blood Watch. Don't worry about completing every quest as you'll be back this way and you've already done quite a bit. Turn in all your quests, clear your inventory, and make a trip to the Exodar if you've gain an even level since you last trained.

WYRMSCAR ISLAND AND THE BLOODCURSED REEF

Back at Blood Watch, there are a great many quests to grab. The section you'll do next has a few difficult fights, so you may want to partner with another adventurer; this isn't necessary, but it does make it much safer.

Speak with Messenger Hermesius, who has an **Urgent Delivery** for you. Accepting his quest doesn't add anything to your log. That's because he dropped a piece of mail in your mailbox. Right click on the mailbox to open it and click the *Letter from the Admiral* to put it in your inventory. Once in your inventory, right-click on the letter to get **Bloodcurse Legacy**. Make sure you also have **A Map to Where?** and **Ysera's Tears** before you head out.

Urgent Delivery	
Faction	Alliance
Location	Blood Watch
Quest Giver	Messenger Hermesius
Quest Completion	Messenger Hermesius
Reward	Chains to The Bloodcurse Legacy

The Bloodcurse Legacy	
Faction	Alliance
Location	Blood Watch
Quest Giver	A Letter from the Admiral
Quest Completion	Captain Edward Hanes
Reward	Chains to The Bloodcursed Naga

Ysera's Tears	
Faction	Alliance
Location	Blood Watch
Quest Giver	Jessera of Mac'Aree
Quest Completion	Jessera of Mac'Aree
Reward	Free Choice of Jessera's Fungus Lined Tunic (Cloth Chest, 28 Armor, +2 STA, +3 INT) or Jessera's Fungus Lined Vest (Leather Chest, 68 Armor, +2 STA, Equip +6 Attack Power) or Jessera's Fungus Lined Hauberk (Mail Chest, 174 Armor, +2 STR, +2 STA)

Your first stop is the Ruins of Loreth'Aman. The Naga are much easier to deal with now that you are a couple levels higher than them, but don't try to run past them. Kill them for easy experience and to relieve stress on your way to the northern part of the ruins. Climb the crumbled stone to get atop the small gazebo. A book lies on the ground. Pick up the book and gain the quest **Deciphering the Book**.

Deciphering the Book	
Faction	Alliance
Location	Ruins of Loreth'Aman
Quest Giver	Battered Ancient Book
Quest Completion	Anchorite Paetheus
Reward	Chains to Nolkai's Words

Swim out to Wyrmscar Island, which is inhabited by undead Veridian Whelps and Broodlings. The Veridian Whelps can put you to sleep (until they hit you again), but the real danger is their brethren. The Veridian Broodlings have a ranged spit attack that poisons you. This is made worse when they hit you with multiple spits since the spits stack. More than a couple of these on you and you're in trouble. The good news is that the spit can be interrupted.

Stick to the beach for now unless you see the bright blue *Ysera's Tears* near trees or bones. You only need two of these, so grab them when you can, but don't wander around the dragonkin if you don't have to.

Another thing to watch for is Prince Toreth. He has a quest and wanders the island. It's easiest to find him on the east side and you have other business over there. Follow the shore east and north until you find Captain Edward Hanes. The Captain wants you to help him get revenge against **The Blood-cursed Naga**.

The Bloodcursed Naga	
Faction	Alliance
Location	Wyrmscale Island
Quest Giver	Captain Edward Hanes
Quest Completion	Captain Edward Hanes
Reward	Chains to The Hopeless Ones...

The Naga swim along the Blood-cursed Reef nearby, but Hanes gives you something to make the hunt easier: the ability to swim faster and breathe underwater for 10 minutes. That's more than enough time to mete out a little vengeance. Dive into the water and begin.

The *Bloodcursed Naga* cast ranged Frost Bolts. Although it's good to keep them interrupted if possible, it's not terribly dangerous for you if you fight them one at a time. They rarely swim near each other, so careful pulling will keep you more than safe. Slay the creatures and return to the Captain.

Each time you are near the Captain, take a look inland for Prince Toreth. Edward's next mission is to help **The Hopeless Ones...**

The Hopeless Ones...	
Faction	Alliance
Location	Wyrmscar Island
Quest Giver	Captain Edward Hanes
Quest Completion	Captain Edward Hanes
Reward	Chains to Ending the Bloodcurse

The Bloodcursed Voyagers wander further away from shore and deeper in the reef. It's a good thing the Captain restores the buff he gave you. Swim out and down to the voyagers. They are neutral and will not attack you unless attacked first. They also won't group up against you, so the fighting is a bit easier, but don't get careless.

You only need four *Bloodcursed Souls*. With 10 minutes of buff duration, you have plenty of time. You can't eat or drink while swimming, so you'll need to just tread water to regenerate mana and health. Take the fights one at a time and avoid dying as that cancels the beautiful buff the Captain gave you.

If At First You Don't Succeed...

Should you die while trying to collect the *Bloodcursed Souls*, you're resurrected without the buff Captain Edward Hanes gave you. Without it, it's very difficult to fight the Bloodcursed Voyagers.

Open your quest log and select the quest. Press the "Abandon quest" button. The quest is removed from your log and any *Bloodcursed Souls* you've already collected are removed from your inventory.

Return to Captain Edward Hanes to restart the quest. He'll recast the buff on you, and you can try again.

Head south to Bloodcurse Isle. It's a long swim, but any time left on Edward's buff makes it much faster. The Bloodcurse Naga on the isle are the same as the ones you fought earlier with only one exception: they're on land now. Kill them as you ascend the island, and watch for any patrollers that might make your life difficult.

At the top of the ramp is a small plateau with the statue of Queen Azshara. Clear the entire plateau before attacking the statue. You have to climb onto the statue before you're close enough to break it. Have full mana and health before you do this as *Atoph* will attack.

Return to the Captain when you have the souls he asked for. Now he wants you help with **Ending the Bloodcurse**. Before you leave the island, however, find Prince Toreth. He's working on **Restoring Sanctity** and could use your help.

Restoring Sanctity	
Faction	Alliance
Location	Wyrmscale Island
Quest Giver	Prince Toreth
Quest Completion	Prince Toreth
Reward	Chains to Into the Dream

Ending the Bloodcurse	
Faction	Alliance
Location	Wyrmscar Island
Quest Giver	Captain Edward Hanes
Quest Completion	Captain Edward Hanes
Reward	Wheel of the Lost Hope (Shield, 395 Armor, 7 Block, +3 STA)

Atoph has high health and high armor and deals high damage. Casters attempting this alone should blast him with everything they have before dropping down to the ramp to the east. This will cause some falling damage, but Atoph will take the long way around and be back at maximum range for another volley.

Have a potion ready or a friend with you and Atoph will die like every other Naga on this island. With the leader destroyed, you are free to rest and descend to the water. There are some respawns, but nothing you can't handle. Swim west and return to Blood Watch.

Take a quick detour after speaking with Anchorite Paetheus about **Nolkai's Words**. In Wrathscale Lair, there is a *Mound of Dirt* that Nolkai hid his belongings in. The Naga are much lower level than you now and pose almost no threat. Grab the box and open it for your reward. Return to Blood Watch and prepare for another extended trip.

Nolkai's Words	
Faction	Alliance
Location	Blood Watch
Quest Giver	Anchorite Paetheus
Quest Completion	Mound of Dirt
Reward	Nolkai's Box (25 silver, Nolkai's Band, Nolkai's Lantern (Off-hand, +3 INT), and Nolkai's Bag (8-slot bag))

There's no avoiding the dragonkin now. Travel the island in the direction that Toreth was patrolling, killing dragonkin along the way. This keeps Toreth as close to you as possible. Rest when you need it as the *Veridian Broodlings* and *Veridian Whelps* are still very dangerous. Return to the Prince when you've killed enough dragonkin.

Toreth tells you that with most of the dragonkin restful once again, only **Razormaw** needs to be dealt with. The great beast flies above the island and will only descend if the bone bundle is burned at the fire atop the hill. He is far too powerful for you now.

Razormaw	
Faction	Alliance
Location	Wyrmscar Island
Quest Giver	Prince Toreth
Quest Completion	Prince Toreth
Reward	Choice of Robe of the Dragon Slayer (Cloth Chest, 30 Armor, +3 STA, +3 INT, Equip Improves spell hit rating by 2), Tunic of the Dragon Slayer (Mail Chest, +3 STR, +3 STA, Equip Improves hit rating by 2), or Vest of the Dragon Slayer (Leather Chest, +3 AGI, +3 STA, Equip Improves hit rating by 2)

RAGEFEATHER RIDGE AND WYRMSCAR ISLAND

It's time to deal with the Wildkin north of Blood Watch. Take care of any errands in town and head out. The Wildkin have taken the bones of the fallen dragons and you need to get them back.

The bones stick out of the ground in the Wildkin camps. The Wildkin aren't particularly dangerous alone, but the camps are fairly close together. Getting more than one enemy doesn't guarantee death, but it makes the fight much harder.

Collect the bones as you head north through the camps. Wyrmscar Island is your next stop when you have all eight bones. Finding Toreth is easier now that he shows up on your mini-map, and he asks for help sending the dragons **Into the Dream**.

Speak with Captain Edward Hanes before leaving the island. Walk back to Blood Watch or use your hearthstone.

Into The Dream	
Faction	Alliance
Location	Wyrmscar Island
Quest Giver	Prince Toreth
Quest Completion	Prince Toreth
Reward	Chains to Razormaw

AMBERWEB PASS AND THE CRYO-CORE

Empty your bags of excess loot and stock up on restoration items. Remember to turn in your *Irradiated Crystal Shards*. Check your quest log and make sure you have **Talk to the Hand**, **The Missing Expedition**, and **Searching for Galaen**.

Follow the road to Vindicator's Rest. Watch for Elder Brown Bears as you likely still need to kill a few. Matis the Cruel wanders the road near Vindicator's Rest; he's an elite enemy and more powerful than you, so avoid him.

Speak with everyone at Vindicator's Rest and collect a new batch of quests. After adding **Cutting a Path**, **Treant Transformation**, and **Oh, What Tangled Webs They Weave** you quest log is looking pretty full again. Grab all of the quests. You won't be doing all of them yet, but you don't want to travel all the way out here just to get a quest again.

The tanglers can root you, while the stompers and Ravagers do a good bit of damage. At half health, the Ravagers become enraged. This increases their damage significantly. Save your instant attacks and spells until they enrage and then blow them down. This keeps the damage you take to a minimum.

As all the quests up here are kill quests, grab a partner if you want more safety or go it alone if you want more of a challenge.

Cutting a Path

Faction	Alliance
Location	Vindicator's Rest
Quest Giver	Scout Jorli
Quest Completion	Scout Jorli
Reward	Experience

Treant Transformation

Faction	Alliance
Location	Vindicator's Rest
Quest Giver	Vindicator Corin
Quest Completion	Vindicator Corin
Reward	Experience

When you've killed all the enemies along the southern river bank, cross the river and engage the spiders. The Myst Spinners can web you and the Myst Leechers can poison you. Being able to cure poison or knowing someone who can is be quite useful, but isn't necessary.

Avoid using area-of-effect abilities near the Webbed Creatures. This will either pop them out of the web or just annoy them. If they're annoyed, you will be stuck in combat (and unable to regain mana or health quickly) until they are dead. Released creatures tend to attack the first thing they see.

Oh, the Tangled Webs They Weave

Faction	Alliance
Location	Vindicator's Rest
Quest Giver	Vindicator Corin
Quest Completion	Vindicator Corin
Reward	Experience

Clear the spiders as you climb the pass. Atop is *Zarakh*. She is massive and mean. Clear the spiders in an area so you have a bit of room to fight her, and pull her alone. Zarakh attacks very quickly and hits reasonably hard. Casters may have a difficult time casting any spells with all the interruption.

Strike out northwest toward Amberweb Pass. *Mutated Tanglers*, *Corrupted Stompers*, and *Enraged Ravagers* are between you and your goal. It's a good thing you have quests to kill all of them!

Use Gift of the Naaru before she closes so she can't increase the casting time and have a potion ready (if you have one). If you can survive the first several seconds of the fight, you're in good shape as her health isn't as high as her damage. Blow her down and retreat down the pass.

You're a good way up, so don't jump down. Take the slow way and walk. Finish the quest by killing the spiders on your way out. Cross the river and return to killing tanglers, stompers, and Ravagers.

Turn southeast and head to the Cryo-Core. There are quest targets all along the route there and you should be finished by time you get there. If you aren't, spend a little longer hunting before engaging the *Sunhawk Reclaimers*.

The Sunhawk Reclaimers use fire magic. Have interrupt abilities ready and keep them from making use of these attacks. They wander close to each other at times, so watch before you attack. They have low health and die quickly.

Make your way into the crater from the west side and move to the opening in the Cryo-Core. There are two enemies immediately inside. Peek in and use a ranged attack against one of them. Quickly move around the doorway so the enemy can't see you. Without line of sight, the Sunhawk Reclaimer is forced to come to you and away from possible reinforcements. Kill it when it turns the corner, then kill its friend.

Just inside is Galaen's Corpse. The spirit of Galaen remains long enough to ask you to notify Morae of **Galaen's Fate**. Examine the book on the ground. It is **Galaen's Journal-The Fate of Vindicator Sarvan**. Exit the wreck the way you entered.

Galaen's Fate

Faction	Alliance
Location	The Cryo-Core
Quest Giver	Galaen's Corpse
Quest Completion	Morae
Reward	Choice of Cryo-Core Attendant's Boots (Cloth Feet, 21 Armor, +3 STA, +2 INT), Lightweight Mesh Boots (Mail Feet, 107 Armor +2 STR, +3 STA) or Technician's Boots (Leather Feet, 50 Armor, +3 AGI, Equip +4 Attack Power)

Galaen's Journal-The Fate of Vindicator Sarvan

Faction	Alliance
Location	The Cryo-Core
Quest Giver	Galaen's Journal
Quest Completion	Vindicator Kuros
Reward	Experience

Kill the reclaimers in the area as you move east. Watch for the *Sunhawk Missive* and *Galaen's Amulet*. Be sure you have both before returning to Blood Watch with the bad news for Morae.

Your bags are quite full, so visit a merchant before you turn in any quests. Sell your ill-gotten goods and speak with everyone for your rewards. Vindicator Boros asks you to speak with Interrogator Elysia as she is skilled in **Translations…** She translates the missive for you and gives you orders to make an **Audience with the Prophet**.

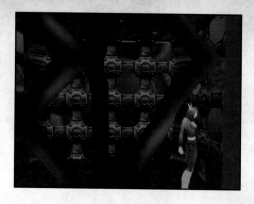

Translations…	
Faction	Alliance
Location	Blood Watch
Quest Giver	Vindicator Boros
Quest Completion	Interrogator Elysia
Reward	Chains to Audience with the Prophet

What We Don't Know…	
Faction	Alliance
Location	Blood Watch
Quest Giver	Exarch Admetius
Quest Completion	Exarch Admetius
Reward	Chains to Vindicator's Rest

Audience with the Prophet	
Faction	Alliance
Location	Blood Watch
Quest Giver	Interrogator Elysia
Quest Completion	Prophet of Velen
Reward	Chains to Truth of Fiction

Speak with the Captive Sunhawk Agent. Continue speaking with her until you've acquired all the information you need. When you return to the Exarch, he orders you to **Vindicator's Rest**. You have business in the Exodar, though.

Vindicator's Rest	
Faction	Alliance
Location	Blood Watch
Quest Giver	Exarch Admetius
Quest Completion	Vindicator Corin
Reward	Chains to Clearing the Way

Don't fly to the Exodar yet. Vindicator Aesom speaks about **What We Know…** and has you talk to Exarch Admetius. The Exarch wants to know **What We Don't Know…** and enlists your aid. He gives you a disguise that lets you pass for a Blood Elf. It's a good thing the guards are in on this!

Take a hippogryph to the Exodar and seek out Prophet Velen. He needs to know if everything is **Truth or Fiction** and sends you back to Blood Watch. Take the time to train while you're here, then make your way to Blood Watch.

What We Know…	
Faction	Alliance
Location	Blood Watch
Quest Giver	Vindicator Aesom
Quest Completion	Exarch Admetius
Reward	Chains to What We Don't Know…

Truth of Fiction	
Faction	Alliance
Location	The Exodar
Quest Giver	Prophet Velen
Quest Completion	Vindicator Boros
Reward	Chains to I Shoot Magic Into the Darkness

FINDING THE SUN PORTAL

Speak with Vindicator Boros before heading to the Warp Piston (**I Shoot Magic Into the Darkness**). This is a quick trip, but stray off the road and finish off any enemies you still have quests for (the Elder Brown Bears for Bear Necessities for example).

I Shoot Magic Into the Darkness	
Faction	Alliance
Location	Blood Watch
Quest Giver	Vindicator Boros
Quest Completion	Vindicator Boros
Reward	Choice of Vindicator's Soft Sole Slippers (Cloth Feet, 17 Armor, +1 STA, +1 INT), Vindicator's Leather Moccasins (Leather Feet, 45 Armor, +1 AGI, +1 STA), or Vindicator's Stompers (Mail Feet, 89 Armor, +2 STA)

Head west to the Cryo-Core and collect the *Medical Supplies*. There are boxes on the ground and the Sunhawk Reclaimers carry them also. Take back what belongs to your people. When you have all 12, return to Blood Watch.

PUSHING TO THE VECTOR COIL

With the medical supplies retrieved, Vindicator Aesom has a good bit of work for you. He wants you to destroy **The Sun Gate**. This may push you to the **Limits of Physical Exhaustion**, but **Don't Drink the Water**.

The Sun Gate	
Faction	Alliance
Location	Blood Watch
Quest Giver	Vindicator Aesom
Quest Completion	The Sun Gate
Reward	Experience

Void Anomalies guard the Warp Piston, but you need to kill these anyway. Use ranged attacks to pull them one at a time as they like to team up. Approach the Warp Piston and verify that the Sun Portal isn't there.

With evidence of a portal at the Warp Piston recently, return to Blood Watch. Cut through Ragefeather Ridge for some easy fighting if you want some quick experience. Vindicator Boros is done for you now, but Vindicator Kuros wants you to take a trip to **The Cryo-Core**.

The Cryo-Core	
Faction	Alliance
Location	Blood Watch
Quest Giver	Vindicator Kuros
Quest Completion	Vindicator Kuros
Reward	Choice of Vindicator's Smasher (Two-hand Mace, 10.7 DPS, +3 STR, +2 STA), Vindicator's Walking Stick (Staff, 10.5 DPS, +2 STA, +3 INT), or Vindicator's Letter Opener (Two-hand Sword, 10.5 DPS, +3 STR, +2 AGI)

Limits of Physical Exhaustion	
Faction	Alliance
Location	Blood Watch
Quest Giver	Vindicator Aesom
Quest Completion	Vindicator Aesom
Reward	Experience

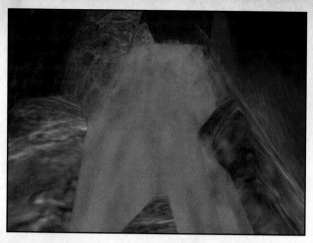

With a number of quests to be completed, head west past the Cryo-Core. South of the Vector Coil is the Sun Gate and one of the Sunhawks' most important camps. Defeating the *Sunhawk Pyromancers* and *Defenders* won't be easy, but that's why you were sent.

Fight your way through the camp. *Void Critters* litter the camp and the bottom of the lake. Kill these as you make your way through the Sunhawk forces.

At the lake, several Sunhawk Portal Controllers hold the *Sun Gate* open. Their entire attention is on the Sun Gate (it has to be), so you can murder them at your leisure. Once all the portal controllers are dead, swim to the Sun Gate and attack it. You have to be right under it to be in range. While you're already wet, kill a few Void Critters to finish the quest.

With the Sun Gate destroyed and the Void Critters decimated, make your way to the road and look for *Matis*. Avoid getting too close to the Vector Coil at this time as the enemies are too powerful for you.

Don't Drink the Water	
Faction	Alliance
Location	Blood Watch
Quest Giver	Vindicator Aesom
Quest Completion	Vindicator Aesom
Reward	Experience

Repair, sell loot, and check your quest log before heading out. Make sure you also have **Vindicator's Rest**, **Matis the Cruel**, and **Critters of the Void**.

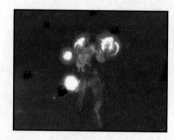

While you look for Matis, make a quick trip to Vindicator's Rest to turn in your quests. When Matis appears, get just in range to use the *Flare Gun* to summon aid. When aid arrives, help bring Matis down.

Head west again and finish killing the Sunhawk Pyromancers and Defenders. Follow the river past the elementals and jump off the waterfall next. The elementals will attack you. Once at the bottom of the waterfall, use the container to get the *Bloodmyst Water Sample*. Use your Hearthstone for a quick return to Blood Watch to turn in your quests.

Watch the exchange between the Image of Velen and Matis to learn more about the Sunhawk.

Critters of the Void	
Faction	Alliance
Location	Vindicator's Rest
Quest Giver	Scout Loryi
Quest Completion	Vindicator Aesom
Reward	Experience

Matis the Cruel	
Faction	Alliance
Location	Blood Watch
Quest Giver	Vindicator Kuros
Quest Completion	Vindicator Kuros
Reward	Choice of Vindicator's Woolies (Cloth Legs, 25 Armor, +4 STA, +3 INT), Vindicator's Leather Chaps (Leather Legs, 60 Armor, +4 AGI, +3 STA), or Vindicator's Iron Legguards (Mail Legs, 132 Armor, +4 STR, +3 STA)

RAZORMAW AND THE VECTOR COIL

There is very little left to do on Bloodmyst Isle, and none of it that you can do alone. Find a friend or few and make your way to Wyrmscar Island.

Stick near Legoso, but let him lead. He's much tougher than you so let him take the hits. Melee classes should wait for Legoso to engage an enemy and only attack an enemy that he has already damaged. Classes with heavier armor (Warriors and Paladins) might consider pulling a single enemy off of Legoso if he has more than 2 enemies on him. Be warned that while he will heal himself, he will not heal you.

Cut your way to the top of Talon's Stand and clear the entire summit. Rest to full health and/or mana and place the *Bundle of Dragon Bones* on the fire to call *Razormaw* to you.

He's very big and not happy. Keep your health high as he will cast fear on you during the fight and you don't want him to get free hits when you're low on health. With friends, this fight is more fun than challenge. Drop down and turn in the quest with Toreth and *Razormaw's Head* to Vindicator's Rest next.

Speak with Vindicator Corin about **Clearing the** Way and Demolitionist Legoso about **Ending Their World**. Legoso wastes no time and sets off at a brisk pace so be ready to follow him.

Casters should plan on staying back as you follow Legoso. Wait for him to engage an enemy before you cast offensive spells and don't heal him until he gets to half health. This will keep most of the enemies beating on him instead of on you.

Follow him to the large red crystal at the base of the Vector Coil. With his help, killing the *Sunhawk Saboteurs* and *Agents* is much easier. He'll plant the charge and set the coil aflame before climbing to the final rise.

Standing in the center of arcing energy is *Sironas*. This Eredar demon is siphoning energy straight from the Vector Coil. Legoso stops this, but Sironas immediately attacks.

Keep her attention on Legoso as she hits very hard and uses Curse of Blood to increase all damage her target takes by 10. All Draenei can use Gift of the Naaru to help keep Legoso healed. Keep pouring on the damage and destroy this abomination.

Return to Vindicator's Rest and then to Blood Watch to turn in your quests. Many people have come to congratulate you on your success. Your friends from Stillpine Hold and Odesyus' Landing have pledged their aid to the Draenei because of your efforts, and Prophet Velen has traveled all the way from the Exodar to tell you of **The Unwritten Prophecy**.

Clearing the Way

Faction	Alliance
Location	Vindicator's Rest
Quest Giver	Vindicator Corin
Quest Completion	Vindicator Corin
Reward	Choice of Flutterer Silk Handwraps (Cloth Hands, 20 Armor, +3 INT, +3 SPI), Ravager Hide Gloves (Leather Hands, 46 Armor, +3 AGI, +3 STA), or Corin's Handguards (Mail Hands, 100 Armor, +3 STR, +3 STA)

Ending Their World

Faction	Alliance
Location	Vindicator's Rest
Quest Giver	Demolitionist Legoso
Quest Completion	Demolitionist Legoso
Reward	Choice of Blade of the Hand (Two-hand Sword, 13.1 DPS, +6 STA, Equip +8 Attack Power), Crossbow of the Hand (Crossbow, 10.9 DPS), Mace of the Hand (One-hand Mace, 10.0 DPS, +3 STR, +3 STA), or Staff of the Hand (Staff, 13.0 DPS, +4 STA, +3 INT, Equip Increases damage and healing done by magical spells and effects by up to 4)

The Unwritten Prophecy

Faction	Alliance
Location	Blood Watch
Quest Giver	Prophet Velen
Quest Completion	Prophet Velen
Reward	Tabard of the Hand and a choice of Signet Ring of the Hand (Ring, +2 INT, Equip Increases spell critical strike rating by 2) or Signet Ring of the Hand (Ring, Equip Improves critical strike rating by 2, +4 Attack Power)

Choose which gift to accept from the Prophet and return to the Exodar to train and prepare yourself for the journey into Azeroth!

WHERE FEW DARE TO TREAD

The maps and legends within provide a wealth of information on the many new zones for the expansion. In earlier chapters, we revealed the zones for the incoming Blood Elves and Draenei. Here, we'll show you a list of the people and places in this re-discovered world.

HELLFIRE PENINSULA

Legend

Herbs	Minerals	Reputation Information
Dreamfoil	Rich Thorium	Thrallmar (Horde)
Felweed	Fel Iron	Mag'Har (Horde)
Dreaming Glory	Khorium	Honor Hold (Alliance)
		Exodar (Alliance)

Map Legend

A Thrallmar

Angela "The Claw" Kestrel	
Anvil	
Apothecary Antonivich	Grand Master Alchemist
Barim Spilthoof	Grand Master Leatherwork
Barley	Wind Rider Master
Battlecryer Blackeye	
Baxter	Chef
Blood Elf Pilgrim	57-59
Caza'rez	
Cookie One-Eye	Food & Drink Vendor
Dalinna	Grand Master Tailor
Falcon Watch Sentinel	59
Far Seer Regulkut	
Felannia	Grand Master Enchanter
Floyd Pinkus	Innkeeper
Forge	
General Krakork	
Huntsman Torf Angerhoof	Stable Master
Injured Thrallmar Grunt	57
Jir'see	
Kaloen	Grand Master Jewelcrafter
Krugosh	Mining Trainer
Mailbox	
Martik Tor'seldori	
Moorutu	Skinning Trainer
Nazgrel	
Quartermaster Urgronn	
Rohok	Grand Master Blacksmith
Ruak Stronghorn	Herbalism Trainer
Shadow Hunter Ty'jin	
Stone Guard Stok'ton	
Thrallmar Grunt	60
Thrallmar Marksman	60
Thrallmar Peon	51
Thrallmar Riding Wolf	56
Thrallmar Wolf Rider	60
Zebig	Grand Master Engineer

B Thrallmar Mine

Dagz	
Foreman Razelcraz	
Gan'arg Sapper	60-61
Maiden of Pain	59
Urga'zz	60

C Stonescythe Canyon

Deranged Helboar	60-61
Marauding Curst Burster	59-60

D Northern Rampart

Shattered Hand Acolyte	62
Shattered Hand Berserker	61
Shattered Hand Guard	62
Shattered Hand Mage	61

E The Dark Portal

Amish Wildhammer	Gryphon Master
Brother Daniels	
Commander Duron	
Dark Cleric Malad	Healing & Sustenance
Lieutenant General Orion	
Nurse Judith	
Quartermaster	Gunman
Rations Vendor	
Supply Master Broog	Supplies
Vlagga Freyfeather	Wind Rider Master

F Supply Caravan

Arcanist Torseldori	
Bloodmage	64-65 Elite
Sergeant Shatterskull	

G Forge Camp: Spite

Forge Camp Legionnaire	60-61 Elite
Gan'arg Servant	60-61
Mo'arg Forgefiend	62 Elite
Sister of Grief	60-61 Elite

H Felspark Ravine

Fel Reaver	70 Elite
Flamewaker Imp	58
Heckling Fel Sprite	58-59
Infernal Warbringer	58-59

I Forge Camp: Rage

Forge Camp Legionnaire	60-61 Elite
Gan'arg Servant	60-61
Mo'arg Forgefiend	62 Elite
Sister of Grief	60-61 Elite

J Forge Camp: Mageddon

Arix'malidash	62 Elite
Forge Camp Legionnaire	60-61 Elite
Gan'arg Servant	60-61

Mo'arg Forgefiend	62 Elite
Sister of Grief	60-61 Elite

K Hellfire Citadel

Drillmaster Zurok	62
Entrance to Citadel Wings	
Force-Copmmander Gorax	63 Elite
Shattered Hand Captain	62-63
Shattered Hand Grunt	62-63
Shattered Hand Neophyte	62
Shattered Hand Warlock	63

L Path of Glory

Shattered Hand Captain	62-63
Shattered Hand Grunt	62-63
Shattered Hand Neophyte	62
Shattered Hand Warlock	63

M Gryphons

Gryphoneer Leafbeard	Gryphon Master
Honor Hold Scout	65 Elite

N The Abyssal Shelf

Fel Reaver Sentry	70 Elite
Gan'arg Peon	68-70 Elite
Mo'arg Overseer	70 Elite

O Reaver's Fall

Armored Wyvern Destroyer	70
Bonechewer Evoker	59-60
Bonechewer Scavenger	59-60
Forward Commander To'arch	65 Elite
Supply Officer Isable	General Goods & Repairs
Wing Commander Brack	Wind Rider Master

P The Legion Front

Doom Whisperer	59-60
Fel Handler	59-60
Legion Antenna: Mageddon	
Netherhound	59-60
Subjugator Yalqiz	62
Wrathguard	59-60

Q The Stair of Destiny

Deathwhisperer	70 Elite
Dread Tactician	70 Elite
Fel Soldier	70 Elite
Pit Commander	70 Elite
Wrath Master	70 Elite

R Void Ridge

Collapsing Voidwalker	61-62
Vacillating Voidwalker	61-62

S Zeth'Gor

Bleeding Hollow Dark Shaman	61
Bleeding Hollow Grunt	60-61
Bleeding Hollow Necrolyte	60
Bleeding Hollow Peon	59-60
Bleeding Hollow Skeleton	60
Bleeding Hollow Tormentor	61
Bleeding Hollow Worg	60
Eye of Grillok	60
Feng	60
Grillok	60
Ripp	58
Starving Helboar	59-60
Warlord Morkh	60
Worg Master Kruush	60

T Spinebreaker Post

Althen the Historian	
Amilya Airheart	Wind Rider Master
Emissary Modiba	
Grelag	
Hagash the Blind	Bowyer
Lukra	General Goods
Mondul	Food & Drink Vendor
Ogath the Mad	
Peon Bolgar	Trade Goods
Stone Guard Ambelan	
Thrallmar Grunt	60
Thrallmar Peon	50

U Expedition Armory

Arch Mage Xintor	61
Commander Hogarth	
Lieutenant Commander Thalvos	
Unyielding Footman	59-60
Unyielding Knight	59-60
Unyielding Sorcerer	59-60

V The Warp Fields

Rogue Voidwalker	60-61
Uncontrolled Voidwalker	60-61

Razorthorn Trail

Razorfang Hatchling	59-60
Razorfang	Ravager 61

W Southern Rampart

Hulking Helboar	61
Shattered Hand Berserker	61-62
Shattered Hand Grenadier	61-62
Shattered Hand Guard	61-62

X Gor'gaz Outpost

Shattered Hand Berserker	61-62

Y Zepplin Crash

Legassi	
"Screaming" Screed Luckheed	

AA The Great Fissure

Blacktalon the Savage	63 Elite
Stonescythe Alpha	61-62
Stonescythe Ambusher	61-62
Stonescythe Whelp	60-61
Tunneler	61-62

AB Falcon Watch

Apothecary Azethen	
Arcanist Calesthris Dawnstar	
Aresella	Medic
Cookpot	
Falcon Watch Ranger	68
Falconer Drenna Riverwind	
Fallesh Sunfallow	Weapon Merchant
Innalia	Wind Rider Master
Innkeeper Bazil Olof'tazun	Innkeeper
Lursa Sunfallow	Reagent Vendor
Magistrix Carinda	
Mailbox	
Orb of Translocation	
Pilgrim Gal'ressa	
Provisioner Valine	Food & Drink Vendor
Ranger Captain Venn'ren	
Recovering Pilgrim	58-60
Ryathen the Somber	
Wanted Poster	

AC Dwarf Camp

Gremni Longbeard	
Mirren Longbeard	

AD Den of Haal'esh

Haal'eshi Talonguard	62-63
Haal'eshi Windwalker	62
Kaliri Matriarch	63
Kaliri Nest	
Kaliri Swooper	60
Wounded Blood Elf Pilgrim	

AE Dustquill Ravine

Quilfang Ravager	62-63
Quilfang Skitterer	61-62

AF Cenarion Post

Amythiel Mistwalker	
Earthbinder Galandria Nightbreeze	
Mahuram Stouthoof	
Thiah Redmane	
Tola'thion	

AG Ruins of Sha'naar

Akoru the Firecaller	
Arzeth the Merciless	63 Elite
Arzeth the Powerless	63
Ayloan the Waterwaker	
Dreghood Brute	57
Dreghood Geomancer	56-57
Illadari Taskmaster	63
Morod the Windstirrer	
Naladu	

AH Thornpoint Hill

Thornfang Ravager	62-63
Thornfang Venomspitter	62-63

AI Fallen Sky Ridge

Raging Colossus	62-63 Elite
Raging Shardling	62-63

AJ Mag'har Post

Debilitated Mag'har Grunt	58
Earthcaller Ryga	
Gorkan Bloodfist	68 Elite
Mag'har Grunt	61
Mag'har Hunter	62-63
Mag'har Watcher	62-63
Provisioner Braknar	

AK Pools of Aggonar

Arazzius the Cruel	63 Elite
Blistering Oozeling	61-62
Blistering Rot	61-62
Mistress of Doom	62
Terrorfiend	61-62

AL Honor Hold

Anvil	
Caretaker Dilandrus	
Explorers' League Archaeologist	54-56
Father Malgor Devidicus	
Field Commander Romus	
Flightmaster Krill Bitterhue	Gryphon Master
Force Commander Danath Trollbane	
Forge	
Gaston	Chef
Gunny	
Hama	Grand Master Tailor
Honor Guard Greyn	
Honor Hold Archer	59-60
Honor Hold Defender	59-60
Humphry	Grand Master Blacksmith
Hurnak Grimmord	Mining Trainer
Injured Nethergarde Infantry	57-58
Injured Stormwind Infantry	57-58
Jelena Nightsky	Skinning Trainer
Lieutenant Chadwick	
Logistics Officer Ulrike	Honor Hold Quartermaster
Magus Filinthus	
Mailbox	
Marshal Isildor	
Master Sergeant Lorin Thalmerok	Stable Master
Nethergarde Infantry	58-60
Prospector Murantus	
Seargent Dalton	
Seer Kryv	
Sid Limbardi	Innkeeper
Stormwind Infantry	57
Tatiana	Grand Master Jewelcrafter
War Horse	56
Warrant Officer Tracy Proudwell	

AM Honor Hold Mine

Foreman Biggums	
Gan'arg Sapper	60-61
Honor Hold Miner	53-54
Maiden of Pain	59

AN Temple of Telhamat

Amaan the Wise	
Anchorite Alendar	
Anchorite Obadei	
Anvil	
Burko	Medic
Caregiver Ophera Windfury	Innkeeper
Elsaana	
Escaped Dreghood	58

Forge	
Ikan	
Kuma	Hippogryph Master
Mailbox	
Provisioner Anir	Food & Drink Vendor
Rumatu	
Scout Vanura	
Talaara	Weapon Merchant
Telhamat Protector	59-60
Vodesiin	Reagent Vendor
Yaluu	

AP Throne of Kil'jaeden

Greater Fel-Spark	70-71
Throne-Guard Champion	72 Elite

Throne-Guard Highlord	72 Elite
Doomforge Automaton	71 Elite
Throne-Guard Sentinel	71 Elite
Throne Hound	71 Elite
Doom Lord Kazzak	World Boss

AD Shatter Point

1	Hulking Helboar	62-63
2	Bonestripper Vulture	61-62
3	Magister Aledis	
4	The Overlook	
5	The Stadium	
6	Broken Hill	

Zangarmarsh

Herbs

Blindweed
Golden Sansam
Felweed
Ragveil
Dreaming Glory
Flame Cap
Withered Giant Corpse
Withered Bog Lord Corpse
Starving Fungal Giant Corpse

Minerals

Fel Iron
Adamantite

Reputation Information

Cenarion Expedition (Both Factions)
Sporeggar (Both Factions)

Map Legend

A Telredor

Anchorite Ahuurn	
Anvil	
Caregiver Abidaar	Innkeeper
Cookpot	
Elevator	
Forge	
Joraal	Stable Master
K. Lee Smallfry	Grand Master Engineer
Mailbox	
Prospector Conall	
Ruam	
Telredor Guard	65 Elite
Vindicator Idaar	

B Zabra'jin

Anvil	
Captured Gnome	Item Repair
Du'ga	Wind Rider Master
Farbosi	
Forge	
Gambarinka	Tradesman
Guard Untula	
Khalan	Stable Master
Mailbox	
Merajit	Innkeeper
Messenger Gazgrigg	
Seer Janidi	Reagent Vendor
Shadow Hunter Denjai	
Tayemba	
Wanted Poster	
Witch Doctor Tor'gash	
Zabra'jin Guard	65 Elite
Zurjaya	Fishing Trainer

C Cenarion Refuge

Anvil	
Campfire	
Expedition Warden	70
Fedryen Swiftspear	Cenarion Expedition Quartermaster
Forge	
Ikeyen	
Innkeeper Coryth Stoktron	
Juno Dufrain	Fishing Supplies
Kameel Longstride	Stable Master
Keleth	
Lauranna Thar'well	
Lethyn Moonfire	
Mailbox	
Naka	Cooking Supplier
Talut	
Wanted Poster	
Warden Hamoot	
Windcaller Blackhoof	
Ysiel Windsinger	

D East Zangarmarsh

Fen Strider	61-62
Marshfang Ripper	60-61
Umbraglow Stinger	60-61
Young Spore Bat	60-61

E Umbrafen Lake/The Lagoon

Mire Hydra	61-62
Umbrafen Eel	61-62

F Umbrafen Village

Boglash	61 Elite
Umbrafen Oracle	60-61
Umbrafen Seer	60-61
Umbrafen Witchdoctor	60-61

G Funggor Cavern

Lord Klaq	62
Marsh Dredger	62
Marsh Lurker	61
Sporelok	61-62

H Darkcrest Shore

Darkcrest Sentry	61
Darkcrest Siren	62-63
Darkcrest Taskmaster	62-63
Dreghood Drudge	62-63

I Darkcrest Enclave

Darkcrest Sentry	61
Darkcrest Siren	62-63
Darkcrest Taskmaster	62-63
Dreghood Drudge	62-63
Steampump Overseer	63

J The Dead Mire

Marshfang Ripper	60
Parched Hydra	62
Sporewing	61
Withered Bog Lord	62
Withered Giant	61

K Swamprat Post

Lorti	Reagent Merchant
Magasha	
Reavij	
Swamprat Guard	65 Elite
Zurai	General Merchant

L Bloodscale Grounds

Bloodscale Overseer	63-64
Bloodscale Sentry	62
Bloodscale Wavecaller	64
Wrekt Slave	63-64

M Northern Zangarmarsh

Bogflare Needler	62-63
Greater Spore Bat	61-62

N Central Zangarmarsh

Bloodthirsty Marshfang	60-61
Fen Strider	61
Spore Bat	60-61

O Feralfen Village

Blacksting	62
Feralfen Druid	61-62
Feralfen Hunter	61-62
Tamed Spore Bat	56-57

P Boha'mu Ruins

Elder Kuruti	62 Elite
Feralfen Druid	61-62
Feralfen Mystic	61-62

Q Southern Zangarmarsh

Fen Strider	61
Marshfang Slicer	62-63
Spore Bat	60-61

R Serpent Lake

Entrance to Coilfang Instances	
Fenclaw Thrasher	64
Mragesh	64
Mudfin Frenzy	62-63
Watcher Jhang	

S Orebor Harborage

Aktu	Armor Merchant

Map Legend

- Cookpot
- Doba — Cooking Supplies
- Ikuti
- Innkeeper Kerp — Innkeeper
- Mailbox
- Muheru the Weaver — Tailoring Supplies
- Orebor Harborage Defender — 65 Elite
- Puluu
- Timothy Daniels
- Wanted Poster

T Hewn Bog
- Ango'rosh Ogre — 62-63
- Ango'rosh Shaman — 62-63

U Bloodscale Enclave
- Bloodscale Enchantress — 64
- Bloodscale Sentry — 62-63
- Bloodscale Slavedriver — 63-64
- Marsh Walker — 63-64
- Wrekt Slave — 63-64

V The Edge
- Greater Spore Bat — 61-62
- Ironspine Gazer — 63-64
- Ironspine Threshalisk — 63

W Daggerfen Village
- Daggerfen Assassin — 62-63
- Daggerfen Muckdweller — 62-63

X Ango'rosh Grounds
- Ango'rosh Brute — 62-63
- Ango'rosh Sentry — 63-64
- Ango'rosh Warlock — 63-64

Y Ango'rosh Stronghold
- Ango'rosh Mauler — 63-64
- Ango'rosh Souleater — 63-64
- Overlord Gorefist — 63

Z Eastern Zangarmarsh
- Greater Spore Bat — 61-62
- Marsh Walker — 63-64
- Marshlight Bleeder — 63-64

AA Marshlight Lake
- Bogstrok Crusher — 62
- Bogstrok Razorclaw — 62

AB Sporeggar
- Fhwoor
- Gshaff
- Gzhun'tt
- Khn'nix
- Msshi'fn
- Sporeggar Harvester — 63-64
- Sporeggar Preserver — 63-64
- T'shu

AC Blade's Run

AC Quagg Ridge
- Bog Lord — 64
- Fungal Giant — 64
- Starving Bog Lord — 63
- Starving Fungal Giant — 63

AD The Spawning Glen
- Mature Spore Sac
- Sporeggar Spawn
- Starving Bog Lord — 63
- Starving Fungal Giant — 62

1 Coosh'coosh — 68 Elite
2 Portal Clearing
3 Leesa'oh
4 Fahssn
5 West Beacon
6 Twinspire Graveyard
7 East Beacon
8 Horde Field Scout
9 Alliance Field Scout
10 Count Ungula — 62

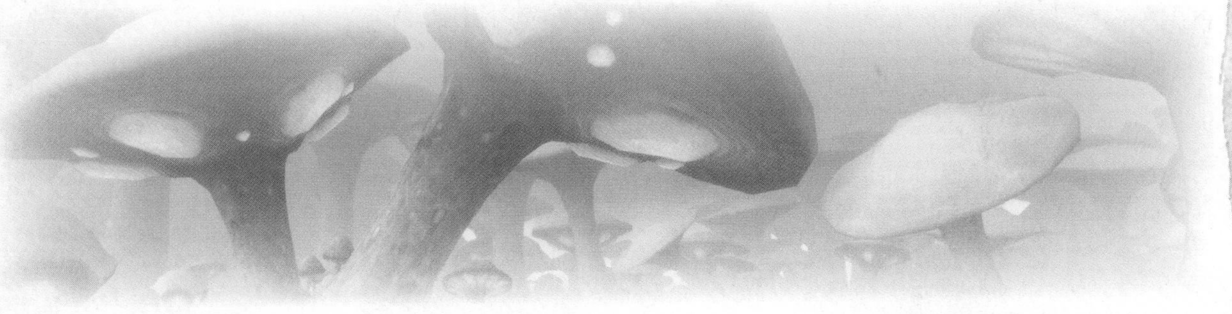

Terokkar Forest

Legend

Herbs

Felweed

Dreaming Glory

Terocone

Minerals

Fel Iron

Adamantite

Khorium

Reputation Information

No specific Reputations, but control of the region in PvP allows characters to collect Spirit Shards from the bosses for all Instances in the zone. These items are handed in to NPCs in Stonebreaker Hold and Allerian Stronghold for various items!

Map Legend

A	Razorthorn Shelf	
B	Veil Shienor	
	Ayit	63
	Shienor Sorcerer	62-63
	Shienor Talonite	62-63
C	Open Forest (Northeast)	
	Dampscale Devourer	63-64
	Ironjaw	63-64
	Royal Teromoth	63-64 Pacify (No Attack for Several Seconds)
	Timber Worg Alpha	64
	Stonegazer	64 Elite
	Warp Stalker	63 Sprint, Movement/Attack Speed Debuff
D	Firewing Point	
	Firewing Bloodwarder	63-64

	Firewing Defender	63-64
	Firewing Warlock	63-64
	Isla Starmane	
	Sharth Voldoun	65 Elite
E	Tuurem	
	Tuuren Hunter	62-63
	Tuuren Scavenger	62-63
	Wrekt Seer	63
F	Cenarion Thicket	
	Dreadfang Lurker	63-64 Very nasty poison attacks
	Empoor	64
	Empoor's Bodyguard	64
	Teromoth	62-63
	Timber Worg	62-63

	Vicious Teromoth	62-63
G	Grangol'var Village	
	Shadowy Advisor	63
	Shadowy Executioner	63-64
	Shadowy Hunter	65
	Shadowy Initiate	62
	Shadowy Laborer	60
	Shadowy Leader	64
	Shadowy Summoner	63-64
H	Veil Skith	
	Skithian Dreadhawk	63-64
	Skithian Windripper	63-64
	Urdak	63

Map Legend

I The Bone Wastes

Bonelasher	64-65
Deathskitter	64 Elite Loot Mob
Der'izu Arcanist	64-65
Der'izu Bandit	64-65
Draenei Skeleton	64-65
Dreadfang Widow	63-64
Floon	
Lost Spirit	64-65

J Auchindoun

Clarissa	
Draenei Pilgrim	
Ha'lei	
Isfar	
Provisioner Tsaalt	Sha'tar Merchant
Ramdor the Mad	

K Veil Lithic

Kokorek	
Mug'gok	Wandering 65
Shalassi Oracle	64-65
Shalassi Talonguard	63-64

L Bleeding Hollow Ruins

Boulderfist Invader	64-65
Kilrath	68 Horde Elite
Unkor the Ruthless	65

M Stonebreaker Hold

Advisor Faila	
Anvil	
Bar Talet	Bowyer
Forge	
Gardok Ripjaw	
Grek	
Grek's Riding Wolf	
Grenk	General Goods
Innkeeper Grilka	Innkeeper
Kerna	Wind Rider Master
Kurgatok	
Mailbox	
Malukaz	
Mawg Grimshot	
Mokasa	
Rakoria	
Rokag	
Rungor	Trade Goods
Smoker	
Spirit Sage Gartok	

Stonebreaker Grunt	65
Stonebreaker Peon	50-51
Tooki	
Trag	Stable Master
Wanted Poster	

N Allerian Stronghold

Allerian Defender	64-66
Allerian Horseman	60
Allerian Peasant	55
Andarl	
Anvil	
Bertelm	
Captain Auric Sunchaser	
Cecil Meyers	Blacksmithing Supplies
Fabian Lanzonelli	General Goods and Bags
Forge	
Furnan Skysoar	Gryphon Master
High Elf Ranger	65
Innkeeper Biribi	Innkeeper
Jenai Starwhisper	
Lady Dena Kennedy	60 Elite
Leeli Longhaggle	Trade Goods
Lemla Hopewing	Apprentice Gryphon Master
Lieutenant Gravelhammer	
Mailbox	
Ros'eleth	
Spirit Sage Zran	
Supply Officer Mills	Rations
Taela Everstride	
Thander	
Wanted Poster	

O Bonechewer Ruins

Bonechewer Backbreaker	63-64
Bonechewer Devastator	63-64
Lisaile Fireweaver	64
Timber Worg Alpha	63-64
Warped Peon	64

P Skethyl Mountains (Flying Mount Required)

Q Veil Shalas

Dugar	63 Horde
Deirom	63 Alliance
Luanga	65 Elite
Shalassi Oracle	64-65
Shalassi Talonguard	63-64

R Veil Reskk

Ashkaz	62

Shienor Sorcerer	63
Shienor Talonite	62-63
Shienor Wing Guard	63

S The Barrier Hills

T Skettis

Skettis Talonite	70
Greater Kaliri	66-68
Skettis Surger	71
Skettis Wing Guard	70
Skettis Windwalker	71
Blackwind Sabrecat	70
Mountain Colossus	72 Elite
Skettis Eviscerator	72
Skettis Time-Shifter	71
Skettis Sentinel	72

U Netherweb Ridge

Dreadfang Widow	63-64

V Blackwind Lake/W Blackwind Valley

Skettis Talonite	70
Greater Kaliri	66-68
Skettis Surger	71
Skettis Wing Guard	70
Skettis Windwalker	71
Blackwind Sabrecat	70
Mountain Colossus	72 Elite

1	Auchenai Crypts	Instance Entrance
2	Mana-Tombs	Instance Entrance
3	Sethekk Halls	Instance Entrance
4	The Shadow Labyrinth	Shadow Labyrinth Key Required
5	Spirit Towers	
6	Silmyr Lake	
	Dampscale Basilisk	62-63
7	Shattrath City	
8	Carrion Hill	
9	Refugee Caravan	
10	Sethekk Tomb	
11	Tomb of Lights	
12	Shadowstalker Kaide	Horde 64
13	Theloria Shadecloak	Alliance 64
14	Prospector Balmoral	Alliance 65
15	Lookout Nodak	Horde 65
16	Levixus the Soul Caller	66 Elite Demon

SHATTRATH CITY

Legend

Herbs	Minerals	Reputation Information
None	None	Scryers (Both Factions)
		The Aldor (Both Factions)
		The Sha'tar (Both Faction)
		Lower City (Both Factions)

A Eastern City Entrance

Broken Refugee	
Dwarf Refugee	
Haggard War Veteran	
Vagabond	
Vagrant	

B World's End Tavern

Albert Quarksprocket	
Haris Pilton	Socialite
Kylene	Barmaid
Leatei	
Mailbox	
Raliq the Drunk	
Sal'salabim	68 Elite
Shaarubo	Bartender
Shattrath Saul	
Tinkerbell	Haris Pilton's Pet

C Northern City Entrance

Haggard War Veteran	

D Mildred's Clinic

Injured Refugee	
Mildred Fletcher	Physician
Refugee Kid	
Seth	
Sha'nir	The Aldor
Zahila	

E Skettis Rise

Araac	Underneath the Rise
Karokka	Poison Supplies
Lissaf	Blade Merchant
Skettis Outcast	

F Crafter's Cubby

Kradu Grimblade	Weapon Crafter
Zula Slagfury	Armor Crafter

G Southern Entrance

Vagabond	
Vagrant	

H Crafter's Market

Aaron Hollman	Blacksmithing Supplies
Cro Threadstrong	Leatherworking Supplies
Darmari	Grand Master Leatherworker
Elin	Tailoring Supplies
Eral	General Goods
Ernie Packwell	Trade Goods
Fantei	Reagent Vendor
Granny Smith	Fruit Seller
Griftah	Amazing Amulets
Jack Trapper	Cook
Jim Saltit	Cooking Supplier
Madame Ruby	Enchanting Supplies
Muffin Man Moser	Bread Merchant
Peasant Refugee	
Seymour	Grand Master Skinner
Viggz Shinesparked	Engineering Supplies

I Aldor Training Area

Aldor Neophyte	70
Aldor Vindicator	70 Elite
Emissary Mordin	63 Elite
Ezekiel	
Grand Anchorite Almonen	70
Harbinger Argomen	
High Exarch Commodus	70
Veteran Vindicator	70

J Aldor Bank

Gromden	Banker
Mailbox	
Mendorn	Banker
Quartermaster Endarin	

K Scryer Bank

Berudan Keysworn	Banker
Inscriber Veredis	Scryer Inscriptions
L'lura Goldspun	Banker
Mailbox	
Quartermaster Enuril	
Scryer Vault Guardian	70

L A'dal's Chamber (East Side)

A'dal	The Sha'tar
Aldor Anchorite	70
Aldor Marksman	70
Aldor Neophyte	70
Harbinger Argomen	
Khadgar	Sons of Lothar
Oric Coe	Alliance 70 Elite
Portal to Darnassus	Alliance Only
Portal to Ironforge	Alliance Only
Portal to Silvermoon City	Horde Only
Portal to Stormwind	Alliance Only
Portal to The Exodar	Alliance Only

M A'Dal's Chamber (West Side)

Aldor Anchorite	70
Aldor Neophyte	70
G'eras Vindicator	70 Elite
G'eras	Dungeon Hard Mode Rewards
Portal to Orgrimmar	Horde Only
Portal to Thunder Bluff	Horde Only
Portal to Undercity	Horde Only
Spymistress Mehlisah Suncrown	

N Scryer's Tier

Scryer Arcane Guardian	70
Scryer Arcanist	60-61
Scryer Retainer	64-66

O East Wing

Dathris Sunstriker	
Innkeeper Haelthol	Innkeeper
Lisrythe Bloodwatch	Fence/Gem Merchant
Mahir Redstroke	Dagger Vendor
Mailbox	
Nalama the Merchant	General Goods
Trader Endernor	Trade Goods
Urumir Stavebright	Staff Vendor

P West Wing

Quelama Greenroad	Wand Vendor
Scryer Arcanist	60-61
Scryer Retainer	64-66
Selanam the Blade	Sword Vendor

Q The Library

Arodis Sunblade	Keeper of Shattari Artifacts
Enchanter Aeldron	Expert Enchanter
Enchanter Salias	Apprentice Enchanter
Enchantress Metura	Journeyman Enchanter
Enchantress Volali	Artisan Enchanter
High Enchanter Bardolan	Master Enchanter
Magister Falris	
Magistrix Fyalenn	
Mi'irku Farstep	Portal Trainer
Olodam Farhollow	
Scryer Arcane Guardian	70
Scryer Arcanist	60-61
Scryer Retainer	64-66
Vinemster Alamaro	Wine Vendor
Voren'thal the Seer	
Yurial Soulwater	Enchanting Supplies

R Aldor Rise

Adyen the Lightwarden	72 Elite
Aldor Anchorite	
Harbinger Erothem	70

S South Rise

Aldor Vindicator	70 Elite
Garul	Food and Drink Vendor
Mailbox	
Minalei	Innkeeper
Neophyte Combatant	70

T North Rise

Ahamen	Staff Vendor
Aldor Anchorite	70
Aldor Vindicator	70 Elite
Hamanar	Grand Master Jewelcrafter
Inessera	Jewelcrafting Supplies Vendor

U Temple of the Aldor

Aldor Anchorite	70
Anchorite Attendant	19
Anchorite Lyteera	
Asuur	Keeper of Shattari Artifacts
Ishanah	High Priestess of the Aldor

V Horde Battlemasters

Keldor the Lost	Horde Arathi Basin Battlemaster
Montok Redhands	Horde Warsong Gulch Battlemaster
Wolf-Sister Maka	Horde Alterac Valley Battlemaster
Yula the Fair	Horde Eye of the Storm Battlemaster

W Alliance Battlemasters

Adam Eternum	Alliance Arathi Basin Battlemaster
Haelga Slatefist	Alliance Alterac Valley Battlemaster
Iravar	Alliance Eye of the Storm Battlemaster
Lylandor	Alliance Warsong Gulch Battlemaster
Battle-Tiger	Adam Eternum's Pet

Map Legend

1	Oloraak	Fish Merchant	4	Arcanist Adyria and Iz'zard	7	Nutral	Flight Master
2	"Dirty" Larry and "Epic" Malone		5	Nicole Bartlett's Boarding House and Mailbox	8	Lathrai	
3	Farmer Griffith and Ewe		6	Harbinger Haronem	The Aldor	9	Exit to Nagrand	

NAGRAND

Legend

Map Legend

Consortium Overseer		
Gezhe		
Zerid		

P Southwind Cleft

Boulderfist Mage	66
Boulderfist Warrior	65-66

Q Halaa

Chief Researcher Kartos	
Halaani Guard	65
Quartermaster Davian Vaclav	Halaa Faction Merchant

R Ancestral Grounds

Agitated Orc Spirit	66-67

S Forge Camp: Fear

Felguard Legionnaire	67-68 Elite
Gan'arg Tinkerer	66-68
Mo'arg Engineer	67-68 Elite
Xirkis, Overseer of Fear	68 Elite

T Forge Camp: Hate

Demos, Overseer of Hate	68 Elite
Fel Cannon: Hate	70
Felguard Legionnaire	67-68 Elite
Gan'arg Tinkerer	66-68
Mo'arg Engineer	67-68 Elite
Mo'arg Master Planner	68 Elite

U Warmaul Hill

Cho'war the Pillager	67 Elite

Earthen Brand	Gurok the Usurper Summoned Here
Mag'har Prisoners	Locked in Cages/Requires Warmaul Prisoner Key
Mountain Gronn	67 Elite
Warmaul Brute	66-67
Warmaul Chef Bufferlo	66 Elite
Warmaul Warlock	66-67

V Northwind Cleft

Boulderfist Mage	65-66
Boulderfist Warrior	65-66
Muck Spawn	65-66

W Laughing Skull Ruins

Blazing Warmaul Pyre	
Gurgthock	
Mogor	67 Elite (Chain Combat Event)
Warmaul Reaver	65-66
Warmaul Shaman	65-66
Zorbo the Advisor	66

X Mag'hari Procession

Elder Ungriz	Horde 68
Elder Yorley	Horde 67
Saurfang the Younger	Horde 70 Elite

Y Sunspring Post

Kurenai Captive	Alliance 62
Mag'har Captive	Horde 62
Murkblood Brute	67
Murkblood Putrifier	65-66
Murkblood Raiders	66-67

Murkblood Scavenger	64
Ortor of Murkblood	67
Sunspring Villager	Corpses

A Lake Sunspring

Lake Surger	65-66
Watoosun's Polluted Essence	66

1 The Twilight Ridge

Deathshadow Archon	70
Deathshadow Spellbinder	70
Deathshadow Overlord	71
Deathshadow Warlock	70
Deathshadow Imp	70
Deathshadow Acolyte	70
Deathshadow Hound	70
Reth'hedron the Subduer	73 Elite

2 The Low Path

3 Lump 65 Sleeping, Charge

4 Clan Watch

5 Wyvern Camps Used to Start Bombing Runs

6 Skysong Lake

7 Abandoned Armory

8 Wazat Tusker 68 Elite

9 Altrius the Sufferer Quest Giver for Forge Camps

BLADE'S EDGE MOUNTAINS

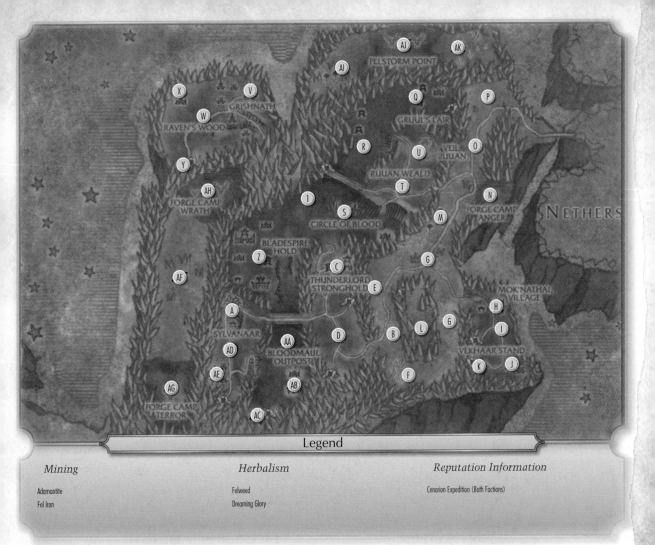

Legend

Mining	Herbalism	Reputation Information
Adamantite	Felweed	Cenarion Expedition (Both Factions)
Fel Iron	Dreaming Glory	

Map Legend

A Sylvanaar

Amerun Leafshade	Hippogryph Master
Borgrim Stouthammer	Quest Giver
Bronwyn Stouthammer	Quest Giver
Cahill	Weaponsmith
Caoileann	Trade Goods
Commander Skyshadow	Quest Giver
Innkeeper Shaunessy	Innkeeper
Kialon Nightblade	Quest Giver
Mailbox	
Moonwell	
Rina Moonspring	Quest Giver
Sylvanaar Sentinel	65
Syvanaar Ancient Protector	70
Tanaide	General Goods

Trayana	Quest Giver

B Toshley's Station

Bembil Knockhammer	General Goods
Bossi Pentapiston	Engineering Supplies
Razak Ironsides	70 Elite
Rip Pedalslam	Gryphon Master
Sassa Weldwell	Trade Goods
Station Bot-Jock	67
Station Guard	70
Station Technician	67
Tally Zapnabber	Quest Giver
Tally's Twin	Quest Giver

C Thunderlord Stronghold

Anvil	
Daga Ramba	Potions

Forge	
Gholah	Innkeeper
Gor'drek	Quest Giver
Karnaze	General Goods
Lor	Stable Master
Mailbox	
Nekthar	Quest Giver
Old Orok	Fruit and Fungus
Orgatha	Axesmith
Pol Snowhoof	Trade Goods
Raiza	Throwing Weapons
Rexxar	72 Elite
Rokgah Bloodgrip	Quest Giver
Threlc	Fishmonger
Thunderlord Grunt	65

Tor'chunk Twoclaws		Quest Giver
Unoke Tenderhoof		Wind Rider Master
Wanted Poster		

D Jagged Ridge

Bladewing Bloodletter	65-66
Thunderlord Dire Wolf	65-66

E Bladespire Outpost

Bladespire Crusher	67
Bladespire Mystic	67

F Singing Ridge

Blade's Edge Rock Flayer	66-67
Lesser Nether Drake	66-67

G Razor Ridge

Daggermaw Lashtail	66-67
Ridgespine Stalker	67
Scalewing Serpent	66
Maggoc	66 Elite

H Mok'Nathal Village

Braagor	Butcher
Erool	Trade Goods
Grikka	Grand Master Leatherworker
Krugash	General Goods
Matron Varah	Innkeeper
Mok'Nathal Hunter	65
Rogar	Leatherworking Supplies
Ruka	Smashing Weapons
Spiritcaller Grakosh	Quest Giver
Spiritcaller Roxnar	Quest Giver
Spiritcaller Skrash	Quest Giver

I Vekhaar Stand

Tawny Silkwing	65-66
Tawny Silkwing Larva	65-66

J Veil Vekh

Angry Arakkoa Pet	61
Vekh'nir Dreadhawk	65-66
Vekh'nir Keeneye	65-66
Vekh'nir Matriarch	66
Vekh'nir Stormcaller	65-66

K Trogma's Claim

Arakkoa Ogre Slave	65-66
Vekh'nir Dreadhawk	65-66
Vekh'nir Stormcaller	65-66

L Death's Door

Deathforge Over-Smith	68
Deathforge Technician	67-68
Eredar Highlord	68 Elite
Maiden of Nightmares	69
Void Terror	68

M Razaani Camp

Fiendling Flest Beast	67

Razaani Nexus Stalker	67-68
Razaani Raider	67-68
Razaani Spell-Thief	67-68
Ridgespine Horror	67

N Forge Camp: Anger

Anger Guard	67-68
Doomcryer	68 Elite
Doomforge Attendant	69
Doomforge Engineer	69
Fel Corrupter	67

O Bladed Gulch

Fel Corrupter	66-67
Felsworn Daggermaw	67
Felsworn Scalewing	67

P Skald

Scalded Basilisk	67-68
Searing Elemental	67-68
Skald Imp	67-68

Q Gruul's Lair

Bladespire Battlemage	67 Elite
Bladespire Chef	67 Elite
Bladespire Enforcer	67 Elite
Bladespire Ravager	67 Elite
Fingrom	67 Elite
Goc	70 Elite

R Bloodmaul Camp

Bloodmaul Battle Worg	66-67
Bloodmaul Bremaster	66
Bloodmaul Mauler	65-66
Bloodmaul Warlock	65-66
Dorgok	66

S Circle of Blood

"Lefty" Puddemup	Arena Battlemaster
Memininie	
Steamwheedle Sam	Arena Promoter

T Ruuan Weald

Expedition Warden	70
Moonwell	
Noko Moonwhisper	Reagent Vendor
Rashere Pridehoof	Trade Goods
Xerintha Ravenoak	Food and Drink
Zenyen Swiftstrider	Trade Goods

U Veil Ruuan

Beryl Silkwing Larva	66-67
Beryl Silkwing	66-67
Ruuan Weald Basilisk	66
Ruuan'ok Cloudgazer	66-67
Ruuan'ok Matriarch	67
Ruuan'ok Ravenguard	66-67
Ruuan'ok Skyfury	66-67

V Grishnath

Grishna Basilisk	67
Grishna Falconwing	67-68
Grishna Harbinger	67-88
Grishna Matriarch	68
Grishna Raven	63-64
Grishna Scorncrow	67-68

W Raven's Wood

Dire Raven	67-68
Raven's Wood Leafbeard	67-68
Raven's Wood Stonebark	68 Elite

X Boulder'mok

Plumpcheek Brute	67-68
Plumpcheek Chieftain	68
Plumpcheek Shaman	67-68

Y Blackwing Coven

Wyrmcult Adept	68
Wyrmcult Blackwhelp	67-68
Wyrmcult Dragon Egg	65
Wyrmcult Zealot	67-68

Z Bladespire Hold

Anvil	
Bladespire Brute	65-66
Bladespire Champion	66
Bladespire Cook	65-66
Bladespire Raptor	65-66
Bladespire Shaman	65-66
Droggam	66
Forge	
Gorr'Dim	67
Grulloc	66 Elite
Korgaah	65
Mugdorg	66
Thunderlord Clan Arrow	
Thunderlord Clan Drum	
Thunderlord Clan Tablet	

AA Bloodmaul Ravine

Bloodmaul Brew Keg	
Bloodmaul Brewmaster	65
Bloodmaul Dire Wolf	65
Bloodmaul Geomancer	65-66
Bloodmaul Skirmisher	65-66
T'chali the Witch Doctor	Quest Giver

AB Bloodmaul Outpost

Bloodmaul Brew Keg	
Bloodmaul Brewmaster	65
Bloodmaul Dire Wolf	65
Bloodmaul Geomancer	65-66
Bloodmaul Skirmisher	65-66
Grimnok Battleborn	67

AC Draenethyst Mine

Bloodmaul Brew Keg	
Bloodmaul Brewmaster	65
Bloodmaul Brute	65-66
Bloodmaul Dire Wolf	65
Bloodmaul Drudger	65-66
Bloodmaul Geomancer	65-66
Bloodmaul Skirmisher	65-66
T'chali's Hookah	

AD The Living Grove

Fey Drake	65-66
Grovestalker Lynx	65-66
Living Grove Defender	65-66
Stronglimb Deeproot	66 Elite

AE Veil Lashh

Lashh'an Kaliri	61-62
Lashh'an Talonite	65-66
Lashh'an Windwalker	65-66
Lashh'an Wing Guard	65-66

AF Vortex Pinnacle

Deathlash Stinger	71
Spire Needler	71-72

Daggertail Lizard	73 Elite
Wrath Corrupter	70-72
Bladespine Basilisk	72
Vortex Walker	71 Elite

AG Forge Camp: Terror

Fear Fiend	70
Legion Fel Cannon MKII	70
Wrath Speaker	70
Vile Fire-Soul	70
Abyssal Flamebringer	71
Terror-Fire Guardian	71
Nightmare Imp	70
Nightmare Weaver	70 Elite
Terrordar the Tormentor	70 Elite

AH Forge Camp: Wrath

Wrath Hound	69
Wrath Reaver	72 Elite
Wrath Fiend	70
Fel Rager	70
Furnace Guard	70
Wrath Speaker	70
Galvanoth	71 Elite

AI Bash'ir Landing

Bash'ir Arcanist	71
Lightning Wasp	70
Unbound Ethereal	70
Bash'ir Raider	70
Bash'ir Spell-Thief	71
Bash'ir Arcanist	72
Deathlash Stinger	72-73
Amberpelt Clefthoof	71
Daggertail Lizard	72

AJ Felstorm Point

Darkflame Infernal	70
Felstorm Corruptor	71
Insidious Familiar	71
Witness of Doom	70
Felstorm Overseer	71

AK Crystal Spine

Shard-Hide Boar	70-71
Warp-Mane Chimaera	72
Shard Stalker	72
Trigul	72 Elite

1 Young Crust Burster	**66-67**

NETHERSTORM

Map To Zoom Out

On map labels:
FORGE BASE GEHENNA
FORGE BASE OBLIVION
RUINS OF FARAHLON
MANAFORGE ARA
MANAFORGE ULTRIS
STORMSPIRE
CELESTIAL RIDGE
ECO-DOME MIDREALM
RUINS OF ENKAAT
AREA 52
MANAFORGE DURO
TEMPEST KE
MANAFORGE B'NAAR
ARKLON RUINS
SUNFURY HOLD
MANAFORGE CORUU
KIRIN'VAR VILLAGE
S

Legend

Mining

Apex 67 Elite	
Farahlon Breaker	69-70
Cragskaar	69 Elite
Adamantite	
Rich Adamantite	

Herbalism

Netherbloom
Felweed
Golden Sansam
Dreaming Glory

Reputation Information

Aldor (Both Factions)
Scryers (Both Factions)
Consortium (Both Factions)

Map Legend

A Area 52

Anchorite Karja	Quest Giver
Area 52 Big Bruiser	70 Elite
Area 52 Bruiser	65
Bill	Quest Giver
Chief Engineer Trep	Quest Giver
Dash	Trade Supplies
Doc	
Exarch Orelis	Quest Giver
Gant	Food & Drink
Innkeeper Remi Dodoso	Innkeeper
Irradiated Worker	61
Kalynna Lathred	
Kizzie	General Supplies
Krexcil	Flight Master
Lee Sparks	The Taskmaster
Magistrix Larynna	Quest Giver
Mailbox	
Nether-Stalker Khay'ji	Quest Giver
Netherstorm Agent	65
Off-Duty Engineer	
Papa Wheeler	Quest Giver
Qiff	Engineering Supplies
Ravandwyr	Quest Giver
Rocket-Chief Fuselage	Quest Giver
Scryer Retainer	65
Seasoned Vindicator	70 Elite
Spymaster Thalodien	Quest Giver
Veronia	Quest Giver
Vixton Pinchwhistle	Arena Vendor
Wanted Poster	
Xyrol	Grand Master Engineer

B B'naar Balista Camp

Captain Arathyn	68
Sunfury Bloodwarder	67-68

C Manaforge B'naar

Arcane Annihilator	68 Elite
B'naar Control Console	
Sunfury Astromancer	67-68
Sunfury Bloodwarder	67-68
Sunfury Captain	68
Sunfury Geologist	67-68
Sunfury Magister	67-68
Sunfury Warp-Engineer	67-68
Sunfury Warp-Master	68

D Southwest Netherstorm

Mana Wraith	67-68
Nether Ray	67-68
Netherrock	68
Shaleskin Flayer	67-68
Sundered Rumbler	67-68
Warp Aberration	67-68

E Ruins of Enkaat

Bot-Specialist Alley	Quest Giver
Disembodied Protector	67-68
Disembodied Vindicator	67-68
Etherlithium Matrix Crystal	Quest Target
Maxx A. Million Mk. I	63
Maxx A. Million Mk. II	65
Maxx A. Million Mk. V	67

F Southwest Cliffs

Nether Ray	67-68
Phase Hunter	67-68

G Camp of Boom

Boom Bot	67-68
Dr. Boom	68

H Arklonis Ridge

Farahlon Giant	67-68

I Arklon Ruins

Artifact Seeker	67-68
Felblade Doomguard	67-68
Pentatharon	69

J The Heap

Ethereal Technology	Quest Target
N. D. Meancamp	Quest Giver
Scrapped Fel Reaver	70 Elite
Warp-Raider Nesaad	69
Zaxxis Raider	67-68

Zaxxis Stalker	67-68	

K Manaforge Coruu

Arcane Annihilator	68 Elite
Arch Mage Adonis	68
Caledis Brightdawn	Quest Giver
Commander Dawnforge	68
Coruu Control Console	
Lariel Sunrunner	Quest Giver
Overseer Seylanna	68
Sunfury Arcanist	67-68
Sunfury Arch Mage	68
Sunfury Guardsman	67-68
Sunfury Guardsman	68
Sunfury Researcher	67-68

L Sunfury Hold

Sunfury Archer	67-68
Sunfury Flamekeeper	68
Sunfury Arch Mage	68
Sunfury Researcher	67-68

M Kirin'Var Village

Abjurist Belmara	68
Battle-Mage Dathric	68
Bessy	Quest Giver
Cohlien Frostweaver	68
Conjurer Luminrath	68
Kirin'Var Apprentice	69
Kirin'Var Ghost	68
Kirin'Var Rune	
Kirin'Var Spectre	68
Rhonsus	69
Severed Defender	68
Severed Spirit	68
Skeletal Stallion	68
Spectral Bovine	5
Tormented Soul	68

M1 Western Kirin'Var Village

Book Shelf	
Dresser	
Foot Locker	
Mageslayer	68-69
Mana Bomb Fragment	
Mana Seeker	68-69
Weapon Rack	

N The Violet Tower

Apprentice Andrethan	Quest Giver
Ar'kelos	68
Archmage Vargoth	Quest Giver
Custodian Dieworth	Quest Giver
Lieutenant-Sorcerer Morran	Quest Giver
Thadell	Quest Giver

O Chapel Yard

Kirin'Var Ghost	68
Naberius	69 Elite
Tormented Citizen	68
Tormented Soul	68

P The Vortex Fields

Apex	67 Elite
Mana Snapper	67
Swiftwing Shredder	69
Warp Chaser	67-68

Q Invasion Point: Destroyer

Drijya	Quest Giver
Warp-Gate Engineer	68-69

R Manaforge Duro

Duro Control Console	
Glacius	67
Nether Anomaly	68
Nether Beast	68
Summoner Kanthin	69
Sunfury Bowman	68-69
Sunfury Centurion	68-69
Sunfury Conjurer	68-69
Sunfury Technician	68

S The Scrap Field

Doomclaw	69
Gan'arg Engineer	68-69
Mo'arg Doomsmith	69

T Midrealm Post

Dealer Dunar	General Provisioner
Gahruj	Quest Giver
Mama Wheeler	Quest Giver
Mehrdad	Quest Giver
Shauly Pore	Quest Giver

U Eco-Dome Midrealm

Barbscale Crocolisk	68-69
Ivory Bell	Quest Target
Ripfang Lynx	68-69
Shimmerwing Moth	68-69

V Central Cliffs

Mana Snapper	67-68
Nether Ray	67-68

W Voidwind Plateau

Craghide Basilisk	68-69
Seeping Sludge	69-70
Shaleskin Ripper	68-69

X Celestial Ridge

Ethereal Teleport Pad	
Jorad Mace	Quest Giver
Nether Dragon	70
Nether Drake	68-69
Shrouded Figure	Quest Giver
Tyri	Quest Giver

Y Protectorate Watch Post

Captain Saeed	71
Commander Ameer	Quest Giver
Dealer Hazzin	General Provisioner
Flesh Handler Viridius	Quest Giver
Professor Dabiri	Quest Giver
Protectorate Avenger	69-70
Protectorate Nether Drake	70
Protectorate Vanguard	70
Researcher Navuud	Quest Giver
Subservient Flesh Beast	61

Wind Trader Marid	Quest Giver

Z Etherium Staging Grounds

Captured Protectorate Vanguard	Quest Giver
Congealed Void Horror	70 Elite
Ethereum Archon	69
Ethereum Assassin	69
Ethereum Gladiator	70
Ethereum Nexus-Stalker	70
Ethereum Overlord	69-70
Ethereum Prison	
Ethereum Researcher	69-70
Ethereum Shocktrooper	69-70
Ethereum Sparring Dummy	68
Ethereum Transponder Zeta	
Void Waste	69
Warden Icoshock	70

AA Access Shaft Zeon

Agent Ya-six	Quest Giver
Arconus the Insatiable	70
Fleshfiend	69-70
Parasitic Fleshbeast	69-70
Withered Corpse	69-70

AB Manaforge Ultris

Dimensius the All-Devouring	70 Elite
Seeping Ooze	70
Seeping Sludge	68-69
Unstable Voidwraith	68-69
Voidshrieker	68-69

AC Ruins of Farahlon

Culuthas	70 Elite
Eye of Culuthas	69-70
Hound of Culuthas	69-70

AD Netherstone

Cragskaar	69 Elite
Farahlon Breaker	69-70

AE Eco-Dome Farfield

Scythetooth Raptor	68-69
Tashar	Quest Giver
Tyrantus	71

AF Forge Base: Gehenna

Fel Imp	68-69
Forgemaster Sil'harad	68 Elite
Gan'arg Technomancer	68-69
Ironspine Forgelord	68
Legion Fel Cannon	70
Wrath Priestess	68-69
Wrathbringer	68-69

AG Forge Base: Oblivion

Cyber-Rage Foregelord	69
Fel Imp	68-69
Forgemaster Morug	68 Elite
Gan'arg Mekgineer	68-69
Legion Fel Cannon	70
Wrath Priestess	68-69
Wrathbringer	68-69

AH Northern Netherstorm

Sundered Thunderer	68-69
Warp Monstrosity	68-69

AI Tuluman's Landing

Kaylaan	Quest Giver
Nether-Stalker Oazul	Quest Giver
Wind Trader Tuluman	Weapon Merchant

AJ Eco-Dome Sutheron

Farahlon Lasher	68-69
Markaru	68
Talbuk Doe	68-69
Talbuk Sire	68-69

AK Eco-Dome Skyperch

Farahlon Lasher	68-69
Talbuk Doe	68-69
Talbuk Sire	68-69

AL The Stormspire

Action Jaxon	Quest Giver
Asarnan	Grand Master Enchanter
Audi the Needle	Quest Giver
Aurine Moonblaze	Quest Giver

Cookpot	
Dealer Aljaan	Trade Goods
Dealer Digriz	General Goods
Dealer Jadyan	Exotic Weapons
Dealer Malij	Enchanting Supplies
Dealer Najeeb	Spare Parts
Dealer Rashaad	Exotic Creatures
Dealer Sadaqat	Potent Potables
Dealer Senzik	Gems and Jewelcrafting
Dealer Zijaad	Arcane Goods
Eyonix	Innkeeper
Ghabar	Quest Giver
Grennik	Flight Master
Image of Nexus-Prince Haramad	Quest Giver
Jazdalaad	Grand Master Jewelcrafter
Karaaz	Consortium Vendor
Mailbox	
Nether-Stalker Nauthis	Quest Giver
Stormspire Nexus-Guard	71 Elite
Zephyrion	Quest Giver
Zuben Elgenubi	Quest Giver
Zuben Eschamali	Quest Giver

AM Manaforge Ara

Ara Control Console	
Daughter of Destiny	70
Mana Beast	69-70
Mo'arg Warp-Master	70
Overseer Azarad	70
Phase Hunter	67-68
Sunfury Blood Knight	70
Sunfury Nethermancer	69-70

AN Socrethar's Seat

Adyen the Lightwarden	71 Elite
Anchorite Karja	71
Exarch Orelis	69
Hatecryer	70
Socrethar	72 Elite
Wrath Lord	70

1	Doctor Vomisa, Ph. T.	Quest Giver
2	Harpax	Flight Master
3	Tempest Keep	
4	Agent Araxes	Quest Giver

SHADOWMOON VALLEY

A Shadowmoon Village (Horde)

Anvil	
Blood Guard Gulmok	
Chief Apothecary Hildagard	
Dama Wildmane	Windrider Keeper
Drek'Gol	Wind Rider Master
Earthmender Splinthoof	
Gedrah	Stable Master
Grokam Deatheye	Weaponsmith
Grutah	Grand Master Blacksmith
Heated Forge	
Infernal Attacker	67-68
Innkeeper Darg Bloodclaw	Innkeeper
Kalara	Trade Goods
Kor'kron Defender	70 Elite
Korthul	Bowyer & Gunsmith
Mailbox	
Olrokk	Riding Instructor
Overlord Or'barokh	
Researcher Tiorus	
Sergeant Kargrul	
Shadowmoon Peon	60
Shadowmoon Scout	67
*Shadowmoon Zealot	67-69
Trop Rendlimb	General Goods
Wanted Poster: Uvuros, Scourge of Shadowmoon	

B Wildhammer Stronghold (Alliance)

Anvil	
Barimoke Wildbeard	
Bron Goldhammer	
Brubeck Stormfoot	Gryphon Master
Brunn Flamebeard	Gryphon Keeper
Celie Steelwing	Cook
Crinn Pathfinder	Stable Master
Daggle Ironshaper	Guns and Ammunition
Dalin Stouthammer	Cooking Supplies
Dreg Cloudsweeper	Innkeeper
Earthmender Sophurus	
Eli Thunderstrike	Sky'ree's Keeper
Gnomus	
Gryphonrider Kieran	
Heated Forge	
Ilsa Blusterbrew	Riding Instructor
Infernal Attacker	67-68
Kurdan Wildhammer	
Mailbox	
Mari Stonehand	Armorsmith
Oran Blusterbrew	Trade Goods
Ordinn Thunderfist	Hammersmith
Salle Sunforge	General Goods
*Shadowmoon Harbinger	68-69

Sky'ree	70 Elite
Thane Yorregar	
Wanted Poster: Uvuros, Scourge of Shadowmoon	
Warcaller Beersnout	
Wildhammer Defender	67
Wildhammer Guard	70 Elite
Wildhammer Scout	
Wing Commander Nuaninn	
Zorus the Judicator	

C Sanctum of the Stars (Scryer)

Allieshor	Flight Master
Alorra	Armor Supplier
Alorya	General Goods Vendor
Arcanist Thelis	
Arrond	Tailoring Supplier
Battlemage Vyara	
Belanna	
Feranin	Provisions Supplier
Furan	
Larissa Sunstrike	
Lelagar	Smithing Supplier
Mailbox	
Roldemar	Innkeeper
Scryer Guardian	70 Elite
Sulamin	
Varen the Reclaimer	

D Altar of Sha'tar (Aldor)

Altar of Sha'tar Vindicator	70 Elite
Anchorite Ceyla	
Caretaker Aluuro	Innkeeper
Darmend	Smithing Supplier
Dearny	Leatherworking Merchant
Denath	
Dorni	General Goods Vendor
Dunaman	Weapons Vendor
Exarch Onaala	
Haaram	
Harbinger Saronen	
Maddix	Flight Master
Mailbox	
Maranem	
Nanomah	Provisions Merchant
Vindicator Aluumen	

E Legion Hold

Deathforged Infernal	68
Fel Reaver Armor	Quest Target
Legion Fel Cannon	67
Legion Teleporter	Quest Target
Mo'arg Weaponsmith	66-67
Morgroron	68 Elite
Overseer Ripsaw	69

Prophetess Cavrylin	69
Shadow Council Warlock	67
Terrormaster	67-68
Wrathwalker	67-68

F The Fetid Pool

Intact Power Core	Quest Target
Mutant Horror	67-68

G Magma Fields

Ever-burning Ash	Quest Target
Felboar	67-68
Felfire Diemetradon	67-68
Vilewing Chimaera	68

H Sketh'lon Wreckage

Asghar	68
Dark Conclave Hawkeye	67
Dark Conclave Ravenguard	68
Dark Conclave Shadowmancer	67-68
Skethyl Owl	68-69

I Illidari Point

Ar'tor, Son of Oronok	
Illidari Deathbringer	69
Illidari Painlasher	68-69
Illidari Satyr	69
Illidari Shocktrooper	68-69
Lothros	70
Painmistress Gabrissa	70

J Slag Watch (Horde)

Mokthar Grimblade	
Scout Zagran	

K Deathforge Tower (Alliance)

Gryphonrider Nordin	
Stormer Ewan Wildwing	

L The Deathforge

Cooling Infernal	68-69
Deathforge Guardian	68-69
Deathforge Imp	67-68
Deathforge Smith	68-69
Deathforge Summoner	68-69
Deathforge Tinkerer	68-69
Dormant Infernal	68-69
Infernal Soul	68
Infernal Oversoul	68
Kagrosh	
Newly Crafted Infernal	68
Warbringer Razuun	69

M The Altar of Damnation

Earthmender	Gorboto
Earthmender	Torlok
*Gul'dan	
*Remnant of Hate	69
*Spirit of the Past	62

The Fel Pits

Enraged Earth Spirit	68-69
Enraged Fire Spirit	68-69
Spawn of Uvuros	69

N Coilskar Point

Coilskar Cobra	68
Coilskar Defender	68
Coilskar Siren	68-69
Coilskar Waterkeeper	69
Enraged Water Spirit	68
Lady Shav'var	69

O Kraator's Shelf

Kraator	68 Elite
Scorchshell Pincer	68

P Shattered Plains

Domesticated Felboar	65-66
Flayer Egg	Quest Target
Ravenous Flayer Matriarch	70 Elite
Ravenous Flayer	69-70
Shadowmoon Tuber Mound	Quest Target

Q Coilskar Cistern

Captured Water Spirit	60-63
Coilskar Chest	
Coilskar Cobra	68
Coilskar Muckwatcher	70
Coilskar Myrmidon	70
Coilskar Sorceress	69-70
Earthmender Wilda	
Enraged Water Spirit	69
Keeper of the Cistern	69

R Ruins of Baa'ri

Ashtongue Warrior	69-70
Illidari Overseer	69
Ashtongue Shaman	70
Ashtongue Worker	69
Ashtongue Handler	69
Elekk Demolisher	69
Oronu the Elder	70

S Arcano-Scorp Station

Arcano-Scorp	70
Greater Felfire Diemetradon	68-69

T The Broken Shelf

Enraged Air Spirit	70
Scorchshell Pincer	68-69

U Ata'mal Terrace

Shadowmoon Chosen	70

Shadowmoon Darkweaver	69-70
Shadowmoon Eye of Kilrogg	70
Shadowmoon Slayer	68-69
Shadowmoon Soulstealer	70 Elite
Shadowsworn Drakonid	70 Elite

V Ruins of Karabor

Alandien	70 Elite
Azaloth	70 Elite
Demon Hunter Initiate	70
Demon Hunter Supplicant	70
Netharel	70 Elite
Spellbound Terrorguard	68
Sunfury Blood Lord	68
Sunfury Eradicator	67-68
Sunfury Summoner	70
Sunfury Warlock	70
Theras	70 Elite
Varedis	70 Elite

W Warden's Cage

Akama	
Ashtongue Deathsworn	
Dreadwarden	70
Illidari Agonizer	67
Illidari Jailor	70
Maiev Shadowsong	
Sanoru	
Zandras	70

X Netherwing Fields

Enraged Air Spirit	70
Mature Netherwing Drake	69-70 Elite
Mordenai	
Neltharaku	
Rocknail Flayer	70
Rocknail Ripper	69
Ruul the Darkener	71 Elite

Y Dragonmaw Fortress

Dragonmaw Drake-Rider	70
Dragonmaw Shaman	69-70
Dragonmaw Subjugator	69
Dragonmaw Wrangler	68-69
Enslaved Netherwing Drake	69
Heated Forge	
Karynaku	
Ruul the Darkener	71 Elite

Z The Altar of Shadows

Ancient Shadowmoon Spirit	

Enraged Air Spirit	70
Greater Felfire Diemetradon	68-69

AA The Path of Conquest

Chancellor Bloodleaf	70 Elite
Corok the Mighty	70 Elite
Eclipsion Cavalier	69-70
Eclipsion Soldier	68-69
Eclipsion Spellbinder	68-69
Son of Corok	68 Elite
Val'zareq the Conqueror	70 Elite

AB Crimson Watch

Crystal Prison	
Illidari Watcher	70 Elite

AC Eclipse Point

Eclipsion Archmage	68-69
Eclipsion Bloodwarder	70 Eclipsion Centurion 68-69
Eclipsion Dragonhawk	67-68
Grand Commander Ruusk	72 Elite
Illidari Slayer	70 Elite

AD Eclipsion Fields

Crazed Colossus	69-70 Elite

AE Sketh'lon Base Camp

Dark Conclave Harbinger	68
Dark Conclave Ritualist	67-68
Dark Conclave Scorncrow	67-68
Dark Conclave Talonite	67
Skethyl Owl	68-69

AG Netherwing Ledge

Dragonmaw Overseer	72
Dragonmaw Peon	68-69
Dragonmaw Skybreaker	70
*Vhel'kur	70 Elite

1 Parshah	
2 Uylaru	**70**
3 Eykenen	**70**
4 Uvuvros	**70 Elite**
5 Grom'tor Son of Oronok	
6 Oronok Torn-heart	
7 Felspine the Greater	**70 Elite**
8 Smith Gorlunk	**70**
9 *Clerics of Karabor	**68-69**
10 *Ghostriders of Karabor (Patrolling)	**70**
11 Haalum	
12 Lakaan	

* Can only be seen using Spectrecles

WORLD DUNGEONS

THE BLOOD FURNACE

DUNGEON INFORMATION

Name:	The Blood Furnace
Location:	Hellfire Peninsula
Faction:	Both
Suggested Levels:	60-63 (group of 5)
Primary Enemies:	Humanoids, Demons
Damage Types:	Physical, Shadow, Nature
Time to Complete:	2 Hours

WHO TO BRING

No class is without use in the Blood Furnace. The Fel Orcs spare no expense at repelling your entry and you should be ready to bring the courageous with you. Below is a table of suggestions based on what each class can do.

Jobs	
Class	Abilities
Druid	Healing, Backup Tanking, DPS, In-fight Recovery, Abolish Poison
Hunter	Ranged DPS, Backup Tanking (Pet), In-combat CC (Freezing Trap), Aspect of the Wild
Mage	Ranged DPS, Burst DPS, In-combat CC (Polymorph), In-combat CC (Frost Nova), Counterspell
Paladin	Healing, Tanking, Mana Recovery, Cleanse, Shadow Resistance Aura
Priest	Healing, Shadow Protection, In-combat CC (Mind Control), Dispel Magic
Rogue	DPS, Burst DPS, Out-of-combat CC (Sap), In-combat CC (Blind), Stuns
Shaman	Healing, Wipe Protection, Poison Cleansing Totem, Nature Resistance Totem
Warlock	Ranged DPS, Devour Magic (Felhunter), In-combat CC (Succubus), In-combat CC (Banish), Wipe Protection, Enslave Demon
Warrior	Tanking, DPS

GETTING TO THE BLOOD FURNACE

As part of Hellfire Citadel, The Blood Furnace stands almost equidistant from either flight point. This is misleading however. The Blood Furnace can only be entered by the highest part of the wall and must be reached via a siege ladder in the southern part of Hellfire.

Alliance parties need only climb the wall on the southern side of the ravine and enter the instance. Horde parties must travel across the Path of Glory to the southern part of the wall and make their way to the instance.

Shadowmoon Adept	61 Elite
Notes: Shadow Bolt	
Shadowmoon Summoner	61 Elite
Notes: Shadow Bolt, Inferno, Summons Succubus	
Shadowmoon Technician	62 Elite
Notes: Proximity Bombs (1800 damage to all in range), Silence	
Shadowmoon Warlock	62 Elite
Notes: Shadow Bolt, Corruption, Curse of Tongues	
The Maker	62 Elite
Notes: Throw Beaker (Throws beaker at target dealing 1000-1200 nature damage and knocks target into air), Domination	
Shadowmoon Channeler	62 Elite
Notes: Shadow Bolt, Mark of Shadow (Magic, All Shadow damage taken is increased by 1,100. 2 minute duration)	

OUT OF THE FIRE AND INTO THE FURNACE

THE ENEMY GARRISON

Broggok	63 Elite
Notes: Poison Bolt (Randomly hits two targets), Poison Cloud (Leaves poison trail), Slime Spray (Poison front cone AoE)	
Fel Orc Neophyte	62 Elite
Notes: Intercept, Enrage (physical damage increased by 122, attack speed increased by 60%)	
Felguard Brute	61 Elite
Notes: Knockback	
Felguard Annihilator	62 Elite
Notes: Intercept, Knockback	
Hellfire Imp	61
Notes: Fire Bolt	
Keli'dan the Breaker	63 Elite
Notes: Burning Nova, Shadow Bolt Volley, Corruption	
Laughing Skull Enforcer	61 Elite
Notes: Shield Bash	
Laughing Skull Legionnaire	61 Elite
Notes: Enrages at 25% health	
Laughing Skull Rogue	61 Elite
Notes: Poison, Stealth, Kidney Shot, Backstab	
Laughing Skull Warden	62 Elite
Notes: Fast attack speed	
Nascent Fel Orc	62
Notes: Thunderclap	

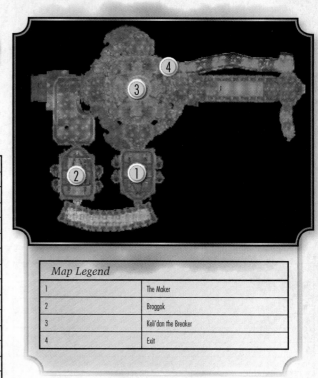

Map Legend	
1	The Maker
2	Broggok
3	Keli'dan the Breaker
4	Exit

THE STAIRS

The Fel Orcs of Hellfire Citadel have been warped and corrupted. They are far stronger and more resilient than normal Orcs and they are multiplying. Intelligence indicates that the Blood Furnace is an essential part of this operation.

Two Laughing Skull Enforcers guard the entrance. While this fight is simple, take the opportunity to discuss battle plans with the party. Use the party symbols to indicate who is targeting what to avoid confusion. Also discuss the attack order so you can keep your party's attacks focused and avoid breaking CC early.

Sample Explanation		
Symbol	Designation	Attack Order
Skull	Tank & DPS	1
Star	Seduce	2
Moon	Polymorph	3

The above example assumes three enemies and a party with a Warlock and Mage. Your party will most likely be different, so take the time to work out the battle strategy before you need it.

There are several groups guarding the bottom of the stairs. Each group consists of two Shadowmoon Adepts and one Hellfire Imp. The Adepts are elite and seem to be the real threat, but they are not. The Imp does immense damage, will not advance on you, and has relatively low health.

If you have a Warlock, keep the Imp banished until the Adepts are killed. Use interrupts to keep the Adepts from using their more powerful attacks. Another option is to have your Warlock enslave the first Imp. This gives your party a rather powerful ally. Be sure the Warlock warns you before he or she releases the Imp though.

If you are without a Warlock, CC as many of the Adepts as you can and kill the Imp quickly. At 1,000 Shadow damage a cast, you can't leave it alive and casting long.

Another pair of Laughing Skull Enforcers guard the stairs. Pull them away from the stairs and kill them as you did the first pair. Ascend the stairs slowly and together. Stealthing enemies wander the stairs and can do decent damage to a caster before the party can react. Alternatively, Hunters can use Flares and humans can use Perception to try to find these stealthed enemies. It's also a good idea to have a tank or another plate-wearer up the stairs first to draw the initial strike.

The enemy groups at the top of the stairs are packed fairly close together and have a wanderer with them. Each group has three Shadowmoon Adepts and one Hellfire Imp. Wait until the Shadowmoon Summoner wanders off to the left side before pulling the right group.

Use a ranged attack then duck into the previous room. By hiding behind a wall you break their line of sight and force them to come to you. Have CC ready when the enemies join you in the previous room. As with the battles at the bottom of the stairs, if you have a Warlock, banish the Imp and kill the Adepts. If you are without a Warlock, CC the Adepts and kill the Imp first.

Wait for the Summoner to wander to the right side once he is clear, pull the front left group into the previous room. Dispatch them as you did the first group. The Summoner is your next target. Use a ranged attack to get his attention and interrupts to keep him from casting. When he joins you, kill him.

The final group is now very much alone. Descend on them and show them the power of Azeroth. Proceed down the hall on your left.

There are two groups of guards. Each has a Laughing Skull Enforcer and Laughing Skull Legionnaire. Kill the Enforcer first as the Legionnaire enrages at low health. Be ready for the Legionnaire and crush it before it can capitalize on the damage increase.

The next set of guards can be dealt with in exactly the same manner. Proceed along the hallway until it connects with a larger room. As with the previous room, there are several groups and a wandering Shadowmoon Warlock. The groups here are much more dangerous than the previous room however.

Each group consists of Shadowmoon Adepts and Summoners. The Adepts aren't nearly as dangerous as the Summoners. In pulls with more than one Summoner, CC one and interrupt the other until its dead. If allowed time, the Summoners call a Succubus to their aid. This may not seem like much, but it can seduce your healer (or someone else) unless killed. If a Summoner calls a Succubus, kill the pet first. You can't afford to have 20% of your party CC'd by a pet.

Pull the first group when the Shadowmoon Warlock is away. Have crowd control and interrupts ready. The fighting is simple as long as the Summoner is locked down or killed quickly.

The wandering Warlock is your next target. Wait for it to move away from the far group and pull it around a wall. Kill it and engage the far group like you did the first. It's more likely than not that this group will have two Summoners, kill one quickly while the other is CC'd.

With the room cleared, only the two guards at the next doorway block your way forward. The Laughing Skull Enforcers aren't anything you haven't fought before. Dispatch them and rest to full as the next area requires more finesse.

THE PRISONS

While there are fewer enemies in each group, they are much more dangerous. Shadowmoon Summoners and Technicians are in pairs throughout the room, while a Laughing Skull Warden and Shadowmoon Technician patrol. The Technicians will be a nuisance through the next several rooms, so you need to learn how to deal with them.

The Shadowmoon Technicians can cast silence. This lasts for several seconds and makes your life much more difficult as tanks won't be able to taunt, healers can't heal, and casters can't bring the hammer. Kill the Technicians quickly to avoid a much more troubling fight.

They also drop Proximity Bombs. Once armed, these will explode and do 1,800 fire damage to any party members nearby when triggered. They are very visible, and should be avoided at all costs. Once the immediate fight is finished, have a Rogue disarm them or a high health party member set them off (after being healed to full). This keeps them from hindering the next fight.

Pull the first group on the left when the patrollers are away and duck around the doorway. Have an interrupt ready to force the Shadowmoon Summoner to come to you. When the enemies reach the doorway, CC the Shadowmoon Technician and kill the Summoner.

If you don't have any ranged interrupts, or if the Summoner resisted the interrupt, the fight is more challenging. CC the Technician as soon as it gets to the doorway. Kill the Succubus first. This leaves the Summoner free to cast, but you need the Succubus down before you engage the Summoner. Once the pet is dead, focus on the Summoner then the Technician.

The group on the right is your next target. Wait for the patrol to wander away before pulling the same way you did before. Continue this until the room is clear of all enemies except the Maker.

There are two doors on each side of the room with captured Orcs within, but they are too far gone for you to help. Rest to full and prepare for a fast and frantic fight.

The Maker has high Health, deals high damage, and has a couple tricks up his sleeve just to make your life more difficult. He can throw beakers at party members that toss them into the air. This effectively CC's the characters for a couple seconds and interrupts any spellcasts. If the tank is thrown into the air, stop attacks until the tank can regain aggro. His Domination ability actually resets aggro, so watch out for it.

The second ability can be just as devastating. The Maker can force a party member to join him for several seconds. This means the fight changes from five on one to four on two. Ignore the controlled character and keep focusing on the Maker.

Kill the Maker and the door forward opens. More of the Blood Furnace's function is revealed by a peak inside the next area. Shadowmoon Technicians stand around pods of some sort where Nascent Fel Orcs are being corrupted.

Pull the group of two Technicians and one Fel Orc into the previous room when the patrolling Laughing Skull Enforcers are away. As the Nascent Fel Orcs are not elite, they should be killed first while the Technicians are CC'd or kept busy. Once the Fel Orc is killed, dispatch the Technicians one at a time. Be watchful of the Proximity Bombs during the fight.

Wait for the Laughing Skull Enforcers patrol to return, then pull them into the previous room. This is another fight that is more to slow you down than to kill you. Slay the Enforcers as you have before.

Send your tank into the hallway and to the left side. It's a dead end, but a Laughing Skull Rogue waits there to ambush an unsuspecting caster. Destroy this Orc with extreme prejudice.

Now that it's safe for the softer party members, move into the hallway. The groups lining the hallway vary in composition, but you've fought all of them before. Watch the two patrolling Laughing Skull Enforcers further down. Don't let these join an existing fight.

Shadowmoon Technicians, Nascent Fel Orcs and various Shadowmoon casters will comprise the groups. The Fel Orcs can be slain quickly and should be your first targets. The Technicians should be controlled until you're ready to deal with them. The casters should be interrupted when possible. To pull the casters to you, hide behind the recessed areas of the walls to break line of sight.

Move through the corridor slowly and rest to regain Health and Mana after each fight. You want to be at your best if something goes wrong. Be sure to uncover and kill the Laughing Skull Rogue at the very end of the hallway before he can jump one of your casters.

Another large room with prison doors on both sides greets you. Shadowmoon Summoners and Technicians fill the room. The entire room needs to be cleared before you can advance, so start pulling the groups.

Pull the groups into the previous hallway. If you have a ranged interrupt, use it to keep the Summoners from calling their pets. Crowd control the Technicians as soon as they get to the hallway and kill the Summoner. The Technicians are easy prey when taken one at a time. Be watchful of the Proximity Bombs they leave.

If you do not have a ranged interrupt, pull the group around the corner. CC the Technicians as soon as they get there and kill any pets the Summoners have called. It's important to keep the Technicians CC'd so they don't silence your party members and the Succubae dead so they don't CC characters.

Fel Orc Neophytes are part of the final groups. Even with an obstructed view, you can now see Broggok. He isn't pretty. Don't get anxious, you'll be fighting him before long.

The Fel Orc Neophytes are fully corrupted and very dangerous. Unlike their Nascent cousins, they are elite. They also enrage themselves on occasion. This burning hatred increases their attack power and attack speed immensely. They can also intercept to stun and damage casters in your party without warning

CC the Neophytes and kill the other enemy first. These fights are more to give you a taste of what you're about to face then to kill you. Don't let anyone touch the lever on the floor until you've rested fully and are ready for a very difficult fight.

Pulling the lever begins an event that will test your group's ability to survive against overwhelming odds. Rather than opening the door to Broggok, it opens one of the prison doors. These prisoners are much more aware than the previous ones, and they aren't your friends.

The enemies will engage you and fight to the death. When they fall, the next door opens and another group charges you. The fights get progressively more difficult as more elite enemies are in each batch. Only after all four of the groups are dead will Broggok come forward. You won't have any time to rest between the Orc battles, so any class that can restore Mana or Health during the fighting will be worth its weight in gold.

Orc Groups

Order	Nascent Fel Orcs	Fel Orc Neophytes
1	4	0
2	3	1
3	2	2
4	1	3

Take stock and make sure you're using all your characters to their fullest. Mages should Conjure Mana Rubies for themselves. Warlocks should provide a Healthstone to each party member. Blessing of Wisdom and Mana Spring Totem are going to be essential in keeping your casters in the fight. Consider passing out potions as well to keep some of the strain from the healers.

The first fight is against four Nascent Fel Orcs. While none of them are elite, avoid using AoE attacks as you need to conserve your Mana. CC some to lessen damage taken by the party, but let melee and wand attacks do the bulk of the damage.

When the last Orc falls, the second fight begins. This fight has one elite enemy and three non-elites. CC the Fel Orc Neophyte. If you have more in-

combat CC, then CC the Nascent Fel Orcs, but the Neophyte needs to be CC'd until the party is ready. Kill the weaker Orcs, then the Neophyte.

The third group is more dangerous then the second. With two Fel Orc Neophytes, two Nascent Fel Orcs, and no rest since the last two fights. The fighting is probably getting a bit chaotic. Watch your Mana and use any timed abilities that regenerate it if you get low. Mana Tide Totem, Innervate, and Evocation are all abilities that can make a huge difference in this event. Using Mana potions is another option to keep you casting.

CC both the Fel Orc Neophytes if you can. With no possibility of additional mobs, use fear spells if you need to. Kill both the Nascent Fel Orcs then focus on the Neophytes one at a time.

The final fight is treacherous. You're low on Mana, low on Health, and the enemy has three Fel Orc Neophytes and a Nascent Fel Orc. Use any AoE CC you have to keep the enemies from dealing any substantial damage. Kill the Nascent Fel Orc and take the Neophytes one at a time. Once you engage the final enemy, pull the fight to the previous hallway. Killing the last Orc releases Broggok and he's not happy.

The Price of Failure

This is one of the 'wipe' fights for players new to the instance. The run from the graveyard is short so don't despair and don't destroy a group by blaming the wipe on a specific person.

Wiping on any of the Orc battles resets the entire event. Discuss what you can do better this time and come at it with a fresh mind and a little bit of petty vengeance.

Dying to Broggok does not reset the Orc encounters however. Once you kill the final Orc, they stay dead.

Broggok engages the party immediately and you won't have time to recover Mana or Health. He uses a variety of abilities that revolve around his use of poisons. His Poison Bolt randomly hits two targets, the Poison Cloud he trails forces players to pay attention so as not to stray into it, and his Slime Spray is a frontal cone, poison AoE. Avoid standing in the green rings and keep Broggok as far from the ranged members as possible. This limits the damage his AoE poison attacks do.

The tank should grab Broggok early and keep him facing away from the party. An easy way to do this is to constantly rotate around his lair. Move whenever Broggok puts a green circle at your feet, but keep Broggok away from the softer party members.

Anything that can cure poison will be used heavily in this fight. Use Aspect of the Wild and Nature Resistance Totem if you have them to reduce the damage each attack does. Try to keep the poison off as many party members as possible.

DPS classes should burn any cooldowns they have that increase damage. This is a make or break fight. Throw everything you have at this disgusting creature. When Broggok crashes to the ground, collect your loot, pat yourselves on the back, and regain Health and Mana…you're not done yet.

THE BLOOD FURNACE

The room beyond is fairly large. Shadowmoon Warlocks with Felguard Brutes patrol. To the left is a large group of three Hellfire Imps and three Shadowmoon Warlocks. When the patrols are away, pull the group and duck around the corner. This forces them to approach you. CC as many as you can when they come around the corner. Kill any Imps that aren't CC'd first. You haven't fought these since the beginning, but their damage is still impressive.

Once the active Imps are dead, kill any active Warlocks before breaking CC. Wait for a patrol to wander near the door and pull it toward you. Kill the

Shadowmoon Warlock first as it buffs the Felguard Brute. Move the party to where the Hellfire Imps were and look for the Laughing Skull Rogue. It's better to kill this treacherous snake on your terms.

The remaining patrol should be getting to your party soon. Engage and destroy it much the way you did the first patrol. Only two Felguard Brutes guard the door that blocks your advance. CC one if you have a Warlock and kill the other. If you are without a Warlock, use ranged snares or a Freezing Trap to keep one ineffective while you kill the other. Finish the final enemy and get your AoEs ready.

The next room contains only one group of enemies, but it's a large group. One Shadowmoon Warlock is surrounded by six Hellfire Imps. These aren't nearly as dangerous as the Imps before. They do less damage and have lower Health, but there are more of them. Pull the group around the corner to clump them all together and use AoE attacks to destroy the Imps. With his helpers dead, the Warlock is doomed.

If you are without sufficient AoE attacks, charge into the room and use burst DPS to kill the Imps as quickly as possible. Once the tank takes the first blast from all the enemies, the healer should use his or her largest heal and duck around the corner. Using a large heal like that will pull aggro from all the enemies that aren't engaged. This is good as they have to run around the corner to attack the healer. The time they spend running is time they don't spend casting.

Once the enemies close with the healer, he or she should run around the corner again (into the room with the party). This will disrupt the enemies again and bring them back to the party. Many of the Imps should be dead at this point and the tank needs to grab the remaining aggro before this little game of tag turns deadly. Handle the remainders as a standard fight.

Take the ramp to the right and start down to the main level. Two Felguard Annihilators guard the ramp. These are stronger than the Felguard Brutes, but can be dealt with in the same fashion. CC one and kill the other. Having a Warlock to Enslave and Banish is ideal, but Frost Nova or other rooting effects work just as well. Having the primary tank hold one while the rest of the party kills the other is the least ideal option, but it is still effective.

The bottom of the ramp leads to much tougher enemies. Groups of one Shadowmoon Warlock and two Felguard Annihilators stand guard. If you can CC an Annihilator do so and kill the Warlock first and the active Annihilator second. The Warlocks can buff the Annihilators just as they could buff the Brutes.

You can also use humanoid based CC on the Warlock and kill the Annihilators first. Be extremely careful using Sap as the second group is very close and you don't want to fight both at once.

With the first group dead, pull the second in the same fashion and rest to full Health and Mana. Through the doorway you can see the goal of your quest. Keli'dan the Breaker stands in the center of five Shadowmoon Channelers.

So Far From the Light

Consider equipping any items that increase your Shadow Protection. Both the Shadowmoon Channelers and Keli'dan use Shadow-based attacks. Any abilities that increase Shadow Protection should be cast or renewed if their duration is getting short. Shadow Protection and Shadow Resistance Aura are great for this.

The Channelers also cast Mark of Shadow. This magic debuff increases Shadow damage taken by 1,100 and lasts for two minutes. Characters with Cleanse, Dispel Magic, or Devour Magic (Felhunter) should be ready to keep this debuff from destroying your party.

Take the time to restore buffs, pass out Shadow Protection Potions, Healthstones, etc. while you discuss the plan ahead. With five elite enemies, you'll need to use every ounce of CC you have.

The Shadowmoon Channelers attack at the same time and cannot be pulled individually. Start the fight with Sap or Mind Control. If your Rogue has Improved Sap, let him or her CC one before you Mind Control. Let the Mind Controlled enemy die before the rest of the party engages. You don't get experience or loot from that enemy, but victory is more important.

Polymorph any you can and have interrupts ready for the enemies that aren't CC'd. If a caster or healer gains aggro, they should duck into the previous room to break los. This gives the rest of the party time to pull the enemy off the endangered.

While Frost Nova won't do much to CC the enemies when used in the large room, pulling the enemies into the previous room before using it is much more useful. This roots the enemies where they can't cast on the party. Other CC abilities that work well are Intimidating Shout, Psychic Scream, and other fear attacks. Keli'dan won't attack until all the Channelers are dead, so fear away!

Use any abilities that regenerate Mana or Health once you get down to the final Channeler. If Innervate, Evocation, or Mana Tide Totem has recycled since you last used them, now is a good time to use them again. Having full Health and Mana when you engage Keli'dan makes the fight much easier.

As soon as the last Shadowmoon Channeler dies, Keli'dan the Breaker attacks. Don't stand near him unless you must. His primary attack is a Shadow Bolt Volley, so it doesn't matter which way he faces, but he also uses Burning Nova. If you have Mark of Shadow on more than a couple party members, this fight quickly devolves into a mad dash of kill before being killed.

Several times during the fight, Keli'dan will stop attacking for a moment and taunt you, "Come closer". Get out of melee range as quickly as you can. Keli'dan casts Burning Nova (5-second cast) followed by his Shadow Bolt Volley. Any characters hit by both of these takes a great deal of damage and may even be killed before the healer can restore their Health. To make matters worse, he becomes invulnerable when he begins casting Burning Nova. Run away as soon as you notice he's stopped taking damage to limit the damage done to your party.

This is the final fight of the instance. Any timed abilities or trinkets that increase your damage or reduces the damage you take should be used. Don't hold anything back as Keli'dan surely isn't. When his corpse is finally beneath your feet, collect your loot and follow the door that opened for a shortcut to the entrance and daylight.

HELLFIRE RAMPARTS

DUNGEON INFORMATION

Name	Hellfire Ramparts
Location	Hellfire Peninsula
Faction	Both
Suggested Levels	59-62 (group of 5)
Primary Enemies	Humanoids, Beasts
Damage Types	Physical, Shadow, Fire
Time to Complete	1-2 Hours

WHO TO BRING

Every class brings something to a group heading into Hellfire Ramparts.
Below is a table of suggestions based on what each class can do.

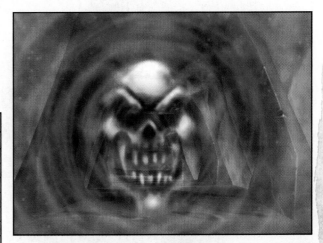

Jobs	
Class	**Abilities**
Druid	Healing, Backup Tanking, DPS, In-combat CC (Hibernate), Remove Curse
Hunter	Ranged DPS, Backup Tanking (Pet), In-combat CC (Freezing Trap)
Mage	Ranged DPS, Burst DPS, In-combat CC (Polymorph), Remove Curse
Paladin	Healing, Tanking, Mana Recovery, Cleanse, Shadow Resistance Aura, Fire Resistance Aura
Priest	Healing, Shadow Protection, In-combat CC (Mind Control)
Rogue	DPS, Burst DPS, Out-of-combat CC (Sap), In-combat CC (Blind), Stuns
Shaman	Healing, Fire Resistance Totem, Wipe Protection
Warlock	Ranged DPS, Devour Magic (Felhunter), In-combat CC (Succubus), Wipe Protection
Warrior	Tanking, DPS

GETTING TO HELLFIRE RAMPARTS

Hellfire Ramparts is one wing of Hellfire Citadel. Situated neatly in the
center of Hellfire Peninsula, it's close to both Horde and Alliance flight
points and graveyards.

Alliance parties can climb the wall on the southern side of the ravine
and drop down to the instance entrance. Horde parties should climb the
wall on the northern side of the ravine and take the ramp down to the
instance entrance.

THE ENEMY GARRISON

Bleeding Hollow Archer	60 Elite
Notes: Ranged Attacks	
Bleeding Hollow Darkcaster	60 Elite
Notes: Shadow bolt	
Bleeding Hollow Scryer	61-62 Elite
Notes: Shadow bolt, Fear, Life Drain	
Bleeding Hollow Seer	60 Elite
Notes: Shadow bolt, Fear	
Bonechewer Beastmaster	60 Elite
Notes: Summons 3 Shattered Hand Warhounds, Stealth Detection	
Bonechewer Destroyer	60 Elite
Notes: Cleave, Mortal Strike, Knockback	
Bonechewer Hungerer	60-61 Elite
Notes: Demoralizing Shout, Disarm	
Bonechewer Ravener	60 Elite
Notes: Kidney Shot	
Bonechewer Ripper	60 Elite
Notes: Enrage	
Felhound	59-60
Notes: Summoned by Omar the Unscarred	
Hellfire Sentry	58 Elite
Note: Kidney Shot, Heightened Stealth Detection	
Hellfire Watcher	60 Elite
Notes: Heal Watchkeeper Gargolmar	
Nazan	62 Elite Boss
Notes: Cone of Fire, Liquid Flame, Fireball	
Omor the Unscarred	62 Elite Boss
Notes: Summons Felhounds (these have the Spell Lock ability which can silence a caster), Treacherous Aura (360-440 damage every second), Shadow Bolt, Orbital Strike (Knocks a target into the air and bounces them around), Shadow Whip (Pulls an airborne target down to the ground), Demonic Shield (Casts when low on health, Reduces all damage by 75% for a short duration)	
Shattered Hand Warhounds	50-60
Notes: Stealth Detection	
Vazruden	62 Elite Boss
Notes: Revenge	
Watchkeeper Gargolmar	62 Elite Boss
Notes: Surge (Works like Intercept, but knocks down all nearby targets), Mortal Wound (Like a stacking Mortal Strike), Overpower, Gains Retaliation at low health	

ATOP THE WALLS

THE RAMPARTS

While the trip in is uneventful, that ends at the instance portal. The rest of the trip is a hard fight through legions of enemies.

Guarding the first bridge is a pair of Bonechewer Hungerers. Wait for the patrolling Bonechewer Ravener to be on the other side of the bridge before pulling the two. The fight is fairly straight-forward.

Take this opportunity to practice the group's crowd control. The fight is small enough that failed crowd control isn't a death sentence and the instance portal is right behind you if anything goes wrong. The party leader should designate a symbol for each type of target and explain the attack order.

Sample Explanation		
Symbol	**Designation**	**Attack Order**
Star	Sap	1
Moon	Polymorph	2
Skull	Tank & DPS	3

This example assumes three enemies and a group with a Rogue and Mage. Your group will be different, so take the time to find what everyone is comfortable with.

With the first two guards out of the way, grab the Bonechewer Ravener next time he wanders to this side of the bridge. Destroy him and dispatch the far two Bonechewer Hungerers in the same way you did the first two.

Cross the bridge and prepare for slightly more difficult fights. There are three enemies in each group and all of them are elite. The Bleeding Hollow Darkcasters and Archers attack from range, so they are good candidates for CC. The Bonechewer Destroyer has a number of melee attacks that make him quite dangerous. Kill him first to keep him from making the life of the caster(s) too difficult.

Keep your backs facing the bridge (or other areas you've cleared) while fighting the Bonechewer Destroyer. He can knock you off the ramparts if you are unlucky. A fall from the ramparts is death no matter who you are. He also has a cleave attack, so keep the Destroyer facing away from melee DPS characters and other soft target party members.

The Bleeding Hollow Darkcaster should be your next target as he can be interrupted and pulled to the group. Without use of his spells, he's little more than a glorified bookworm. With only one enemy left, the Bleeding Hollow Archer won't last long.

Move to the next group and handle it much the same. Continue along the rampart until you reach the group of two Bonechewer Hungerers and two Shattered Hand Warhounds. The Warhounds are not elite and can be killed quickly. CC the Hungerers until the Warhounds have been dispatched. Avoid using AoE attacks on the Warhounds; breaking CC on either or both of the Hungerers will prove to be deadly to the character who cast the AoE.

Do not attempt to use Sap on enemies near the Warhounds. The Warhounds can smell through stealth and alert others to your presence. If the only in-combat CC you have in the party is Hibernate, the tactics should change slightly. Hibernate one of the Warhounds; kill the other Warhound, then the two Hungerers. Kill the final Warhound last.

Once again, the enemies have upped the ante. There is a group of three Bleeding Hollow Seers surrounding a Bonechewer Ripper. This fight is going to test your CC capabilities as well as your pulling. All four enemies are elite and the Seers can cast fear.

CC as many of the Seers as possible and pull the fight back. As the Seers can fear, you don't want to fight near another group. One bad fear and you'll be fighting far more than you can handle.

Kill the active Seers first. If you have an off-tank, they should hold the Ripper away from the rest of the party until all non CC'd Seers are dead. Focus on the Ripper next, then the remaining Seers one at a time.

THE CORRIDOR

A Bonechewer Beastmaster and two Bonechewer Destroyers stand before you. Don't pull this group yet. Wait for the patrolling Bonechewer Hungerer with his two Shattered Hand Warhounds. When they are closest to you, pull them away from the Destroyers and Beastmaster.

Pulling these prior to the Beastmaster fight keeps them from joining when you least want them to. CC the Hungerer well away from the Beastmaster and kill the two Warhounds. Once the Warhounds are dead, finish the Hungerer and rest to full.

The next fight looks much easier than it is. Rest to full Mana and Health before beginning the fight. Two Bonechewer Destroyers stand near a Bonechewer Beastmaster. Do not attempt to Sap any of the targets as the Beastmaster can smell through stealth. CC one of the Destroyers as soon as the fight starts.

If you have spare CC, use it on the Beastmaster while you kill the second Destroyer. Keep the first Destroyer CC'd as you move to the Beastmaster. During the fight, he will summon several Shattered Hand Warhounds.

Hold the Beastmaster while you destroy all the Warhounds he summoned. They aren't elite, but will do incredible damage if allowed to chew on a caster. With all his friends dead, finish off the Beastmaster and the last Destroyer.

Learning the Ropes

This is one of the 'wipe' fights for players new to the instance. The run from the graveyard is short so don't despair and don't destroy a group by blaming the wipe on a specific person. Examine what you could have done better and note it for future runs as you make your way back to the instance.

The next fight is against another group of four elite enemies. One Bonechewer Ravener and one Bonechewer Destroyer are guarding two Bleeding Hollow Darkcasters. If you have enough in-combat CC, keep the Darkcasters from participating in the fight while you kill the Ravener and Destroyer. The Destroyer does more damage than the Ravener, but the Ravener will stun your tank repeatedly. A stunned tank can't control aggro, so kill the Ravener first. The rest of the fight is simple. Kill the Destroyer, than the Darkcasters one at a time.

If you are short on in-combat CC, kill the Darkcasters first, while the tank holds the Ravener and Destroyer away from the party. With stuns and knockbacks on the tank, losing aggro is expected. Kill the Darkcasters quickly and move on to the Ravener and Destroyer.

Many of the next fights involve both elite enemies and the Shattered Hand Warhounds. CC the elite enemies and kill the Warhounds. This tactic is extremely useful and keep you safe until you see Watchkeeper Gargolmar and his Hellfire Watchers patrolling.

This is the first boss and should not be taken lightly. Wait for him to patrol away and pull the enemy groups on each side of the corridor. The fights are similar to what you've done before and the enemies need to be cleared before you engage Gargolmar. Take a moment to regain Health and Mana before pulling Gargolmar's group.

Gargolmar inflicts high melee damage and can surge to intercept the party member furthest from him knocking all nearby targets down. The tank should hold Gargolmar while the rest of the group kills the two Hellfire Watchers. The Watchers heal Gargolmar if allowed to live. CC one if you have in-combat CC and kill the other. If you don't have any in-combat CC, have someone with interrupts keep the second Hellfire Watcher ineffective while the party kills the first.

Pet classes can leave their pet at range to take the brunt of Gargolmar's surges. This keeps the more fragile party members safe from his attention. With both the Watchers dead, show Gargolmar the power of Azeroth! Gargolmar's abilities can wreak havoc on your party, so watch out! His Mortal Wound stacks, but is like Mortal Strike in all other ways. This prevents healing and inflicts a considerable amount of damage. His Overpower and Retaliation (which counters melee attacks) are just like the Warrior abilities and can inflict serious damage to all members, especially non-plate wearers.

Jumping Ahead

If your party is experienced with Hellfire Ramparts and in a hurry, the next few groups on the right side of the corridor can be skipped by sticking to the left side. This should only be done by experienced parties as most characters can benefit from the practice, the reputation, and the item drops.

On the right are two more groups very similar to what you've already fought. With all the patrollers removed, these are straightforward fights. CC the casters, kill any non-elites, and then kill the elites one at a time.

The doorway at the end of the corridor is guarded by two Bonechewer Hungerers. You've fought these before and they aren't a threat if your party has made it this far. Kill them and enter the staircase. Approach the top of the staircase carefully as a large and challenging fight awaits you in the next corridor.

Four Bleeding Hollow Scryers surround one Bonechewer Ripper in the next hallway. The Scryers cast Shadow bolt and Fear and can be quite dangerous with so many of them. The Ripper can enrage as well.

Pull them with a ranged attack and wait for the Scryers to start casting. As soon as they begin casting, duck around the corner and back onto the stairs. This gives you time as they will try to complete their castings before they realize you are out of line of sight. Once they realize this, they will run to the stairs to start casting again.

Jump on the Ripper and kill him quickly. Use AoE CC abilities to keep the Scryers from doing anything useful. Psychic Scream and Intimidating Shout are good examples of these. If you are without AoE CC, use what CC you can and burn through the enemies at maximum speed. The less CC you have, the more damage you have, so use it.

Once the Ripper and a couple of the Scryers are down, the battle becomes much easier. It's far harder to die in a couple seconds when there are only two enemies. Once the encounter is done, rest to regain lost Mana and Health.

The doorway at the end of the corridor is guarded by two Bonechewer Destroyers. When your party is ready, pull and kill these two overmatched guards. The open area beyond is of much more concern.

THE PLATFORMS

There are groups on the left, on the right, in the center, and roaming the area. Wait for the roaming group to be away before pulling the group to the right back into the hallway.

If you fight them at the edge of the open area, the patrolling group will join. Have someone who isn't the tank pull this group and run back to the staircase and around the corner. This forces the two Bleeding Hollow Archers to run down the hallway and to their doom. Use in-combat CC to hold the Archers while you dispatch the Destroyer then the Archers.

Omor casts a rather damaging curse. Anyone able to remove curses should be prepared to do so. The curse causes massive Shadow damage to all members near the afflicted.

Equipping items that increase your Shadow Resistance can make this less painful, but nothing beats removal.

The roaming Bonechewer Ravener and two Shattered Hand Warhounds are your next targets. Wait for them to patrol away from the other groups and pull them into the hallway. Kill the dogs first and the Ravener won't stand a chance.

The area is much manageable now. The group to the left consists of one Bleeding Hollow Darkcaster, one Bonechewer Hungerer, and two Bonechewer Destroyers. CC the Destroyers and rush the group. Kill the Darkcaster first as it won't have time to be effective before you're finished with it. The Hungerer is your second target and finish with the Destroyers.

The final group on the platform should be very scared. Charge them and kill the Darkcaster, then the Warhound before engaging the melee enemies. Both the Darkcaster and Warhound have lower Health and neither last long.

After exiting the platform area, take the entrance guarded by two Bonechewer Hungerers. Kill the Hungerers and proceed to Omor the Unscarred.

Two Darkcasters guard access to Omor. These can be kill without angering Omor, but don't charge them. Use any ranged interrupts you have and get CC ready. Pull one and interrupt the first to force it to come to you; CC the other. Bring the other Darkcaster to clear the way to Omor.

Omor isn't someone to be taken lightly. He has reasonable Health, summons friends, and casts a curse that can affect an entire party if you aren't careful. Your tank should charge in and hold Omor as close to the center of the platform as possible. Ranged DPS should spread out while still being in healing range.

This keeps your party out of range of the curse without reducing their effectiveness. If anyone gets cursed near you, move away from them to avoid taking damage. The Shadow damage can easily cause a wipe if you don't keep track of it.

Several times throughout the fight, Omor will summon Felhounds to aid him. These Felhounds have the Spell Lock ability that can destroy a party since it prevents casters from casting. Omor also has the Orbital Whip ability (which launches a target into the air and bounces them around) and the Shadow Whip ability (that pulls the target back to the ground). This can effectively keep a member of the party out of the fight. Burst DPS classes should destroy these before they can cause a problem for your healer. Casters should watch their Health as Omor casts Demonic Shield when he reaches low Health. Avoid using any of your large spells during the last few moments of his life.

With all of this in mind, the fight will go smoothly. Keep your party healed and Omor falls. Collect your booty and return to the central platform for the final few fights.

Vazruden the Herald flies over the final platform. There is a small group of enemies guarding the bridge, but they are of little consequence. Kill them, but don't pull the Hellfire Sentries. Rest to full Health and Mana and prepare for a frantic fight.

The Fires From Above

Vazruden the Herald employs a number of fire attacks throughout the fight. Consider using Fire Protection Potions and equipping items that increase your Fire Resistance to make the fight less stressful.

Pulling the Hellfire Sentries begins the final fight. While they aren't of consequence, Vazruden jumps off his dragon and engages you as soon as you kill the Sentries. Vazruden does high physical damage, but he's not your primary concern. Nazan breathes fire from the sky and small areas burn with dragonfire for a short time as a result. Do not stand in these flaming circles. The damage they do is immense.

Slowly kill Vazruden while dodging the breath attacks of Nazan. Hold as much of your Mana as you can as things get much worse later. When Vazruden gets low on Health, he'll summon his dragon to land and fight with him. Finish Vazruden quickly and turn your attention to Nazan.

Even on the ground, Nazan is terribly dangerous. His physical attacks aren't that strong, but he still uses a Fireball attack that leaves Liquid Flame on the ground. Be careful! While his physical attacks aren't strong, Vazruden's spells can alter the tide of battle in a second!

The tank needs to keep Nazan facing away from the party without standing in a circle of fire. Use all your Mana on your fastest damaging spells. Use any timers you have to increase your damage output. Keep the tank up as best you can with rapid fire healing. This is a race to see who can kill who first.

If your party stays out of the circles of fire, the healer should have enough Mana to keep the tank alive long enough for the party to kill the dragon. If the tank goes down, abandon all hope of healing people and switch to all out DPS. The only way to win is to kill the beast before it kills you.

Resurrect any party members that died in the engagement, collect your loot and head home.

Slave Pens

DUNGEON INFORMATION

Name:	Slave Pens
Location:	Zangarmarsh
Faction:	Both
Suggested Levels:	61-65 (group of 5)
Primary Enemies:	Humanoids
Damage Types:	Physical, Frost, Nature
Time to Complete:	2 Hours

WHO TO BRING

No one is without a place or use in Slave Pens. While avoiding redundancy is important, so many classes bring multiple abilities to a group that it's very easy to have two of the same class performing very different roles.

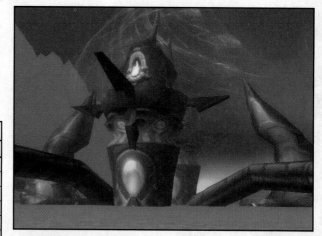

Jobs	
Class	**Abilities**
Druid	Healing, Backup Tanking, DPS
Hunter	Ranged DPS, Backup Tanking (Pet), In-combat CC (Freezing Trap), Aspect of the Wild
Mage	Ranged DPS, Burst DPS, In-combat CC (Polymorph)
Paladin	Healing, Tanking, Mana Recovery, Cleanse, Frost Resistance Aura
Priest	Healing, In-combat CC (Mind Control)
Rogue	DPS, Burst DPS, Out-of-combat CC (Sap), In-combat CC (Blind), Stuns
Shaman	Healing, Frost Resistance Totem, Wipe Protection
Warlock	Ranged DPS, In-combat CC (Succubus), Wipe Protection
Warrior	Tanking, DPS

GETTING TO THE SLAVE PENS

The Slave Pens is one of the many wings of Coilfang Reservoir. Horde parties can fly into Zabra'jin while Alliance parties fly into Telredor.

At the center of Serpent Lake is the Coilfang Reservoir. Dive beneath the water at the center of the pumping station and look for the drain. Swim through the drain and surface within the Reservoir. The Slave Pens are the western most instance portal.

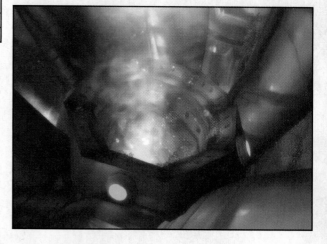

The Slave Pens, while a stand alone instance, is meant to be part of the larger Coilfang Reservoir. The level difference between each wing is substantial enough that parties aren't likely to run one wing after another, but each wing is fairly short.

DOWN THE DRAIN

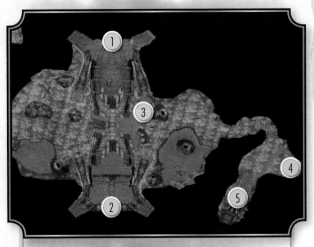

THE SLAVES AND THEIR KEEPERS

Bogstrok	62 Elite
Notes: Piercing Jab (139-161% weapon damage and reduces target's armor by 15% for 20 sec.)	
Coilfang Champion	62 Elite
Notes: Intimidating Shout, Cleave	
Coilfang Collaborator	62 Elite
Notes: Cripple (Reduces movement speed by 50%, increases swing time by 100%), Enrage	
Coilfang Defender	63 Elite
Notes: Spell Shield (reflects magic attacks when active)	
Coilfang Enchantress	62-63 Elite
Notes: Frost Bolt, Entangling Roots, Lightning Storm	
Coilfang Observer	62 Elite
Notes: Immolate, Accompanied by Coilfang Ray	
Coilfang Ray	64 Elite
Notes: Psychic Horror (6 second Horror)	
Coilfang Scale-Healer	63 Elite
Notes: Heal, Holy Nova	
Coilfang Slavehandler	63 Elite
Notes: Rend, Hamstring	
Coilfang Soothsayer	62 Elite
Notes: Decayed Intelligence (Magic, Intellect reduced by 25%, Area of Effect, Lasts 15 seconds)	
Coilfang Technician	62-63 Elite
Notes: Rain of Fire	
Greater Bogstrok	62 Elite
Notes: Decayed Strength (Disease, Strength reduced by 25)	
Mennu the Betrayer	64 Elite Boss
Notes: Lightning Bolt	
Quagmirran	64 Elite Boss
Notes: Poison Bolt Volley (AoE), Cleave, Uppercut (Damage & Knock back), Acid Geyser (AoE nature damage)	
Rokmar the Clacker	64 Elite Boss
Notes: Water Spit (AoE), Grievous Wounds (Bleed for 685-815 until they're healed)	
Wastewalker Slave	63 Elite
Notes: Amplify Magic, Fireball, Frost Bolt	
Wastewalker Taskmaster	63 Elite
Notes: Cripple (Reduces movement speed by 50%, increases swing time by 100%)	
Wastewalker Worker	62 Elite

Map Legend	
1	Mennu the Betrayer
2	Weeder Greenthumb
3	Rokmar the Clacker
4	Naturalist Bite
5	Quagmirran

A DAMP BEGINNING

At first, there is little sign of Naga presence in the Slave Pens. Bogstrok and Greater Bogstrok patrol the area in groups of three. These patrols move very quickly and cannot be safely bypassed.

Though quite monstrous looking, the Bogstrok are considered humanoid. This opens a variety of CC options including Polymorph, Freezing Trap, Blind, and Fear. Avoid using Fear as you don't need the fight to be any larger.

Gather aggro on the tank and slug away at the chitin-covered foes one at a time. While they aren't terribly dangerous, they present ideal practice for your party's fire control. Use the raid symbols to let everyone know what is getting CC'd and what order to kill the enemies in. No enemy will last long with your entire party firing at them.

Sample Explanation		
Symbol	Designation	Attack Order
Star	Sap	2
Skull	Tank & DPS	1
Moon	Polymorph	3

The first group was probably a little rough. The second group has the same composition and presents another try at perfection. Keep your tank's health high and all aggro on the tank as the Bogstroks do a good bit of damage.

Continue down the tunnel until it widens. Several Naga guard are watching over Broken slaves. This can be used to your advantage. The slaves only fight you while the Naga stands. Concentrate all your fire on the Coilfang Slavehandler and kill him quickly. When the Naga falls, the Wastewalker Workers will thank you for their freedom and run away.

Use a ranged attack to pull the enemies to you. This keeps you from fighting both groups at once. The first group consists of one Coilfang Slavehandler and three Wastewalker Workers.

The next group is similar to the first with only minor differences. Instead of three Wastewalker Workers, there are two Wastewalker Slaves. The Slaves cast spells from range. This can be a problem as they do not realize they are free if the Slavehandler dies too far away. Drag the fight to the Slaves and kill the Naga first. Should they continue attacking you when the Naga falls, you have no choice but to kill them.

A pair of Coilfang Champions patrols ahead. Pull these back to your party as you don't want to fight them near the room ahead. CC one and pull the other to you. The tank should hold the target away from as much of the party as possible as Coilfang Champions use Intimidating Shout. This single ability can cause your entire party to run in fear if used close enough. Kill the Champions one at a time before proceeding.

As the Slavehandler is elite, he won't drop fast. Use CC to keep the Workers from dealing significant damage or have your tank hold the attention of all four enemies. Avoid using area of effect attacks as the Workers will continue attacking you if you do too much damage to them.

Further down, the tunnel opens into a large cavern. Several groups of Naga and Bogstrok patrol. The enemy has established forces in the entire cavern, but you only have a few objectives. You can skip many of the enemies without endangering your mission. Should you want the additional experience or treasure, kill any mobs not mentioned in this walkthrough.

Hold your party at the entrance of the cavern for the time being. To the right are four Naga and a pet; a Coilfang Observer, two Coilfang Champions, a Coilfang Scale-Healer, and a Coilfang Ray. Remember that the Champions can fear several members of your party at once.

Pull the group and CC as many of the Champions as possible. Use the tunnel wall to break line of sight and force the enemies to close the distance. The Scale-Healer uses Holy Nova and does damage to any of your party in range and heal its companions. Keep it away from the bulk of the party and kill it first. The Coilfang Ray can fear one person at a time, but only uses it on a party member that doesn't have aggro. This means that the Ray won't fear your tank.

The patrol is next. Rest while you wait for it to patrol near your group. Use a ranged attack to pull the Coilfang Enchantresses and Champion. As before, CC the Champion until the softer targets are dealt with. The Enchantresses use area of effect attacks and should be kept away from as many party members as possible. If you have extra CC, keep one of the Enchantresses held while the party kills the other. Clean the mobs up one at a time and prepare to pull the Bogstrok on the bridge.

You've fought groups of Bogstrok before and these are no different. Use the same tactics of CC and focused firing that you used at the beginning of the instance.

Jumping Ahead

Many of the enemies within Slave Pens can be avoided. If your party is in need of practice, experience, or loot, take the time to clear any groups not mentioned here.

THE COILFANG STRONGHOLD

The Coilfang Defenders are fairly sturdy, but don't deal much damage unless you cast at them while they have a spell shield up. When the shield is up, all spells are reflected back at the caster. Stop casting when the shield goes up and kill the two annoyances.

Move into the passage and engage the two wander Coilfang Technicians. Have interrupts ready as the Technicians can cast AoE fire spells. These are channeled spells, so any interruption stops the rest of the spell.

Once the Scale-Healer is dead, turn your focus to the Coilfang Ray. Renew the CC on the Champions as needed. If either breaks free, an off-tank or pet should grab them and keep them away from the party. This ensures they can't fear everyone. Kill the Observer next and the Champions last.

To the right, Mennu the Betrayer paces up and down a ramp. There are groups of Coilfang Collaborators and Technicians at the bottom of the ramp. When Mennu is at the top of the ramp, pull the first group into the corridor. The Broken here are different. These have chosen to join forces with the Naga and will fight to the death. Deal with the Technician first while keeping the Collaborators CCd. The Collaborators enrage at low health, so keep your fire focused.

When they have been killed, rest to full Health and Mana and prepare to pull Mennu into the corridor. Mennu uses many of the same abilities Shamans do. He has a number of totems with various effects ranging from healing to AoE damage. Have a Hunter, or melee member (who isn't the tank) keep the totems destroyed during the fight.

Keep the tank's Health well above half as Mennu has a number of instant spells that can inflict a great bit of damage quickly. Hold your interrupts for his heals. When green energy surrounds his hands, use your interrupts. With his heals disabled and his totems destroyed, Mennu doesn't have much to rely on and won't survive your group's attack.

Remain at the bottom of the ramp and have your puller grab the group of two Coilfang Collaborators and one Technician. As before, CC the Collaborators until the Technician is dead. The Broken enrage at low Health, so be ready for the burst damage increase. Keep your tank's Health high and kill them one at a time to avoid two enraged enemies.

Ascend the ramp and be ready for another fight. A pair of Coilfang Technicians patrol along each bridge above. There are only two so the fights are fairly easy. Immediately rest after the first fight and prepare for the second. Though you only need to clear one bridge, clearing both will save you headache and a possible wipe ahead.

Follow a bridge to the center of the area and several more groups of enemies. Where the bridges connect, there is a group of two Coilfang Defenders and one Coilfang Collaborator.

Pull the fight to you as another group patrols on the other side of the walkway. CC the Defenders and kill the Collaborator first. With their spell shield, the Defenders take longer to kill while the Collaborator is less defensive.

Charge the next group now that the path is clear. The Coilfang Technician is flanked by two Coilfang Collaborators. CC the Collaborators first and kill the Technician. Have interrupts ready to keep it from using its Rain of Fire. Once the Coilfang is dead, focus on the kill the Collaborators one at a time.

Both of the bridges have been destroyed and there is no way to proceed except jumping into the water below. It's deep enough that you won't take damage from the fall. Do not jump toward the ledges below. Jump toward the center of the water instead.

Keep most of your party in the water and have your highest level member creep onto the broken portion of wall. There are three patrols nearby; one on each side and one on the ramp ahead. When all three are away, signal the party to ascend the broken wall and climb onto the wall to the left. Follow the wall as far as you can and wait. This gives the entire party a chance to see the Coilfang Enchantress and two Coilfang Technicians patrolling below. Decide CC and attack order before dropping down and engaging the enemy group.

The Enchantress is a high priority target. She can deal decent damage and turn your party members against you. Keep her spells interrupted and destroy her quickly while keeping the Technicians CCd. Once the Enchantress is dead, kill the Technicians one at a time and look around. There is a passage to the left, but you need to get to the top of the ramp before taking it.

One Coilfang Technician and two Collaborators patrol the ramp. When your party is ready, pull them into the passage. Breaking line of sight forces the enemy to come to you and keeps them from getting help from the other patrol. CC the Collaborators and kill the Technician first. Watch the last patrol and make your way up the ramp when it's clear.

Weeder Greenthumb isn't in the best shape, but now you know. Examine the body if you have the quest. With one Druid found, it's time to exit the Naga Stronghold and head into the deepest part of the dungeon. Take the passage out. Only two Coilfang Champions are guarding it.

Keep in mind the fear Coilfang Champions use when you engage them. CC one and kill the other to keep them from fearing your entire group for long periods. When both enemies are dead, rest to full Health and Mana while you look around.

THE DEEPER TUNNELS

Don't get too used to the expansive cavern. You'll be back in cramped quarters soon. For now, there is a group of four Bogstrok that need to be killed. This is a simple and straight forward fight. CC as many as you can and kill them one at a time. Avoid using AoE attacks as your tank may not be able to keep the entire group from eating your casters.

Another fight that will truly test your party's CC and focus fire capability is ahead. A Coilfang Tempest, a Scale-Healer, an Observer, and a Ray stand guard near the center of the area. As before, the Scale-Healer should be your first target. CC as many of the others as you can starting with the Tempest.

Keep the fight away from as many party members as possible. The Scale-Healer uses Holy Nova and the Ray uses Psychic Horror. These abilities can make a fight very chaotic. Once the Scale-Healer is dead, turn to the Ray and destroy it. Kill the Observer and Tempest last.

When the bodies of your enemies litter the floor around you, rest to full Health and Mana before engaging Rokmar.

A Cold Reception

Rokmar is physically impressive. He deals high physical damage and has high Health. He also casts spells that can't be interrupted! He has a powerful bleed attack that can only be removed by healing the afflicted to 90% or better.

He uses a Water Spit. This Frost attack hits your entire party for moderate damage. Consider using any Frost Resistant abilities or gear you have and keep your member's Health high during the engagement.

Rokmar doesn't have any abilities that incapacitate your tank, so aggro shouldn't be a problem. Give the tank a few seconds to build aggro, and then start doing damage. Keep Entangling Roots dispelled from your tank. It doesn't CC your tank, but makes it more difficult to hold aggro.

Rokmar's Water Spit isn't a cone effect. It doesn't matter which way Rokmar is facing. As long as you are within range and line of sight, you will get hit by this. Be ready to use Potions, Bandages, or Healthstones if your healer falls behind. He or she will have enough work to do just keeping the tank alive against this giant crustacean.

This fight will give your healer a taste of what's in store. Use more Mana-efficient heals on the tank when he or she needs it. Cast faster heals on each party member after a Water Spit. It's important to get the weakest party members first as Rokmar will occasionally cast a second volley quickly after the first. Rokmar's Grievous Wounds ability is also one to pay attention to. It causes a bleed effect of 685-815 until the target is healed.

When the Clacker falls, resurrect the fallen, collect your loot and continue your journey. The next group of Naga is similar to the previous; one Coilfang Scale-Healer, one Observer, one Ray, and two Tempests.

Wait for the two patrolling Coilfang Defenders to move away before using a ranged attack to pull the larger group. As before, CC the Tempests and focus all fire on the Scale-Healer. If you are short on CC, have an off-tank or pet hold the two Tempests away from the party. When the Scale-Healer falls, engage the Ray and Observer. Leave the Tempests for last and kill them one at a time.

Engage the Defenders when they patrol back toward you. There are only two and you've fought them before. Keep your fire focuses and eliminate the Naga. The group on the left side of the ramp is your next target.

Two Coilfang Champions stand with an Enchantress and a Soothsayer. CC the Champions to keep them from fearing your group around and kill the casters first. Pull the fight back if the Champions break CC as you don't want to be feared into the next group.

Another large group stands on the right side of the ramp. Two Coilfang Tempests, an Observer, a Ray, and a Scale-Healer comprise the group. Start the fight by CCing as many Naga as possible. The Tempests make great CC targets followed by the Observer and the Ray. Kill the Scale-Healer first as it can draw the fight out significantly. If you are short on CC, have a pet or off-tank hold the two Tempests away from the party while you kill the first three. When the enemies are dead, rest while waiting for the patrol to come to the top of the ramp.

When the two Coilfang Champions, one Soothsayer, and one Enchantress stop at the top of the ramp, pull them. As before, CC the Champions and kill the casters first. This fight is marginally safer than the previous, but don't relax too much.

With the patrol dead, the passage is much safer for a short while. Ahead are two pair of Wastewalkers. Ignore these entirely as they will not attack unless you strike first.

There are four Bogstrok in the group ahead and all look very similar. When you begin the fight, pull the non-CC'd enemies away from the CC'd enemies. This keeps focusing fire simple and avoids accidentally breaking CC with AoE abilities. Use this same tactic on the next group of three Bogstrok.

Take a moment to rest. You want full Health and Mana for the next fight. Two Coilfang Defenders and two Coilfang Observers guard a cage. The Defenders take a lot of punishment before going down, so CC these first. Have an off-tank or pet hold the second Observer while the party kills the first. Use interrupts to keep the damage your party takes to a minimum. Kill the second Observer once the first is dead. Finish the fight by killing the Defenders one at a time. *Do not* let anyone speak with the Naturalist Bite in the cage until the party has a chance to rest.

Once again, take a moment to rest to full Health and Mana. Speak with the Druid when your party is ready. This triggers a fight against a Coilfang Enchantress, a Soothsayer and a Champion.

As the enemy forces you into combat, out of combat CC isn't an option. CC the Champion immediately as it can use its AoE fear to disrupt your party. With the Champion dealt with for now, CC the Soothsayer or have someone with interrupts keep it from casting. Focus all your fire on the Enchantress. It's very important to keep it from casting as they can turn your party members against you!

Focus all your DPS on the Enchantress and then the Soothsayer. Keep the Champion CC'd until both casters are dead. Once he is alone, kill the Champion and rest for the fight against Quagmirran.

A Sticky Situation

Quagmirran is a mountain of mold that submerges itself in slime. Perhaps it's no wonder that his most damaging attacks are Nature-based.

Several times during the fight, Quagmirran uses an AoE Poison Bolt. This does significant Nature damage immediately and even more Nature damage over time. Be ready to use Cure Poison, Abolish Poison, or Poison Cleansing Totem to counter this. He also has a severe acid spit attack that harms those in front of him.

Equipping items and trinkets that increase your Nature Resistance is highly recommended. Abilities such as Nature Resist Totem and Aspect of the Wild make the fight much easier.

Once the Naga ambush is dealt with, Quagmirran comes out of the water at the end of the tunnel. This keeps you from having to engage him while holding your breath. Send your tank in and blast away. Use your highest damage attacks and any trinkets that increase your damage output.

This entire fight is a race. Quagmirran hits very hard and uses Cleave. Any melee DPS should stand behind Quagmirran or risk taking damage very quickly. As the tank will have priority for heals, have potions and Health-stones (if you have a Warlock) ready. Quagmirran's final two abilities are Uppercut and Acid Geyser. His Uppercut damages the target and has a knock back and the Acid Geyser is a channeled ability which rains poison on nearby targets and inflicts nature damage the entire time.

There are no fights after Quagmirran. If you've been holding any timed abilities or trinkets for a rainy day, now's the time to use them. With Quagmirran's damage output, your healer *will* run out of Mana. Kill Quagmirran as quickly as possible. If your tank or healer goes down, keep blasting away. The only way to win the fight is for Quagmirran to die.

With the hulking mass of Quagmirran decaying, resurrect the fallen, collect your loot and make your way out of the instance. If you want to walk out, follow the tunnel back to Rokmar's room and jump into the water on the left. There is a ramp across the water that leads you to the front of the dungeon.

UNDERBOG

DUNGEON INFORMATION

Name:	Underbog
Location:	Zangarmarsh
Faction:	Both
Suggested Levels:	62-65 (group of 5)
Primary Enemies:	Humanoids, Elementals
Damage Types:	Physical, Nature
Time to Complete:	2-3 Hours

WHO TO BRING

Every class has something to do in the Underbog. In fact, most classes have several things to do.

Bite-sized Pieces

The size and level deviance of Coilfang Reservoir is immense. To make the instance friendlier, it's been broken into several wings. This allows groups with more time to run it several times in an evening, or groups with less time to still run it.

Jobs

Class	Abilities
Druid	Healing, Backup Tanking, DPS, Abolish Disease
Hunter	Ranged DPS, Backup Tanking (Pet), In-combat CC (Freezing Trap), Aspect of the Wild
Mage	Ranged DPS, Burst DPS, In-combat CC (Polymorph)
Paladin	Healing, Tanking, Mana Recovery, Cleanse
Priest	Healing, In-combat CC (Mind Control)
Rogue	DPS, Burst DPS, Out-of-combat CC (Sap), In-combat CC (Blind), Stuns
Shaman	Healing, Nature Resistance Totem, Poison Cleansing Totem, Wipe Protection
Warlock	Ranged DPS, In-combat CC (Succubus, Banish), Wipe Protection
Warrior	Tanking, DPS

GETTING TO UNDERBOG

Underbog is one of the many wings of Coilfang Reservoir. Horde parties can fly into Zabra'jin while Alliance parties fly into Telredor.

At the center of Serpent Lake is the Coilfang Reservoir. Dive beneath the water at the center of the pumping station and look for the drain. Swim through the drain and surface within the Reservoir. Underbog is the eastern most instance portal.

THE ENEMY GARRISON

Bog Giant	63 Elite
Notes: Enrage, Fungal Decay (Disease. Nature damage every 3 seconds. Movement speed reduced by 40%)	
Claw	65 Elite Boss
Notes: Echoing Roar (Reduces nearby targets armor by 75% for 20 sec.), Maul	
Fen Ray	64 Elite
Notes: Horror	
Ghaz'an	65 Elite Boss
Notes: Tail Sweep (Damage and knock back), Acid Spit (AoE frontal cone poison attack)	
Hungarfen	65 Elite Boss
Notes: Foul Spores (Drains health from nearby targets while Hungarfen channels)	
Lykul Stinger	64 Elite
Notes: Frenzy	
Lykul Wasp	63-64 Elite
Notes: Ranged poison attack	
Murkblood Healer	64 Elite
Notes: Healer	
Murkblood Oracle	63-64 Elite
Notes: Fireball	
Murkblood Tribesman	63-64 Elite
Notes: Enrages	
Swamplord Musel'ek	65 Elite Boss
Notes: Multishot, Freeze trap, Raptor Strike, Deterrence	
The Black Stalker	65 Elite Boss
Notes: Chain lightning, Static Charge, Levitate, Suspend	
Underbat	62-63 Elite
Notes: Knockdown	
Underbog Frenzy	63-64 Elite
Notes: Aquatic	
Underbog Lord	64 Elite
Notes: Fungal Rot	
Underbog Lurker	62 Elite
Notes: Fungal Decay (Disease. Nature damage every 3 seconds. Movement speed reduced by 40%)	
Underbog Shambler	62-63 Elite
Notes: Fungal Decay (Disease. Nature damage every 3 seconds. Movement speed reduced by 40%)	
Wrathfin Myrmidon	63-64 Elite
Notes: Coral Cut (Physical damage every 3 sec. for 15 sec.)	
Wrathfin Sentry	64 Elite
Notes: Stealth Detection	
Wrathfin Warrior	64 Elite
Notes: Enrages at low health, Heroic Strike, Shield Bash	

CLOGGING THE DRAINS

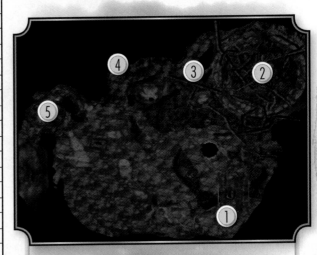

Map Legend	
1	Hungarfen
2	Ghaz'an
3	Earthbinder Rayge
4	Swamplord Musel'ek and Claw
5	The Black Stalker

CLIMBING THE RAMPS

You start in a tunnel with enemies patrolling nearby. The Underbats can be pulled singly or as a group. The first couple of fights are very easy. The Underbats have only a knockdown as a special ability. If your group includes a Warlock, use these to grab a couple easy Soul Shards.

The easy fights don't last long. As the passage opens into an immense cavern, a group of Underbog Lurkers and an Underbog Shambler patrol ahead. These creatures are immune to many forms of CC. Only Freezing Trap, Fear, and Banish are effective and using Fear with other enemies close by is begging for problems.

Use the raid symbols to designate which enemies to CC and what order to kill them in. This keeps your party from breaking CC and allow you to kill each enemy much quicker.

Sample Explanation		
Symbol	Designation	Attack Order
Skull	Tank & DPS	1
Blue Box	Freezing Trap	2
Moon	Banish	3

This example assumes three enemies and a group with both a Hunter and a Warlock. Your group will be different so take the time to get comfortable with the raid symbols. Time spent now will more than make up for itself by the end of the instance.

Follow the wall to the left as you move ahead. To the right is a group very similar in makeup to the previous fight. If your party had trouble with the previous fight, pull the group to the right for a little more practice before you get to the tougher opponents.

Pull the group of three Underbats ahead. While only having a knockdown and not doing much damage, having three of the Underbats on your tank can be very frustrating. A tank that is knocked down can't hold aggro, so use Polymorph or Freezing Trap to CC what you can. If you are short on CC, use other Warriors, Paladins, Hunter Pets, or Warlock Pets to hold aggro from the other Underbats until the first is dead.

Using off-tanks increases the damage the party takes over all, but having a tank that is unable to hold aggro because he or she is constantly knocked down is even worse. Kill the Underbats one at a time.

Near the water and to the left is a group of three Underbog Lurkers. Pull and CC these just as you did earlier. If you are short on CC, have your tank hold all the active enemies and bring them down one at a time. Don't use AoE's unless your tank feels comfortable holding aggro against an AoE.

With the path clear, move to the edge of the water. Don't enter the water as Underbog Frenzies are waiting for a taste of your flesh. Watch the patrolling Underbats and Bog Giant. Pull the Bog Giant when the Underbats are away. The Bog Giant hits fairly hard and can disease your party members. Have abilities to cure disease ready and kill the Giant.

The patrolling Underbats are your next target. Pull them to you and kill them one at a time. Remember that they have a knockdown and the tank has a harder time holding aggro. Focusing your fire makes the tank's job much easier.

Follow the waterline until you get to the ramp. Underbog Lurkers and Shamblers guard the bottom of the ramp while several enemies patrol the length of the ramp. When the patrols are away, pull the Underbogs to you and destroy them one at a time. Avoid falling into the water nearby as the Underbog Frenzies are still looking to take a nibble out of you.

Wait for the patrollers to come down the ramp before you pull them. Take the Bog Giant first. Keep your tank's Health high as the Giant can inflict some troubling hits and you don't want to lose your tank due to an untimely critical.

Pull the group of Underbats next. You've fought them before so use the techniques that have worked for you. CC them if you have the classes to do so. Use off-tanks if you don't have the abilities to CC them. Ascend the ramp when the way is clear.

Once Hungarfen throws the vines away and comes at you again, finish the awful creature. Collect the **Underspore Frond** nearby if you have the quest for it. Rest at the next bridge and prepare for the pulls to resume.

A group of four Underbats patrols on the next rise. Pull them across the bridge when the patrolling Bog Giant is away. As all of the Underbats can knock your tank down, be very careful to focus fire. The tank won't be able to run around gathering loose aggro. Polymorph, Hibernate, and Freezing Trap and work against the Underbats. As you're pulling them across the bridge, Fear is a relatively safe option as well.

Two Bog Giants stand in front of Hungarfen. The good news is that these two can be pulled before you engage Hungarfen. The bad news is that you will get both and neither is vulnerable to many forms of CC. If you have a Hunter, use Freezing Trap for one while the party focuses on the other. Using an off-tank for the second Bog Giant is also feasible.

Keep your damage focused on one Giant at a time. Their high Health means they won't go down fast and your healer will run out of Mana keeping two tanks at high Health. When both Giants are dead, rest to full Mana and Health. Hungarfen will the first true test of your party.

All Mucked Up

This is one of the 'wipe' fights for players new to the instance. The run from the graveyard is short so don't despair and don't destroy a group by blaming the wipe on a specific person. Examine what you could have done better and note it for future runs as you make your way back to the instance.

Hungarfen has immense Health and does incredible physical damage. These aspects alone are major trouble but they are not the true power of this beast. Throughout much of the fight, Hungarfen drops mushrooms on the group. These will increase in size until they pop and infect any party members near them with Spore Cloud that deals 360 to 450 damage every 2 sec. for 20 sec..

That means this has to be a moving battle. Everyone in the party must be constant aware of their surrounds and move away from any mushrooms growing near them. Keeping Hungarfen's attention on the tank won't be difficult as long as the tank is kept alive.

When Hungarfen reaches 10% Health, he casts Fungal Spores. It drains health from all nearby targets and heals Hungarfen for a few seconds. To negate this ability, run away until he stops using the ability and resumes combat as before. Take this time to heal the party up to full and be ready for when Hungarfen reengages.

When the Underbats are dead, pull the Bog Giant. Being alone, he won't pose any significant threat. Keep your tank's health high and the enemy away from the softer party members and you'll be fine. Repeat this several times as you move across the bridge and left around the pillar.

Watch for the Sanquine Hibiscus as you move. They are groundspawns and quest items. There are only two more Bog Giants before the enemies greatly change. Pull the final Bog Giant when the Wrathfin Myrmidons are at the top of the ramp to avoid a much larger engagement.

THE TANK

With the Bog Giant out of the way, move your party to the bottom of the ramp and against the wall. The enemies in this section are primarily humanoid. Polymorph, Mind Control, Seduce, Sap, and Freezing Trap are all valid forms of CC.

When the two wandering Wrathfin Myrmidons are at the bottom of the ramp, pull them. This engages only the two and leaves the Naga at the top of the ramp for next pull. The Myrmidons are melee enemies and will engage your tank directly. Kill them one at a time, but don't move up the ramp yet.

Have your puller move to the top of the ramp and watch for the patrol in the corridor ahead. When you see the patrol move away from the doorway, pull the two Wrathfin Sentries to the bottom of the ramp. Don't CC them until they get to the ramp as the patrol can add if it encounters a CC'd target.

Ascend the bridge and prepare for a much larger fight. Wait for the patrol to move away again before pulling the group to the right, just inside the doorway. There are four enemies in this group so CC and raid symbols will make your lives much easier.

Murkblood Healers are Too Good to Live

The Murkblood Healers are very powerful. They have both a single target heal and an AoE heal that is far more powerful than anything you have access to. They are so powerful that your entire attack plan hinges upon how to deal with them.

If you have a Priest, use Mind Control. You can either let the other enemies kill the Healer for you, or use the Healer to keep your party alive while the other enemies are dispatched.

If you do not have a Priest in your party, kill the Murkblood Healer first. Do not attempt any other form of CC. If the CC is broken early, the Healer can restore the Health of all other enemies very quickly.

The group consists of two Murkblood Spearmen, one Murkblood Healer, and one Wrathfin Warrior. Use the wall to break line of sight and force the enemies to come out of the corridor. Allow them to join you on the platform before you CC any. This is important as you don't want the patrol to join the fight.

CC the Spearmen and deal with the Healer and Warrior first. Once the Healer and Warrior are dead (or controlled), kill the Spearmen one at a time and watch the patrol again. As the patrol moves down the corridor, pull the group just inside and to the left of the doorway.

There are only three enemies in this group; one Murkblood Healer and two Murkblood Spearmen. Deal with this group much the same way you did with the previous group. CC the Spearmen as they join you on the platform and deal with the Healer first. When the Healer is taken care of, kill the Spearmen one at a time. Pull the patrol next time you see it.

Kill the Myrmidons and move your party into the corridor and to the right. This is a dead end, but gives you a better view of the next few pulls. The hallway continues west and there are several groups of enemies along the walls.

Rest up and prepare for the next couple fights. Wait for the larger patrol to move away before pulling the group of three. One is a Murkblood Oracle and casts at you from range. Use a ranged interrupt or duck out the door to force it to close with you. If you leave it at range, the patrol will add and overwhelm your party.

Deal with the Healer first, then the Oracle, then the Tribesman. This drops the enemies very quickly and opens your party to the least amount of damage. Grab the patrol as it comes back your direction. As the group is very large, CC will be important.

The Murkblood Healer must be dealt with first. CC the Murkblood Tribesman and Spearman. The Wrathfin Warrior can be CC'd until the Healer is dead if you have extra CC. Kill the Warrior, then the Spearman, and finally the Tribesman. Avoid using Fear as there are many enemies close by.

When the group is dead, move down the hall to the bottom of the ramp. Rest here while your puller ascends the ramp to get the next group. There are four enemies in this group just as there were in the last. Deal with them in the same fashion.

Move up the ramp and take a moment to look around. Groups of Naga stand along the path to the right and Ghaz'an swims in the water below.

Pull the groups along the walkway to the right one at a time. You've fought them all before and ducking down the stairs will force them to close with you. This keeps them well away from the other groups and avoids potential wipe situations.

Deal with the Healers first, then the casters, then the melee enemies to kill as quickly as possible. Watch the center of the room as you kill the groups. Ghaz'an climbs the pipes and perches atop the central platform.

Charge Ghaz'an and immediately face it away from the party; non-tank members should remain on Ghaz'an's flank and not stand right behind him to avoid the Tail Sweep!. It has a cone effect poison attack. If only the tank is in front of it, only the tank gets hit. Ghaz'an is fairly simple if you keep it facing away from the party. Its melee hits aren't terrible and its Health isn't as high as Hungarfen's. Party members behind Ghaz'an should avoid being too close to the edge as Ghaz'an's tail has a knockback effect.

When the water is calm again, jump out of the hole in the northern side of the tank. Make sure you have at least half your Health before jumping as it's embarrassing to die when no enemies are in sight. Recover from the fall before continuing.

The Druids and Getting Out

Follow the tunnel until it forks. On the left path is Earthbinder Rayge. Speak with him briefly for **Lost in Action** before moving your party back to the fork. Only the puller should descend down the right path for now. The next two pulls have three Fen Rays in each.

Hold your party at the bottom of the ramp and send your puller forward. There is another group of Fen Rays that needs to be pulled back. Destroy these as you have the others but don't move forward yet. Once again, send your puller ahead.

Bring the group of two Fen Rays and one Lykul Wasp back to the group. Kill the Rays first as they interfere with standard group procedure by fearing your members around. Once the Rays are dealt with, kill the Wasp.

Each Fen Ray has an AoE Horror effect. It lasts only a couple seconds, but cannot be broken and they can use it several times in the fight. Focus fire and destroy the Rays one at a time. The fight can be fairly chaotic, but keep your cool and maintain aggro on the tank to get through it.

Pull the Fen Rays all the way back up the ramp to the group. As they have a horror ability, you don't want them sending a party member into another group. This extra room gives you more CC options against the Fen Rays. While Hibernate, Polymorph, and Freezing Trap would be the standard options against them, Fear and Scare Beast are safe to use with the added room.

CC as many as you can to keep the fight from becoming a nightmare and kill them one at a time. When the first group is dead, grab the second. The party should remain at the fork until both Fen Ray groups have been dispatched.

A group of two Fen Rays is next. It's a smaller group, so you can handle it without worry if you've gotten this far. Once this group is dead, move forward until you can see the last group of Fen Rays.

Two Fen Rays and a Lykul Wasp hover just before a boss encounter. Pull the fight well back as you don't want to be feared into either of the bosses or the patrolling Bog Giant. As before, kill the Rays first and the Wasp last.

Have your party rest while your puller hugs the left wall. Do not engage Swamplord Musel'ek or Claw yet. A Bog Giant patrols on the left and will make the boss fight much more difficult if it's allowed to join. Wait for it to patrol close to you and pull it back to the group. Kill it as you have in the past and rest to full in preparation of the next encounter.

Move your group to the bottom of the ramp and engage the flying bugs. One Lykul Wasp and two Lykul Stingers make up the group. Destroy the Wasp first as its ranged poison attack can make the life of a caster very difficult. Be ready to use a shield or throw heals a bit faster when the Stingers glow red. This signals their Frenzy and the increase in attack speed and overall damage. Keep a close eye on your tank's Health during this.

Musel'ek and Claw attack as a pair and are both immune to CC. Both do incredible damage and Claw has immense Health. This means that Musel'ek needs to die first. If you have an off-tank as well as your primary tank, have the off-tank hold Claw. The primary tank will need to hold Musel'ek as he hits pretty hard. Voidwalkers and Hunter Pets can off-tank Claw if you need, but Druids, Warriors, and Paladins are better suited for it.

172

Use your most powerful attacks to bring Musel'ek down quickly, but don't use abilities that have substantial timers as there is a more difficult encounter shortly. Your healer will be strained at the start of the fight keeping two tanks alive. Casters shouldn't worry about conserving Mana in the beginning. Blow everything your have to kill Musel'ek.

Once Musel'ek is dead, the fight gets much simpler. Keep you tank above half Health in case Claw gets a couple critical strikes in a row. Lay into him with everything you have left. When Claw is defeated, he reverts to become Windcaller Claw. Speak with him before continuing

Move along the path to the south. An Underbog Lord stands guard over the way forward. While not a full boss, the Underbog Lord is pretty nasty. He can instantly stack five Fungal Rots on a target, so keep him looking at the same target as much as possible. Bring the Lord down as quickly as you can without using your timed abilities. Once again, rest to full Health.

When you see the bodies of the Fen Rays littering the floor, you're close. Around the corner, the passage opens into a large room. Engage the Black Stalker when you party is ready.

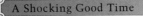

The Black Stalker uses a multitude of lightning-based attacks. While it isn't as pertinent for the casters of the group to have high Nature Resistance, it's quite useful for the tank.

Consider using items, potions, and abilities to increase your party's Nature Resistance with special attention to your tank as he or she is likely to get hit with many of the attacks. Nature Resistance Totem and Aspect of the Wild are both very potent.

Spread your ranged attackers about the room so none are close to each other, but all are in healing range. The tank should hold the Stalker at the southern portion to the room. Dismiss any pets as they are a liability to your survival.

The Black Stalker doesn't have as much Health as Hungarfen did, but it is far more damaging. It deals physical damage and has Chain Lightning (instant multiple target Nature damage), and Static Charge (debuff that damages all party members near the afflicted). As the Chain Lightning can bounce from your tank, to a pet, back to your tank, it's important that no pets join the tank in melee.

Keeping your party spread out will reduce the damage done by Static Field. This debuff can not by dispelled, so reducing the damage is the best you can do. The Black Stalker can also throw members into the air and hold them there. This is devastating to melee characters, but casters can still use spells when held in the air. Don't panic and keep being as useful as possible. If a healer is pulled into the air make sure the tank moves into healing range. Melee party members should switch to a ranged weapon until they fall back to the ground.

As soon as the fight starts, use all your timed abilities. This is the final fight of the dungeon and The Black Stalker is quite lethal. There is little rhyme or reason to which attack it uses when. Positioning is the best defense you have so blast away with everything in your arsenal.

When the smoldering corpse of the Stalker falls, take its head if you have the quest. Resurrect any members who fell and take the path further to leave the dungeon.

CRAFTING AND SKILL ITEMS

Alchemy

Created Item	Skill Lvl	Source	Reagent(s)
Minor Healing Potion	N/A	Special	1 Peacebloom, 1 Silverleaf, 1 Empty Vial
Elixir of Lion's Strength	N/A	Special	1 Earthroot, 1 Silverleaf, 1 Empty Vial
Elixir of Minor Defense	N/A	Special	2 Silverleaf, 1 Empty Vial
Weak Troll's Blood Potion	15	Trained	1 Peacebloom, 2 Earthroot, 1 Empty Vial
Minor Mana Potion	25	Trained	1 Mageroyal, 1 Silverleaf, 1 Empty Vial
Minor Rejuvenation Potion	40	Trained	2 Mageroyal, 1 Peacebloom, 1 Empty Vial
Elixir of Minor Fortitude	50	Trained	2 Earthroot, 1 Peacebloom, 1 Empty Vial
Elixir of Minor Agility	50	Found	1 Swiftthistle, 1 Silverleaf, 1 Empty Vial
Discolored Healing Potion	50	Found	1 Discolored Worg Heart, 1 Peacebloom, 1 Empty Vial
Lesser Healing Potion	55	Trained	1 Minor Healing Potion, 1 Briarthorn
Swiftness Potion	60	Found	1 Swiftthistle, 1 Briarthorn, 1 Empty Vial
Rage Potion	60	Found	1 Sharp Claw, 1 Briarthorn, 1 Empty Vial
Elixir of Tongues	70	Found	2 Earthroot, 2 Mageroyal, 1 Empty Vial
Blackmouth Oil	80	Trained	2 Oily Blackmouth, 1 Empty Vial
Elixir of Wisdom	90	Trained	1 Mageroyal, 2 Briarthorn, 1 Empty Vial
Elixir of Water Breathing	90	Trained	1 Stranglekelp, 2 Blackmouth Oil, 1 Empty Vial
Elixir of Giant Growth	90	Found	1 Deviate Fish, 1 Earthroot, 1 Empty Vial
Holy Protection Potion	100	Found	1 Bruiseweed, 1 Swiftthistle, 1 Empty Vial
Swim Speed Potion	100	Trained	1 Swiftthistle, 1 Blackmouth Oil, 1 Empty Vial
Minor Magic Resistance Potion	110	Found	3 Mageroyal, 1 Wild Steelbloom, 1 Empty Vial
Healing Potion	110	Trained	1 Bruiseweed, 1 Briarthorn, 1 Leaded Vial
Lesser Mana Potion	120	Trained	1 Mageroyal, 1 Stranglekelp, 1 Empty Vial
Elixir of Poison Resistance	120	Found	1 Large Venom Sac, 1 Bruiseweed, 1 Leaded Vial
Strong Troll's Blood Potion	125	Trained	2 Bruiseweed, 2 Briarthorn, 1 Leaded Vial
Cowardly Flight Potion	125	Found	1 Delicate Feather, 1 Kingsblood, 1 Leaded Vial
Elixir of Defense	130	Trained	1 Wild Steelbloom, 1 Stranglekelp, 1 Leaded Vial
Fire Oil	130	Trained	2 Firefin Snapper, 1 Empty Vial
Shadow Protection Potion	135	Found	1 Grave Moss, 1 Kingsblood, 1 Leaded Vial

Alchemy

Created Item	Skill Lvl	Source	Reagent(s)
Elixir of Lesser Agility	140	Found	1 Wild Steelbloom, 1 Swiftthistle, 1 Leaded Vial
Elixir of Firepower	140	Trained	2 Fire Oil, 1 Kingsblood, 1 Leaded Vial
Elixir of Ogre's Strength	150	Found	1 Earthroot, 1 Kingsblood, 1 Leaded Vial
Free Action Potion	150	Found	2 Blackmouth Oil, 1 Stranglekelp, 1 Leaded Vial
Greater Healing Potion	155	Trained	1 Liferoot, 1 Kingsblood, 1 Leaded Vial
Mana Potion	160	Trained	1 Stranglekelp, 1 Kingsblood, 1 Leaded Vial
Lesser Invisibility Potion	165	Trained	1 Fadeleaf, 1 Wild Steelbloom, 1 Leaded Vial
Shadow Oil	165	Found	4 Fadeleaf, 4 Grave Moss, 1 Leaded Vial
Fire Protection Potion	165	Found	1 Small Flame Sac, 1 Fire Oil, 1 Leaded Vial
Elixir of Fortitude	175	Trained	1 Wild Steelbloom, 1 Goldthorn, 1 Leaded Vial
Great Rage Potion	175	Found	1 Large Fang, 1 Kingsblood, 1 Leaded Vial
Mighty Troll's Blood Potion	180	Found	1 Liferoot, 1 Bruiseweed, 1 Leaded Vial
Elixir of Agility	185	Trained	1 Stranglekelp, 1 Goldthorn, 1 Leaded Vial
Frost Protection Potion	190	Found	1 Wintersbite, 1 Goldthorn, 1 Leaded Vial
Nature Protection Potion	190	Found	1 Liferoot, 1 Stranglekelp, 1 Leaded Vial
Elixir of Frost Power	190	Found	2 Wintersbite, 1 Khadgar's Whisker, 1 Leaded Vial
Elixir of Detect Lesser Invisibility	195	Found	1 Khadgar's Whisker, 1 Fadeleaf, 1 Leaded Vial
Elixir of Greater Defense	195	Trained	1 Wild Steelbloom, 1 Goldthorn, 1 Leaded Vial
Frost Oil	200	Found	4 Khadgar's Whisker, 2 Wintersbite, 1 Leaded Vial
Catseye Elixir	200	Trained	1 Goldthorn, 1 Fadeleaf, 1 Leaded Vial
Oil of Immolation	205	Trained	1 Firebloom, 1 Goldthorn, 1 Crystal Vial
Greater Mana Potion	205	Trained	1 Khadgar's Whisker, 1 Goldthorn, 1 Leaded Vial
Magic Resistance Potion	210	Found	1 Khadgar's Whisker, 1 Purple Lotus, 1 Crystal Vial
Goblin Rocket Fuel	210	Found	1 Firebloom, 1 Volatile Rum, 1 Leaded Vial

Created Item	Skill Lvl	Source	Reagent(s)
Lesser Stoneshield Potion	215	Found	1 Mithril Ore, 1 Goldthorn, 1 Leaded Vial
Superior Healing Potion	215	Trained	1 Sungrass, 1 Khadgar's Whisker, 1 Crystal Vial
Elixir of Greater Water Breathing	215	Trained	1 Ichor of Undeath, 2 Purple Lotus, 1 Crystal Vial
Gurubashi Mojo Madness	300	Special	1 Blood of Heroes, 1 Massive Mojo, 6 Powerful Mojo, 1 Black Lotus
Wildvine Potion	225	Found	1 Wildvine, 1 Purple Lotus, 1 Crystal Vial
Philosopher's Stone	225	Found	4 Iron Bar, 1 Black Vitriol, 4 Purple Lotus, 4 Firebloom
Transmute: Iron to Gold	225	Found	1 Iron Bar
Transmute: Mithril to Truesilver	225	Found	1 Mithril Bar
Elixir of Detect Undead	230	Trained	1 Arthas' Tears, 1 Crystal Vial
Dreamless Sleep Potion	230	Trained	3 Purple Lotus, 1 Crystal Vial
Arcane Elixir	235	Trained	1 Blindweed, 1 Goldthorn, 1 Crystal Vial
Invisibility Potion	235	Found	1 Ghost Mushroom, 1 Sungrass, 1 Crystal Vial
Elixir of Greater Intellect	235	Trained	1 Blindweed, 1 Khadgar's Whisker, 1 Crystal Vial
Gift of Arthas	240	Found	1 Arthas' Tears, 1 Blindweed, 1 Crystal Vial
Elixir of Greater Agility	240	Trained	1 Sungrass, 1 Goldthorn, 1 Crystal Vial
Elixir of Dream Vision	240	Found	3 Purple Lotus, 1 Crystal Vial
Elixir of Giants	245	Found	1 Sungrass, 1 Gromsblood, 1 Crystal Vial
Ghost Dye	245	Found	2 Ghost Mushroom, 1 Purple Dye, 1 Crystal Vial
Elixir of Shadow Power	250	Found	3 Ghost Mushroom, 1 Crystal Vial
Elixir of Demonslaying	250	Found	1 Gromsblood, 1 Ghost Mushroom, 1 Crystal Vial
Elixir of Detect Demon	250	Trained	2 Gromsblood, 1 Crystal Vial
Stonescale Oil	250	Trained	1 Stonescale Eel, 1 Leaded Vial
Limited Invulnerability Potion	250	Found	2 Blindweed, 1 Ghost Mushroom, 1 Crystal Vial
Elixir of Greater Firepower	250	Found	3 Fire Oil, 3 Firebloom, 1 Crystal Vial
Mighty Rage Potion	255	Found	3 Gromsblood, 1 Crystal Vial
Superior Mana Potion	260	Found	2 Sungrass, 2 Blindweed, 1 Crystal Vial
Elixir of Superior Defense	265	Found	2 Stonescale Oil, 1 Sungrass, 1 Crystal Vial
Elixir of the Sages	270	Found	1 Dreamfoil, 2 Plaguebloom, 1 Crystal Vial
Transmute: Arcanite	275	Found	1 Thorium Bar, 1 Arcane Crystal
Major Healing Potion	275	Found	2 Golden Sansam, 1 Mountain Silversage, 1 Crystal Vial
Elixir of Brute Force	275	Found	2 Gromsblood, 2 Plaguebloom, 1 Crystal Vial
Transmute: Air to Fire	275	Found	1 Essence of Air
Transmute: Earth to Water	275	Found	1 Essence of Earth
Transmute: Earth to Life	275	Found	1 Essence of Earth
Transmute: Fire to Earth	275	Found	1 Essence of Fire

Created Item	Skill Lvl	Source	Reagent(s)
Transmute: Undeath to Water	275	Found	1 Essence of Undeath
Transmute: Water to Air	275	Found	1 Essence of Water
Transmute: Water to Undeath	275	Found	1 Essence of Water
Transmute: Life to Earth	275	Found	1 Living Essence
Mageblood Potion	275	Found	1 Dreamfoil, 2 Plaguebloom, 1 Crystal Vial
Greater Dreamless Sleep Potion	275	Found	2 Dreamfoil, 1 Golden Sansam, 1 Crystal Vial
Greater Stoneshield Potion	280	Found	3 Stonescale Oil, 1 Thorium Ore, 1 Crystal Vial
Elixir of the Mongoose	280	Found	2 Mountain Silversage, 2 Plaguebloom, 1 Crystal Vial
Purification Potion	285	Found	2 Icecap, 2 Plaguebloom, 1 Crystal Vial
Greater Arcane Elixir	285	Found	3 Dreamfoil, 1 Mountain Silversage, 1 Crystal Vial
Living Action Potion	285	Found	2 Icecap, 2 Mountain Silversage, 2 Heart of the Wild, 1 Crystal Vial
Greater Fire Protection Potion	290	Found	1 Elemental Fire, 1 Dreamfoil, 1 Crystal Vial
Greater Frost Protection Potion	290	Found	1 Elemental Water, 1 Dreamfoil, 1 Crystal Vial
Greater Nature Protection Potion	290	Found	1 Elemental Earth, 1 Dreamfoil, 1 Crystal Vial
Greater Arcane Protection Potion	290	Found	1 Dream Dust, 1 Dreamfoil, 1 Crystal Vial
Greater Shadow Protection Potion	290	Found	1 Shadow Oil, 1 Dreamfoil, 1 Crystal Vial
Major Troll's Blood Potion	290	Found	1 Gromsblood, 2 Plaguebloom, 1 Crystal Vial
Major Mana Potion	295	Found	3 Dreamfoil, 2 Icecap, 1 Crystal Vial
Flask of the Titans	300	Found	30 Gromsblood, 10 Stonescale Oil, 1 Black Lotus, 1 Crystal Vial
Flask of Distilled Wisdom	300	Found	30 Dreamfoil, 10 Icecap, 1 Black Lotus, 1 Crystal Vial
Flask of Supreme Power	300	Found	30 Dreamfoil, 10 Mountain Silversage, 1 Black Lotus, 1 Crystal Vial
Flask of Chromatic Resistance	300	Found	30 Icecap, 10 Mountain Silversage, 1 Black Lotus, 1 Crystal Vial
Major Rejuvenation Potion	300	Found	1 Heart of the Wild, 4 Golden Sansam, 4 Dreamfoil, 1 Imbued Vial
Transmute: Elemental Fire	300	Found	1 Heart of Fire
Volatile Healing Potion	300	Trained	1 Golden Sansam, 1 Felweed, 1 Imbued Vial
Onslaught Elixir	300	Trained	1 Mountain Silversage, 1 Felweed, 1 Imbued Vial
Adept's Elixir	300	Trained	1 Dreamfoil, 1 Felweed, 1 Imbued Vial
Elixir of Camouflage	305	Found	1 Ragveil, 1 Felweed, 1 Imbued Vial

Created Item	Skill Lvl	Source	Reagent(s)
Elixir of Major Strength	305	Trained	1 Mountain Silversage, 1 Felweed, 1 Imbued Vial
Elixir of Healing Power	310	Trained	1 Golden Sansam, 1 Dreaming Glory, 1 Imbued Vial
Unstable Mana Potion	310	Trained	2 Ragveil, 1 Felweed, 1 Imbued Vial
Sneaking Potion	315	Found	2 Ragveil, 1 Felweed, 1 Imbued Vial
Elixir of Mastery	315	Trained	3 Terocone, 1 Felweed, 1 Imbued Vial
Elixir of Major Frost Power	320	Found	2 Mote of Water, 1 Ancient Lichen, 1 Imbued Vial
Insane Strength Potion	320	Found	3 Terocone, 1 Imbued Vial
Elixir of the Searching Eye	325	Found	2 Ragveil, 1 Terocone, 1 Imbued Vial
Super Healing Potion	325	Trained	2 Dreaming Glory, 1 Felweed, 1 Imbued Vial
Mercurial Stone	325	Trained	1 Primal Earth, 1 Primal Life, 1 Primal Mana
Elixir of Major Agility	330	Found	1 Terocone, 2 Felweed, 1 Imbued Vial
Shrouding Potion	335	Found	3 Ragveil, 1 Netherbloom, 1 Imbued Vial
Fel Strength Elixir	335	Found	2 Terocone, 2 Nightmare Vine, 1 Imbued Vial
Super Mana Potion	340	Found	2 Netherbloom, 1 Felweed, 1 Imbued Vial
Elixir of Major Firepower	345	Found	3 Mote of Fire, 1 Ancient Lichen, 1 Imbued Vial
Elixir of Major Defense	345	Found	3 Ancient Lichen, 1 Terocone, 1 Imbued Vial
Fel Regeneration Potion	345	Found	2 Felweed, 3 Nightmare Vine, 1 Imbued Vial
Alchemist's Stone	350	Found	1 Philosopher's Stone, 1 Earthstorm Diamond, 1 Skyfire Diamond, 2 Fel Lotus, 5 Primal Might
Elixir of Major Shadow Power	350	Found	1 Ancient Lichen, 1 Nightmare Vine, 1 Imbued Vial
Major Dreamless Sleep Potion	350	Found	1 Dreaming Glory, 1 Nightmare Vine, 1 Imbued Vial
Heroic Potion	350	Found	2 Terocone, 1 Ancient Lichen, 1 Imbued Vial
Haste Potion	350	Found	2 Terocone, 1 Netherbloom, 1 Imbued Vial
Destruction Potion	350	Found	2 Nightmare Vine, 1 Netherbloom, 1 Imbued Vial
Transmute: Primal Air to Fire	350	Found	1 Primal Air
Transmute: Primal Earth to Water	350	Found	1 Primal Earth
Transmute: Primal Fire to Earth	350	Found	1 Primal Fire
Transmute: Primal Water to Air	350	Found	1 Primal Water
Transmute: Primal Might	350	Found	1 Primal Earth, 1 Primal Water, 1 Primal Air, 1 Primal Fire, 1 Primal Mana

Created Item	Skill Lvl	Source	Reagent(s)
Transmute: Earthstorm Diamond	350	Found	3 Deep Peridot, 3 Shadow Draenite, 3 Golden Draenite, 2 Primal Earth, 2 Primal Water
Transmute: Skyfire Diamond	350	Found	3 Blood Garnet, 3 Flame Spessarite, 3 Azure Moonstone, 2 Primal Fire, 2 Primal Air
Elixir of Major Mageblood	355	Found	1 Ancient Lichen, 1 Netherbloom, 1 Imbued Vial
Major Arcane Protection Potion	360	Found	1 Primal Mana, 1 Mana Thistle, 1 Imbued Vial
Major Fire Protection Potion	360	Found	1 Primal Fire, 1 Mana Thistle, 1 Imbued Vial
Major Frost Protection Potion	360	Found	1 Primal Water, 1 Mana Thistle, 1 Imbued Vial
Major Holy Protection Potion	360	Found	1 Primal Life, 1 Primal Water, 1 Imbued Vial
Major Nature Protection Potion	360	Found	1 Primal Life, 1 Mana Thistle, 1 Imbued Vial
Major Shadow Protection Potion	360	Found	1 Primal Shadow, 1 Mana Thistle, 1 Imbued Vial
Fel Mana Potion	360	Found	1 Mana Thistle, 2 Nightmare Vine, 1 Imbued Vial
Elixir of Empowerment	365	Found	1 Netherbloom, 1 Mana Thistle, 1 Imbued Vial
Ironshield Potion	365	Found	2 Ancient Lichen, 1 Primal Earth, 1 Imbued Vial
Transmute: Primal Earth to Life	N/A	Special	1 Primal Earth
Transmute: Primal Fire to Mana	N/A	Special	1 Primal Fire
Transmute: Primal Life to Earth	N/A	Special	1 Primal Life
Transmute: Primal Mana to Fire	N/A	Special	1 Primal Mana
Transmute: Primal Shadow to Water	N/A	Special	1 Primal Shadow
Transmute: Primal Water to Shadow	N/A	Special	1 Primal Water
Super Rejuvination Potion	N/A	Special	2 Mana Thistle, 1 Dreaming Glory, 1 Netherbloom, 1 Imbued Vial
Flask of Arcane Fortification	N/A	Special	1 Fel Lotus, 10 Mana Thistle, 20 Netherbloom, 1 Imbued Vial
Flask of the Fortification	N/A	Special	1 Fel Lotus, 10 Mana Thistle, 20 Ancient Lichen, 1 Imbued Vial
Flask of Mighty Restoration	N/A	Special	1 Fel Lotus, 10 Mana Thistle, 20 Dreaming Glory, 1 Imbued Vial
Flask of Relentless Assault	N/A	Special	1 Fel Lotus, 10 Mana Thistle, 20 Terocone, 1 Imbued Vial
Flask of Shadow Fortification	N/A	Special	1 Fel Lotus, 10 Mana Thistle, 20 Nightmare Vine, 1 Imbued Vial

Blacksmithing

Created Item	Skill Lvl	Source	Reagent(s)
Copper Chain Pants	1	Trained	4 Copper Bar
Rough Sharpening Stone	N/A	Special	1 Rough Stone
Rough Weightstone	N/A	Special	1 Rough Stone, 1 Linen Cloth
Copper Bracers	N/A	Special	2 Copper Bar
Rough Copper Vest	N/A	Special	4 Copper Bar
Copper Mace	15	Trained	6 Copper Bar, 1 Weak Flux, 2 Linen Cloth
Copper Axe	20	Trained	6 Copper Bar, 1 Weak Flux, 2 Linen Cloth
Copper Chain Boots	20	Trained	8 Copper Bar
Copper Shortsword	25	Trained	6 Copper Bar, 1 Weak Flux, 2 Linen Cloth
Rough Grinding Stone	25	Trained	2 Rough Stone
Copper Dagger	30	Trained	6 Copper Bar, 1 Weak Flux, 1 Rough Grinding Stone, 1 Light Leather
Copper Claymore	30	Trained	10 Copper Bar, 2 Weak Flux, 1 Rough Grinding Stone, 1 Light Leather
Copper Chain Belt	35	Trained	6 Copper Bar
Copper Battle Axe	35	Trained	12 Copper Bar, 2 Weak Flux, 2 Malachite, 2 Rough Grinding Stone, 2 Light Leather
Copper Chain Vest	35	Found	8 Copper Bar, 2 Rough Grinding Stone
Runed Copper Gauntlets	40	Trained	8 Copper Bar, 2 Rough Grinding Stone
Runed Copper Pants	45	Trained	8 Copper Bar, 2 Fine Thread, 3 Rough Grinding Stone
Gemmed Copper Gauntlets	60	Found	8 Copper Bar, 1 Tigerseye, 1 Malachite
Coarse Sharpening Stone	65	Trained	1 Coarse Stone
Coarse Weightstone	65	Trained	1 Coarse Stone, 1 Wool Cloth
Heavy Copper Maul	65	Trained	12 Copper Bar, 2 Weak Flux, 2 Light Leather
Runed Copper Belt	70	Trained	10 Copper Bar
Thick War Axe	70	Trained	10 Copper Bar, 2 Weak Flux, 2 Silver Bar, 2 Rough Grinding Stone, 2 Light Leather
Ironforge Chain	70	Found	12 Copper Bar, 2 Malachite, 2 Rough Grinding Stone
Coarse Grinding Stone	75	Trained	2 Coarse Stone
Runed Copper Breastplate	80	Found	12 Copper Bar, 1 Shadowgem, 2 Rough Grinding Stone
Runed Copper Bracers	90	Trained	10 Copper Bar, 3 Rough Grinding Stone
Heavy Copper Broadsword	95	Trained	14 Copper Bar, 2 Weak Flux, 2 Tigerseye, 2 Medium Leather
Rough Bronze Boots	95	Trained	6 Bronze Bar, 6 Rough Grinding Stone
Rough Bronze Bracers	100	Found	4 Bronze Bar
Silver Rod	100	Trained	1 Silver Bar, 2 Rough Grinding Stone
Ironforge Breastplate	100	Found	16 Copper Bar, 2 Tigerseye, 3 Rough Grinding Stone
Silver Skeleton Key	100	Trained	1 Silver Bar, 1 Rough Grinding Stone
Thick Bronze Darts	100	Trained	6 Bronze Bar, 2 Rough Grinding Stone, 1 Medium Leather
Rough Bronze Leggings	105	Trained	6 Bronze Bar
Rough Bronze Cuirass	105	Trained	7 Bronze Bar

Blacksmithing

Created Item	Skill Lvl	Source	Reagent(s)
Big Bronze Knife	105	Trained	6 Bronze Bar, 4 Weak Flux, 2 Rough Grinding Stone, 1 Tigerseye, 1 Medium Leather
Bronze Mace	110	Trained	6 Bronze Bar, 4 Weak Flux, 1 Medium Leather
Rough Bronze Shoulders	110	Trained	5 Bronze Bar, 1 Coarse Grinding Stone
Pearl-handled Dagger	110	Trained	6 Bronze Bar, 1 Strong Flux, 2 Small Lustrous Pearl, 2 Coarse Grinding Stone
Bronze Axe	115	Trained	7 Bronze Bar, 4 Weak Flux, 1 Medium Leather
Patterned Bronze Bracers	120	Trained	5 Bronze Bar, 2 Coarse Grinding Stone
Bronze Shortsword	120	Trained	5 Bronze Bar, 4 Weak Flux, 2 Medium Leather
Heavy Sharpening Stone	125	Trained	1 Heavy Stone
Heavy Weightstone	125	Trained	1 Heavy Stone, 1 Wool Cloth
Deadly Bronze Poniard	125	Found	4 Bronze Bar, 1 Strong Flux, 1 Swiftness Potion, 2 Shadowgem, 2 Coarse Grinding Stone, 2 Medium Leather
Silvered Bronze Shoulders	125	Found	8 Bronze Bar, 2 Silver Bar, 2 Coarse Grinding Stone
Heavy Grinding Stone	125	Trained	3 Heavy Stone
Bronze Warhammer	125	Trained	8 Bronze Bar, 1 Strong Flux, 1 Medium Leather
Heavy Bronze Mace	130	Trained	8 Bronze Bar, 1 Strong Flux, 1 Moss Agate, 1 Shadowgem, 2 Coarse Grinding Stone, 2 Medium Leather
Silvered Bronze Boots	130	Trained	6 Bronze Bar, 1 Silver Bar, 2 Coarse Grinding Stone
Silvered Bronze Breastplate	130	Found	10 Bronze Bar, 2 Silver Bar, 2 Coarse Grinding Stone
Bronze Greatsword	130	Trained	12 Bronze Bar, 2 Strong Flux, 2 Medium Leather
Silvered Bronze Gauntlets	135	Trained	8 Bronze Bar, 1 Silver Bar, 2 Coarse Grinding Stone
Bronze Battle Axe	135	Trained	14 Bronze Bar, 1 Strong Flux, 2 Medium Leather
Iridescent Hammer	140	Found	10 Bronze Bar, 1 Strong Flux, 1 Iridescent Pearl, 2 Coarse Grinding Stone, 2 Medium Leather
Ironforge Gauntlets	140	Found	8 Bronze Bar, 3 Shadowgem, 4 Coarse Grinding Stone
Shining Silver Breastplate	145	Trained	20 Bronze Bar, 2 Moss Agate, 2 Lesser Moonstone, 2 Iridescent Pearl, 4 Silver Bar
Mighty Iron Hammer	145	Found	6 Iron Bar, 2 Strong Flux, 1 Elixir of Ogre's Strength, 2 Lesser Moonstone, 2 Coarse Grinding Stone, 2 Medium Leather
Green Iron Boots	145	Found	6 Iron Bar, 2 Coarse Grinding Stone, 1 Green Dye
Green Iron Gauntlets	150	Found	4 Iron Bar, 2 Small Lustrous Pearl, 2 Coarse Grinding Stone, 1 Green Dye

Created Item	Skill Lvl	Source	Reagent(s)
Iron Shield Spike	150	Found	6 Iron Bar, 4 Coarse Grinding Stone
Iron Buckle	150	Trained	1 Iron Bar
Golden Rod	150	Trained	1 Gold Bar, 2 Coarse Grinding Stone
Golden Skeleton Key	150	Trained	1 Gold Bar, 1 Heavy Grinding Stone
Solid Iron Maul	155	Found	8 Iron Bar, 2 Strong Flux, 1 Heavy Grinding Stone, 4 Silver Bar, 2 Heavy Leather
Green Iron Leggings	155	Trained	8 Iron Bar, 1 Heavy Grinding Stone, 1 Green Dye
Silvered Bronze Leggings	155	Found	12 Bronze Bar, 4 Silver Bar, 2 Coarse Grinding Stone
Hardened Iron Shortsword	160	Found	6 Iron Bar, 2 Strong Flux, 1 Heavy Grinding Stone, 2 Lesser Moonstone, 3 Heavy Leather
Green Iron Shoulders	160	Found	7 Iron Bar, 1 Heavy Grinding Stone, 1 Green Dye
Barbaric Iron Shoulders	160	Found	8 Iron Bar, 4 Sharp Claw, 2 Heavy Grinding Stone
Barbaric Iron Breastplate	160	Found	20 Iron Bar, 4 Heavy Grinding Stone
Green Iron Bracers	165	Trained	6 Iron Bar, 1 Green Dye
Iron Counterweight	165	Found	4 Iron Bar, 2 Coarse Grinding Stone, 1 Lesser Moonstone
Golden Iron Destroyer	170	Found	10 Iron Bar, 4 Gold Bar, 2 Lesser Moonstone, 2 Strong Flux, 2 Heavy Leather, 2 Heavy Grinding Stone
Green Iron Helm	170	Trained	12 Iron Bar, 1 Citrine, 1 Green Dye
Golden Scale Leggings	170	Found	10 Iron Bar, 2 Gold Bar, 1 Heavy Grinding Stone
Jade Serpentblade	175	Found	8 Iron Bar, 2 Strong Flux, 2 Heavy Grinding Stone, 2 Jade, 3 Heavy Leather
Golden Scale Shoulders	175	Found	6 Steel Bar, 2 Gold Bar, 1 Heavy Grinding Stone
Barbaric Iron Helm	175	Found	10 Iron Bar, 2 Large Fang, 2 Sharp Claw
Moonsteel Broadsword	180	Found	8 Steel Bar, 2 Strong Flux, 2 Heavy Grinding Stone, 3 Lesser Moonstone, 3 Heavy Leather
Green Iron Hauberk	180	Trained	20 Iron Bar, 4 Heavy Grinding Stone, 2 Jade, 2 Moss Agate, 1 Green Leather Armor
Barbaric Iron Boots	180	Found	12 Iron Bar, 4 Large Fang, 2 Heavy Grinding Stone
Glinting Steel Dagger	180	Trained	10 Steel Bar, 2 Strong Flux, 1 Moss Agate, 1 Elemental Earth, 1 Heavy Leather
Massive Iron Axe	185	Found	14 Iron Bar, 2 Strong Flux, 2 Heavy Grinding Stone, 4 Gold Bar, 2 Heavy Leather
Polished Steel Boots	185	Found	8 Steel Bar, 1 Citrine, 1 Lesser Moonstone, 2 Heavy Grinding Stone
Golden Scale Bracers	185	Trained	5 Steel Bar, 2 Heavy Grinding Stone

Created Item	Skill Lvl	Source	Reagent(s)
Barbaric Iron Gloves	185	Found	14 Iron Bar, 3 Heavy Grinding Stone, 2 Large Fang
Golden Scale Coif	190	Found	8 Steel Bar, 2 Gold Bar, 2 Heavy Grinding Stone
Steel Weapon Chain	190	Found	8 Steel Bar, 2 Heavy Grinding Stone, 4 Heavy Leather
Searing Golden Blade	190	Found	10 Steel Bar, 4 Gold Bar, 2 Elemental Fire, 2 Heavy Leather
Edge of Winter	190	Found	10 Steel Bar, 1 Frost Oil, 2 Elemental Water, 2 Elemental Air, 2 Heavy Leather
Golden Scale Cuirass	195	Found	12 Steel Bar, 2 Gold Bar, 4 Heavy Grinding Stone
Frost Tiger Blade	200	Found	8 Steel Bar, 2 Strong Flux, 2 Heavy Grinding Stone, 2 Jade, 1 Frost Oil, 4 Heavy Leather
Shadow Crescent Axe	200	Found	10 Steel Bar, 2 Strong Flux, 3 Heavy Grinding Stone, 2 Citrine, 1 Shadow Oil, 3 Heavy Leather
Golden Scale Boots	200	Found	10 Steel Bar, 4 Gold Bar, 4 Heavy Grinding Stone
Steel Breastplate	200	Trained	16 Steel Bar, 3 Heavy Grinding Stone
Solid Sharpening Stone	200	Trained	1 Solid Stone
Solid Weightstone	200	Trained	1 Solid Stone, 1 Silk Cloth
Solid Grinding Stone	200	Trained	4 Solid Stone
Inlaid Mithril Cylinder	200	Found	5 Mithril Bar, 1 Gold Bar, 1 Truesilver Bar
Truesilver Rod	200	Trained	1 Truesilver Bar, 1 Heavy Grinding Stone
Truesilver Skeleton Key	200	Trained	1 Truesilver Bar, 1 Solid Grinding Stone
Whirling Steel Axes	200	Trained	5 Steel Bar, 2 Elemental Air, 2 Heavy Grinding Stone, 1 Heavy Leather
Heavy Mithril Shoulder	205	Trained	8 Mithril Bar, 6 Heavy Leather
Heavy Mithril Gauntlet	205	Trained	6 Mithril Bar, 4 Mageweave Cloth
Golden Scale Gauntlets	205	Found	10 Steel Bar, 4 Gold Bar, 4 Heavy Grinding Stone
Mithril Scale Pants	210	Trained	12 Mithril Bar
Heavy Mithril Pants	210	Found	10 Mithril Bar
Heavy Mithril Axe	210	Trained	12 Mithril Bar, 2 Citrine, 1 Solid Grinding Stone, 4 Heavy Leather
Steel Plate Helm	215	Trained	14 Steel Bar, 1 Solid Grinding Stone
Mithril Scale Bracers	215	Found	8 Mithril Bar
Mithril Shield Spike	215	Found	4 Mithril Bar, 2 Truesilver Bar, 4 Solid Grinding Stone
Mithril Scale Gloves	220	Found	8 Mithril Bar, 6 Heavy Leather, 4 Mageweave Cloth
Ornate Mithril Pants	220	Found	12 Mithril Bar, 1 Truesilver Bar, 1 Solid Grinding Stone
Ornate Mithril Gloves	220	Found	10 Mithril Bar, 6 Mageweave Cloth, 1 Truesilver Bar, 1 Solid Grinding Stone
Blue Glittering Axe	220	Found	16 Mithril Bar, 2 Aquamarine, 1 Solid Grinding Stone, 4 Thick Leather

Created Item	Skill Lvl	Source	Reagent(s)
Ornate Mithril Shoulder	225	Found	12 Mithril Bar, 1 Truesilver Bar, 6 Thick Leather
Truesilver Gauntlets	225	Trained	10 Mithril Bar, 8 Truesilver Bar, 3 Aquamarine, 3 Citrine, 1 Guardian Gloves, 2 Solid Grinding Stone
Wicked Mithril Blade	225	Found	14 Mithril Bar, 4 Truesilver Bar, 1 Solid Grinding Stone, 2 Thick Leather
Orcish War Leggings	230	Found	12 Mithril Bar, 1 Elemental Earth
Heavy Mithril Breastplate	230	Trained	16 Mithril Bar
Mithril Coif	230	Trained	10 Mithril Bar, 6 Mageweave Cloth
Big Black Mace	230	Trained	16 Mithril Bar, 1 Black Pearl, 4 Shadowgem, 1 Solid Grinding Stone, 2 Thick Leather
Mithril Spurs	235	Found	4 Mithril Bar, 3 Solid Grinding Stone
Mithril Scale Shoulders	235	Found	14 Mithril Bar, 4 Thick Leather
Heavy Mithril Boots	235	Trained	14 Mithril Bar, 4 Thick Leather
The Shatterer	235	Trained	24 Mithril Bar, 4 Core of Earth, 6 Truesilver Bar, 5 Citrine, 5 Jade, 4 Solid Grinding Stone, 4 Thick Leather
Ornate Mithril Breastplate	240	Found	16 Mithril Bar, 6 Truesilver Bar, 1 Heart of Fire, 1 Solid Grinding Stone
Dazzling Mithril Rapier	240	Found	14 Mithril Bar, 1 Aquamarine, 2 Lesser Moonstone, 2 Moss Agate, 1 Solid Grinding Stone, 2 Mageweave Cloth
Heavy Mithril Helm	245	Found	14 Mithril Bar, 1 Aquamarine
Truesilver Breastplate	245	Trained	12 Mithril Bar, 12 Truesilver Bar, 2 Star Ruby, 2 Black Pearl, 2 Solid Grinding Stone
Ornate Mithril Boots	245	Found	14 Mithril Bar, 2 Truesilver Bar, 4 Thick Leather, 1 Solid Grinding Stone, 1 Aquamarine
Ornate Mithril Helm	245	Found	16 Mithril Bar, 2 Truesilver Bar, 1 Solid Grinding Stone
Phantom Blade	245	Trained	28 Mithril Bar, 6 Breath of Wind, 8 Truesilver Bar, 2 Lesser Invisibility Potion, 6 Aquamarine, 4 Solid Grinding Stone, 2 Thick Leather
Runed Mithril Hammer	245	Found	18 Mithril Bar, 2 Core of Earth, 1 Solid Grinding Stone, 4 Thick Leather
Blight	250	Trained	28 Mithril Bar, 10 Ichor of Undeath, 10 Truesilver Bar, 6 Solid Grinding Stone, 6 Thick Leather
Dense Sharpening Stone	250	Trained	1 Dense Stone
Dense Weightstone	250	Trained	1 Dense Stone, 1 Runecloth
Dense Grinding Stone	250	Trained	4 Dense Stone
Thorium Armor	250	Found	16 Thorium Bar, 1 Blue Sapphire, 4 Yellow Power Crystal
Thorium Belt	250	Found	12 Thorium Bar, 4 Red Power Crystal

Created Item	Skill Lvl	Source	Reagent(s)
Ebon Shiv	255	Found	12 Mithril Bar, 6 Truesilver Bar, 2 Star Ruby, 1 Solid Grinding Stone, 2 Thick Leather
Thorium Bracers	255	Found	12 Thorium Bar, 4 Blue Power Crystal
Truesilver Champion	260	Trained	30 Mithril Bar, 16 Truesilver Bar, 6 Star Ruby, 4 Breath of Wind, 8 Solid Grinding Stone, 6 Thick Leather
Radiant Belt	260	Found	10 Thorium Bar, 2 Heart of Fire
Thorium Greatsword	260	Found	16 Thorium Bar, 2 Dense Grinding Stone, 4 Rugged Leather
Earthforged Leggings	260	Trained	16 Mithril Bar, 2 Core of Earth
Light Earthforged Blade	260	Trained	12 Mithril Bar, 4 Core of Earth
Light Emberforged Hammer	260	Trained	12 Mithril Bar, 4 Heart of Fire
Light Skyforged Axe	260	Trained	12 Mithril Bar, 4 Breath of Wind
Windforged Leggings	260	Trained	16 Mithril Bar, 2 Breath of Wind
Dark Iron Pulverizer	265	Found	18 Dark Iron Bar, 4 Heart of Fire
Imperial Plate Shoulders	265	Found	12 Thorium Bar, 6 Rugged Leather
Imperial Plate Belt	265	Found	10 Thorium Bar, 6 Rugged Leather
Dark Iron Mail	270	Found	10 Dark Iron Bar, 2 Heart of Fire
Radiant Breastplate	270	Found	18 Thorium Bar, 2 Heart of Fire, 1 Star Ruby
Imperial Plate Bracers	270	Found	12 Thorium Bar
Wildthorn Mail	270	Found	40 Thorium Bar, 2 Enchanted Thorium Bar, 4 Living Essence, 4 Wildvine, 1 Huge Emerald
Bleakwood Hew	270	Found	30 Thorium Bar, 6 Living Essence, 6 Wildvine, 6 Large Opal, 2 Dense Grinding Stone, 8 Rugged Leather
Inlaid Thorium Hammer	270	Found	30 Thorium Bar, 4 Gold Bar, 2 Truesilver Bar, 2 Blue Sapphire, 4 Rugged Leather
Dark Iron Sunderer	275	Found	26 Dark Iron Bar, 4 Heart of Fire
Thorium Shield Spike	275	Found	4 Thorium Bar, 4 Dense Grinding Stone, 2 Essence of Earth
Ornate Thorium Handaxe	275	Found	20 Thorium Bar, 2 Large Opal, 2 Dense Grinding Stone, 4 Rugged Leather
Dawn's Edge	275	Found	30 Thorium Bar, 4 Enchanted Thorium Bar, 4 Star Ruby, 4 Blue Sapphire, 2 Dense Grinding Stone, 4 Rugged Leather
Arcanite Skeleton Key	275	Trained	1 Arcanite Bar, 1 Dense Grinding Stone
Arcanite Rod	275	Trained	3 Arcanite Bar, 1 Dense Grinding Stone
Dark Iron Shoulders	280	Found	6 Dark Iron Bar, 1 Heart of Fire
Thorium Boots	280	Found	20 Thorium Bar, 8 Rugged Leather, 4 Green Power Crystal
Thorium Helm	280	Found	24 Thorium Bar, 1 Star Ruby, 4 Yellow Power Crystal
Huge Thorium Battleaxe	280	Found	40 Thorium Bar, 6 Dense Grinding Stone, 6 Rugged Leather

Created Item	Skill Lvl	Source	Reagent(s)
Enchanted Battlehammer	280	Found	20 Thorium Bar, 6 Enchanted Thorium Bar, 2 Huge Emerald, 4 Powerful Mojo, 4 Rugged Leather
Blazing Rapier	280	Found	10 Enchanted Thorium Bar, 4 Essence of Fire, 4 Heart of Fire, 2 Azerothian Diamond, 2 Dense Grinding Stone
Dark Iron Plate	285	Found	20 Dark Iron Bar, 8 Heart of Fire
Radiant Gloves	285	Found	18 Thorium Bar, 4 Heart of Fire
Demon Forged Breastplate	285	Found	40 Thorium Bar, 10 Demonic Rune, 4 Blue Sapphire, 4 Star Ruby
Rune Edge	285	Found	30 Thorium Bar, 2 Large Opal, 2 Dense Grinding Stone, 4 Rugged Leather
Serenity	285	Found	6 Enchanted Thorium Bar, 2 Arcanite Bar, 4 Powerful Mojo, 2 Large Opal, 2 Blue Sapphire, 1 Huge Emerald
Radiant Boots	290	Found	14 Thorium Bar, 4 Heart of Fire
Dawnbringer Shoulders	290	Found	20 Thorium Bar, 4 Arcanite Bar, 2 Huge Emerald, 2 Essence of Water
Fiery Plate Gauntlets	290	Found	20 Thorium Bar, 6 Enchanted Thorium Bar, 2 Essence of Fire, 4 Star Ruby
Volcanic Hammer	290	Found	30 Thorium Bar, 4 Heart of Fire, 4 Star Ruby, 4 Rugged Leather
Corruption	290	Found	40 Thorium Bar, 2 Arcanite Bar, 16 Demonic Rune, 8 Essence of Undeath, 2 Blue Sapphire, 2 Dense Grinding Stone, 4 Rugged Leather
Heavy Timbermaw Belt	290	Found	12 Thorium Bar, 3 Essence of Earth, 3 Living Essence
Girdle of the Dawn	290	Found	8 Thorium Bar, 6 Truesilver Bar, 1 Righteous Orb
Imperial Plate Boots	295	Found	18 Thorium Bar
Imperial Plate Helm	295	Found	18 Thorium Bar, 1 Star Ruby
Radiant Circlet	295	Found	18 Thorium Bar, 4 Heart of Fire
Storm Gauntlets	295	Found	20 Thorium Bar, 4 Enchanted Thorium Bar, 4 Essence of Water, 4 Blue Sapphire
Dark Iron Bracers	295	Found	4 Dark Iron Bar, 2 Fiery Core, 2 Lava Core
Fiery Chain Girdle	295	Found	6 Dark Iron Bar, 3 Fiery Core, 3 Lava Core
Thorium Leggings	300	Found	26 Thorium Bar, 4 Red Power Crystal
Imperial Plate Chest	300	Found	20 Thorium Bar
Runic Plate Shoulders	300	Found	20 Thorium Bar, 2 Arcanite Bar, 6 Gold Bar
Runic Plate Boots	300	Found	20 Thorium Bar, 2 Arcanite Bar, 10 Silver Bar
Whitesoul Helm	300	Found	20 Thorium Bar, 4 Enchanted Thorium Bar, 6 Truesilver Bar, 6 Gold Bar, 2 Azerothian Diamond
Radiant Leggings	300	Found	20 Thorium Bar, 4 Heart of Fire
Runic Plate Helm	300	Found	30 Thorium Bar, 2 Arcanite Bar, 2 Truesilver Bar, 1 Huge Emerald
Imperial Plate Leggings	300	Found	24 Thorium Bar

Created Item	Skill Lvl	Source	Reagent(s)
Helm of the Great Chief	300	Found	40 Thorium Bar, 4 Enchanted Thorium Bar, 60 Jet Black Feather, 6 Large Opal, 2 Huge Emerald
Lionheart Helm	300	Found	80 Thorium Bar, 12 Arcanite Bar, 40 Wicked Claw, 10 Blue Sapphire, 4 Azerothian Diamond
Runic Breastplate	300	Found	40 Thorium Bar, 2 Arcanite Bar, 1 Star Ruby
Runic Plate Leggings	300	Found	40 Thorium Bar, 2 Arcanite Bar, 1 Star Ruby
Stronghold Gauntlets	300	Found	15 Arcanite Bar, 20 Enchanted Thorium Bar, 10 Essence of Earth, 4 Blue Sapphire, 4 Large Opal
Enchanted Thorium Helm	300	Found	6 Arcanite Bar, 16 Enchanted Thorium Bar, 6 Essence of Earth, 2 Large Opal, 1 Azerothian Diamond
Enchanted Thorium Leggings	300	Found	10 Arcanite Bar, 20 Enchanted Thorium Bar, 6 Essence of Water, 2 Blue Sapphire, 1 Huge Emerald
Enchanted Thorium Breastplate	300	Found	8 Arcanite Bar, 24 Enchanted Thorium Bar, 4 Essence of Earth, 4 Essence of Water, 2 Huge Emerald, 2 Azerothian Diamond
Invulnerable Mail	300	Found	30 Arcanite Bar, 30 Enchanted Thorium Bar, 6 Huge Emerald, 6 Azerothian Diamond
Blood Talon	300	Found	10 Enchanted Thorium Bar, 10 Arcanite Bar, 8 Demonic Rune, 10 Star Ruby, 2 Dense Grinding Stone
Darkspear	300	Found	20 Enchanted Thorium Bar, 20 Powerful Mojo, 2 Huge Emerald, 2 Azerothian Diamond, 2 Dense Grinding Stone
Hammer of the Titans	300	Found	50 Thorium Bar, 15 Arcanite Bar, 4 Guardian Stone, 6 Enchanted Leather, 10 Essence of Earth
Arcanite Champion	300	Found	15 Arcanite Bar, 8 Azerothian Diamond, 1 Righteous Orb, 4 Large Opal, 8 Enchanted Leather, 2 Dense Grinding Stone
Annihilator	300	Found	40 Thorium Bar, 12 Arcanite Bar, 10 Essence of Undeath, 8 Huge Emerald, 2 Dense Grinding Stone, 4 Enchanted Leather
Frostguard	300	Found	18 Arcanite Bar, 8 Blue Sapphire, 8 Azerothian Diamond, 4 Essence of Water, 2 Dense Grinding Stone, 4 Enchanted Leather
Masterwork Stormhammer	300	Found	20 Enchanted Thorium Bar, 8 Huge Emerald, 8 Large Opal, 6 Essence of Earth, 4 Enchanted Leather
Arcanite Reaper	300	Found	20 Arcanite Bar, 6 Enchanted Leather, 2 Dense Grinding Stone

Created Item	Skill Lvl	Source	Reagent(s)
Heartseeker	300	Found	10 Arcanite Bar, 10 Enchanted Thorium Bar, 2 Enchanted Leather, 6 Star Ruby, 6 Azerothian Diamond, 6 Large Opal, 4 Dense Grinding Stone
Dark Iron Leggings	300	Found	16 Dark Iron Bar, 4 Fiery Core, 6 Lava Core
Fiery Chain Shoulders	300	Found	16 Dark Iron Bar, 4 Fiery Core, 5 Lava Core
Dark Iron Destroyer	300	Found	18 Dark Iron Bar, 12 Lava Core, 2 Blood of the Mountain, 2 Enchanted Leather
Dark Iron Reaver	300	Found	16 Dark Iron Bar, 12 Fiery Core, 2 Blood of the Mountain, 2 Enchanted Leather
Sulfuron Hammer	300	Found	8 Sulfuron Ingot, 20 Dark Iron Bar, 50 Arcanite Bar, 25 Essence of Fire, 10 Blood of the Mountain, 10 Lava Core, 10 Fiery Core
Elemental Sharpening Stone	300	Found	2 Elemental Earth, 3 Dense Stone
Heavy Timbermaw Boots	300	Found	4 Arcanite Bar, 6 Essence of Earth, 6 Living Essence
Gloves of the Dawn	300	Found	2 Arcanite Bar, 10 Truesilver Bar, 1 Righteous Orb
Dark Iron Helm	300	Found	4 Lava Core, 2 Fiery Core, 4 Dark Iron Bar
Dark Iron Gauntlets	300	Found	3 Lava Core, 5 Fiery Core, 4 Core Leather, 4 Dark Iron Bar, 2 Blood of the Mountain
Black Amnesty	300	Found	3 Lava Core, 6 Fiery Core, 12 Arcanite Bar, 1 Blood of the Mountain, 4 Dark Iron Bar
Blackfury	300	Found	5 Lava Core, 2 Fiery Core, 16 Arcanite Bar, 6 Dark Iron Bar
Ebon Hand	300	Found	4 Lava Core, 7 Fiery Core, 12 Arcanite Bar, 8 Dark Iron Bar, 4 Azerothian Diamond
Blackguard	300	Found	6 Lava Core, 6 Fiery Core, 10 Arcanite Bar, 6 Dark Iron Bar, 12 Guardian Stone
Nightfall	300	Found	8 Lava Core, 5 Fiery Core, 10 Arcanite Bar, 12 Dark Iron Bar, 4 Huge Emerald
Bloodsoul Breastplate	300	Found	20 Thorium Bar, 10 Souldarite, 2 Bloodvine, 2 Star Ruby
Bloodsoul Gauntlets	300	Found	12 Thorium Bar, 6 Souldarite, 2 Bloodvine, 4 Enchanted Leather
Bloodsoul Shoulders	300	Found	16 Thorium Bar, 8 Souldarite, 2 Bloodvine, 1 Star Ruby
Darksoul Breastplate	300	Found	20 Thorium Bar, 14 Souldarite, 2 Large Opal
Darksoul Leggings	300	Found	18 Thorium Bar, 12 Souldarite, 2 Large Opal
Darksoul Shoulders	300	Found	16 Thorium Bar, 10 Souldarite, 1 Large Opal
Dark Iron Boots	300	Found	3 Lava Core, 3 Fiery Core, 4 Core Leather, 6 Dark Iron Bar

Blacksmithing

Created Item	Skill Lvl	Source	Reagent(s)
Darkrune Breastplate	300	Found	20 Thorium Bar, 10 Dark Rune, 10 Truesilver Bar
Darkrune Gauntlets	300	Found	12 Thorium Bar, 6 Dark Rune, 6 Truesilver Bar, 2 Enchanted Leather
Darkrune Helm	300	Found	16 Thorium Bar, 8 Dark Rune, 8 Truesilver Bar, 1 Black Diamond
Heavy Obsidian Belt	300	Found	14 Small Obsidian Shard, 4 Enchanted Thorium Bar, 2 Essence of Earth
Light Obsidian Belt	300	Found	14 Small Obsidian Shard, 4 Enchanted Leather
Jagged Obsidian Shield	300	Found	8 Large Obsidian Shard, 24 Small Obsidian Shard, 8 Enchanted Thorium Bar, 4 Essence of Earth
Black Grasp of the Destroyer	300	Found	8 Large Obsidian Shard, 24 Small Obsidian Shard, 8 Enchanted Leather, 1 Flask of Supreme Power
Obsidian Mail Tunic	300	Found	15 Large Obsidian Shard, 36 Small Obsidian Shard, 12 Enchanted Leather, 10 Guardian Stone, 4 Azerothian Diamond
Thick Obsidian Breastplate	300	Found	18 Large Obsidian Shard, 40 Small Obsidian Shard, 12 Enchanted Thorium Bar, 10 Essence of Earth, 4 Huge Emerald
Persuader	300	Found	15 Arcanite Bar, 10 Dark Iron Bar, 20 Essence of Undeath, 20 Dark Rune, 10 Devilsaur Leather, 2 Skin of Shadow
Titanic Leggings	300	Found	12 Arcanite Bar, 20 Enchanted Thorium Bar, 10 Essence of Earth, 2 Flask of the Titans
Sageblade	300	Found	12 Arcanite Bar, 2 Nexus Crystal, 2 Flask of Supreme Power, 4 Enchanted Leather
Icebane Bracers	300	Found	4 Frozen Rune, 12 Thorium Bar, 2 Arcanite Bar, 2 Essence of Water
Icebane Breastplate	300	Found	7 Frozen Rune, 16 Thorium Bar, 2 Arcanite Bar, 4 Essence of Water
Icebane Gauntlets	300	Found	5 Frozen Rune, 12 Thorium Bar, 2 Arcanite Bar, 2 Essence of Water
Ironvine Breastplate	300	Found	12 Enchanted Thorium Bar, 2 Bloodvine, 2 Arcanite Bar, 2 Living Essence
Ironvine Gloves	300	Found	8 Enchanted Thorium Bar, 1 Bloodvine, 2 Living Essence
Ironvine Belt	300	Found	6 Enchanted Thorium Bar, 2 Living Essence
Fel Iron Plate Gloves	300	Trained	4 Fel Iron Bar
Fel Iron Chain Coif	300	Trained	4 Fel Iron Bar
Fel Sharpening Stone	300	Trained	1 Fel Iron Bar, 1 Mote of Earth
Fel Iron Rod	300	Trained	6 Fel Iron Bar
Fel Weightstone	300	Trained	1 Fel Iron Bar, 1 Netherweave Cloth
Enchanted Thorium Blades	300	Trained	2 Enchanted Thorium Bar, 6 Thorium Bar, 1 Rugged Leather
Fel Iron Plate Belt	305	Trained	4 Fel Iron Bar
Fel Iron Chain Gloves	310	Trained	5 Fel Iron Bar

Blacksmithing

Created Item	Skill Lvl	Source	Reagent(s)
Fel Iron Hatchet	310	Trained	9 Fel Iron Bar
Fel Iron Plate Boots	315	Trained	6 Fel Iron Bar
Fel Iron Plate Pants	315	Trained	8 Fel Iron Bar
Fel Iron Chain Bracers	315	Trained	6 Fel Iron Bar
Fel Iron Hammer	315	Trained	10 Fel Iron Bar
Fel Iron Chain Tunic	320	Trained	9 Fel Iron Bar
Fel Iron Greatsword	320	Trained	12 Fel Iron Bar
Fel Iron Breastplate	325	Trained	10 Fel Iron Bar
Adamantite Maul	325	Found	8 Adamantite Bar
Lesser Rune of Warding	325	Trained	1 Adamantite Bar
Adamantite Cleaver	330	Found	8 Adamantite Bar
Adamantite Dagger	330	Found	7 Adamantite Bar, 2 Knothide Leather
Great Earthforged Hammer	330	Trained	12 Adamantite Bar, 6 Primal Earth
Heavy Earthforged Breastplate	330	Trained	8 Adamantite Bar, 4 Primal Earth
Lavaforged Warhammer	330	Trained	8 Adamantite Bar, 6 Primal Fire
Skyforged Great Axe	330	Trained	10 Adamantite Bar, 6 Primal Air
Stoneforged Claymore	330	Trained	10 Adamantite Bar, 6 Primal Earth
Stormforged Axe	330	Trained	8 Adamantite Bar, 3 Primal Water, 3 Primal Air
Stormforged Hauberk	330	Trained	8 Adamantite Bar, 2 Primal Water, 2 Primal Air
Windforged Rapier	330	Trained	6 Adamantite Bar, 6 Primal Air
Adamantite Rapier	335	Found	12 Adamantite Bar
Adamantite Plate Bracers	335	Found	8 Adamantite Bar, 2 Primal Earth, 6 Primal Fire
Adamantite Plate Gloves	335	Found	12 Adamantite Bar, 2 Knothide Leather, 4 Primal Earth, 4 Primal Fire
Adamantite Breastplate	340	Found	20 Adamantite Bar, 6 Primal Earth, 6 Primal Fire
Lesser Rune of Shielding	340	Found	1 Adamantite Bar
Flamebane Bracers	350	Found	6 Fel Iron Bar, 3 Primal Water, 2 Primal Fire
Adamantite Sharpening Stone	350	Found	1 Adamantite Bar, 2 Mote of Earth
Greater Rune of Warding	350	Found	1 Khorium Bar
Adamantite Rod	350	Found	10 Adamantite Bar
Breastplate of Kings	350	Trained	8 Primal Might, 6 Hardened Adamantite Bar, 6 Eternium Bar, 8 Khorium Bar
Drakefist Hammer	350	Trained	20 Primal Fire, 20 Primal Earth, 12 Eternium Bar, 8 Khorium Bar
Lionheart Blade	350	Trained	10 Primal Might, 14 Khorium Bar, 6 Hardened Adamantite Bar
Nether Chain Shirt	350	Trained	20 Primal Shadow, 20 Primal Air, 6 Hardened Adamantite Bar, 4 Felsteel Bar, 8 Khorium Bar
Fireguard	350	Trained	20 Primal Shadow, 20 Primal Mana, 14 Felsteel Bar

Blacksmithing

Created Item	Skill Lvl	Source	Reagent(s)
The Planar Edge	350	Trained	5 Primal Might, 20 Primal Shadow, 2 Hardened Adamantite Bar, 12 Felsteel Bar
Thunder	350	Trained	20 Primal Air, 20 Primal Water, 6 Hardened Adamantite Bar, 12 Khorium Bar
Lunar Crescent	350	Trained	12 Primal Air, 12 Primal Earth, 4 Primal Might, 22 Eternium Bar
Adamantite Weightstone	350	Found	1 Adamantite Bar, 2 Netherweave Cloth
Felsteel Whisper Knives	350	Trained	6 Felsteel Bar, 2 Primal Air, 2 Primal Fire, 1 Heavy Knothide Leather
Enchanted Adamantite Belt	355	Found	2 Hardened Adamantite Bar, 8 Arcane Dust, 2 Large Prismatic Shard
Enchanted Adamantite Boots	355	Found	3 Hardened Adamantite Bar, 12 Arcane Dust, 2 Large Prismatic Shard
Flamebane Helm	355	Found	12 Fel Iron Bar, 5 Primal Water, 3 Primal Fire
Enchanted Adamantite Breastplate	360	Found	4 Hardened Adamantite Bar, 20 Arcane Dust, 4 Large Prismatic Shard
Flamebane Gloves	360	Found	8 Fel Iron Bar, 4 Primal Water, 4 Primal Fire
Felsteel Gloves	360	Found	6 Felsteel Bar
Felsteel Leggings	360	Found	8 Felsteel Bar
Khorium Belt	360	Found	3 Khorium Bar, 2 Primal Water, 2 Primal Mana
Khorium Pants	360	Found	6 Khorium Bar, 4 Primal Water, 4 Primal Mana
Felsteel Shield Spike	360	Found	4 Felsteel Bar, 4 Primal Fire, 4 Primal Earth
Enchanted Adamantite Leggings	365	Found	4 Hardened Adamantite Bar, 24 Arcane Dust, 4 Large Prismatic Shard
Flamebane Breastplate	365	Found	16 Fel Iron Bar, 6 Primal Water, 4 Primal Fire
Felsteel Helm	365	Found	8 Felsteel Bar
Khorium Boots	365	Found	4 Khorium Bar, 3 Primal Water, 3 Primal Mana
Ragesteel Gloves	365	Found	8 Fel Iron Bar, 6 Primal Fire, 3 Khorium Bar, 2 Elixir of Major Strength
Ragesteel Helm	365	Found	10 Fel Iron Bar, 10 Primal Fire, 4 Khorium Bar, 4 Elixir of Major Strength
Felfury Gauntlets	365	Found	10 Felsteel Bar, 3 Primal Might, 1 Primal Nether
Gauntlets of the Iron Tower	365	Found	10 Hardened Adamantite Bar, 2 Primal Might, 15 Primal Earth, 1 Primal Nether
Steelgrip Gauntlets	365	Found	10 Felsteel Bar, 5 Primal Might, 1 Primal Nether
Storm Helm	365	Found	8 Hardened Adamantite Bar, 16 Primal Air, 16 Primal Water, 1 Primal Nether
Helm of the Stalwart Defender	365	Found	8 Hardened Adamantite Bar, 22 Primal Earth, 12 Primal Mana, 1 Primal Nether

Blacksmithing

Created Item	Skill Lvl	Source	Reagent(s)
Oathkeeper's Helm	365	Found	8 Hardened Adamantite Bar, 3 Primal Might, 18 Primal Life, 1 Primal Nether
Black Felsteel Bracers	365	Found	6 Felsteel Bar, 15 Primal Shadow, 1 Primal Nether
Bracers of the Green Fortress	365	Found	6 Hardened Adamantite Bar, 20 Primal Life, 1 Primal Nether
Blessed Bracers	365	Found	6 Hardened Adamantite Bar, 2 Primal Might, 15 Primal Water, 1 Primal Nether
Felsteel Longblade	365	Found	10 Felsteel Bar, 8 Primal Might, 2 Primal Nether
Khorium Champion	365	Found	20 Khorium Bar, 2 Hardened Adamantite Bar, 6 Primal Might, 2 Primal Nether
Fel Edged Battleaxe	365	Found	10 Felsteel Bar, 8 Primal Might, 2 Primal Nether
Felsteel Reaper	365	Found	10 Felsteel Bar, 8 Primal Might, 2 Primal Nether
Runic Hammer	365	Found	5 Hardened Adamantite Bar, 8 Primal Might, 2 Primal Nether
Fel Hardened Maul	365	Found	10 Felsteel Bar, 8 Primal Might, 2 Primal Nether
Eternium Runed Blade	365	Found	4 Felsteel Bar, 10 Eternium Bar, 8 Primal Might, 2 Primal Nether
Dirge	365	Found	10 Felsteel Bar, 8 Primal Might, 2 Primal Nether
Hand of Eternity	365	Found	4 Hardened Adamantite Bar, 10 Eternium Bar, 8 Primal Might, 2 Primal Nether
Ragesteel Breastplate	370	Found	12 Fel Iron Bar, 10 Primal Fire, 6 Khorium Bar, 4 Elixir of Major Strength
Swiftsteel Gloves	370	Found	6 Felsteel Bar, 2 Large Prismatic Shard, 4 Elixir of Major Agility, 4 Primal Air
Earthpeace Breastplate	370	Found	4 Hardened Adamantite Bar, 6 Primal Life, 4 Primal Earth
Greater Rune of Shielding	375	Found	1 Eternium Bar
Eternium Rod	375	Found	4 Eternium Bar
Black Planar Edge	375	Trained	1 The Planar Edge, 12 Primal Nether, 6 Felsteel Bar
Bulwark of Kings	375	Trained	1 Breastplate of Kings, 10 Primal Nether, 10 Primal Mana
Deep Thunder	375	Trained	1 Thunder, 12 Primal Nether, 10 Primal Mana

Blacksmithing

Created Item	Skill Lvl	Source	Reagent(s)
Dragonmaw	375	Trained	1 Drakefist Hammer, 12 Primal Nether, 2 Primal Might
Lionheart Champion	375	Trained	1 Lionheart Blade, 12 Primal Nether, 2 Primal Might
Mooncleaver	375	Trained	1 Lunar Crescent, 12 Primal Nether, 10 Primal Mana
Blazeguard	375	Trained	1 Fireguard, 12 Primal Nether, 10 Primal Air
Twisting Nether Chain Shirt	375	Trained	1 Nether Chain Shirt, 10 Primal Nether, 10 Primal Mana
Embrace of the Twisting Nether	375	Trained	1 Twisting Nether Chain Shirt, 5 Nether Vortex
Bulwark of the Ancient Kings	375	Trained	1 Bulwark of Kings, 5 Nether Vortex
Blazefury	375	Trained	1 Blazeguard, 20 Nether Vortex
Lionheart Executioner	375	Trained	1 Lionheart Champion, 20 Nether Vortex
Wicked Edge of the Planes	375	Trained	1 Black Planar Edge, 20 Nether Vortex
Bloodmoon	375	Trained	1 Mooncleaver, 20 Nether Vortex
Dragonstrike	375	Trained	1 Dragonmaw, 20 Nether Vortex
Stormherald	375	Trained	1 Deep Thunder, 20 Nether Vortex
Belt of the Guardian	375	Found	5 Nether Vortex, 2 Hardened Adamantite Bar, 4 Primal Water
Red Belt of Battle	375	Found	5 Nether Vortex, 2 Hardened Adamantite Bar, 4 Primal Fire
Boots of the Protector	375	Found	2 Primal Nether, 4 Hardened Adamantite Bar, 12 Primal Water
Red Havoc Boots	375	Found	2 Primal Nether, 4 Hardened Adamantite Bar, 12 Primal Fire
Wildguard Breastplate	375	Found	8 Felsteel Bar, 12 Primal Life, 12 Primal Shadow, 1 Primal Nether
Wildguard Leggings	375	Found	8 Felsteel Bar, 12 Primal Life, 12 Primal Shadow, 1 Primal Nether
Wildguard Helm	375	Found	8 Felsteel Bar, 12 Primal Life, 12 Primal Shadow, 1 Primal Nether
Iceguard Breastplate	375	Found	8 Khorium Bar, 12 Primal Water, 12 Primal Fire, 1 Primal Nether
Iceguard Leggings	375	Found	8 Khorium Bar, 12 Primal Water, 12 Primal Fire, 1 Primal Nether
Iceguard Helm	375	Found	8 Khorium Bar, 12 Primal Water, 12 Primal Fire, 1 Primal Nether

Cooking

Created Item	Skill Lvl	Source	Reagent(s)
Basic Campfire	N/A	Special	1 Simple Wood
Charred Wolf Meat	N/A	Special	1 Stringy Wolf Meat
Brilliant Smallfish	1	Found	1 Raw Brilliant Smallfish
Slitherskin Mackerel	1	Found	1 Raw Slitherskin Mackerel
Herb Baked Egg	1	Found	1 Small Egg, 1 Mild Spices
Crispy Bat Wing	1	Found	1 Meaty Bat Wing, 1 Mild Spices
Gingerbread Cookie	1	Found	1 Small Egg, 1 Holiday Spices
Lynx Steak	1	Found	1 Lynx Meat
Roasted Moongraze Tenderloin	1	Found	1 Moongraze Stag Tenderloin
Spice Bread	1	Trained	1 Simple Flour, 1 Mild Spices
Spiced Wolf Meat	10	Trained	1 Stringy Wolf Meat, 1 Mild Spices
Beer Basted Boar Ribs	10	Found	1 Crag Boar Rib, 1 Rhapsody Malt
Kaldorei Spider Kabob	10	Found	1 Small Spider Leg
Scorpid Surprise	20	Found	1 Scorpid Stinger
Roasted Kodo Meat	35	Found	1 Kodo Meat, 1 Mild Spices
Egg Nog	35	Found	1 Small Egg, 1 Ice Cold Milk, 1 Holiday Spirits, 1 Holiday Spices
Smoked Bear Meat	40	Found	1 Bear Meat
Coyote Steak	50	Trained	1 Coyote Meat
Goretusk Liver Pie	50	Found	1 Goretusk Liver, 1 Mild Spices
Fillet of Frenzy	50	Found	1 Soft Frenzy Flesh, 1 Mild Spices
Strider Stew	50	Found	1 Strider Meat, 1 Shiny Red Apple
Boiled Clams	50	Trained	1 Clam Meat, 1 Refreshing Spring Water
Longjaw Mud Snapper	50	Found	1 Raw Longjaw Mud Snapper
Loch Frenzy Delight	50	Found	1 Raw Loch Frenzy, 1 Mild Spices
Rainbow Fin Albacore	50	Found	1 Raw Rainbow Fin Albacore
Bat Bites	50	Found	1 Bat Flesh
Blood Sausage	60	Found	1 Bear Meat, 1 Boar Intestines, 1 Spider Ichor
Thistle Tea	60	Found	1 Swiftthistle, 1 Refreshing Spring Water
Goldthorn Tea	N/A	Special	1 Goldthorn, 1 Refreshing Spring Water
Crunchy Spider Surprise	60	Found	1 Crunchy Spider Leg
Westfall Stew	75	Found	1 Stringy Vulture Meat, 1 Murloc Eye, 1 Goretusk Snout
Crab Cake	75	Trained	1 Crawler Meat, 1 Mild Spices
Dry Pork Ribs	80	Trained	1 Boar Ribs, 1 Mild Spices
Crocolisk Steak	80	Found	1 Crocolisk Meat, 1 Mild Spices
Smoked Sagefish	80	Found	1 Raw Sagefish, 1 Mild Spices
Cooked Crab Claw	85	Found	1 Crawler Claw, 1 Mild Spices
Savory Deviate Delight	85	Found	1 Deviate Fish, 1 Mild Spices
Murloc Fin Soup	90	Found	2 Murloc Fin, 1 Hot Spices
Dig Rat Stew	90	Found	1 Dig Rat
Clam Chowder	90	Found	1 Clam Meat, 1 Ice Cold Milk, 1 Mild Spices
Redridge Goulash	100	Found	1 Crisp Spider Meat, 1 Tough Condor Meat

Cooking

Created Item	Skill Lvl	Source	Reagent(s)
Seasoned Wolf Kabob	100	Found	2 Lean Wolf Flank, 1 Stormwind Seasoning Herbs
Crispy Lizard Tail	100	Found	1 Thunder Lizard Tail, 1 Hot Spices
Bristle Whisker Catfish	100	Found	1 Raw Bristle Whisker Catfish
Succulent Pork Ribs	110	Found	2 Boar Ribs, 1 Hot Spices
Gooey Spider Cake	110	Found	2 Gooey Spider Leg, 1 Hot Spices
Big Bear Steak	110	Found	1 Big Bear Meat, 1 Hot Spices
Lean Venison	110	Found	1 Stag Meat, 4 Mild Spices
Crocolisk Gumbo	120	Found	1 Tender Crocolisk Meat, 1 Hot Spices
Hot Lion Chops	125	Found	1 Lion Meat, 1 Hot Spices
Goblin Deviled Clams	125	Trained	1 Tangy Clam Meat, 1 Hot Spices
Lean Wolf Steak	125	Found	1 Lean Wolf Flank, 1 Mild Spices
Curiously Tasty Omelet	130	Found	1 Raptor Egg, 1 Hot Spices
Tasty Lion Steak	150	Found	2 Lion Meat, 1 Soothing Spices
Heavy Crocolisk Stew	150	Found	2 Tender Crocolisk Meat, 1 Soothing Spices
Soothing Turtle Bisque	175	Found	1 Turtle Meat, 1 Soothing Spices
Barbecued Buzzard Wing	175	Found	1 Buzzard Wing, 1 Hot Spices
Giant Clam Scorcho	175	Found	1 Giant Clam Meat, 1 Hot Spices
Rockscale Cod	175	Found	1 Raw Rockscale Cod
Roast Raptor	175	Found	1 Raptor Flesh, 1 Hot Spices
Hot Wolf Ribs	175	Found	1 Red Wolf Meat, 1 Hot Spices
Jungle Stew	175	Found	1 Tiger Meat, 1 Refreshing Spring Water, 2 Shiny Red Apple
Carrion Surprise	175	Found	1 Mystery Meat, 1 Hot Spices
Mystery Stew	175	Found	1 Mystery Meat, 1 Skin of Dwarven Stout
Mithril Headed Trout	175	Found	1 Raw Mithril Head Trout
Sagefish Delight	175	Found	1 Raw Greater Sagefish, 1 Hot Spices
Dragonbreath Chili	200	Found	1 Mystery Meat, 1 Small Flame Sac, 1 Hot Spices
Heavy Kodo Stew	200	Found	2 Heavy Kodo Meat, 1 Soothing Spices, 1 Refreshing Spring Water
Spider Sausage	200	Trained	2 White Spider Meat
Spiced Chili Crab	225	Found	1 Tender Crab Meat, 2 Hot Spices
Monster Omelet	225	Found	1 Giant Egg, 2 Soothing Spices
Cooked Glossy Mightfish	225	Found	1 Raw Glossy Mightfish, 1 Soothing Spices
Spotted Yellowtail	225	Found	1 Raw Spotted Yellowtail
Filet of Redgill	225	Found	1 Raw Redgill
Undermine Clam Chowder	225	Found	2 Zesty Clam Meat, 1 Hot Spices, 1 Ice Cold Milk
Tender Wolf Steak	225	Found	1 Tender Wolf Meat, 1 Soothing Spices
Grilled Squid	240	Found	1 Winter Squid, 1 Soothing Spices
Hot Smoked Bass	240	Found	1 Raw Summer Bass, 2 Hot Spices
Nightfin Soup	250	Found	1 Raw Nightfin Snapper, 1 Refreshing Spring Water
Poached Sunscale Salmon	250	Found	1 Raw Sunscale Salmon
Lobster Stew	275	Found	1 Darkclaw Lobster, 1 Refreshing Spring Water

Cooking

Created Item	Skill Lvl	Source	Reagent(s)
Mightfish Steak	275	Found	1 Large Raw Mightfish, 1 Hot Spices, 1 Soothing Spices
Baked Salmon	275	Found	1 Raw Whitescale Salmon, 1 Soothing Spices
Runn Tum Tuber Surprise	275	Found	1 Runn Tum Tuber, 1 Soothing Spices
Smoked Desert Dumplings	285	Special	1 Sandworm Meat, 1 Soothing Spices
Dirge's Kickin' Chimaerok Chops	300	Found	1 Hot Spices, 1 Goblin Rocket Fuel, 1 Deeprock Salt, 1 Chimaerok Tenderloin
Buzzard Bites	300	Found	1 Buzzard Meat
Ravager Dog	300	Found	1 Ravager Flesh
Blackened Trout	300	Found	1 Barbed Gill Trout
Feltail Delight	300	Found	1 Spotted Feltail
Clam Bar	300	Found	2 Jaggal Clam Meat, 1 Soothing Spices
Sporeling Snack	310	Found	1 Strange Spores
Blackened Sporefish	310	Found	1 Zangarian Sporefish
Blackened Basilisk	315	Found	1 Chunk o' Basilisk
Grilled Mudfish	320	Found	1 Figluster's Mudfish
Poached Bluefish	320	Found	1 Icefin Bluefish
Roasted Clefthoof	325	Found	1 Clefthoof Meat
Warp Burger	325	Found	1 Warped Flesh
Talbuk Steak	325	Found	1 Talbuk Venison
Golden Fish Sticks	325	Found	1 Golden Darter
Crunchy Serpent	335	Found	1 Serpent Flesh
Mok'Nathal Shortribs	335	Found	1 Raptor Ribs
Spicy Crawdad	350	Found	1 Furious Crawdad

Enchanting

Created Item	Skill Lvl	Source	Reagent(s)
Enchant Bracer - Minor Health	N/A	Special	1 Strange Dust
Runed Copper Rod	N/A	Special	1 Copper Rod, 1 Strange Dust, 1 Lesser Magic Essence
Enchant Bracer - Minor Deflection	N/A	Special	1 Lesser Magic Essence, 1 Strange Dust
Lesser Magic Wand	10	Trained	1 Simple Wood, 1 Lesser Magic Essence
Enchant Chest - Minor Health	15	Trained	1 Strange Dust
Enchant Chest - Minor Absorption	40	Trained	2 Strange Dust, 1 Lesser Magic Essence
Enchant Chest - Minor Mana	40	Found	1 Lesser Magic Essence
Enchant Cloak - Minor Resistance	45	Trained	1 Strange Dust, 2 Lesser Magic Essence
Minor Wizard Oil	45	Found	2 Strange Dust, 1 Maple Seed, 1 Empty Vial
Enchant Bracer - Minor Stamina	50	Trained	3 Strange Dust
Enchant Chest - Lesser Health	60	Trained	2 Strange Dust, 2 Lesser Magic Essence
Enchant Bracer - Minor Spirit	60	Found	2 Lesser Magic Essence
Enchant Cloak - Minor Protection	70	Trained	3 Strange Dust, 1 Greater Magic Essence
Greater Magic Wand	70	Trained	1 Simple Wood, 1 Greater Magic Essence
Enchant Chest - Lesser Mana	80	Found	1 Greater Magic Essence, 1 Lesser Magic Essence
Enchant Bracer - Minor Agility	80	Trained	2 Strange Dust, 1 Greater Magic Essence
Enchant Bracer - Minor Strength	80	Found	5 Strange Dust
Enchant Weapon - Minor Beastslayer	90	Found	4 Strange Dust, 2 Greater Magic Essence
Enchant Weapon - Minor Striking	90	Trained	2 Strange Dust, 1 Greater Magic Essence, 1 Small Glimmering Shard
Enchant 2H Weapon - Minor Impact	100	Trained	4 Strange Dust, 1 Small Glimmering Shard
Enchant 2H Weapon - Lesser Intellect	100	Found	3 Greater Magic Essence
Runed Silver Rod	100	Trained	1 Silver Rod, 6 Strange Dust, 3 Greater Magic Essence, 1 Runed Copper Rod
Enchant Shield - Minor Stamina	105	Trained	1 Lesser Astral Essence, 2 Strange Dust
Enchant 2H Weapon - Lesser Spirit	110	Found	1 Lesser Astral Essence, 6 Strange Dust
Enchant Cloak - Minor Agility	110	Found	1 Lesser Astral Essence

Created Item	Skill Lvl	Source	Reagent(s)
Enchant Cloak - Lesser Protection	115	Trained	6 Strange Dust, 1 Small Glimmering Shard
Enchant Shield - Lesser Protection	115	Found	1 Lesser Astral Essence, 1 Strange Dust, 1 Small Glimmering Shard
Enchant Chest - Health	120	Trained	4 Strange Dust, 1 Lesser Astral Essence
Enchant Bracer - Lesser Spirit	120	Found	2 Lesser Astral Essence
Enchant Cloak - Lesser Fire Resistance	125	Trained	1 Fire Oil, 1 Lesser Astral Essence
Enchant Boots - Minor Stamina	125	Found	8 Strange Dust
Enchant Boots - Minor Agility	125	Found	6 Strange Dust, 2 Lesser Astral Essence
Enchant Shield - Lesser Spirit	130	Trained	2 Lesser Astral Essence, 4 Strange Dust
Enchant Bracer - Lesser Stamina	130	Trained	2 Soul Dust
Enchant Cloak - Lesser Shadow Resistance	135	Found	1 Greater Astral Essence, 1 Shadow Protection Potion
Enchant Weapon - Lesser Striking	140	Trained	2 Soul Dust, 1 Large Glimmering Shard
Enchant Bracer - Lesser Strength	140	Found	2 Soul Dust
Enchant Chest - Lesser Absorption	140	Trained	2 Strange Dust, 1 Greater Astral Essence, 1 Large Glimmering Shard
Enchant 2H Weapon - Lesser Impact	145	Trained	3 Soul Dust, 1 Large Glimmering Shard
Enchant Chest - Mana	145	Trained	1 Greater Astral Essence, 2 Lesser Astral Essence
Enchant Gloves - Mining	145	Found	1 Soul Dust, 3 Iron Ore
Enchant Gloves - Herbalism	145	Found	1 Soul Dust, 3 Kingsblood
Enchant Gloves - Fishing	145	Found	1 Soul Dust, 3 Blackmouth Oil
Enchant Bracer - Lesser Intellect	150	Trained	2 Greater Astral Essence
Enchant Chest - Minor Stats	150	Trained	1 Greater Astral Essence, 1 Soul Dust, 1 Large Glimmering Shard
Runed Golden Rod	150	Trained	1 Golden Rod, 1 Iridescent Pearl, 2 Greater Astral Essence, 2 Soul Dust, 1 Runed Silver Rod
Minor Mana Oil	150	Found	3 Soul Dust, 2 Maple Seed, 1 Leaded Vial
Enchant Shield - Lesser Stamina	155	Trained	1 Lesser Mystic Essence, 1 Soul Dust
Enchant Cloak - Defense	155	Trained	1 Small Glowing Shard, 3 Soul Dust
Lesser Mystic Wand	155	Trained	1 Star Wood, 1 Lesser Mystic Essence, 1 Soul Dust
Enchant Boots - Lesser Agility	160	Trained	1 Soul Dust, 1 Lesser Mystic Essence
Enchant Chest - Greater Health	160	Trained	3 Soul Dust

Created Item	Skill Lvl	Source	Reagent(s)
Enchant Bracer - Spirit	165	Trained	1 Lesser Mystic Essence
Enchant Boots - Lesser Stamina	170	Trained	4 Soul Dust
Enchant Bracer - Lesser Deflection	170	Found	1 Lesser Mystic Essence, 2 Soul Dust
Enchant Bracer - Stamina	170	Trained	6 Soul Dust
Enchant Weapon - Lesser Beastslayer	175	Found	1 Lesser Mystic Essence, 2 Large Fang, 1 Small Glowing Shard
Enchant Weapon - Lesser Elemental Slayer	175	Found	1 Lesser Mystic Essence, 1 Elemental Earth, 1 Small Glowing Shard
Enchant Cloak - Fire Resistance	175	Trained	1 Lesser Mystic Essence, 1 Elemental Fire
Greater Mystic Wand	175	Trained	1 Star Wood, 1 Greater Mystic Essence, 1 Vision Dust
Enchant Shield - Spirit	180	Trained	1 Greater Mystic Essence, 1 Vision Dust
Enchant Bracer - Strength	180	Trained	1 Vision Dust
Enchant Chest - Greater Mana	185	Trained	1 Greater Mystic Essence
Enchant Boots - Lesser Spirit	190	Found	1 Greater Mystic Essence, 2 Lesser Mystic Essence
Enchant Weapon - Winter's Might	190	Found	3 Greater Mystic Essence, 3 Vision Dust, 1 Large Glowing Shard, 2 Wintersbite
Enchant Shield - Lesser Block	195	Found	2 Greater Mystic Essence, 2 Vision Dust, 1 Large Glowing Shard
Enchant Weapon - Striking	195	Trained	2 Greater Mystic Essence, 1 Large Glowing Shard
Enchant 2H Weapon - Impact	200	Trained	4 Vision Dust, 1 Large Glowing Shard
Enchant Gloves - Skinning	200	Found	1 Vision Dust, 3 Green Whelp Scale
Enchant Chest - Lesser Stats	200	Trained	2 Greater Mystic Essence, 2 Vision Dust, 1 Large Glowing Shard
Runed Truesilver Rod	200	Trained	1 Truesilver Rod, 1 Black Pearl, 2 Greater Mystic Essence, 2 Vision Dust, 1 Runed Golden Rod
Lesser Wizard Oil	200	Found	3 Vision Dust, 2 Stranglethorn Seed, 1 Leaded Vial
Enchant Cloak - Greater Defense	205	Trained	3 Vision Dust
Enchant Cloak - Resistance	205	Trained	1 Lesser Nether Essence
Enchant Gloves - Agility	210	Trained	1 Lesser Nether Essence, 1 Vision Dust
Enchant Shield - Stamina	210	Found	5 Vision Dust
Enchant Bracer - Intellect	210	Trained	2 Lesser Nether Essence
Enchant Boots - Stamina	215	Trained	5 Vision Dust
Enchant Gloves - Advanced Mining	215	Found	3 Vision Dust, 3 Truesilver Bar
Enchant Bracer - Greater Spirit	220	Found	3 Lesser Nether Essence, 1 Vision Dust
Enchant Chest - Superior Health	220	Trained	6 Vision Dust

Created Item	Skill Lvl	Source	Reagent(s)
Enchant Gloves - Advanced Herbalism	225	Found	3 Vision Dust, 3 Sungrass
Enchant Cloak - Lesser Agility	225	Found	2 Lesser Nether Essence
Enchant Gloves - Strength	225	Trained	2 Lesser Nether Essence, 3 Vision Dust
Enchant Boots - Minor Speed	225	Trained	1 Small Radiant Shard, 1 Aquamarine, 1 Lesser Nether Essence
Enchant Shield - Greater Spirit	230	Trained	1 Greater Nether Essence, 2 Dream Dust
Enchant Weapon - Demonslaying	230	Found	1 Small Radiant Shard, 2 Dream Dust, 1 Elixir of Demonslaying
Enchant Chest - Superior Mana	230	Trained	1 Greater Nether Essence, 2 Lesser Nether Essence
Enchant Bracer - Deflection	235	Found	1 Greater Nether Essence, 2 Dream Dust
Enchant Shield - Frost Resistance	235	Found	1 Large Radiant Shard, 1 Frost Oil
Enchant Boots - Agility	235	Trained	2 Greater Nether Essence
Enchant 2H Weapon - Greater Impact	240	Trained	2 Large Radiant Shard, 2 Dream Dust
Enchant Bracer - Greater Strength	240	Trained	2 Dream Dust, 1 Greater Nether Essence
Enchant Chest - Stats	245	Trained	1 Large Radiant Shard, 3 Dream Dust, 2 Greater Nether Essence
Enchant Weapon - Greater Striking	245	Trained	2 Large Radiant Shard, 2 Greater Nether Essence
Enchant Bracer - Greater Stamina	245	Found	5 Dream Dust
Enchant Gloves - Riding Skill	250	Found	2 Large Radiant Shard, 3 Dream Dust
Enchant Gloves - Minor Haste	250	Trained	2 Large Radiant Shard, 2 Wildvine
Enchanted Leather	250	Trained	1 Rugged Leather, 1 Lesser Eternal Essence
Enchanted Thorium	250	Trained	1 Thorium Bar, 3 Dream Dust
Lesser Mana Oil	250	Found	3 Dream Dust, 2 Purple Lotus, 1 Crystal Vial
Enchant Bracer - Greater Intellect	255	Found	3 Lesser Eternal Essence
Enchant Boots - Greater Stamina	260	Found	10 Dream Dust
Enchant Weapon - Fiery Weapon	265	Found	4 Small Radiant Shard, 1 Essence of Fire
Smoking Heart of the Mountain	265	Found	1 Blood of the Mountain, 1 Essence of Fire, 3 Small Brilliant Shard
Enchant Cloak - Greater Resistance	265	Found	2 Lesser Eternal Essence, 1 Heart of Fire, 1 Core of Earth, 1 Globe of Water, 1 Breath of Wind, 1 Ichor of Undeath
Enchant Shield - Greater Stamina	265	Found	10 Dream Dust

Created Item	Skill Lvl	Source	Reagent(s)
Enchant Bracer - Superior Spirit	270	Found	3 Lesser Eternal Essence, 10 Dream Dust
Enchant Gloves - Greater Agility	270	Found	3 Lesser Eternal Essence, 3 Illusion Dust
Enchant Boots - Spirit	275	Found	2 Greater Eternal Essence, 1 Lesser Eternal Essence
Enchant Chest - Major Health	275	Found	6 Illusion Dust, 1 Small Brilliant Shard
Wizard Oil	275	Found	3 Illusion Dust, 2 Firebloom, 1 Crystal Vial
Enchant Shield - Superior Spirit	280	Found	2 Greater Eternal Essence, 4 Illusion Dust
Enchant Weapon - Icy Chill	285	Found	4 Small Brilliant Shard, 1 Essence of Water, 1 Essence of Air, 1 Icecap
Enchant Cloak - Superior Defense	285	Found	8 Illusion Dust
Enchant Chest - Major Mana	290	Found	3 Greater Eternal Essence, 1 Small Brilliant Shard
Runed Arcanite Rod	290	Found	1 Arcanite Rod, 1 Golden Pearl, 10 Illusion Dust, 4 Greater Eternal Essence, 1 Runed Truesilver Rod, 2 Large Brilliant Shard
Enchant Weapon - Strength	290	Found	6 Large Brilliant Shard, 6 Greater Eternal Essence, 4 Illusion Dust, 2 Essence of Earth
Enchant Weapon - Agility	290	Found	6 Large Brilliant Shard, 6 Greater Eternal Essence, 4 Illusion Dust, 2 Essence of Air
Enchant Bracer - Mana Regeneration	290	Found	16 Illusion Dust, 4 Greater Eternal Essence, 2 Essence of Water
Enchant 2H Weapon - Agility	290	Found	10 Large Brilliant Shard, 6 Greater Eternal Essence, 14 Illusion Dust, 4 Essence of Air
Enchant Gloves - Greater Strength	295	Found	4 Greater Eternal Essence, 4 Illusion Dust
Enchant Boots - Greater Agility	295	Found	8 Greater Eternal Essence
Enchant Bracer - Superior Strength	295	Found	6 Illusion Dust, 6 Greater Eternal Essence
Enchant 2H Weapon - Superior Impact	295	Found	4 Large Brilliant Shard, 10 Illusion Dust
Enchant Weapon - Unholy Weapon	295	Found	4 Large Brilliant Shard, 4 Essence of Undeath
Enchant 2H Weapon - Major Intellect	300	Found	12 Greater Eternal Essence, 2 Large Brilliant Shard
Enchant Weapon - Superior Striking	300	Found	2 Large Brilliant Shard, 10 Greater Eternal Essence
Enchant Bracer - Superior Stamina	300	Found	15 Illusion Dust
Enchant Weapon - Crusader	300	Found	4 Large Brilliant Shard, 2 Righteous Orb
Enchant Chest - Greater Stats	300	Found	4 Large Brilliant Shard, 15 Illusion Dust, 10 Greater Eternal Essence
Enchant Weapon - Lifestealing	300	Found	6 Large Brilliant Shard, 6 Essence of Undeath, 6 Living Essence

Enchanting

Created Item	Skill Lvl	Source	Reagent(s)
Enchant 2H Weapon - Major Spirit	300	Found	12 Greater Eternal Essence, 2 Large Brilliant Shard
Enchant Weapon - Spell Power	300	Found	4 Large Brilliant Shard, 12 Greater Eternal Essence, 4 Essence of Fire, 4 Essence of Water, 4 Essence of Air, 2 Golden Pearl
Enchant Weapon - Healing Power	300	Found	4 Large Brilliant Shard, 8 Greater Eternal Essence, 6 Living Essence, 6 Essence of Water, 1 Righteous Orb
Enchant Bracer - Healing Power	300	Found	2 Large Brilliant Shard, 20 Illusion Dust, 4 Greater Eternal Essence, 6 Living Essence
Enchant Weapon - Mighty Spirit	300	Found	10 Large Brilliant Shard, 8 Greater Eternal Essence, 15 Illusion Dust
Enchant Weapon - Mighty Intellect	300	Found	15 Large Brilliant Shard, 12 Greater Eternal Essence, 20 Illusion Dust
Enchant Gloves - Threat	300	Found	4 Nexus Crystal, 6 Large Brilliant Shard, 8 Larval Acid
Enchant Gloves - Shadow Power	300	Found	3 Nexus Crystal, 10 Large Brilliant Shard, 6 Essence of Undeath
Enchant Gloves - Frost Power	300	Found	3 Nexus Crystal, 10 Large Brilliant Shard, 4 Essence of Water
Enchant Gloves - Fire Power	300	Found	2 Nexus Crystal, 10 Large Brilliant Shard, 4 Essence of Fire
Enchant Gloves - Healing Power	300	Found	3 Nexus Crystal, 8 Large Brilliant Shard, 1 Righteous Orb
Enchant Gloves - Superior Agility	300	Found	3 Nexus Crystal, 8 Large Brilliant Shard, 4 Essence of Air
Enchant Cloak - Greater Fire Resistance	300	Found	3 Nexus Crystal, 8 Large Brilliant Shard, 4 Essence of Fire
Enchant Cloak - Greater Nature Resistance	300	Found	2 Nexus Crystal, 8 Large Brilliant Shard, 4 Living Essence
Enchant Cloak - Stealth	300	Found	3 Nexus Crystal, 8 Large Brilliant Shard, 2 Black Lotus
Enchant Cloak - Subtlety	300	Found	4 Nexus Crystal, 6 Large Brilliant Shard, 2 Black Diamond
Enchant Cloak - Dodge	300	Found	3 Nexus Crystal, 8 Large Brilliant Shard, 8 Guardian Stone
Brilliant Wizard Oil	300	Found	2 Large Brilliant Shard, 3 Firebloom, 1 Imbued Vial
Brilliant Mana Oil	300	Found	2 Large Brilliant Shard, 3 Purple Lotus, 1 Imbued Vial
Runed Fel Iron Rod	300	Trained	1 Fel Iron Rod, 4 Greater Eternal Essence, 6 Large Brilliant Shard, 1 Runed Arcanite Rod
Enchant Chest - Restore Mana Prime	300	Trained	2 Lesser Planar Essence, 2 Arcane Dust
Enchant Bracer - Assault	300	Trained	6 Arcane Dust
Enchant Bracer - Brawn	305	Trained	6 Arcane Dust
Enchant Boots - Vitality	305	Found	6 Arcane Dust, 4 Major Healing Potion, 4 Major Mana Potion

Enchanting

Created Item	Skill Lvl	Source	Reagent(s)
Enchant Gloves - Blasting	305	Trained	1 Lesser Planar Essence, 4 Arcane Dust
Enchant Bracer - Major Intellect	305	Trained	3 Lesser Planar Essence
Enchant Shield - Tough Shield	310	Trained	6 Arcane Dust, 10 Primal Earth
Enchant Cloak - Major Armor	310	Trained	8 Arcane Dust
Superior Mana Oil	310	Found	3 Arcane Dust, 1 Netherbloom, 1 Imbued Vial
Enchant Gloves - Assault	310	Trained	8 Arcane Dust
Enchant Cloak - Greater Agility	310	Trained	1 Greater Planar Essence, 4 Arcane Dust, 1 Primal Air
Enchant Bracer - Stats	315	Trained	6 Arcane Dust, 6 Lesser Planar Essence
Enchant Chest - Exceptional Health	315	Trained	8 Arcane Dust, 4 Major Healing Potion, 2 Large Brilliant Shard
Enchant Bracer - Major Defense	320	Found	2 Small Prismatic Shard, 10 Arcane Dust
Enchant Boots - Fortitude	320	Found	12 Arcane Dust
Enchant Chest - Major Spirit	320	Trained	2 Greater Planar Essence
Enchant Bracer - Superior Healing	325	Found	4 Greater Planar Essence, 4 Primal Life
Enchant Shield - Intellect	325	Found	4 Greater Planar Essence
Enchant Chest - Exceptional Mana	325	Found	1 Large Prismatic Shard, 4 Major Mana Potion, 3 Greater Planar Essence
Arcane Dust	325	Found	1 Arcane Crystal
Enchant Cloak - Spell Penetration	325	Found	2 Greater Planar Essence, 6 Arcane Dust, 2 Primal Mana
Enchant Shield - Major Stamina	325	Found	15 Arcane Dust
Prismatic Sphere	325	Trained	4 Large Prismatic Shard
Enchant Cloak - Major Resistance	330	Found	4 Greater Planar Essence, 4 Primal Fire, 4 Primal Air, 4 Primal Earth, 4 Primal Water
Enchant Bracer - Restore Mana Prime	335	Found	8 Greater Planar Essence
Large Prismatic Shard	335	Found	3 Small Prismatic Shard
Enchant Shield - Shield Block	340	Found	12 Arcane Dust, 4 Greater Planar Essence, 10 Primal Earth
Enchant Boots - Dexterity	340	Found	8 Greater Planar Essence, 8 Arcane Dust
Enchant Weapon - Major Striking	340	Found	2 Large Prismatic Shard, 6 Greater Planar Essence, 6 Arcane Dust
Enchant Weapon - Major Intellect	340	Found	2 Large Prismatic Shard, 10 Greater Planar Essence
Superior Wizard Oil	340	Found	3 Arcane Dust, 1 Nightmare Vine, 1 Imbued Vial
Enchant Gloves - Major Strength	340	Trained	12 Arcane Dust, 1 Greater Planar Essence
Enchant Chest - Exceptional Stats	345	Found	4 Large Prismatic Shard, 4 Arcane Dust, 4 Greater Planar Essence

Enchanting

Created Item	Skill Lvl	Source	Reagent(s)
Enchant Chest - Major Resilience	345	Found	4 Greater Planar Essence, 10 Arcane Dust
Enchant Bracer - Fortitude	350	Found	1 Large Prismatic Shard, 10 Greater Planar Essence, 20 Arcane Dust
Enchant Weapon - Potency	350	Found	4 Large Prismatic Shard, 5 Greater Planar Essence, 20 Arcane Dust
Enchant 2H Weapon - Savagery	350	Found	4 Large Prismatic Shard, 40 Arcane Dust
Enchant Weapon - Major Spellpower	350	Found	8 Large Prismatic Shard, 8 Greater Planar Essence
Runed Adamantite Rod	350	Found	1 Adamantite Rod, 8 Greater Planar Essence, 8 Large Prismatic Shard, 1 Primal Might, 1 Runed Fel Iron Rod
Enchant Gloves - Major Healing	350	Found	6 Greater Planar Essence, 6 Large Prismatic Shard, 6 Primal Life
Enchant Cloak - Greater Arcane Resistance	350	Found	4 Large Prismatic Shard, 8 Primal Mana
Enchant Cloak - Greater Shadow Resistance	350	Found	4 Large Prismatic Shard, 8 Primal Shadow
Enchant Weapon - Major Healing	350	Found	8 Large Prismatic Shard, 8 Primal Water, 8 Primal Life
Void Sphere	350	Trained	2 Void Crystal
Enchant Bracer - Spellpower	360	Found	6 Large Prismatic Shard, 8 Primal Fire, 8 Primal Water
Enchant Ring - Striking	360	Found	8 Large Prismatic Shard, 24 Arcane Dust
Enchant Ring - Spellpower	360	Found	8 Large Prismatic Shard, 8 Greater Planar Essence
Enchant Shield - Resistance	360	Found	6 Large Prismatic Shard, 3 Primal Earth, 3 Primal Fire, 3 Primal Air, 3 Primal Water
Enchant 2H Weapon - Major Agility	360	Found	8 Large Prismatic Shard, 6 Greater Planar Essence, 20 Arcane Dust

Enchanting

Created Item	Skill Lvl	Source	Reagent(s)
Enchant Weapon - Battlemaster	360	Found	2 Void Crystal, 8 Large Prismatic Shard, 8 Primal Water
Enchant Weapon - Spellsurge	360	Found	12 Large Prismatic Shard, 10 Greater Planar Essence, 20 Arcane Dust
Enchant Gloves - Spell Strike	360	Found	8 Greater Planar Essence, 2 Arcane Dust, 2 Large Prismatic Shard
Enchant Gloves - Major Spellpower	360	Found	6 Greater Planar Essence, 6 Large Prismatic Shard, 6 Primal Mana
Enchant Boots - Cat's Swiftness	360	Found	8 Large Prismatic Shard, 8 Primal Air
Enchant Boots - Boar's Speed	360	Found	8 Large Prismatic Shard, 8 Primal Earth
Enchant Ring - Healing Power	370	Found	8 Large Prismatic Shard, 10 Greater Planar Essence, 20 Arcane Dust
Enchant Boots - Surefooted	370	Found	2 Void Crystal, 4 Large Prismatic Shard, 1 Primal Nether
Enchant Ring - Stats	375	Found	6 Void Crystal, 6 Large Prismatic Shard
Enchant Weapon - Mongoose	375	Found	6 Void Crystal, 10 Large Prismatic Shard, 8 Greater Planar Essence, 40 Arcane Dust
Enchant Weapon - Sunfire	375	Found	6 Void Crystal, 10 Large Prismatic Shard, 8 Greater Planar Essence, 10 Primal Fire, 2 Primal Might
Enchant Weapon - Soulfrost	375	Found	6 Void Crystal, 10 Large Prismatic Shard, 8 Greater Planar Essence, 10 Primal Water, 10 Primal Shadow
Runed Eternium Rod	375	Found	1 Eternium Rod, 12 Greater Planar Essence, 2 Void Crystal, 4 Primal Might, 1 Runed Adamantite Rod

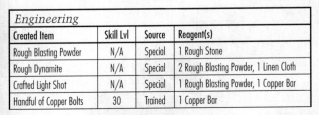

Engineering

Created Item	Skill Lvl	Source	Reagent(s)
Rough Blasting Powder	N/A	Special	1 Rough Stone
Rough Dynamite	N/A	Special	2 Rough Blasting Powder, 1 Linen Cloth
Crafted Light Shot	N/A	Special	1 Rough Blasting Powder, 1 Copper Bar
Handful of Copper Bolts	30	Trained	1 Copper Bar

Engineering

Created Item	Skill Lvl	Source	Reagent(s)
Rough Copper Bomb	30	Trained	1 Copper Bar, 1 Handful of Copper Bolts, 2 Rough Blasting Powder, 1 Linen Cloth
Copper Tube	50	Trained	2 Copper Bar, 1 Weak Flux
Rough Boomstick	50	Trained	1 Copper Tube, 1 Handful of Copper Bolts, 1 Wooden Stock

Created Item	Skill Lvl	Source	Reagent(s)
Arclight Spanner	50	Trained	6 Copper Bar
Crude Scope	60	Trained	1 Copper Tube, 1 Malachite, 1 Handful of Copper Bolts
Copper Modulator	65	Trained	2 Handful of Copper Bolts, 1 Copper Bar, 2 Linen Cloth
Mechanical Squirrel	75	Found	1 Copper Modulator, 1 Handful of Copper Bolts, 1 Copper Bar, 2 Malachite
Coarse Blasting Powder	75	Trained	1 Coarse Stone
Crafted Heavy Shot	75	Trained	1 Coarse Blasting Powder, 1 Copper Bar
Coarse Dynamite	75	Trained	3 Coarse Blasting Powder, 1 Linen Cloth
Target Dummy	85	Trained	1 Copper Modulator, 2 Handful of Copper Bolts, 1 Bronze Bar, 1 Wool Cloth
Silver Contact	90	Trained	1 Silver Bar
Small Seaforium Charge	100	Found	2 Coarse Blasting Powder, 1 Copper Modulator, 1 Light Leather, 1 Refreshing Spring Water
Flying Tiger Goggles	100	Trained	6 Light Leather, 2 Tigerseye
Practice Lock	100	Trained	1 Bronze Bar, 2 Handful of Copper Bolts, 1 Weak Flux
EZ-Thro Dynamite	100	Found	4 Coarse Blasting Powder, 1 Wool Cloth
Deadly Blunderbuss	105	Trained	2 Copper Tube, 4 Handful of Copper Bolts, 1 Wooden Stock, 2 Medium Leather
Large Copper Bomb	105	Trained	3 Copper Bar, 4 Coarse Blasting Powder, 1 Silver Contact
Bronze Tube	105	Trained	2 Bronze Bar, 1 Weak Flux
Standard Scope	110	Trained	1 Bronze Tube, 1 Moss Agate
Lovingly Crafted Boomstick	120	Found	2 Bronze Tube, 2 Handful of Copper Bolts, 1 Heavy Stock, 3 Moss Agate
Shadow Goggles	120	Found	4 Medium Leather, 2 Shadowgem
Small Bronze Bomb	120	Trained	4 Coarse Blasting Powder, 2 Bronze Bar, 1 Silver Contact, 1 Wool Cloth
Whirring Bronze Gizmo	125	Trained	2 Bronze Bar, 1 Wool Cloth
Flame Deflector	125	Found	1 Whirring Bronze Gizmo, 1 Small Flame Sac
Heavy Blasting Powder	125	Trained	1 Heavy Stone
Heavy Dynamite	125	Trained	2 Heavy Blasting Powder, 1 Wool Cloth
Crafted Solid Shot	125	Trained	1 Heavy Blasting Powder, 1 Bronze Bar
Gnomish Universal Remote	125	Found	6 Bronze Bar, 1 Whirring Bronze Gizmo, 2 Flask of Oil, 1 Tigerseye, 1 Malachite
Small Blue Rocket	125	Found	1 Coarse Blasting Powder, 1 Medium Leather
Small Green Rocket	125	Found	1 Coarse Blasting Powder, 1 Medium Leather
Small Red Rocket	125	Found	1 Coarse Blasting Powder, 1 Medium Leather
Silver-plated Shotgun	130	Trained	2 Bronze Tube, 2 Whirring Bronze Gizmo, 1 Heavy Stock, 3 Silver Bar

Engineering

Created Item	Skill Lvl	Source	Reagent(s)
Goblin Rocket Boots	130	Found	1 Black Mageweave Boots, 2 Mithril Tube, 4 Heavy Leather, 2 Goblin Rocket Fuel, 1 Unstable Trigger
Ornate Spyglass	135	Trained	2 Bronze Tube, 2 Whirring Bronze Gizmo, 1 Copper Modulator, 1 Moss Agate
Big Bronze Bomb	140	Trained	2 Heavy Blasting Powder, 3 Bronze Bar, 1 Silver Contact
Minor Recombobulator	140	Found	1 Bronze Tube, 2 Whirring Bronze Gizmo, 2 Medium Leather, 1 Moss Agate
Bronze Framework	145	Trained	2 Bronze Bar, 1 Medium Leather, 1 Wool Cloth
Moonsight Rifle	145	Found	3 Bronze Tube, 3 Whirring Bronze Gizmo, 1 Heavy Stock, 2 Lesser Moonstone
Explosive Sheep	150	Trained	1 Bronze Framework, 1 Whirring Bronze Gizmo, 2 Heavy Blasting Powder, 2 Wool Cloth
Green Tinted Goggles	150	Trained	4 Medium Leather, 2 Moss Agate, 1 Flying Tiger Goggles
Aquadynamic Fish Attractor	150	Trained	2 Bronze Bar, 1 Nightcrawlers, 1 Coarse Blasting Powder
Gold Power Core	150	Trained	1 Gold Bar
Red Firework	150	Found	1 Heavy Blasting Powder, 1 Heavy Leather
Green Firework	150	Found	1 Heavy Blasting Powder, 1 Heavy Leather
Blue Firework	150	Found	1 Heavy Blasting Powder, 1 Heavy Leather
Ice Deflector	155	Found	1 Whirring Bronze Gizmo, 1 Frost Oil
Iron Strut	160	Trained	2 Iron Bar
Discombobulator Ray	160	Found	3 Whirring Bronze Gizmo, 2 Silk Cloth, 1 Jade, 1 Bronze Tube
Portable Bronze Mortar	165	Found	4 Bronze Tube, 1 Iron Strut, 4 Heavy Blasting Powder, 4 Medium Leather
Goblin Jumper Cables	165	Found	6 Iron Bar, 2 Whirring Bronze Gizmo, 2 Flask of Oil, 2 Silk Cloth, 2 Shadowgem, 1 Fused Wiring
Gyrochronatom	170	Trained	1 Iron Bar, 1 Gold Power Core
Iron Grenade	175	Trained	1 Iron Bar, 1 Heavy Blasting Powder, 1 Silk Cloth
Compact Harvest Reaper Kit	175	Trained	2 Iron Strut, 1 Bronze Framework, 2 Gyrochronatom, 4 Heavy Leather
Solid Blasting Powder	175	Trained	2 Solid Stone
Solid Dynamite	175	Trained	1 Solid Blasting Powder, 1 Silk Cloth
Bright-Eye Goggles	175	Found	6 Heavy Leather, 2 Citrine
Gyromatic Micro-Adjustor	175	Trained	4 Steel Bar
Large Blue Rocket	175	Found	1 Heavy Blasting Powder, 1 Heavy Leather
Large Green Rocket	175	Found	1 Heavy Blasting Powder, 1 Heavy Leather
Large Red Rocket	175	Found	1 Heavy Blasting Powder, 1 Heavy Leather
Accurate Scope	180	Found	1 Bronze Tube, 1 Jade, 1 Citrine
Advanced Target Dummy	185	Trained	1 Iron Strut, 1 Bronze Framework, 1 Gyrochronatom, 4 Heavy Leather

Created Item	Skill Lvl	Source	Reagent(s)
Craftsman's Monocle	185	Found	6 Heavy Leather, 2 Citrine
Flash Bomb	185	Found	1 Blue Pearl, 1 Heavy Blasting Powder, 1 Silk Cloth
Big Iron Bomb	190	Trained	3 Iron Bar, 3 Heavy Blasting Powder, 1 Silver Contact
SnowMaster 9000	190	Found	8 Mithril Bar, 4 Gyrochronatom, 4 Snowball, 1 Frost Oil
Goblin Land Mine	195	Found	3 Heavy Blasting Powder, 2 Iron Bar, 1 Gyrochronatom
Mithril Tube	195	Trained	3 Mithril Bar
Mechanical Dragonling	200	Found	1 Bronze Framework, 4 Iron Strut, 4 Gyrochronatom, 2 Citrine, 1 Fused Wiring
Gnomish Cloaking Device	200	Found	4 Gyrochronatom, 2 Jade, 2 Lesser Moonstone, 2 Citrine, 1 Fused Wiring
Large Seaforium Charge	200	Found	2 Solid Blasting Powder, 2 Heavy Leather, 1 Refreshing Spring Water
Unstable Trigger	200	Trained	1 Mithril Bar, 1 Mageweave Cloth, 1 Solid Blasting Powder
Mechanical Repair Kit	200	Trained	1 Mithril Bar, 1 Mageweave Cloth, 1 Solid Blasting Powder
EZ-Thro Dynamite II	200	Found	1 Solid Blasting Powder, 2 Mageweave Cloth
Fire Goggles	205	Trained	1 Green Tinted Goggles, 2 Citrine, 2 Elemental Fire, 4 Heavy Leather
Mithril Blunderbuss	205	Trained	1 Mithril Tube, 1 Unstable Trigger, 1 Heavy Stock, 4 Mithril Bar, 2 Elemental Fire
Goblin Rocket Fuel Recipe	205	Trained	1 Blank Parchment, 1 Engineer's Ink
Goblin Mortar	205	Trained	2 Mithril Tube, 4 Mithril Bar, 5 Solid Blasting Powder, 1 Gold Power Core, 1 Elemental Fire
Goblin Mining Helmet	205	Trained	8 Mithril Bar, 1 Citrine, 4 Elemental Earth
Goblin Construction Helmet	205	Trained	8 Mithril Bar, 1 Citrine, 4 Elemental Fire
Goblin Sapper Charge	205	Trained	1 Mageweave Cloth, 3 Solid Blasting Powder, 1 Unstable Trigger
Inlaid Mithril Cylinder Plans	205	Trained	1 Blank Parchment, 1 Engineer's Ink
Gnomish Shrink Ray	205	Trained	1 Mithril Tube, 1 Unstable Trigger, 4 Mithril Bar, 4 Flask of Mojo, 2 Jade
Lil' Smoky	205	Found	1 Core of Earth, 2 Gyrochronatom, 1 Fused Wiring, 2 Mithril Bar, 1 Truesilver Bar
Pet Bombling	205	Found	1 Big Iron Bomb, 1 Heart of Fire, 1 Fused Wiring, 6 Mithril Bar
Hi-Impact Mithril Slugs	210	Trained	1 Mithril Bar, 1 Solid Blasting Powder
Deadly Scope	210	Found	1 Mithril Tube, 2 Aquamarine, 2 Thick Leather
Gnomish Goggles	210	Trained	1 Fire Goggles, 1 Mithril Tube, 2 Gold Power Core, 2 Flask of Mojo, 2 Heavy Leather

Created Item	Skill Lvl	Source	Reagent(s)
Gnomish Net-o-Matic Projector	210	Trained	1 Mithril Tube, 2 Shadow Silk, 4 Thick Spider's Silk, 2 Solid Blasting Powder, 4 Mithril Bar
Mithril Casing	215	Trained	3 Mithril Bar
Mithril Frag Bomb	215	Trained	1 Mithril Casing, 1 Unstable Trigger, 1 Solid Blasting Powder
Gnomish Harm Prevention Belt	215	Trained	1 Dusky Belt, 4 Mithril Bar, 2 Truesilver Bar, 1 Unstable Trigger, 2 Aquamarine
Catseye Ultra Goggles	220	Found	4 Thick Leather, 2 Aquamarine, 1 Catseye Elixir
Mithril Heavy-bore Rifle	220	Found	2 Mithril Tube, 1 Unstable Trigger, 1 Heavy Stock, 6 Mithril Bar, 2 Citrine
Spellpower Goggles Xtreme	225	Found	4 Thick Leather, 2 Star Ruby
Parachute Cloak	225	Found	4 Bolt of Mageweave, 2 Shadow Silk, 1 Unstable Trigger, 4 Solid Blasting Powder
Gnomish Rocket Boots	225	Trained	1 Black Mageweave Boots, 2 Mithril Tube, 4 Heavy Leather, 8 Solid Blasting Powder, 4 Gyrochronatom
Blue Rocket Cluster	225	Found	1 Solid Blasting Powder, 1 Thick Leather
Green Rocket Cluster	225	Found	1 Solid Blasting Powder, 1 Thick Leather
Red Rocket Cluster	225	Found	1 Solid Blasting Powder, 1 Thick Leather
Firework Launcher	225	Found	1 Inlaid Mithril Cylinder, 1 Goblin Rocket Fuel, 1 Unstable Trigger, 1 Mithril Casing
Deepdive Helmet	230	Found	8 Mithril Bar, 1 Mithril Casing, 1 Truesilver Bar, 4 Tigerseye, 4 Malachite
Rose Colored Goggles	230	Trained	6 Thick Leather, 2 Star Ruby
Goblin Bomb Dispenser	230	Trained	2 Mithril Casing, 4 Solid Blasting Powder, 6 Truesilver Bar, 1 Unstable Trigger, 2 Accurate Scope
Gnomish Battle Chicken	230	Trained	1 Mithril Casing, 6 Truesilver Bar, 6 Mithril Bar, 2 Inlaid Mithril Cylinder, 1 Gold Power Core, 2 Jade
Hi-Explosive Bomb	235	Trained	2 Mithril Casing, 1 Unstable Trigger, 2 Solid Blasting Powder
The Big One	235	Trained	1 Mithril Casing, 1 Goblin Rocket Fuel, 6 Solid Dynamite, 1 Unstable Trigger
Gnomish Mind Control Cap	235	Trained	10 Mithril Bar, 4 Truesilver Bar, 1 Gold Power Core, 2 Star Ruby, 4 Mageweave Cloth
Sniper Scope	240	Found	1 Mithril Tube, 1 Star Ruby, 2 Truesilver Bar
Gnomish Death Ray	240	Trained	2 Mithril Tube, 1 Unstable Trigger, 1 Essence of Undeath, 4 Ichor of Undeath, 1 Inlaid Mithril Cylinder
Goblin Dragon Gun	240	Trained	2 Mithril Tube, 4 Goblin Rocket Fuel, 6 Mithril Bar, 6 Truesilver Bar, 1 Unstable Trigger

Created Item	Skill Lvl	Source	Reagent(s)
The Mortar: Reloaded	N/A	Special	1 Goblin Mortar, 1 Mithril Bar, 3 Solid Blasting Powder
Mithril Gyro-Shot	245	Trained	2 Mithril Bar, 2 Solid Blasting Powder
Green Lens	245	Trained	8 Thick Leather, 3 Jade, 3 Aquamarine, 2 Heart of the Wild, 2 Wildvine
Goblin Rocket Helmet	245	Trained	1 Goblin Construction Helmet, 4 Goblin Rocket Fuel, 4 Mithril Bar, 1 Unstable Trigger
Mithril Mechanical Dragonling	250	Found	14 Mithril Bar, 4 Heart of Fire, 4 Truesilver Bar, 2 Inlaid Mithril Cylinder, 2 Goblin Rocket Fuel, 2 Star Ruby
Salt Shaker	250	Trained	1 Mithril Casing, 6 Thorium Bar, 1 Gold Power Core, 4 Unstable Trigger
Dense Blasting Powder	250	Trained	2 Dense Stone
Dense Dynamite	250	Trained	2 Dense Blasting Powder, 3 Runecloth
Snake Burst Firework	250	Found	2 Dense Blasting Powder, 2 Runecloth, 1 Deeprock Salt
Thorium Grenade	260	Found	1 Thorium Widget, 3 Thorium Bar, 3 Dense Blasting Powder, 3 Runecloth
Thorium Rifle	260	Found	2 Mithril Tube, 2 Mithril Casing, 2 Thorium Widget, 4 Thorium Bar, 1 Deadly Scope
Thorium Widget	260	Found	3 Thorium Bar, 1 Runecloth
Truesilver Transformer	260	Found	2 Truesilver Bar, 2 Elemental Earth, 1 Elemental Air
Gyrofreeze Ice Reflector	260	Found	6 Thorium Widget, 2 Truesilver Transformer, 2 Blue Sapphire, 4 Essence of Fire, 2 Frost Oil, 4 Icecap
World Enlarger	260	Found	1 Mithril Casing, 2 Thorium Widget, 1 Gold Power Core, 1 Unstable Trigger, 1 Citrine
Ultrasafe Transporter - Gadgetzan	N/A	Special	12 Mithril Bar, 2 Truesilver Transformer, 4 Core of Earth, 2 Globe of Water, 4 Aquamarine, 1 Inlaid Mithril Cylinder
Dimensional Ripper - Everlook	N/A	Special	10 Mithril Bar, 1 Truesilver Transformer, 4 Heart of Fire, 2 Star Ruby, 1 The Big One
Lifelike Mechanical Toad	265	Found	1 Living Essence, 4 Thorium Widget, 1 Gold Power Core, 1 Rugged Leather
Goblin Jumper Cables XL	265	Found	2 Thorium Widget, 2 Truesilver Transformer, 2 Fused Wiring, 2 Ironweb Spider Silk, 2 Star Ruby
Alarm-O-Bot	265	Found	4 Thorium Bar, 2 Thorium Widget, 4 Rugged Leather, 1 Star Ruby, 1 Fused Wiring
Spellpower Goggles Xtreme Plus	270	Found	1 Spellpower Goggles Xtreme, 4 Star Ruby, 2 Enchanted Leather, 8 Runecloth
Dark Iron Rifle	275	Found	2 Thorium Tube, 6 Dark Iron Bar, 2 Deadly Scope, 2 Blue Sapphire, 2 Large Opal, 4 Rugged Leather

Created Item	Skill Lvl	Source	Reagent(s)
Masterwork Target Dummy	275	Found	1 Mithril Casing, 1 Thorium Tube, 2 Thorium Widget, 1 Truesilver Bar, 2 Rugged Leather, 4 Runecloth
Thorium Tube	275	Found	6 Thorium Bar
Major Recombobulator	275	Found	2 Thorium Tube, 1 Truesilver Transformer, 2 Runecloth
Powerful Seaforium Charge	275	Found	2 Thorium Widget, 3 Dense Blasting Powder, 2 Rugged Leather, 1 Refreshing Spring Water
Large Blue Rocket Cluster	275	Found	1 Dense Blasting Powder, 1 Rugged Leather
Large Green Rocket Cluster	275	Found	1 Dense Blasting Powder, 1 Rugged Leather
Large Red Rocket Cluster	275	Found	1 Dense Blasting Powder, 1 Rugged Leather
Firework Cluster Launcher	275	Found	4 Inlaid Mithril Cylinder, 4 Goblin Rocket Fuel, 2 Truesilver Transformer, 1 Mithril Casing
Steam Tonk Controller	275	Found	2 Thorium Widget, 1 Mithril Casing, 1 Gold Power Core
Delicate Arcanite Converter	285	Found	1 Arcanite Bar, 1 Ironweb Spider Silk
Dark Iron Bomb	285	Found	2 Thorium Widget, 1 Dark Iron Bar, 3 Dense Blasting Powder, 3 Runecloth
Thorium Shells	285	Found	2 Thorium Bar, 1 Dense Blasting Powder
Voice Amplification Modulator	290	Found	2 Delicate Arcanite Converter, 1 Gold Power Core, 1 Thorium Widget, 1 Large Opal
Master Engineer's Goggles	290	Found	1 Fire Goggles, 2 Huge Emerald, 4 Enchanted Leather
Hyper-Radiant Flame Reflector	290	Found	4 Dark Iron Bar, 3 Truesilver Transformer, 6 Essence of Water, 4 Star Ruby, 2 Azerothian Diamond
Arcane Bomb	300	Found	1 Delicate Arcanite Converter, 3 Thorium Bar, 1 Runecloth
Arcanite Dragonling	300	Found	1 Mithril Mechanical Dragonling, 8 Delicate Arcanite Converter, 10 Enchanted Thorium Bar, 6 Thorium Widget, 4 Gold Power Core, 6 Enchanted Leather
Flawless Arcanite Rifle	300	Found	10 Arcanite Bar, 2 Thorium Tube, 2 Essence of Fire, 2 Essence of Earth, 2 Azerothian Diamond, 2 Enchanted Leather
Field Repair Bot 74A	300	Found	12 Thorium Bar, 4 Rugged Leather, 1 Fused Wiring, 2 Elemental Earth, 1 Elemental Fire
Biznicks 247x128 Accurascope	300	Found	2 Lava Core, 2 Essence of Earth, 4 Delicate Arcanite Converter, 6 Dark Iron Bar, 1 Thorium Tube
Core Marksman Rifle	300	Found	4 Fiery Core, 2 Lava Core, 6 Arcanite Bar, 2 Delicate Arcanite Converter, 2 Thorium Tube

Created Item	Skill Lvl	Source	Reagent(s)
Force Reactive Disk	300	Found	6 Arcanite Bar, 2 Delicate Arcanite Converter, 8 Essence of Air, 12 Living Essence, 8 Essence of Earth
Ultra-Flash Shadow Reflector	300	Found	8 Dark Iron Bar, 4 Truesilver Transformer, 6 Living Essence, 4 Essence of Undeath, 2 Azerothian Diamond, 2 Large Opal
Bloodvine Goggles	300	Found	4 Bloodvine, 5 Souldarite, 2 Delicate Arcanite Converter, 8 Powerful Mojo, 4 Enchanted Leather
Bloodvine Lens	300	Found	5 Bloodvine, 5 Souldarite, 1 Delicate Arcanite Converter, 8 Powerful Mojo, 4 Enchanted Leather
Tranquil Mechanical Yeti	N/A	Special	1 Cured Rugged Hide, 4 Thorium Widget, 2 Globe of Water, 2 Truesilver Transformer, 1 Gold Power Core
Elemental Blasting Powder	300	Trained	1 Mote of Fire, 1 Mote of Earth
Fel Iron Casing	300	Trained	3 Fel Iron Bar
Handful of Fel Iron Bolts	300	Trained	1 Fel Iron Bar
Fel Iron Bomb	305	Trained	1 Fel Iron Casing, 2 Handful of Fel Iron Bolts, 1 Elemental Blasting Powder
Zapthrottle Mote Extractor	305	Found	2 Fel Iron Casing, 2 Handful of Fel Iron Bolts, 4 Primal Life, 1 Delicate Arcanite Converter
Fel Iron Shells	310	Trained	2 Fel Iron Bar, 1 Elemental Blasting Powder
Fel Iron Musket	320	Trained	2 Thorium Tube, 3 Fel Iron Casing, 4 Handful of Fel Iron Bolts
Adamantite Grenade	325	Trained	4 Adamantite Bar, 2 Handful of Fel Iron Bolts, 1 Elemental Blasting Powder
Crashin' Thrashin' Robot	325	Found	1 Adamantite Frame, 2 Fel Iron Casing, 1 Gold Power Core, 2 Handful of Fel Iron Bolts
Fel Iron Toolbox	325	Found	1 Fel Iron Casing, 5 Fel Iron Bar, 2 Handful of Fel Iron Bolts
Adamantite Frame	325	Trained	4 Adamantite Bar, 1 Primal Earth
Critter Enlarger	325	Found	1 Adamantite Frame, 2 Handful of Fel Iron Bolts, 1 Gold Power Core
The Bigger One	325	Trained	3 Fel Iron Casing, 6 Elemental Blasting Powder, 3 Arcane Powder, 2 Handful of Fel Iron Bolts
Gnomish Flame Turret	325	Trained	1 Adamantite Frame, 2 Handful of Fel Iron Bolts, 1 Primal Fire, 1 Thorium Tube
Healing Potion Injector	330	Found	1 Fel Iron Casing, 1 Handful of Fel Iron Bolts, 2 Knothide Leather, 20 Super Healing Potion
Adamantite Scope	335	Found	1 Thorium Tube, 8 Adamantite Bar, 2 Golden Draenite
White Smoke Flare	335	Found	1 Elemental Blasting Powder, 1 Netherweave Cloth

Created Item	Skill Lvl	Source	Reagent(s)
Red Smoke Flare	335	Found	1 Elemental Blasting Powder, 1 Netherweave Cloth, 1 Red Dye
Blue Smoke Flare	335	Found	1 Elemental Blasting Powder, 1 Netherweave Cloth, 1 Blue Dye
Green Smoke Flare	335	Found	1 Elemental Blasting Powder, 1 Netherweave Cloth, 1 Green Dye
Adamantite Shells	335	Found	2 Adamantite Bar, 1 Elemental Blasting Powder
Purple Smoke Flare	335	Found	1 Elemental Blasting Powder, 1 Netherweave Cloth, 1 Purple Dye
Dimensional Ripper - Area 52	N/A	Special	1 Adamantite Frame, 2 Primal Fire, 2 The Bigger One, 4 Handful of Fel Iron Bolts, 1 Khorium Power Core
Ultrasafe Transporter - Toshley's Station	N/A	Special	1 Adamantite Frame, 2 Primal Air, 2 Felsteel Stabilizer, 4 Handful of Fel Iron Bolts, 1 Khorium Power Core
Cogspinner Goggles	340	Found	4 Heavy Knothide Leather, 2 Blood Garnet, 8 Arcane Dust
Power Amplification Goggles	340	Found	4 Heavy Knothide Leather, 2 Flame Spessarite, 8 Arcane Dust
Super Sapper Charge	340	Trained	4 Netherweave Cloth, 4 Elemental Blasting Powder, 1 Primal Mana
Gnomish Poultryizer	340	Trained	2 Hardened Adamantite Tube, 2 Khorium Power Core, 10 Arcane Dust, 2 Large Prismatic Shard
Mana Potion Injector	345	Found	1 Fel Iron Casing, 1 Handful of Fel Iron Bolts, 2 Knothide Leather, 20 Super Mana Potion
Adamantite Rifle	350	Found	2 Thorium Tube, 2 Adamantite Frame, 4 Handful of Fel Iron Bolts
Ultra-Spectropic Detection Goggles	350	Found	4 Heavy Knothide Leather, 2 Khorium Bar, 2 Deep Peridot, 2 Small Prismatic Shard
Khorium Toolbox	350	Found	1 Fel Iron Casing, 5 Khorium Bar, 2 Handful of Fel Iron Bolts
Hardened Adamantite Tube	350	Trained	3 Hardened Adamantite Bar
Khorium Power Core	350	Trained	3 Khorium Bar, 1 Primal Fire
Felsteel Stabilizer	350	Trained	2 Felsteel Bar
Elemental Seaforium Charge	350	Found	2 Elemental Blasting Powder, 1 Fel Iron Casing, 1 Handful of Fel Iron Bolts
Goblin Rocket Launcher	350	Trained	2 Hardened Adamantite Tube, 1 Khorium Power Core, 2 Felsteel Stabilizer, 6 Primal Fire, 6 Primal Earth, 2 Delicate Arcanite Converter
Nigh Invulnerability Belt	350	Trained	8 Heavy Knothide Leather, 4 Khorium Power Core, 10 Primal Life, 10 Primal Shadow, 2 Delicate Arcanite Converter
Rocket Boots Xtreme	355	Found	8 Heavy Knothide Leather, 2 Khorium Power Core, 2 Hardened Adamantite Tube, 4 Felsteel Stabilizer

Engineering

Created Item	Skill Lvl	Source	Reagent(s)
Felsteel Boomstick	360	Found	1 Hardened Adamantite Tube, 4 Felsteel Stabilizer, 4 Handful of Fel Iron Bolts
Hyper-Vision Goggles	360	Found	4 Heavy Knothide Leather, 2 Khorium Bar, 2 Nightseye, 2 Large Prismatic Shard
Khorium Scope	360	Found	1 Hardened Adamantite Tube, 4 Khorium Bar, 2 Dawnstone
Ornate Khorium Rifle	375	Found	2 Hardened Adamantite Tube, 12 Khorium Bar, 4 Handful of Fel Iron Bolts, 2 Noble Topaz
Stabilized Eternium Scope	375	Found	2 Hardened Adamantite Tube, 6 Felsteel Stabilizer, 2 Star of Elune
Foreman's Enchanted Helmet	375	Trained	4 Shadowweave Cloth, 12 Primal Mana, 12 Primal Air
Foreman's Reinforced Helmet	375	Trained	8 Hardened Adamantite Bar, 12 Primal Earth, 12 Primal Fire
Gnomish Power Goggles	375	Trained	4 Spellfire Cloth, 8 Primal Fire, 8 Primal Air, 8 Primal Earth, 8 Primal Water, 2 Talasite
Gnomish Battle Goggles	375	Trained	8 Heavy Knothide Leather, 12 Primal Shadow, 12 Primal Earth, 12 Primal Fire, 2 Living Ruby

First Aid

Created Item	Skill Lvl	Source	Reagent(s)
Linen Bandage	N/A	Special	1 Linen Cloth
Heavy Linen Bandage	40	Trained	2 Linen Cloth
Wool Bandage	80	Trained	1 Wool Cloth
Anti-Venom	80	Trained	1 Small Venom Sac
Heavy Wool Bandage	115	Trained	2 Wool Cloth
Strong Anti-Venom	130	Found	1 Large Venom Sac
Silk Bandage	150	Trained	1 Silk Cloth
Heavy Silk Bandage	180	Found	2 Silk Cloth
Mageweave Bandage	210	Found	1 Mageweave Cloth
Heavy Mageweave Bandage	240	Special	2 Mageweave Cloth
Runecloth Bandage	260	Special	1 Runecloth
Heavy Runecloth Bandage	290	Special	2 Runecloth
Powerful Anti-Venom	300	Found	1 Huge Venom Sac
Netherweave Bandage	330	Found	1 Netherweave Cloth
Heavy Netherweave Bandage	360	Found	2 Netherweave Cloth

Created Item	Skill Lvl	Source	Reagent(s)
Delicate Copper Wire	N/A	Special	2 Copper Bar
Braided Copper Ring	N/A	Special	2 Delicate Copper Wire
Woven Copper Ring	N/A	Special	2 Delicate Copper Wire, 1 Copper Bar
Rough Stone Statue	N/A	Special	8 Rough Stone
Heavy Copper Ring	5	Trained	4 Copper Bar, 2 Delicate Copper Wire
Malachite Pendant	20	Trained	1 Malachite, 1 Delicate Copper Wire
Tigerseye Band	20	Trained	1 Tigerseye, 1 Delicate Copper Wire
Inlaid Malachite Ring	30	Trained	2 Malachite, 2 Copper Bar
Ornate Tigerseye Necklace	30	Trained	2 Tigerseye, 2 Copper Bar, 1 Delicate Copper Wire
Bronze Setting	50	Trained	2 Bronze Bar
Elegant Silver Ring	50	Trained	1 Silver Bar
Solid Bronze Ring	50	Trained	4 Bronze Bar
Thick Bronze Necklace	50	Trained	2 Bronze Bar, 1 Shadowgem, 1 Delicate Copper Wire
Coarse Stone Statue	50	Trained	8 Coarse Stone
Simple Pearl Ring	60	Trained	1 Small Lustrous Pearl, 1 Bronze Setting, 2 Copper Bar
Bronze Band of Force	65	Trained	2 Bronze Bar, 1 Bronze Setting, 3 Malachite, 3 Tigerseye, 2 Shadowgem
Gloom Band	70	Trained	2 Shadowgem, 1 Bronze Setting, 2 Delicate Copper Wire
Brilliant Necklace	75	Trained	4 Bronze Bar, 1 Bronze Setting, 1 Moss Agate
Ring of Silver Might	80	Trained	2 Silver Bar
Bronze Torc	80	Trained	6 Bronze Bar, 1 Bronze Setting, 1 Lesser Moonstone
Heavy Silver Ring	90	Trained	2 Silver Bar, 1 Bronze Setting, 1 Moss Agate, 1 Lesser Moonstone
Ring of Twilight Shadows	100	Trained	2 Shadowgem, 2 Bronze Bar
Heavy Jade Ring	105	Trained	1 Jade, 1 Bronze Setting, 2 Iron Bar
Amulet of the Moon	110	Found	2 Lesser Moonstone, 1 Bronze Setting
Barbaric Iron Collar	110	Trained	8 Iron Bar, 2 Large Fang, 2 Bronze Setting
Heavy Stone Statue	110	Trained	8 Heavy Stone
Moonsoul Crown	120	Trained	3 Lesser Moonstone, 3 Small Lustrous Pearl, 4 Soul Dust, 4 Silver Bar, 2 Mana Potion
Pendant of the Agate Shield	120	Found	1 Moss Agate, 1 Bronze Setting
Wicked Moonstone Ring	125	Found	1 Lesser Moonstone, 1 Shadow Oil, 4 Iron Bar
Heavy Iron Knuckles	125	Found	8 Iron Bar, 2 Elixir of Ogre's Strength
Golden Dragon Ring	135	Trained	1 Jade, 2 Gold Bar, 2 Delicate Copper Wire
Silver Rose Pendant	145	Found	1 Moss Agate, 1 Jade, 2 Silver Bar, 2 Bronze Setting
Heavy Golden Necklace of Battle	150	Found	1 Gold Bar, 2 Moss Agate, 1 Elixir of Ogre's Strength
Mithril Filigree	150	Trained	2 Mithril Bar

Created Item	Skill Lvl	Source	Reagent(s)
Blazing Citrine Ring	150	Found	1 Citrine, 4 Mithril Bar
Jade Pendant of Blasting	160	Found	1 Jade, 3 Mithril Filigree
The Jade Eye	170	Found	1 Jade, 2 Elemental Earth
Engraved Truesilver Ring	170	Trained	1 Truesilver Bar, 2 Gold Bar
Solid Stone Statue	175	Trained	10 Solid Stone
Citrine Ring of Rapid Healing	180	Trained	1 Citrine, 2 Elemental Water, 2 Mithril Bar
Golden Ring of Power	180	Trained	4 Gold Bar, 1 Lesser Moonstone, 1 Jade, 1 Citrine
Citrine Pendant of Golden Healing	190	Found	1 Citrine, 2 Elemental Water, 2 Gold Bar, 1 Bronze Setting
Figurine - Jade Owl	200	Trained	4 Jade, 2 Truesilver Bar, 4 Vision Dust, 4 Mithril Filigree
Figurine - Golden Hare	200	Found	6 Gold Bar, 2 Cut Citrine
Truesilver Commander's Ring	200	Trained	3 Truesilver Bar, 2 Star Ruby, 2 Citrine
Aquamarine Signet	210	Trained	3 Aquamarine, 4 Flask of Mojo
Figurine - Black Pearl Panther	215	Found	4 Black Pearl, 4 Flask of Mojo
Aquamarine Pendant of the Warrior	220	Trained	1 Aquamarine, 2 Flask of Mojo, 3 Mithril Filigree
Ruby Crown of Restoration	225	Found	2 Star Ruby, 2 Black Pearl, 4 Truesilver Bar, 4 Thorium Setting, 4 Greater Mana Potion
Thorium Setting	225	Trained	3 Thorium Bar
Figurine - Truesilver Crab	225	Found	2 Aquamarine, 4 Truesilver Bar, 2 Core of Earth, 2 Globe of Water, 4 Flask of Mojo
Dense Stone Statue	225	Trained	10 Dense Stone
Red Ring of Destruction	230	Trained	1 Star Ruby, 1 Citrine, 1 Thorium Setting
Figurine - Truesilver Boar	235	Found	2 Star Ruby, 4 Truesilver Bar, 2 Heart of Fire, 2 Breath of Wind, 4 Flask of Mojo
Ruby Pendant of Fire	235	Trained	1 Star Ruby, 1 Thorium Setting
Truesilver Healing Ring	240	Trained	2 Truesilver Bar, 4 Heart of the Wild
The Aquamarine Ward	245	Found	1 Aquamarine, 2 Truesilver Bar, 1 Thorium Setting, 2 Mithril Bar
Gem Studded Band	250	Found	2 Aquamarine, 2 Citrine, 4 Thorium Setting, 2 Truesilver Bar
Opal Necklace of Impact	250	Found	2 Large Opal, 2 Thorium Setting, 4 Truesilver Bar, 2 Large Radiant Shard, 2 Mithril Filigree
Figurine - Ruby Serpent	260	Found	2 Star Ruby, 2 Essence of Fire, 4 Flask of Big Mojo, 2 Truesilver Bar
Simple Opal Ring	260	Trained	2 Large Opal, 1 Thorium Setting, 2 Thorium Bar
Diamond Focus Ring	265	Trained	1 Azerothian Diamond, 1 Thorium Setting
Sapphire Signet	275	Trained	4 Blue Sapphire, 2 Truesilver Bar, 1 Thorium Setting
Emerald Crown of Destruction	275	Found	2 Huge Emerald, 2 Large Opal, 2 Blue Sapphire, 2 Arcanite Bar, 6 Thorium Bar

Created Item	Skill Lvl	Source	Reagent(s)
Onslaught Ring	280	Trained	8 Thorium Bar, 2 Powerful Mojo, 2 Essence of Earth
Sapphire Pendant of Winter Night	280	Trained	1 Blue Sapphire, 2 Essence of Undeath, 1 Essence of Water, 1 Thorium Setting
Glowing Thorium Band	280	Trained	2 Azerothian Diamond, 1 Thorium Bar, 1 Thorium Setting
Figurine - Emerald Owl	285	Found	2 Huge Emerald, 2 Arcanite Bar, 2 Thorium Bar, 4 Powerful Mojo
Ring of Bitter Shadows	285	Found	1 Arcanite Bar, 4 Essence of Undeath, 2 Demonic Rune
Living Emerald Pendant	290	Trained	2 Huge Emerald, 4 Living Essence, 4 Powerful Mojo
Emerald Lion Ring	290	Trained	2 Huge Emerald, 1 Thorium Bar, 1 Thorium Setting
Figurine - Black Diamond Crab	300	Found	4 Pristine Black Diamond, 4 Black Diamond, 2 Azerothian Diamond, 2 Arcanite Bar, 4 Thorium Bar
Figurine - Dark Iron Scorpid	300	Found	4 Dark Iron Bar, 2 Arcanite Bar, 2 Star Ruby
Teardrop Blood Garnet	300	Found	1 Blood Garnet
Inscribed Flame Spessarite	300	Found	1 Flame Spessarite
Radiant Deep Peridot	300	Found	1 Deep Peridot
Glowing Shadow Draenite	300	Found	1 Shadow Draenite
Brilliant Golden Draenite	300	Found	1 Golden Draenite
Solid Azure Moonstone	300	Found	1 Azure Moonstone
Primal Stone Statue	300	Found	1 Primal Earth
Necklace of the Diamond Tower	305	Found	2 Azerothian Diamond, 2 Thorium Setting, 2 Arcanite Bar
Bold Blood Garnet	305	Found	1 Blood Garnet
Luminous Flame Spessarite	305	Found	1 Flame Spessarite
Jagged Deep Peridot	305	Found	1 Deep Peridot
Royal Shadow Draenite	305	Found	1 Shadow Draenite
Gleaming Golden Draenite	305	Found	1 Golden Draenite
Sparkling Azure Moonstone	305	Found	1 Azure Moonstone
Bright Blood Garnet	305	Found	1 Blood Garnet
Band of Natural Fire	310	Trained	1 Flame Spessarite, 4 Essence of Fire, 4 Living Essence
Fel Iron Blood Ring	310	Trained	1 Fel Iron Bar, 2 Blood Garnet
Golden Draenite Ring	310	Trained	1 Fel Iron Bar, 2 Golden Draenite
Arcanite Sword Pendant	315	Found	4 Arcanite Bar, 4 Essence of Earth, 4 Essence of Air
Runed Blood Garnet	315	Found	1 Blood Garnet
Glinting Flame Spessarite	315	Found	1 Flame Spessarite
Enduring Deep Peridot	315	Found	1 Deep Peridot
Shifting Shadow Draenite	315	Found	1 Shadow Draenite
Thick Golden Draenite	315	Found	1 Golden Draenite
Stormy Azure Moonstone	315	Found	1 Azure Moonstone

Created Item	Skill Lvl	Source	Reagent(s)
Azure Moonstone Ring	320	Trained	1 Fel Iron Bar, 2 Azure Moonstone, 1 Deep Peridot
Blood Crown	325	Found	8 Thorium Bar, 2 Blood of the Mountain, 4 Star Ruby, 2 Blood of Heroes
Delicate Blood Garnet	325	Found	1 Blood Garnet
Potent Flame Spessarite	325	Found	1 Flame Spessarite
Dazzling Deep Peridot	325	Found	1 Deep Peridot
Sovereign Shadow Draenite	325	Found	1 Shadow Draenite
Rigid Golden Draenite	325	Found	1 Golden Draenite
Lustrous Azure Moonstone	325	Found	1 Azure Moonstone
Smooth Golden Draenite	325	Found	1 Golden Draenite
Mercurial Adamantite	325	Trained	4 Adamantite Powder, 1 Primal Earth
Thick Adamantite Necklace	335	Trained	2 Adamantite Bar, 1 Mercurial Adamantite
Heavy Adamantite Ring	335	Trained	1 Adamantite Bar, 1 Mercurial Adamantite
Heavy Felsteel Ring	345	Found	2 Felsteel Bar, 4 Mercurial Adamantite
Bright Living Ruby	350	Found	1 Living Ruby
Brilliant Dawnstone	350	Found	1 Dawnstone
Dazzling Talasite	350	Found	1 Talasite
Delicate Living Ruby	350	Found	1 Living Ruby
Enduring Talasite	350	Found	1 Talasite
Inscribed Noble Topaz	350	Found	1 Noble Topaz
Flashing Living Ruby	350	Found	1 Living Ruby
Gleaming Dawnstone	350	Found	1 Dawnstone
Glinting Noble Topaz	350	Found	1 Noble Topaz
Glowing Nightseye	350	Found	1 Nightseye
Jagged Talasite	350	Found	1 Talasite
Luminous Noble Topaz	350	Found	1 Noble Topaz
Lustrous Star of Elune	350	Found	1 Star of Elune
Mystic Dawnstone	350	Found	1 Dawnstone
Potent Noble Topaz	350	Found	1 Noble Topaz
Radiant Talasite	350	Found	1 Talasite
Rigid Dawnstone	350	Found	1 Dawnstone
Royal Nightseye	350	Found	1 Nightseye
Runed Living Ruby	350	Source	1 Living Ruby
Shifting Nightseye	350	Found	1 Nightseye
Smooth Dawnstone	350	Found	1 Dawnstone
Sovereign Nightseye	350	Found	1 Nightseye
Solid Star of Elune	350	Found	1 Star of Elune
Sparkling Star of Elune	350	Found	1 Star of Elune
Stormy Star of Elune	350	Found	1 Star of Elune
Subtle Living Ruby	350	Found	1 Living Ruby
Teardrop Living Ruby	350	Found	1 Living Ruby
Thick Dawnstone	350	Found	1 Dawnstone
Bold Living Ruby	350	Found	1 Living Ruby
Khorium Band of Shadows	350	Found	2 Khorium Bar, 3 Mercurial Adamantite, 3 Primal Shadow

Jewelcrafting

Created Item	Skill Lvl	Source	Reagent(s)
Khorium Band of Frost	355	Found	2 Khorium Bar, 4 Mercurial Adamantite, 3 Primal Water
Khorium Inferno Band	355	Found	2 Khorium Bar, 4 Mercurial Adamantite, 3 Primal Fire
Delicate Eternium Ring	355	Found	1 Eternium Bar, 5 Mercurial Adamantite
Thick Felsteel Necklace	355	Found	2 Felsteel Bar, 3 Mercurial Adamantite
Living Ruby Pendant	355	Found	4 Khorium Bar, 1 Mercurial Adamantite, 1 Living Ruby
Khorium Band of Leaves	360	Found	2 Khorium Bar, 4 Mercurial Adamantite, 3 Primal Life
Pendant of Frozen Flame	360	Found	2 Felsteel Bar, 6 Primal Water, 4 Primal Fire, 1 Mercurial Adamantite
Pendant of Thawing	360	Found	2 Felsteel Bar, 6 Primal Fire, 4 Primal Water, 1 Mercurial Adamantite
Pendant of Withering	360	Found	2 Felsteel Bar, 6 Primal Shadow, 4 Primal Life, 1 Mercurial Adamantite
Pendant of Shadow's End	360	Found	2 Felsteel Bar, 6 Primal Life, 4 Primal Shadow, 1 Mercurial Adamantite
Pendant of the Null Rune	360	Found	2 Felsteel Bar, 8 Primal Mana, 1 Mercurial Adamantite
Braided Eternium Chain	360	Found	2 Eternium Bar, 3 Mercurial Adamantite
Eye of the Night	360	Found	2 Hardened Adamantite Bar, 2 Mercurial Adamantite, 1 Nightseye
Ring of Arcane Shielding	360	Found	2 Eternium Bar, 8 Primal Mana
Arcane Khorium Band	365	Found	2 Khorium Bar, 4 Mercurial Adamantite, 3 Primal Mana
Blazing Eternium Band	365	Found	2 Eternium Bar, 4 Mercurial Adamantite, 4 Primal Fire
Embrace of the Dawn	365	Found	2 Eternium Bar, 4 Mercurial Adamantite, 2 Golden Draenite
Chain of the Twilight Owl	365	Found	2 Khorium Bar, 4 Mercurial Adamantite, 2 Azure Moonstone
Bracing Earthstorm Diamond	365	Found	1 Earthstorm Diamond
Brutal Earthstorm Diamond	365	Found	1 Earthstorm Diamond
Insightful Earthstorm Diamond	365	Found	1 Earthstorm Diamond
Powerful Earthstorm Diamond	365	Found	1 Earthstorm Diamond
Tenacious Earthstorm Diamond	365	Found	1 Earthstorm Diamond
Destructive Skyfire Diamond	365	Found	1 Skyfire Diamond
Enigmatic Skyfire Diamond	365	Found	1 Skyfire Diamond
Mystical Skyfire Diamond	365	Found	1 Skyfire Diamond
Swift Skyfire Diamond	365	Found	1 Skyfire Diamond
Coronet of the Verdant Flame	370	Found	20 Khorium Bar, 20 Primal Life, 2 Talasite, 5 Mercurial Adamantite

Jewelcrafting

Created Item	Skill Lvl	Source	Reagent(s)
Circlet of Arcane Might	370	Found	20 Felsteel Bar, 20 Primal Mana, 2 Star of Elune, 5 Mercurial Adamantite
Figurine - Felsteel Boar	370	Found	8 Felsteel Bar, 2 Blood Garnet, 4 Primal Earth
Figurine - Dawnstone Crab	370	Found	4 Khorium Bar, 2 Dawnstone, 4 Golden Draenite
Figurine - Living Ruby Serpent	370	Found	2 Felsteel Bar, 2 Living Ruby, 4 Primal Fire
Figurine - Talasite Owl	370	Found	2 Eternium Bar, 2 Talasite, 4 Primal Mana
Figurine - Nightseye Panther	370	Found	6 Hardened Adamantite Bar, 2 Nightseye, 2 Primal Shadow
The Frozen Eye	375	Found	4 Mercurial Adamantite, 2 Khorium Bar, 6 Primal Water, 6 Primal Fire
The Natural Ward	375	Found	4 Mercurial Adamantite, 2 Felsteel Bar, 6 Primal Life, 6 Primal Shadow

Leatherworking

Created Item	Skill Lvl	Source	Reagent(s)
Handstitched Leather Boots	N/A	Special	2 Light Leather, 1 Coarse Thread
Light Armor Kit	N/A	Special	1 Light Leather
Light Leather	N/A	Special	3 Ruined Leather Scraps
Handstitched Leather Vest	N/A	Special	3 Light Leather, 1 Coarse Thread
Handstitched Leather Cloak	N/A	Special	2 Light Leather, 1 Coarse Thread
Handstitched Leather Bracers	N/A	Special	2 Light Leather, 3 Coarse Thread
Handstitched Leather Pants	15	Trained	4 Light Leather, 1 Coarse Thread
Handstitched Leather Belt	25	Trained	6 Light Leather, 1 Coarse Thread
Light Leather Quiver	30	Trained	4 Light Leather, 2 Coarse Thread
Small Leather Ammo Pouch	30	Trained	3 Light Leather, 4 Coarse Thread
Cured Light Hide	35	Trained	1 Light Hide, 1 Salt
Rugged Leather Pants	35	Found	5 Light Leather, 5 Coarse Thread
Embossed Leather Vest	40	Trained	8 Light Leather, 4 Coarse Thread
Kodo Hide Bag	40	Found	3 Thin Kodo Leather, 4 Light Leather, 1 Coarse Thread
Embossed Leather Boots	55	Trained	8 Light Leather, 5 Coarse Thread

Created Item	Skill Lvl	Source	Reagent(s)
Embossed Leather Gloves	55	Trained	3 Light Leather, 2 Coarse Thread
Embossed Leather Cloak	60	Trained	5 Light Leather, 2 Coarse Thread
White Leather Jerkin	60	Found	8 Light Leather, 2 Coarse Thread, 1 Bleach
Light Leather Bracers	70	Trained	6 Light Leather, 4 Coarse Thread
Fine Leather Gloves	75	Found	1 Cured Light Hide, 4 Light Leather, 2 Coarse Thread
Embossed Leather Pants	75	Trained	1 Cured Light Hide, 6 Light Leather, 2 Coarse Thread
Fine Leather Belt	80	Trained	6 Light Leather, 2 Coarse Thread
Fine Leather Cloak	85	Trained	10 Light Leather, 2 Fine Thread
Fine Leather Tunic	85	Trained	3 Cured Light Hide, 6 Light Leather, 4 Coarse Thread
Fine Leather Boots	90	Found	7 Light Leather, 2 Coarse Thread
Murloc Scale Belt	90	Found	8 Slimy Murloc Scale, 6 Light Leather, 1 Fine Thread
Deviate Scale Cloak	90	Found	4 Deviate Scale, 1 Cured Light Hide, 1 Fine Thread
Moonglow Vest	90	Found	6 Light Leather, 1 Cured Light Hide, 4 Coarse Thread, 1 Small Lustrous Pearl
Murloc Scale Breastplate	95	Found	12 Slimy Murloc Scale, 1 Cured Light Hide, 8 Light Leather, 1 Fine Thread
Light Leather Pants	95	Trained	10 Light Leather, 1 Cured Light Hide, 1 Fine Thread
Medium Armor Kit	100	Trained	4 Medium Leather, 1 Coarse Thread
Dark Leather Boots	100	Trained	4 Medium Leather, 2 Fine Thread, 1 Gray Dye
Dark Leather Tunic	100	Found	6 Medium Leather, 1 Fine Thread, 1 Gray Dye
Hillman's Leather Vest	100	Found	1 Fine Leather Tunic, 2 Cured Light Hide, 2 Coarse Thread
Cured Medium Hide	100	Trained	1 Medium Hide, 1 Salt
Black Whelp Cloak	100	Found	12 Black Whelp Scale, 4 Medium Leather, 1 Fine Thread
Medium Leather	100	Trained	4 Light Leather
Black Whelp Tunic	100	Found	8 Medium Leather, 8 Black Whelp Scale, 1 Cured Light Hide, 2 Fine Thread
Fine Leather Pants	105	Found	8 Medium Leather, 1 Bolt of Woolen Cloth, 1 Fine Thread
Deviate Scale Gloves	105	Found	5 Deviate Scale, 2 Fine Thread
Dark Leather Cloak	110	Trained	8 Medium Leather, 1 Fine Thread, 1 Gray Dye
Dark Leather Pants	115	Trained	12 Medium Leather, 1 Gray Dye, 1 Fine Thread
Deviate Scale Belt	115	Found	6 Perfect Deviate Scale, 4 Deviate Scale, 2 Fine Thread
Toughened Leather Armor	120	Trained	10 Medium Leather, 2 Cured Light Hide, 2 Fine Thread

Leatherworking

Created Item	Skill Lvl	Source	Reagent(s)
Dark Leather Gloves	120	Found	1 Fine Leather Gloves, 1 Cured Medium Hide, 1 Fine Thread, 1 Gray Dye
Hillman's Belt	120	Found	8 Medium Leather, 1 Elixir of Wisdom, 2 Fine Thread
Red Whelp Gloves	120	Found	6 Red Whelp Scale, 4 Medium Leather, 1 Fine Thread
Nimble Leather Gloves	120	Trained	1 Elixir of Minor Agility, 6 Medium Leather, 1 Fine Thread
Dark Leather Belt	125	Trained	1 Fine Leather Belt, 1 Cured Medium Hide, 2 Fine Thread, 1 Gray Dye
Guardian Cloak	125	Found	14 Heavy Leather, 2 Bolt of Silk Cloth, 2 Silken Thread
Fletcher's Gloves	125	Trained	8 Medium Leather, 4 Long Tail Feather, 2 Fine Thread
Hillman's Shoulders	130	Trained	1 Cured Medium Hide, 4 Medium Leather, 1 Fine Thread
Toughened Leather Gloves	135	Trained	4 Medium Leather, 2 Cured Medium Hide, 2 Elixir of Defense, 2 Spider's Silk, 2 Fine Thread
Herbalist's Gloves	135	Found	8 Medium Leather, 4 Kingsblood, 2 Fine Thread
Earthen Leather Shoulders	135	Found	6 Medium Leather, 1 Elemental Earth, 1 Fine Thread
Dark Leather Shoulders	140	Found	12 Medium Leather, 1 Elixir of Lesser Agility, 1 Gray Dye, 2 Fine Thread
Pilferer's Gloves	140	Found	10 Medium Leather, 2 Lucky Charm, 2 Fine Thread
Hillman's Leather Gloves	145	Trained	14 Medium Leather, 4 Fine Thread
Heavy Earthen Gloves	145	Found	12 Medium Leather, 2 Elemental Earth, 2 Bolt of Woolen Cloth, 2 Fine Thread
Hillman's Cloak	150	Trained	5 Heavy Leather, 2 Fine Thread
Barbaric Gloves	150	Found	6 Heavy Leather, 2 Large Fang, 1 Fine Thread
Cured Heavy Hide	150	Trained	1 Heavy Hide, 3 Salt
Heavy Armor Kit	150	Trained	5 Heavy Leather, 1 Fine Thread
Heavy Quiver	150	Trained	8 Heavy Leather, 2 Fine Thread
Heavy Leather Ammo Pouch	150	Trained	8 Heavy Leather, 2 Fine Thread
Heavy Leather	150	Trained	5 Medium Leather
Heavy Leather Ball	150	Found	2 Heavy Leather, 1 Fine Thread
Green Leather Armor	155	Found	9 Heavy Leather, 2 Green Dye, 4 Fine Thread
Barbaric Bracers	155	Found	8 Heavy Leather, 2 Cured Heavy Hide, 4 Small Lustrous Pearl, 1 Raptor Hide, 4 Large Fang
Green Leather Belt	160	Trained	1 Cured Heavy Hide, 5 Heavy Leather, 1 Fine Thread, 1 Green Dye, 1 Iron Buckle
Guardian Pants	160	Trained	12 Heavy Leather, 2 Bolt of Silk Cloth, 2 Fine Thread

Created Item	Skill Lvl	Source	Reagent(s)
Raptor Hide Belt	165	Found	4 Raptor Hide, 4 Heavy Leather, 2 Fine Thread
Raptor Hide Harness	165	Found	6 Raptor Hide, 4 Heavy Leather, 2 Fine Thread
Dusky Leather Leggings	165	Found	10 Heavy Leather, 1 Black Dye, 2 Fine Thread
Guardian Belt	170	Found	2 Cured Heavy Hide, 4 Heavy Leather, 1 Fine Thread, 1 Iron Buckle
Thick Murloc Armor	170	Found	12 Thick Murloc Scale, 1 Cured Heavy Hide, 10 Heavy Leather, 3 Fine Thread
Barbaric Leggings	170	Found	10 Heavy Leather, 2 Fine Thread, 1 Moss Agate
Guardian Armor	175	Found	2 Cured Heavy Hide, 12 Heavy Leather, 1 Shadow Oil, 2 Fine Thread
Barbaric Shoulders	175	Trained	8 Heavy Leather, 1 Cured Heavy Hide, 2 Fine Thread
Dusky Leather Armor	175	Trained	10 Heavy Leather, 1 Shadow Oil, 2 Fine Thread
Green Whelp Armor	175	Found	4 Green Whelp Scale, 10 Heavy Leather, 2 Fine Thread
Green Leather Bracers	180	Trained	2 Cured Heavy Hide, 6 Heavy Leather, 1 Green Dye, 1 Fine Thread
Frost Leather Cloak	180	Trained	6 Heavy Leather, 2 Elemental Earth, 2 Elemental Water, 2 Fine Thread
Gem-studded Leather Belt	185	Found	4 Cured Heavy Hide, 2 Iridescent Pearl, 2 Jade, 1 Citrine, 1 Fine Thread
Dusky Bracers	185	Trained	16 Heavy Leather, 1 Black Dye, 2 Silken Thread
Barbaric Harness	190	Trained	14 Heavy Leather, 2 Fine Thread, 1 Iron Buckle
Murloc Scale Bracers	190	Found	16 Thick Murloc Scale, 1 Cured Heavy Hide, 14 Heavy Leather, 1 Silken Thread
Guardian Gloves	190	Trained	4 Heavy Leather, 1 Cured Heavy Hide, 1 Silken Thread
Green Whelp Bracers	190	Found	6 Green Whelp Scale, 8 Heavy Leather, 2 Silken Thread
Gloves of the Greatfather	190	Found	8 Heavy Leather, 4 Elemental Earth, 1 Silken Thread
Guardian Leather Bracers	195	Found	6 Heavy Leather, 2 Cured Heavy Hide, 1 Silken Thread
Dusky Belt	195	Trained	10 Heavy Leather, 2 Bolt of Silk Cloth, 2 Black Dye, 1 Iron Buckle
Barbaric Belt	200	Found	6 Heavy Leather, 2 Cured Heavy Hide, 2 Coarse Gorilla Hair, 1 Great Rage Potion, 1 Silken Thread, 1 Iron Buckle
Dusky Boots	200	Found	8 Heavy Leather, 2 Shadowcat Hide, 1 Shadow Oil, 2 Silken Thread
Swift Boots	200	Found	10 Heavy Leather, 2 Swiftness Potion, 2 Thick Spider's Silk, 1 Silken Thread
Cured Thick Hide	200	Trained	1 Thick Hide, 1 Deeprock Salt

Created Item	Skill Lvl	Source	Reagent(s)
Thick Armor Kit	200	Trained	5 Thick Leather, 1 Silken Thread
Comfortable Leather Hat	200	Found	12 Heavy Leather, 2 Cured Heavy Hide, 2 Silken Thread
Thick Leather	200	Trained	6 Heavy Leather
Shadowskin Gloves	200	Found	6 Thick Leather, 8 Shadowcat Hide, 2 Black Pearl, 2 Cured Heavy Hide, 4 Shadowgem, 1 Heavy Silken Thread
Nightscape Tunic	205	Trained	7 Thick Leather, 2 Silken Thread
Nightscape Headband	205	Trained	5 Thick Leather, 2 Silken Thread
Turtle Scale Gloves	205	Found	6 Thick Leather, 8 Turtle Scale, 1 Heavy Silken Thread
Turtle Scale Breastplate	210	Trained	6 Thick Leather, 12 Turtle Scale, 1 Heavy Silken Thread
Nightscape Shoulders	210	Found	8 Thick Leather, 6 Mageweave Cloth, 3 Silken Thread
Turtle Scale Bracers	210	Trained	8 Thick Leather, 12 Turtle Scale, 1 Heavy Silken Thread
Big Voodoo Robe	215	Found	10 Thick Leather, 4 Flask of Mojo, 1 Heavy Silken Thread
Tough Scorpid Breastplate	220	Found	12 Thick Leather, 12 Scorpid Scale, 4 Silken Thread
Wild Leather Shoulders	220	Found	10 Thick Leather, 1 Wildvine, 1 Cured Thick Hide
Big Voodoo Mask	220	Found	8 Thick Leather, 6 Flask of Mojo, 1 Heavy Silken Thread
Tough Scorpid Bracers	220	Found	10 Thick Leather, 4 Scorpid Scale, 2 Silken Thread
Tough Scorpid Gloves	225	Found	6 Thick Leather, 8 Scorpid Scale, 2 Silken Thread
Wild Leather Vest	225	Found	12 Thick Leather, 2 Wildvine, 1 Cured Thick Hide
Wild Leather Helmet	225	Found	10 Thick Leather, 2 Wildvine, 1 Cured Thick Hide
Dragonscale Gauntlets	225	Trained	24 Thick Leather, 12 Worn Dragonscale, 4 Heavy Silken Thread, 2 Cured Thick Hide
Wolfshead Helm	225	Trained	18 Thick Leather, 2 Thick Wolfhide, 8 Wicked Claw, 4 Heavy Silken Thread, 2 Cured Thick Hide
Quickdraw Quiver	225	Trained	12 Thick Leather, 1 Cured Thick Hide, 1 Elixir of Agility, 4 Silken Thread
Thick Leather Ammo Pouch	225	Trained	10 Thick Leather, 1 Cured Thick Hide, 1 Elixir of Greater Defense, 6 Silken Thread
Nightscape Pants	230	Trained	14 Thick Leather, 4 Silken Thread
Nightscape Cloak	230	Found	12 Thick Leather, 4 Silken Thread
Turtle Scale Helm	230	Trained	14 Thick Leather, 24 Turtle Scale, 1 Heavy Silken Thread
Gauntlets of the Sea	230	Trained	20 Thick Leather, 8 Globe of Water, 2 Core of Earth, 1 Cured Thick Hide, 4 Heavy Silken Thread

Created Item	Skill Lvl	Source	Reagent(s)
Tough Scorpid Boots	235	Found	12 Thick Leather, 12 Scorpid Scale, 6 Silken Thread
Turtle Scale Leggings	235	Trained	14 Thick Leather, 28 Turtle Scale, 1 Heavy Silken Thread
Nightscape Boots	235	Trained	16 Thick Leather, 2 Heavy Silken Thread
Big Voodoo Pants	240	Found	10 Thick Leather, 6 Flask of Big Mojo, 2 Heavy Silken Thread
Big Voodoo Cloak	240	Found	14 Thick Leather, 4 Flask of Big Mojo, 2 Heavy Silken Thread
Tough Scorpid Shoulders	240	Found	12 Thick Leather, 16 Scorpid Scale, 2 Heavy Silken Thread
Wild Leather Boots	245	Found	14 Thick Leather, 4 Wildvine, 2 Cured Thick Hide
Tough Scorpid Leggings	245	Found	14 Thick Leather, 8 Scorpid Scale, 2 Heavy Silken Thread
Tough Scorpid Helm	250	Found	10 Thick Leather, 20 Scorpid Scale, 2 Heavy Silken Thread
Wild Leather Leggings	250	Found	16 Thick Leather, 6 Wildvine, 2 Cured Thick Hide
Wild Leather Cloak	250	Found	16 Thick Leather, 6 Wildvine, 2 Cured Thick Hide
Helm of Fire	250	Trained	40 Thick Leather, 8 Heart of Fire, 4 Core of Earth, 2 Cured Thick Hide, 4 Heavy Silken Thread
Feathered Breastplate	250	Trained	40 Thick Leather, 40 Jet Black Feather, 2 Black Pearl, 4 Cured Thick Hide, 4 Heavy Silken Thread
Cured Rugged Hide	250	Trained	1 Rugged Hide, 1 Refined Deeprock Salt
Rugged Armor Kit	250	Trained	5 Rugged Leather
Rugged Leather	250	Trained	6 Thick Leather
Dragonscale Breastplate	255	Trained	40 Thick Leather, 30 Worn Dragonscale, 4 Heavy Silken Thread, 4 Cured Thick Hide
Heavy Scorpid Bracers	255	Found	4 Rugged Leather, 4 Heavy Scorpid Scale, 1 Rune Thread
Wicked Leather Gauntlets	260	Found	8 Rugged Leather, 1 Black Dye, 1 Rune Thread
Green Dragonscale Breastplate	260	Found	20 Rugged Leather, 25 Green Dragonscale, 2 Rune Thread
Blackstorm Leggings	260	Trained	10 Rugged Leather, 8 Breath of Wind, 2 Cured Thick Hide, 1 Rune Thread
Dragonstrike Leggings	260	Trained	10 Rugged Leather, 10 Worn Dragonscale, 2 Heart of Fire, 2 Cured Thick Hide, 1 Rune Thread
Wildfeather Leggings	260	Trained	10 Rugged Leather, 40 Jet Black Feather, 4 Wildvine, 2 Cured Thick Hide, 1 Rune Thread
Heavy Scorpid Vest	265	Found	6 Rugged Leather, 6 Heavy Scorpid Scale, 1 Rune Thread

Created Item	Skill Lvl	Source	Reagent(s)
Wicked Leather Bracers	265	Found	8 Rugged Leather, 1 Black Dye, 1 Rune Thread
Chimeric Gloves	265	Found	6 Rugged Leather, 6 Chimera Leather, 1 Rune Thread
Runic Leather Gauntlets	270	Found	10 Rugged Leather, 6 Runecloth, 1 Rune Thread
Volcanic Leggings	270	Found	6 Rugged Leather, 1 Essence of Fire, 1 Core of Earth, 1 Rune Thread
Green Dragonscale Leggings	270	Found	20 Rugged Leather, 25 Green Dragonscale, 1 Rune Thread
Living Shoulders	270	Found	12 Rugged Leather, 4 Living Essence, 1 Rune Thread
Ironfeather Shoulders	270	Found	24 Rugged Leather, 80 Ironfeather, 2 Jade, 1 Rune Thread
Chimeric Boots	275	Found	4 Rugged Leather, 8 Chimera Leather, 1 Rune Thread
Heavy Scorpid Gauntlets	275	Found	6 Rugged Leather, 8 Heavy Scorpid Scale, 1 Rune Thread
Runic Leather Bracers	275	Found	6 Rugged Leather, 1 Black Pearl, 6 Runecloth, 1 Rune Thread
Frostsaber Boots	275	Found	4 Rugged Leather, 6 Frostsaber Leather, 1 Rune Thread
Stormshroud Pants	275	Found	16 Rugged Leather, 2 Essence of Water, 2 Essence of Air, 1 Rune Thread
Warbear Harness	275	Found	28 Rugged Leather, 12 Warbear Leather, 1 Rune Thread
Heavy Scorpid Belt	280	Found	6 Rugged Leather, 8 Heavy Scorpid Scale, 1 Rune Thread
Wicked Leather Headband	280	Found	12 Rugged Leather, 1 Black Dye, 1 Rune Thread
Runic Leather Belt	280	Found	12 Rugged Leather, 10 Runecloth, 1 Rune Thread
Chimeric Leggings	280	Found	8 Rugged Leather, 8 Chimera Leather, 1 Rune Thread
Green Dragonscale Gauntlets	280	Trained	20 Rugged Leather, 30 Green Dragonscale, 1 Cured Rugged Hide, 2 Rune Thread
Frostsaber Leggings	285	Found	6 Rugged Leather, 8 Frostsaber Leather, 1 Rune Thread
Heavy Scorpid Leggings	285	Found	8 Rugged Leather, 12 Heavy Scorpid Scale, 1 Rune Thread
Volcanic Breastplate	285	Found	8 Rugged Leather, 1 Essence of Fire, 1 Essence of Earth, 1 Rune Thread
Blue Dragonscale Breastplate	285	Found	28 Rugged Leather, 30 Blue Dragonscale, 1 Cured Rugged Hide, 1 Rune Thread
Living Leggings	285	Found	16 Rugged Leather, 6 Living Essence, 1 Cured Rugged Hide, 1 Rune Thread
Stormshroud Armor	285	Found	16 Rugged Leather, 3 Essence of Water, 3 Essence of Air, 1 Cured Rugged Hide, 1 Rune Thread

Leatherworking

Created Item	Skill Lvl	Source	Reagent(s)
Warbear Woolies	285	Found	24 Rugged Leather, 14 Warbear Leather, 1 Rune Thread
Chimeric Vest	290	Found	10 Rugged Leather, 10 Chimera Leather, 1 Rune Thread
Black Dragonscale Breastplate	290	Found	40 Rugged Leather, 60 Black Dragonscale, 1 Cured Rugged Hide, 2 Rune Thread
Devilsaur Gauntlets	290	Found	30 Rugged Leather, 8 Devilsaur Leather, 1 Rune Thread
Ironfeather Breastplate	290	Found	40 Rugged Leather, 120 Ironfeather, 1 Jade, 1 Cured Rugged Hide, 1 Rune Thread
Runic Leather Headband	290	Found	14 Rugged Leather, 10 Runecloth, 1 Rune Thread
Wicked Leather Pants	290	Found	16 Rugged Leather, 1 Cured Rugged Hide, 3 Black Dye, 1 Rune Thread
Might of the Timbermaw	290	Found	30 Rugged Leather, 2 Powerful Mojo, 4 Living Essence, 2 Cured Rugged Hide, 2 Rune Thread
Dawn Treaders	290	Found	30 Rugged Leather, 2 Guardian Stone, 4 Essence of Water, 2 Cured Rugged Hide, 2 Rune Thread
Blue Dragonscale Shoulders	295	Found	28 Rugged Leather, 30 Blue Dragonscale, 2 Enchanted Leather, 1 Cured Rugged Hide, 1 Rune Thread
Frostsaber Gloves	295	Found	6 Rugged Leather, 10 Frostsaber Leather, 1 Rune Thread
Heavy Scorpid Helm	295	Found	8 Rugged Leather, 12 Heavy Scorpid Scale, 1 Cured Rugged Hide, 1 Rune Thread
Stormshroud Shoulders	295	Found	12 Rugged Leather, 3 Essence of Water, 3 Essence of Air, 2 Enchanted Leather, 1 Rune Thread
Corehound Boots	295	Found	20 Core Leather, 6 Fiery Core, 2 Lava Core, 2 Rune Thread
Red Dragonscale Breastplate	300	Found	40 Rugged Leather, 30 Red Dragonscale, 1 Rune Thread
Black Dragonscale Shoulders	300	Found	44 Rugged Leather, 45 Black Dragonscale, 2 Enchanted Leather, 1 Cured Rugged Hide, 1 Rune Thread
Devilsaur Leggings	300	Found	30 Rugged Leather, 14 Devilsaur Leather, 1 Cured Rugged Hide, 1 Rune Thread
Living Breastplate	300	Found	16 Rugged Leather, 8 Living Essence, 2 Mooncloth, 1 Cured Rugged Hide, 2 Rune Thread
Onyxia Scale Cloak	300	Found	1 Scale of Onyxia, 1 Cindercloth Cloak, 1 Rune Thread
Runic Leather Pants	300	Found	18 Rugged Leather, 12 Runecloth, 2 Enchanted Leather, 1 Rune Thread
Wicked Leather Belt	300	Found	14 Rugged Leather, 2 Black Dye, 2 Rune Thread

Leatherworking

Created Item	Skill Lvl	Source	Reagent(s)
Heavy Scorpid Shoulders	300	Found	14 Rugged Leather, 14 Heavy Scorpid Scale, 1 Cured Rugged Hide, 2 Rune Thread
Runic Leather Armor	300	Found	22 Rugged Leather, 4 Enchanted Leather, 16 Runecloth, 1 Cured Rugged Hide, 2 Rune Thread
Volcanic Shoulders	300	Found	10 Rugged Leather, 1 Essence of Fire, 1 Essence of Earth, 2 Rune Thread
Wicked Leather Armor	300	Found	20 Rugged Leather, 2 Cured Rugged Hide, 2 Felcloth, 4 Black Dye, 2 Rune Thread
Black Dragonscale Leggings	300	Found	40 Rugged Leather, 60 Black Dragonscale, 4 Enchanted Leather, 1 Cured Rugged Hide, 2 Rune Thread
Frostsaber Tunic	300	Found	12 Rugged Leather, 12 Frostsaber Leather, 1 Cured Rugged Hide, 2 Rune Thread
Onyxia Scale Breastplate	300	Found	40 Rugged Leather, 12 Scale of Onyxia, 60 Black Dragonscale, 2 Rune Thread
Runic Leather Shoulders	300	Found	16 Rugged Leather, 4 Enchanted Leather, 18 Runecloth, 1 Cured Rugged Hide, 2 Rune Thread
Molten Helm	300	Found	15 Core Leather, 3 Fiery Core, 6 Lava Core, 2 Rune Thread
Black Dragonscale Boots	300	Found	6 Enchanted Leather, 30 Black Dragonscale, 4 Fiery Core, 3 Lava Core, 2 Rune Thread
Core Armor Kit	300	Found	3 Core Leather, 2 Rune Thread
Girdle of Insight	300	Found	12 Rugged Leather, 12 Powerful Mojo, 2 Cured Rugged Hide, 4 Rune Thread
Mongoose Boots	300	Found	12 Rugged Leather, 6 Essence of Air, 4 Black Diamond, 2 Cured Rugged Hide, 4 Rune Thread
Swift Flight Bracers	300	Found	12 Rugged Leather, 8 Larval Acid, 60 Ironfeather, 4 Cured Rugged Hide, 4 Rune Thread
Chromatic Cloak	300	Found	30 Rugged Leather, 12 Brilliant Chromatic Scale, 30 Black Dragonscale, 30 Red Dragonscale, 5 Cured Rugged Hide, 8 Rune Thread
Hide of the Wild	300	Found	30 Rugged Leather, 12 Living Essence, 10 Essence of Water, 8 Larval Acid, 3 Cured Rugged Hide, 8 Rune Thread
Shifting Cloak	300	Found	30 Rugged Leather, 12 Essence of Air, 4 Skin of Shadow, 8 Guardian Stone, 4 Cured Rugged Hide, 8 Rune Thread
Timbermaw Brawlers	300	Found	8 Enchanted Leather, 6 Powerful Mojo, 6 Living Essence, 2 Cured Rugged Hide, 2 Ironweb Spider Silk
Golden Mantle of the Dawn	300	Found	8 Enchanted Leather, 4 Living Essence, 4 Guardian Stone, 2 Cured Rugged Hide, 2 Rune Thread

Created Item	Skill Lvl	Source	Reagent(s)
Lava Belt	300	Found	5 Lava Core, 4 Cured Rugged Hide, 4 Ironweb Spider Silk
Chromatic Gauntlets	300	Found	5 Fiery Core, 2 Lava Core, 4 Core Leather, 4 Brilliant Chromatic Scale, 4 Cured Rugged Hide, 4 Ironweb Spider Silk
Corehound Belt	300	Found	8 Fiery Core, 12 Core Leather, 10 Enchanted Leather, 4 Cured Rugged Hide, 4 Ironweb Spider Silk
Molten Belt	300	Found	2 Fiery Core, 7 Lava Core, 6 Essence of Earth, 4 Cured Rugged Hide, 4 Ironweb Spider Silk
Blood Tiger Breastplate	300	Found	35 Primal Tiger Leather, 2 Bloodvine, 3 Cured Rugged Hide, 3 Rune Thread
Blood Tiger Shoulders	300	Found	25 Primal Tiger Leather, 2 Bloodvine, 3 Cured Rugged Hide, 3 Rune Thread
Primal Batskin Bracers	300	Found	8 Primal Bat Leather, 3 Cured Rugged Hide, 4 Living Essence, 3 Rune Thread
Primal Batskin Gloves	300	Found	10 Primal Bat Leather, 4 Cured Rugged Hide, 4 Living Essence, 3 Rune Thread
Primal Batskin Jerkin	300	Found	14 Primal Bat Leather, 5 Cured Rugged Hide, 4 Living Essence, 4 Rune Thread
Blue Dragonscale Leggings	300	Trained	28 Rugged Leather, 36 Blue Dragonscale, 2 Cured Rugged Hide, 2 Rune Thread
Spitfire Bracers	300	Found	1 Light Silithid Carapace, 20 Silithid Chitin, 2 Essence of Fire
Spitfire Gauntlets	300	Found	2 Light Silithid Carapace, 30 Silithid Chitin, 2 Essence of Fire, 1 Cured Rugged Hide
Spitfire Breastplate	300	Found	3 Light Silithid Carapace, 40 Silithid Chitin, 2 Essence of Fire, 2 Cured Rugged Hide
Sandstalker Bracers	300	Found	1 Heavy Silithid Carapace, 20 Silithid Chitin, 2 Larval Acid
Sandstalker Gauntlets	300	Found	2 Heavy Silithid Carapace, 30 Silithid Chitin, 2 Larval Acid, 1 Cured Rugged Hide
Sandstalker Breastplate	300	Found	3 Heavy Silithid Carapace, 40 Silithid Chitin, 2 Larval Acid, 2 Cured Rugged Hide
Dreamscale Breastplate	300	Found	12 Enchanted Leather, 6 Dreamscale, 4 Living Essence, 4 Cured Rugged Hide, 6 Ironweb Spider Silk
Stormshroud Gloves	300	Found	6 Enchanted Leather, 4 Essence of Water, 4 Essence of Air, 2 Cured Rugged Hide, 2 Ironweb Spider Silk
Icy Scale Bracers	300	Found	4 Frozen Rune, 16 Heavy Scorpid Scale, 2 Essence of Water, 2 Cured Rugged Hide, 4 Ironweb Spider Silk
Icy Scale Breastplate	300	Found	7 Frozen Rune, 24 Heavy Scorpid Scale, 2 Essence of Water, 4 Cured Rugged Hide, 4 Ironweb Spider Silk
Icy Scale Gauntlets	300	Found	5 Frozen Rune, 16 Heavy Scorpid Scale, 2 Essence of Water, 3 Cured Rugged Hide, 4 Ironweb Spider Silk

Created Item	Skill Lvl	Source	Reagent(s)
Polar Bracers	300	Found	4 Frozen Rune, 12 Enchanted Leather, 2 Essence of Water, 2 Cured Rugged Hide, 4 Ironweb Spider Silk
Polar Gloves	300	Found	5 Frozen Rune, 12 Enchanted Leather, 2 Essence of Water, 3 Cured Rugged Hide, 4 Ironweb Spider Silk
Polar Tunic	300	Found	7 Frozen Rune, 16 Enchanted Leather, 2 Essence of Water, 4 Cured Rugged Hide, 4 Ironweb Spider Silk
Bramblewood Belt	300	Found	4 Enchanted Leather, 2 Living Essence, 1 Cured Rugged Hide
Bramblewood Boots	300	Found	6 Enchanted Leather, 2 Larval Acid, 2 Living Essence, 2 Cured Rugged Hide
Bramblewood Helm	300	Found	12 Enchanted Leather, 2 Bloodvine, 2 Living Essence, 2 Cured Rugged Hide
Knothide Leather	300	Trained	5 Knothide Leather Scraps
Knothide Armor Kit	300	Trained	6 Knothide Leather
Felscale Gloves	300	Trained	5 Knothide Leather, 1 Fel Scales, 2 Rune Thread
Scaled Draenic Pants	300	Trained	6 Knothide Leather, 3 Fel Scales, 2 Rune Thread
Thick Draenic Gloves	300	Trained	6 Knothide Leather, 2 Rune Thread
Wild Draenish Boots	300	Trained	6 Knothide Leather, 3 Rune Thread
Comfortable Insoles	300	Found	2 Knothide Leather
Gordok Ogre Suit	N/A	Special	4 Rugged Leather, 2 Bolt of Runecloth, 1 Ogre Tannin, 1 Rune Thread
Felscale Boots	310	Trained	8 Knothide Leather, 1 Fel Scales, 2 Rune Thread
Scaled Draenic Gloves	310	Trained	8 Knothide Leather, 1 Fel Scales, 2 Rune Thread
Wild Draenish Gloves	310	Trained	9 Knothide Leather, 3 Rune Thread
Thick Draenic Pants	315	Trained	10 Knothide Leather, 2 Rune Thread
Felscale Pants	320	Trained	10 Knothide Leather, 3 Fel Scales, 3 Rune Thread
Thick Draenic Boots	320	Trained	10 Knothide Leather, 3 Rune Thread
Wild Draenish Leggings	320	Trained	13 Knothide Leather, 3 Rune Thread
Heavy Knothide Leather	325	Found	5 Knothide Leather
Vindicator's Armor Kit	325	Found	3 Heavy Knothide Leather, 1 Primal Earth
Magister's Armor Kit	325	Found	3 Heavy Knothide Leather, 1 Primal Mana
Scaled Draenic Vest	325	Trained	12 Knothide Leather, 3 Fel Scales, 3 Rune Thread
Reinforced Mining Bag	325	Found	6 Heavy Knothide Leather, 4 Primal Earth
Thick Draenic Vest	330	Trained	14 Knothide Leather, 3 Rune Thread
Wild Draenish Vest	330	Trained	15 Knothide Leather, 3 Rune Thread
Golden Dragonstrike Breastplate	330	Trained	20 Knothide Leather, 8 Black Dragonscale, 3 Primal Fire, 2 Rune Thread
Living Crystal Breastplate	330	Trained	20 Knothide Leather, 12 Crystal Infused Leather, 3 Primal Life, 2 Rune Thread

Leatherworking

Created Item	Skill Lvl	Source	Reagent(s)
Primalstorm Breastplate	330	Trained	20 Knothide Leather, 2 Primal Air, 2 Primal Earth, 2 Rune Thread
Felscale Breastplate	335	Trained	14 Knothide Leather, 3 Fel Scales, 3 Rune Thread
Scaled Draenic Boots	335	Trained	12 Knothide Leather, 2 Fel Scales, 3 Rune Thread
Cobrahide Leg Armor	335	Found	4 Heavy Knothide Leather, 2 Cobra Scales, 4 Primal Air
Clefthide Leg Armor	335	Found	4 Heavy Knothide Leather, 8 Thick Clefthoof Leather, 4 Primal Earth
Fel Leather Gloves	340	Found	6 Heavy Knothide Leather, 6 Fel Hide, 6 Primal Shadow, 3 Rune Thread
Netherfury Belt	340	Found	4 Heavy Knothide Leather, 8 Crystal Infused Leather, 3 Primal Water, 3 Primal Mana, 2 Rune Thread
Netherfury Leggings	340	Found	8 Heavy Knothide Leather, 12 Crystal Infused Leather, 5 Primal Water, 5 Primal Mana, 2 Rune Thread
Shadow Armor Kit	340	Found	4 Heavy Knothide Leather, 4 Primal Life
Flame Armor Kit	340	Found	4 Heavy Knothide Leather, 4 Primal Water
Frost Armor Kit	340	Found	4 Heavy Knothide Leather, 4 Primal Fire
Nature Armor Kit	340	Found	4 Heavy Knothide Leather, 4 Primal Shadow
Arcane Armor Kit	340	Found	4 Heavy Knothide Leather, 4 Primal Mana
Drums of War	340	Trained	2 Heavy Knothide Leather, 1 Primal Fire, 2 Thick Clefthoof Leather
Drums of Speed	345	Found	2 Heavy Knothide Leather, 1 Primal Air
Riding Crop	350	Found	4 Heavy Knothide Leather, 1 Primal Might, 6 Arcane Dust, 1 Small Prismatic Shard
Stylin' Purple Hat	350	Found	6 Heavy Knothide Leather, 2 Cobra Scales, 8 Primal Shadow, 4 Zhevra Leather, 3 Rune Thread
Stylin' Adventure Hat	350	Found	6 Heavy Knothide Leather, 2 Cobra Scales, 8 Primal Life, 4 Zhevra Leather, 3 Rune Thread
Stylin' Jungle Hat	350	Found	6 Heavy Knothide Leather, 2 Cobra Scales, 8 Primal Earth, 3 Rune Thread
Stylin' Crimson Hat	350	Found	6 Heavy Knothide Leather, 2 Cobra Scales, 8 Primal Fire, 4 Zhevra Leather, 3 Rune Thread
Fel Leather Boots	350	Found	10 Heavy Knothide Leather, 8 Fel Hide, 8 Primal Shadow, 3 Rune Thread
Fel Leather Leggings	350	Found	10 Heavy Knothide Leather, 10 Fel Hide, 10 Primal Shadow, 3 Rune Thread
Felstalker Belt	350	Found	6 Heavy Knothide Leather, 4 Fel Hide, 8 Crystal Infused Leather, 6 Primal Air, 2 Rune Thread
Netherfury Boots	350	Found	6 Heavy Knothide Leather, 10 Crystal Infused Leather, 4 Primal Water, 4 Primal Mana, 2 Rune Thread

Leatherworking

Created Item	Skill Lvl	Source	Reagent(s)
Enchanted Felscale Boots	350	Found	4 Heavy Knothide Leather, 10 Fel Scales, 6 Primal Mana
Enchanted Felscale Gloves	350	Found	4 Heavy Knothide Leather, 10 Fel Scales, 6 Primal Mana
Enchanted Felscale Leggings	350	Found	6 Heavy Knothide Leather, 12 Fel Scales, 8 Primal Mana
Flamescale Belt	350	Found	4 Heavy Knothide Leather, 8 Crystal Infused Leather, 3 Primal Fire, 3 Primal Water
Flamescale Boots	350	Found	4 Heavy Knothide Leather, 8 Crystal Infused Leather, 3 Primal Fire, 3 Primal Water
Flamescale Leggings	350	Found	6 Heavy Knothide Leather, 12 Crystal Infused Leather, 4 Primal Fire, 4 Primal Water
Enchanted Clefthoof Boots	350	Found	4 Heavy Knothide Leather, 16 Thick Clefthoof Leather, 6 Primal Mana
Enchanted Clefthoof Gloves	350	Found	4 Heavy Knothide Leather, 16 Thick Clefthoof Leather, 6 Primal Mana
Enchanted Clefthoof Leggings	350	Found	6 Heavy Knothide Leather, 24 Thick Clefthoof Leather, 8 Primal Mana
Blastguard Belt	350	Found	4 Heavy Knothide Leather, 6 Fel Hide, 3 Primal Fire, 3 Primal Water
Blastguard Boots	350	Found	4 Heavy Knothide Leather, 8 Fel Hide, 3 Primal Fire, 3 Primal Water
Blastguard Pants	350	Found	6 Heavy Knothide Leather, 10 Fel Hide, 4 Primal Fire, 4 Primal Water
Drums of Restoration	350	Found	2 Heavy Knothide Leather, 2 Primal Life
Heavy Clefthoof Leggings	355	Found	6 Heavy Knothide Leather, 34 Thick Clefthoof Leather, 4 Primal Earth, 2 Rune Thread
Heavy Clefthoof Boots	355	Found	4 Heavy Knothide Leather, 20 Thick Clefthoof Leather, 4 Primal Earth, 2 Rune Thread
Heavy Clefthoof Vest	360	Found	6 Heavy Knothide Leather, 40 Thick Clefthoof Leather, 4 Primal Earth, 2 Rune Thread
Felstalker Bracer	360	Found	6 Heavy Knothide Leather, 6 Fel Hide, 6 Crystal Infused Leather, 4 Primal Air, 2 Rune Thread
Felstalker Breastplate	360	Found	10 Heavy Knothide Leather, 4 Fel Hide, 8 Crystal Infused Leather, 8 Primal Air, 2 Rune Thread
Drums of Battle	365	Found	2 Heavy Knothide Leather, 1 Primal Fire, 1 Primal Earth
Nethercobra Leg Armor	365	Found	4 Heavy Knothide Leather, 4 Cobra Scales, 8 Primal Air, 1 Primal Nether
Nethercleft Leg Armor	365	Found	4 Heavy Knothide Leather, 16 Thick Clefthoof Leather, 8 Primal Earth, 1 Primal Nether

Created Item	Skill Lvl	Source	Reagent(s)
Cobrascale Gloves	365	Found	4 Heavy Knothide Leather, 8 Cobra Scales, 12 Primal Air, 12 Primal Shadow, 1 Primal Nether
Cobrascale Hood	365	Found	6 Heavy Knothide Leather, 10 Cobra Scales, 15 Primal Air, 15 Primal Shadow, 1 Primal Nether
Earthen Netherscale Boots	365	Found	4 Heavy Knothide Leather, 24 Nether Dragonscales, 22 Primal Earth, 4 Primal Mana, 1 Primal Nether
Gloves of the Living Touch	365	Found	4 Heavy Knothide Leather, 16 Primal Life, 12 Primal Earth, 1 Primal Nether
Hood of Primal Life	365	Found	6 Heavy Knothide Leather, 20 Primal Life, 8 Primal Water, 1 Primal Nether
Living Dragonscale Helm	365	Found	6 Heavy Knothide Leather, 28 Nether Dragonscales, 12 Primal Life, 12 Primal Mana, 1 Primal Nether
Netherdrake Gloves	365	Found	4 Heavy Knothide Leather, 24 Nether Dragonscales, 14 Primal Fire, 10 Primal Mana, 1 Primal Nether
Netherdrake Helm	365	Found	6 Heavy Knothide Leather, 28 Nether Dragonscales, 18 Primal Fire, 12 Primal Mana, 1 Primal Nether
Thick Netherscale Breastplate	365	Found	8 Heavy Knothide Leather, 32 Nether Dragonscales, 20 Primal Earth, 8 Primal Air, 1 Primal Nether
Windslayer Wraps	365	Found	4 Heavy Knothide Leather, 12 Wind Scales, 18 Primal Earth, 8 Primal Air, 1 Primal Nether
Windscale Hood	365	Found	6 Heavy Knothide Leather, 20 Wind Scales, 18 Primal Air, 10 Primal Mana, 1 Primal Nether
Windstrike Gloves	365	Found	4 Heavy Knothide Leather, 14 Wind Scales, 14 Primal Air, 10 Primal Fire, 1 Primal Nether
Drums of Panic	370	Found	2 Heavy Knothide Leather, 2 Primal Shadow
Ebon Netherscale Belt	375	Trained	6 Heavy Knothide Leather, 24 Nether Dragonscales, 12 Primal Fire, 12 Primal Shadow, 1 Primal Nether
Ebon Netherscale Bracers	375	Trained	4 Heavy Knothide Leather, 18 Nether Dragonscales, 8 Primal Fire, 8 Primal Shadow
Ebon Netherscale Breastplate	375	Trained	8 Heavy Knothide Leather, 30 Nether Dragonscales, 16 Primal Fire, 16 Primal Shadow, 2 Primal Nether
Netherstrike Belt	375	Trained	6 Heavy Knothide Leather, 24 Nether Dragonscales, 12 Primal Mana, 12 Primal Air, 1 Primal Nether
Netherstrike Bracers	375	Trained	4 Heavy Knothide Leather, 18 Nether Dragonscales, 8 Primal Mana, 8 Primal Air

Created Item	Skill Lvl	Source	Reagent(s)
Netherstrike Breastplate	375	Trained	8 Heavy Knothide Leather, 30 Nether Dragonscales, 16 Primal Mana, 16 Primal Air, 2 Primal Nether
Primalstrike Belt	375	Trained	6 Heavy Knothide Leather, 5 Primal Might, 1 Primal Nether
Primalstrike Bracers	375	Trained	4 Heavy Knothide Leather, 3 Primal Might
Primalstrike Vest	375	Trained	8 Heavy Knothide Leather, 6 Primal Might, 2 Primal Nether
Windhawk Belt	375	Trained	6 Heavy Knothide Leather, 16 Wind Scales, 12 Primal Air, 2 Primal Might, 1 Primal Nether
Windhawk Bracers	375	Trained	4 Heavy Knothide Leather, 12 Wind Scales, 8 Primal Air, 1 Primal Might
Windhawk Hauberk	375	Trained	8 Heavy Knothide Leather, 20 Wind Scales, 16 Primal Air, 3 Primal Might, 2 Primal Nether
Belt of Natural Power	375	Found	5 Nether Vortex, 4 Heavy Knothide Leather, 4 Primal Life, 2 Rune Thread
Belt of Deep Shadow	375	Found	5 Nether Vortex, 4 Heavy Knothide Leather, 4 Primal Shadow, 2 Rune Thread
Belt of the Black Eagle	375	Found	4 Nether Vortex, 4 Heavy Knothide Leather, 4 Primal Air, 6 Wind Scales, 2 Rune Thread
Monsoon Belt	375	Found	4 Nether Vortex, 4 Heavy Knothide Leather, 4 Primal Water, 6 Wind Scales, 2 Rune Thread
Boots of Natural Grace	375	Found	2 Primal Nether, 4 Heavy Knothide Leather, 12 Primal Life, 2 Rune Thread
Boots of Utter Darkness	375	Found	2 Primal Nether, 4 Heavy Knothide Leather, 12 Primal Shadow, 2 Rune Thread
Boots of the Crimson Hawk	375	Found	2 Primal Nether, 4 Heavy Knothide Leather, 10 Primal Air, 6 Wind Scales, 2 Rune Thread
Hurricane Boots	375	Found	2 Primal Nether, 4 Heavy Knothide Leather, 10 Primal Water, 6 Wind Scales, 2 Rune Thread

Poisons

Created Item	Skill Lvl	Source	Reagent(s)
Instant Poison	N/A	Special	1 Dust of Decay, 1 Empty Vial
Crippling Poison	1	Trained	1 Essence of Pain, 1 Empty Vial
Mind-numbing Poison	100	Trained	1 Dust of Decay, 1 Essence of Pain, 1 Empty Vial
Instant Poison II	120	Trained	3 Dust of Decay, 1 Leaded Vial
Deadly Poison	130	Trained	1 Deathweed, 1 Leaded Vial
Wound Poison	140	Trained	1 Essence of Pain, 1 Deathweed, 1 Leaded Vial
Blinding Powder	150	Trained	1 Fadeleaf
Instant Poison III	160	Trained	1 Dust of Deterioration, 1 Leaded Vial
Deadly Poison II	170	Trained	2 Deathweed, 1 Leaded Vial
Mind-numbing Poison II	170	Trained	4 Dust of Decay, 4 Essence of Pain, 1 Leaded Vial
Wound Poison II	180	Trained	1 Essence of Pain, 2 Deathweed, 1 Leaded Vial
Instant Poison IV	200	Trained	2 Dust of Deterioration, 1 Crystal Vial
Deadly Poison III	210	Trained	3 Deathweed, 1 Crystal Vial
Wound Poison III	220	Trained	1 Essence of Agony, 2 Deathweed, 1 Crystal Vial
Crippling Poison II	230	Trained	3 Essence of Agony, 1 Crystal Vial
Instant Poison V	240	Trained	3 Dust of Deterioration, 1 Crystal Vial
Mind-numbing Poison III	240	Trained	2 Dust of Deterioration, 2 Essence of Agony, 1 Crystal Vial
Deadly Poison IV	250	Trained	5 Deathweed, 1 Crystal Vial
Wound Poison IV	260	Trained	2 Essence of Agony, 2 Deathweed, 1 Crystal Vial
Instant Poison VI	280	Trained	4 Dust of Deterioration, 1 Crystal Vial
Deadly Poison V	280	Trained	7 Deathweed, 1 Crystal Vial
Deadly Poison VI	290	Trained	1 Maiden's Anguish, 1 Crystal Vial
Wound Poison V	300	Trained	3 Essence of Agony, 3 Deathweed, 1 Crystal Vial
Instant Poison VII	320	Trained	1 Maiden's Anguish, 1 Dust of Deterioration, 1 Crystal Vial
Deadly Poison VII	330	Trained	1 Maiden's Anguish, 1 Deathweed, 1 Crystal Vial
Anesthetic Poison	340	Trained	4 Lethargy Root, 1 Deathweed, 1 Crystal Vial

Tailoring

Created Item	Skill Lvl	Source	Reagent(s)
Bolt of Linen Cloth	N/A	Special	2 Linen Cloth
Linen Cloak	N/A	Special	1 Bolt of Linen Cloth, 1 Coarse Thread
Brown Linen Shirt	N/A	Special	1 Bolt of Linen Cloth, 1 Coarse Thread
Simple Linen Pants	N/A	Special	1 Bolt of Linen Cloth, 1 Coarse Thread
White Linen Shirt	1	Trained	1 Bolt of Linen Cloth, 1 Coarse Thread, 1 Bleach
Brown Linen Vest	10	Trained	1 Bolt of Linen Cloth, 1 Coarse Thread
Linen Belt	15	Trained	1 Bolt of Linen Cloth, 1 Coarse Thread
Simple Linen Boots	20	Trained	2 Bolt of Linen Cloth, 1 Light Leather, 1 Coarse Thread
Brown Linen Pants	30	Trained	2 Bolt of Linen Cloth, 1 Coarse Thread
Brown Linen Robe	30	Trained	3 Bolt of Linen Cloth, 1 Coarse Thread
White Linen Robe	30	Trained	3 Bolt of Linen Cloth, 1 Coarse Thread, 1 Bleach
Heavy Linen Gloves	35	Trained	2 Bolt of Linen Cloth, 1 Coarse Thread
Red Linen Robe	40	Found	3 Bolt of Linen Cloth, 2 Coarse Thread, 2 Red Dye
Red Linen Shirt	40	Trained	2 Bolt of Linen Cloth, 1 Coarse Thread, 1 Red Dye
Blue Linen Shirt	40	Trained	2 Bolt of Linen Cloth, 1 Coarse Thread, 1 Blue Dye
Simple Dress	40	Trained	2 Bolt of Linen Cloth, 1 Coarse Thread, 1 Blue Dye, 1 Bleach
Linen Bag	45	Trained	3 Bolt of Linen Cloth, 3 Coarse Thread
Blue Linen Vest	55	Found	3 Bolt of Linen Cloth, 1 Coarse Thread, 1 Blue Dye
Red Linen Vest	55	Found	3 Bolt of Linen Cloth, 1 Coarse Thread, 1 Red Dye
Reinforced Linen Cape	60	Trained	2 Bolt of Linen Cloth, 3 Coarse Thread
Green Linen Bracers	60	Trained	3 Bolt of Linen Cloth, 2 Coarse Thread, 1 Green Dye
Linen Boots	65	Trained	3 Bolt of Linen Cloth, 1 Coarse Thread, 1 Light Leather
Barbaric Linen Vest	70	Trained	4 Bolt of Linen Cloth, 1 Light Leather, 1 Fine Thread
Green Linen Shirt	70	Trained	3 Bolt of Linen Cloth, 1 Fine Thread, 1 Green Dye
Handstitched Linen Britches	70	Trained	4 Bolt of Linen Cloth, 2 Fine Thread
Red Linen Bag	70	Found	4 Bolt of Linen Cloth, 1 Fine Thread, 1 Red Dye
Blue Linen Robe	70	Found	4 Bolt of Linen Cloth, 2 Coarse Thread, 2 Blue Dye
Bolt of Woolen Cloth	75	Trained	3 Wool Cloth
Woolen Cape	75	Trained	1 Bolt of Woolen Cloth, 1 Fine Thread
Simple Kilt	75	Trained	4 Bolt of Linen Cloth, 1 Fine Thread
Soft-soled Linen Boots	80	Trained	5 Bolt of Linen Cloth, 2 Light Leather, 1 Fine Thread
Woolen Bag	80	Trained	3 Bolt of Woolen Cloth, 1 Fine Thread

Tailoring

Created Item	Skill Lvl	Source	Reagent(s)
Green Woolen Vest	85	Trained	2 Bolt of Woolen Cloth, 2 Fine Thread, 1 Green Dye
Heavy Woolen Gloves	85	Trained	3 Bolt of Woolen Cloth, 1 Fine Thread
Pearl-clasped Cloak	90	Trained	3 Bolt of Woolen Cloth, 2 Fine Thread, 1 Small Lustrous Pearl
Green Woolen Robe	90	Found	3 Bolt of Woolen Cloth, 2 Fine Thread, 1 Green Dye
Woolen Boots	95	Trained	4 Bolt of Woolen Cloth, 2 Fine Thread, 2 Light Leather
Red Woolen Boots	95	Found	4 Bolt of Woolen Cloth, 2 Light Leather, 1 Fine Thread, 2 Red Dye
Green Woolen Bag	95	Found	4 Bolt of Woolen Cloth, 1 Green Dye, 1 Fine Thread
Gray Woolen Shirt	100	Trained	2 Bolt of Woolen Cloth, 1 Fine Thread, 1 Gray Dye
Heavy Woolen Cloak	100	Found	3 Bolt of Woolen Cloth, 2 Fine Thread, 2 Small Lustrous Pearl
Blue Overalls	100	Found	4 Bolt of Woolen Cloth, 2 Fine Thread, 2 Blue Dye
Gray Woolen Robe	105	Found	4 Bolt of Woolen Cloth, 3 Fine Thread, 1 Gray Dye
Double-stitched Woolen Shoulders	110	Trained	3 Bolt of Woolen Cloth, 2 Fine Thread
Heavy Woolen Pants	110	Trained	5 Bolt of Woolen Cloth, 4 Fine Thread
Stylish Red Shirt	110	Trained	3 Bolt of Woolen Cloth, 2 Red Dye, 1 Fine Thread
White Woolen Dress	110	Trained	3 Bolt of Woolen Cloth, 4 Bleach, 1 Fine Thread
Red Woolen Bag	115	Found	4 Bolt of Woolen Cloth, 1 Red Dye, 1 Fine Thread
Greater Adept's Robe	115	Found	5 Bolt of Woolen Cloth, 3 Fine Thread, 3 Red Dye
Reinforced Woolen Shoulders	120	Found	6 Bolt of Woolen Cloth, 2 Medium Leather, 2 Fine Thread
Stylish Blue Shirt	120	Found	4 Bolt of Woolen Cloth, 2 Blue Dye, 1 Gray Dye, 1 Fine Thread
Stylish Green Shirt	120	Found	4 Bolt of Woolen Cloth, 2 Green Dye, 1 Gray Dye, 1 Fine Thread
Colorful Kilt	120	Found	5 Bolt of Woolen Cloth, 3 Red Dye, 1 Fine Thread
Bolt of Silk Cloth	125	Trained	4 Silk Cloth
Phoenix Pants	125	Found	6 Bolt of Woolen Cloth, 1 Iridescent Pearl, 3 Fine Thread
Spidersilk Boots	125	Trained	2 Bolt of Silk Cloth, 4 Medium Leather, 4 Spider's Silk, 2 Iridescent Pearl
Phoenix Gloves	125	Found	4 Bolt of Woolen Cloth, 1 Iridescent Pearl, 4 Fine Thread, 2 Bleach
Gloves of Meditation	130	Trained	4 Bolt of Woolen Cloth, 3 Fine Thread, 1 Elixir of Wisdom

Tailoring

Created Item	Skill Lvl	Source	Reagent(s)
Bright Yellow Shirt	135	Found	1 Bolt of Silk Cloth, 1 Yellow Dye, 1 Fine Thread
Lesser Wizard's Robe	135	Trained	2 Bolt of Silk Cloth, 2 Fine Thread, 2 Spider's Silk
Spider Silk Slippers	140	Found	3 Bolt of Silk Cloth, 1 Spider's Silk, 2 Fine Thread
Azure Silk Pants	140	Trained	4 Bolt of Silk Cloth, 2 Blue Dye, 3 Fine Thread
Boots of Darkness	140	Found	3 Bolt of Silk Cloth, 2 Medium Leather, 1 Shadow Protection Potion, 2 Fine Thread
Azure Silk Gloves	145	Found	3 Bolt of Silk Cloth, 2 Heavy Leather, 2 Blue Dye, 2 Fine Thread
Azure Silk Hood	145	Trained	2 Bolt of Silk Cloth, 2 Blue Dye, 1 Fine Thread
Hands of Darkness	145	Found	3 Bolt of Silk Cloth, 2 Heavy Leather, 2 Shadow Protection Potion, 2 Fine Thread
Azure Silk Vest	150	Trained	5 Bolt of Silk Cloth, 4 Blue Dye
Small Silk Pack	150	Trained	3 Bolt of Silk Cloth, 2 Heavy Leather, 3 Fine Thread
Robes of Arcana	150	Found	4 Bolt of Silk Cloth, 2 Fine Thread, 2 Spider's Silk
Truefaith Gloves	150	Found	3 Bolt of Silk Cloth, 2 Heavy Leather, 4 Healing Potion, 1 Fine Thread
Dark Silk Shirt	155	Found	2 Bolt of Silk Cloth, 2 Gray Dye, 1 Fine Thread
White Swashbuckler's Shirt	160	Trained	3 Bolt of Silk Cloth, 2 Bleach, 1 Silken Thread
Silk Headband	160	Trained	3 Bolt of Silk Cloth, 2 Fine Thread
Enchanter's Cowl	165	Found	3 Bolt of Silk Cloth, 2 Fine Thread, 2 Thick Spider's Silk
Green Silk Armor	165	Found	5 Bolt of Silk Cloth, 2 Green Dye, 1 Silken Thread
Shadow Hood	170	Found	4 Bolt of Silk Cloth, 1 Silken Thread, 1 Shadow Oil
Formal White Shirt	170	Trained	3 Bolt of Silk Cloth, 2 Bleach, 1 Fine Thread
Earthen Vest	170	Trained	3 Bolt of Silk Cloth, 1 Elemental Earth, 2 Fine Thread
Bolt of Mageweave	175	Trained	5 Mageweave Cloth
Boots of the Enchanter	175	Found	4 Bolt of Silk Cloth, 1 Silken Thread, 2 Thick Spider's Silk
Green Silk Pack	175	Found	4 Bolt of Silk Cloth, 3 Heavy Leather, 3 Fine Thread, 1 Green Dye
Red Swashbuckler's Shirt	175	Trained	3 Bolt of Silk Cloth, 2 Red Dye, 1 Silken Thread
Azure Silk Belt	175	Trained	4 Bolt of Silk Cloth, 1 Elemental Water, 2 Blue Dye, 2 Fine Thread, 1 Iron Buckle
Crimson Silk Belt	175	Trained	4 Bolt of Silk Cloth, 1 Iron Buckle, 2 Red Dye, 1 Silken Thread

Tailoring

Created Item	Skill Lvl	Source	Reagent(s)
Azure Silk Cloak	175	Found	3 Bolt of Silk Cloth, 2 Blue Dye, 2 Fine Thread
Spider Belt	180	Found	4 Bolt of Silk Cloth, 2 Thick Spider's Silk, 1 Iron Buckle
Green Silken Shoulders	180	Trained	5 Bolt of Silk Cloth, 2 Silken Thread
Crimson Silk Cloak	180	Found	5 Bolt of Silk Cloth, 2 Red Dye, 2 Fire Oil, 1 Silken Thread
Long Silken Cloak	185	Trained	4 Bolt of Silk Cloth, 1 Mana Potion, 1 Silken Thread
Rich Purple Silk Shirt	185	Found	4 Bolt of Silk Cloth, 1 Purple Dye, 1 Silken Thread
Black Silk Pack	185	Found	5 Bolt of Silk Cloth, 1 Black Dye, 4 Fine Thread
Crimson Silk Vest	185	Trained	4 Bolt of Silk Cloth, 2 Red Dye, 2 Fine Thread
Robe of Power	190	Trained	2 Bolt of Mageweave, 2 Elemental Earth, 2 Elemental Water, 2 Elemental Fire, 2 Elemental Air, 2 Silken Thread
Crimson Silk Shoulders	190	Found	5 Bolt of Silk Cloth, 2 Fire Oil, 2 Red Dye, 2 Silken Thread
Azure Shoulders	190	Found	6 Bolt of Silk Cloth, 2 Naga Scale, 2 Blue Dye, 2 Silken Thread
Green Holiday Shirt	190	Found	5 Bolt of Silk Cloth, 4 Green Dye, 1 Silken Thread
Earthen Silk Belt	195	Found	5 Bolt of Silk Cloth, 4 Elemental Earth, 4 Heavy Leather, 1 Iron Buckle, 2 Silken Thread
Crimson Silk Pantaloons	195	Trained	4 Bolt of Silk Cloth, 2 Red Dye, 2 Silken Thread
Icy Cloak	200	Found	3 Bolt of Mageweave, 2 Silken Thread, 1 Frost Oil, 2 Thick Spider's Silk
Star Belt	200	Found	4 Bolt of Mageweave, 4 Heavy Leather, 1 Citrine, 1 Iron Buckle, 1 Silken Thread
Black Swashbuckler's Shirt	200	Found	5 Bolt of Silk Cloth, 1 Black Dye, 1 Silken Thread
Crimson Silk Robe	205	Found	8 Bolt of Silk Cloth, 4 Elemental Fire, 2 Mana Potion, 4 Red Dye, 1 Silken Thread
Black Mageweave Vest	205	Trained	2 Bolt of Mageweave, 3 Silken Thread
Black Mageweave Leggings	205	Trained	2 Bolt of Mageweave, 3 Silken Thread
Crimson Silk Gloves	210	Trained	6 Bolt of Silk Cloth, 2 Elemental Fire, 2 Fire Oil, 2 Thick Leather, 4 Red Dye, 2 Silken Thread
Black Mageweave Robe	210	Trained	3 Bolt of Mageweave, 1 Heavy Silken Thread
Black Mageweave Gloves	215	Trained	2 Bolt of Mageweave, 2 Heavy Silken Thread
Red Mageweave Vest	215	Found	3 Bolt of Mageweave, 2 Red Dye, 1 Heavy Silken Thread

Tailoring

Created Item	Skill Lvl	Source	Reagent(s)
White Bandit Mask	215	Found	1 Bolt of Mageweave, 1 Bleach, 1 Heavy Silken Thread
Red Mageweave Pants	215	Found	3 Bolt of Mageweave, 2 Red Dye, 1 Heavy Silken Thread
Orange Mageweave Shirt	215	Trained	1 Bolt of Mageweave, 1 Orange Dye, 1 Heavy Silken Thread
Stormcloth Pants	220	Found	4 Bolt of Mageweave, 2 Globe of Water, 2 Heavy Silken Thread
Stormcloth Gloves	220	Found	3 Bolt of Mageweave, 2 Globe of Water, 2 Heavy Silken Thread
Orange Martial Shirt	220	Found	2 Bolt of Mageweave, 2 Orange Dye, 1 Heavy Silken Thread
Mageweave Bag	225	Trained	4 Bolt of Mageweave, 2 Silken Thread
Red Mageweave Gloves	225	Found	3 Bolt of Mageweave, 2 Red Dye, 2 Heavy Silken Thread
Dreamweave Gloves	225	Trained	4 Bolt of Mageweave, 4 Wildvine, 2 Heart of the Wild, 2 Heavy Silken Thread
Stormcloth Vest	225	Found	5 Bolt of Mageweave, 3 Globe of Water, 2 Heavy Silken Thread
Cindercloth Robe	225	Trained	5 Bolt of Mageweave, 2 Heart of Fire, 2 Heavy Silken Thread
Dreamweave Vest	225	Trained	6 Bolt of Mageweave, 6 Wildvine, 2 Heart of the Wild, 2 Heavy Silken Thread
Enchanted Mageweave Pouch	225	Found	4 Bolt of Mageweave, 4 Vision Dust, 2 Heavy Silken Thread
Black Mageweave Headband	230	Trained	3 Bolt of Mageweave, 2 Heavy Silken Thread
Black Mageweave Boots	230	Trained	3 Bolt of Mageweave, 2 Heavy Silken Thread, 2 Thick Leather
Black Mageweave Shoulders	230	Trained	3 Bolt of Mageweave, 2 Heavy Silken Thread
Lavender Mageweave Shirt	230	Found	2 Bolt of Mageweave, 2 Purple Dye, 2 Heavy Silken Thread
Simple Black Dress	235	Trained	3 Bolt of Mageweave, 1 Black Dye, 1 Heavy Silken Thread, 1 Bleach
Red Mageweave Shoulders	235	Found	4 Bolt of Mageweave, 2 Red Dye, 3 Heavy Silken Thread
Red Mageweave Bag	235	Trained	4 Bolt of Mageweave, 2 Red Dye, 2 Heavy Silken Thread
Pink Mageweave Shirt	235	Found	3 Bolt of Mageweave, 1 Pink Dye, 1 Heavy Silken Thread
Admiral's Hat	240	Found	3 Bolt of Mageweave, 6 Long Elegant Feather, 2 Heavy Silken Thread
Stormcloth Headband	240	Found	4 Bolt of Mageweave, 4 Globe of Water, 2 Heavy Silken Thread
Red Mageweave Headband	240	Found	4 Bolt of Mageweave, 2 Red Dye, 2 Heavy Silken Thread
Tuxedo Shirt	240	Found	4 Bolt of Mageweave, 2 Heavy Silken Thread

Tailoring

Created Item	Skill Lvl	Source	Reagent(s)
Shadowweave Pants	N/A	Special	3 Bolt of Mageweave, 2 Shadow Silk, 1 Heavy Silken Thread
Shadowweave Robe	N/A	Special	3 Bolt of Mageweave, 2 Shadow Silk, 1 Heavy Silken Thread
Shadowweave Gloves	N/A	Special	5 Bolt of Mageweave, 5 Shadow Silk, 2 Heavy Silken Thread
Shadowweave Shoulders	N/A	Special	5 Bolt of Mageweave, 4 Shadow Silk, 2 Heavy Silken Thread
Shadowweave Boots	N/A	Special	6 Bolt of Mageweave, 6 Shadow Silk, 3 Heavy Silken Thread, 2 Thick Leather
Shadowweave Mask	245	Found	2 Bolt of Mageweave, 8 Shadow Silk, 2 Heavy Silken Thread
Stormcloth Shoulders	245	Found	5 Bolt of Mageweave, 6 Globe of Water, 3 Heavy Silken Thread
Cindercloth Boots	245	Trained	5 Bolt of Mageweave, 1 Heart of Fire, 3 Heavy Silken Thread, 2 Thick Leather
Tuxedo Pants	245	Found	4 Bolt of Mageweave, 3 Heavy Silken Thread
Stormcloth Boots	250	Found	6 Bolt of Mageweave, 6 Globe of Water, 3 Heavy Silken Thread, 2 Thick Leather
White Wedding Dress	250	Found	5 Bolt of Mageweave, 3 Heavy Silken Thread
Dreamweave Circlet	250	Trained	8 Bolt of Mageweave, 4 Wildvine, 2 Heart of the Wild, 3 Heavy Silken Thread, 1 Truesilver Bar, 1 Jade
Tuxedo Jacket	250	Found	5 Bolt of Mageweave, 3 Heavy Silken Thread
Bolt of Runecloth	250	Trained	5 Runecloth
Mooncloth	250	Found	2 Felcloth
Mooncloth Boots	N/A	Special	6 Bolt of Runecloth, 4 Mooncloth, 2 Black Pearl, 1 Rune Thread
Festival Dress	250	Found	4 Bolt of Runecloth, 2 Firebloom, 2 Red Dye, 1 Rune Thread
Festive Red Pant Suit	250	Found	4 Bolt of Runecloth, 2 Firebloom, 2 Red Dye, 1 Rune Thread
Runecloth Belt	255	Trained	3 Bolt of Runecloth, 1 Rune Thread
Frostweave Tunic	255	Found	5 Bolt of Runecloth, 2 Globe of Water, 1 Rune Thread
Frostweave Robe	255	Found	5 Bolt of Runecloth, 2 Globe of Water, 1 Rune Thread
Runecloth Robe	260	Found	5 Bolt of Runecloth, 1 Ironweb Spider Silk, 1 Rune Thread
Runecloth Bag	260	Found	5 Bolt of Runecloth, 2 Rugged Leather, 1 Rune Thread
Runecloth Tunic	260	Found	5 Bolt of Runecloth, 1 Ironweb Spider Silk, 1 Rune Thread
Cindercloth Vest	260	Found	5 Bolt of Runecloth, 2 Heart of Fire, 1 Rune Thread

Tailoring

Created Item	Skill Lvl	Source	Reagent(s)
Soul Pouch	260	Found	6 Bolt of Runecloth, 4 Rugged Leather, 2 Ichor of Undeath, 1 Rune Thread
Runecloth Cloak	265	Found	4 Bolt of Runecloth, 1 Ironweb Spider Silk, 1 Rune Thread
Ghostweave Belt	265	Found	3 Bolt of Runecloth, 2 Ghost Dye, 1 Ironweb Spider Silk, 1 Rune Thread
Frostweave Gloves	265	Found	3 Bolt of Runecloth, 1 Essence of Water, 1 Rune Thread
Cindercloth Gloves	270	Found	4 Bolt of Runecloth, 2 Heart of Fire, 1 Rune Thread
Brightcloth Gloves	270	Found	4 Bolt of Runecloth, 2 Gold Bar, 1 Rune Thread
Ghostweave Gloves	270	Found	4 Bolt of Runecloth, 2 Ghost Dye, 1 Ironweb Spider Silk, 1 Rune Thread
Brightcloth Robe	270	Found	5 Bolt of Runecloth, 2 Gold Bar, 1 Rune Thread
Ghostweave Vest	275	Found	6 Bolt of Runecloth, 4 Ghost Dye, 1 Ironweb Spider Silk, 1 Rune Thread
Runecloth Gloves	275	Found	4 Bolt of Runecloth, 4 Rugged Leather, 1 Rune Thread
Cindercloth Cloak	275	Found	5 Bolt of Runecloth, 1 Essence of Fire, 1 Rune Thread
Felcloth Pants	275	Found	5 Bolt of Runecloth, 2 Felcloth, 1 Rune Thread
Brightcloth Cloak	275	Found	4 Bolt of Runecloth, 2 Gold Bar, 1 Rune Thread
Wizardweave Leggings	275	Found	6 Bolt of Runecloth, 1 Dream Dust, 1 Rune Thread
Cloak of Fire	275	Found	6 Bolt of Runecloth, 4 Essence of Fire, 4 Heart of Fire, 4 Elemental Fire, 1 Rune Thread
Enchanted Runecloth Bag	275	Found	5 Bolt of Runecloth, 2 Greater Eternal Essence, 2 Rune Thread
Cenarion Herb Bag	275	Found	5 Bolt of Runecloth, 10 Purple Lotus, 8 Morrowgrain, 2 Rune Thread
Runecloth Boots	280	Found	4 Bolt of Runecloth, 2 Ironweb Spider Silk, 4 Rugged Leather, 1 Rune Thread
Frostweave Pants	280	Found	6 Bolt of Runecloth, 1 Essence of Water, 1 Rune Thread
Cindercloth Pants	280	Found	6 Bolt of Runecloth, 1 Essence of Fire, 1 Rune Thread
Robe of Winter Night	285	Found	10 Bolt of Runecloth, 12 Felcloth, 4 Essence of Undeath, 4 Essence of Water, 1 Rune Thread
Felcloth Boots	285	Found	6 Bolt of Runecloth, 2 Felcloth, 4 Rugged Leather, 1 Rune Thread
Runecloth Pants	285	Found	6 Bolt of Runecloth, 2 Ironweb Spider Silk, 1 Rune Thread
Felcloth Bag	285	Found	12 Felcloth, 6 Enchanted Leather, 2 Dark Rune, 4 Ironweb Spider Silk

Created Item	Skill Lvl	Source	Reagent(s)
Brightcloth Pants	290	Found	6 Bolt of Runecloth, 4 Gold Bar, 1 Ironweb Spider Silk, 1 Rune Thread
Mooncloth Leggings	290	Found	6 Bolt of Runecloth, 4 Mooncloth, 1 Rune Thread
Ghostweave Pants	290	Found	6 Bolt of Runecloth, 4 Ghost Dye, 1 Rune Thread
Felcloth Hood	290	Found	5 Bolt of Runecloth, 2 Felcloth, 1 Rune Thread
Wisdom of the Timbermaw	290	Found	8 Bolt of Runecloth, 3 Essence of Earth, 3 Living Essence, 2 Ironweb Spider Silk
Argent Boots	290	Found	6 Bolt of Runecloth, 4 Enchanted Leather, 2 Golden Pearl, 2 Guardian Stone, 2 Ironweb Spider Silk
Runecloth Headband	295	Found	4 Bolt of Runecloth, 2 Ironweb Spider Silk, 1 Rune Thread
Gordok Ogre Suit	N/A	Special	2 Bolt of Runecloth, 4 Rugged Leather, 1 Ogre Tannin, 1 Rune Thread
Mooncloth Bag	300	Found	4 Bolt of Runecloth, 1 Mooncloth, 1 Rune Thread
Wizardweave Robe	300	Found	8 Bolt of Runecloth, 2 Dream Dust, 1 Rune Thread
Mooncloth Vest	300	Found	6 Bolt of Runecloth, 4 Mooncloth, 1 Rune Thread
Mooncloth Shoulders	300	Found	5 Bolt of Runecloth, 5 Mooncloth, 1 Rune Thread
Runecloth Shoulders	300	Found	7 Bolt of Runecloth, 2 Ironweb Spider Silk, 4 Rugged Leather, 1 Rune Thread
Wizardweave Turban	300	Found	6 Bolt of Runecloth, 4 Dream Dust, 1 Star Ruby, 1 Rune Thread
Felcloth Robe	300	Found	8 Bolt of Runecloth, 3 Felcloth, 2 Demonic Rune, 2 Rune Thread
Mooncloth Circlet	300	Found	4 Bolt of Runecloth, 6 Mooncloth, 1 Azerothian Diamond, 2 Enchanted Leather, 2 Rune Thread
Felcloth Shoulders	300	Found	7 Bolt of Runecloth, 3 Felcloth, 2 Demonic Rune, 4 Rugged Leather, 2 Rune Thread
Gloves of Spell Mastery	300	Found	10 Bolt of Runecloth, 10 Mooncloth, 10 Ghost Dye, 6 Golden Pearl, 6 Huge Emerald, 8 Enchanted Leather, 2 Rune Thread
Bottomless Bag	300	Found	8 Bolt of Runecloth, 12 Mooncloth, 2 Large Brilliant Shard, 2 Core Leather, 2 Rune Thread
Truefaith Vestments	300	Found	12 Bolt of Runecloth, 10 Mooncloth, 4 Righteous Orb, 4 Golden Pearl, 10 Ghost Dye, 2 Rune Thread
Robe of the Archmage	300	Found	12 Bolt of Runecloth, 10 Essence of Fire, 10 Essence of Air, 10 Essence of Earth, 10 Essence of Water, 2 Rune Thread

Created Item	Skill Lvl	Source	Reagent(s)
Robe of the Void	300	Found	12 Bolt of Runecloth, 20 Demonic Rune, 40 Felcloth, 12 Essence of Fire, 12 Essence of Undeath, 2 Rune Thread
Flarecore Mantle	300	Found	12 Bolt of Runecloth, 4 Fiery Core, 4 Lava Core, 6 Enchanted Leather, 2 Rune Thread
Flarecore Gloves	300	Found	8 Bolt of Runecloth, 6 Fiery Core, 4 Essence of Fire, 2 Enchanted Leather, 2 Rune Thread
Flarecore Wraps	300	Found	6 Mooncloth, 8 Fiery Core, 2 Essence of Fire, 6 Enchanted Leather, 4 Rune Thread
Belt of the Archmage	300	Found	16 Bolt of Runecloth, 10 Ghost Dye, 10 Mooncloth, 12 Essence of Water, 12 Essence of Fire, 6 Large Brilliant Shard, 6 Rune Thread
Felcloth Gloves	300	Found	12 Bolt of Runecloth, 20 Felcloth, 6 Demonic Rune, 8 Essence of Undeath, 2 Rune Thread
Inferno Gloves	300	Found	12 Bolt of Runecloth, 10 Essence of Fire, 2 Star Ruby, 2 Rune Thread
Mooncloth Gloves	300	Found	12 Bolt of Runecloth, 6 Mooncloth, 2 Golden Pearl, 2 Rune Thread
Cloak of Warding	300	Found	12 Bolt of Runecloth, 4 Guardian Stone, 1 Arcanite Bar, 2 Rune Thread
Mooncloth Robe	300	Found	6 Bolt of Runecloth, 4 Mooncloth, 2 Golden Pearl, 2 Rune Thread
Mantle of the Timbermaw	300	Found	5 Mooncloth, 5 Essence of Earth, 5 Living Essence, 2 Ironweb Spider Silk
Argent Shoulders	300	Found	5 Mooncloth, 2 Guardian Stone, 2 Ironweb Spider Silk
Flarecore Robe	300	Found	10 Mooncloth, 2 Fiery Core, 3 Lava Core, 6 Essence of Fire, 4 Ironweb Spider Silk
Flarecore Leggings	300	Found	8 Mooncloth, 5 Fiery Core, 3 Lava Core, 10 Essence of Fire, 4 Ironweb Spider Silk
Bloodvine Boots	300	Found	3 Mooncloth, 3 Bloodvine, 4 Enchanted Leather, 4 Bolt of Runecloth, 4 Ironweb Spider Silk
Bloodvine Leggings	300	Found	4 Mooncloth, 4 Bloodvine, 4 Powerful Mojo, 4 Bolt of Runecloth, 2 Ironweb Spider Silk
Bloodvine Vest	300	Found	3 Mooncloth, 5 Bloodvine, 4 Powerful Mojo, 4 Bolt of Runecloth, 2 Ironweb Spider Silk
Runed Stygian Belt	300	Found	2 Bolt of Runecloth, 6 Dark Rune, 2 Felcloth, 2 Enchanted Leather, 2 Ironweb Spider Silk
Runed Stygian Boots	300	Found	4 Bolt of Runecloth, 6 Dark Rune, 4 Felcloth, 2 Enchanted Leather, 2 Ironweb Spider Silk
Runed Stygian Leggings	300	Found	6 Bolt of Runecloth, 8 Dark Rune, 6 Felcloth, 2 Ironweb Spider Silk

Tailoring

Created Item	Skill Lvl	Source	Reagent(s)
Core Felcloth Bag	300	Found	20 Felcloth, 16 Core Leather, 8 Bloodvine, 4 Essence of Fire, 4 Ironweb Spider Silk
Bolt of Netherweave	300	Trained	6 Netherweave Cloth
Big Bag of Enchantment	300	Found	6 Bolt of Runecloth, 4 Large Brilliant Shard, 4 Enchanted Leather, 4 Ironweb Spider Silk
Satchel of Cenarius	300	Found	6 Bolt of Runecloth, 2 Mooncloth, 1 Black Lotus, 4 Ironweb Spider Silk
Gaea's Embrace	300	Found	1 Bloodvine, 2 Mooncloth, 4 Living Essence, 4 Ironweb Spider Silk
Glacial Cloak	300	Found	5 Frozen Rune, 4 Bolt of Runecloth, 2 Essence of Water, 4 Ironweb Spider Silk
Glacial Gloves	300	Found	5 Frozen Rune, 4 Bolt of Runecloth, 4 Essence of Water, 4 Ironweb Spider Silk
Glacial Vest	300	Found	7 Frozen Rune, 8 Bolt of Runecloth, 6 Essence of Water, 8 Ironweb Spider Silk
Glacial Wrists	300	Found	4 Frozen Rune, 2 Bolt of Runecloth, 2 Essence of Water, 4 Ironweb Spider Silk
Sylvan Crown	300	Found	4 Bolt of Runecloth, 2 Mooncloth, 2 Living Essence, 2 Ironweb Spider Silk
Sylvan Shoulders	300	Found	2 Bolt of Runecloth, 4 Living Essence, 2 Ironweb Spider Silk
Sylvan Vest	300	Found	4 Bolt of Runecloth, 2 Bloodvine, 2 Living Essence, 2 Ironweb Spider Silk
Netherweave Net	300	Trained	3 Netherweave Cloth
Netherweave Bracers	310	Trained	3 Bolt of Netherweave, 1 Rune Thread
Netherweave Belt	310	Trained	3 Bolt of Netherweave, 1 Rune Thread
Netherweave Bag	315	Trained	4 Bolt of Netherweave, 1 Rune Thread
Netherweave Gloves	320	Trained	4 Bolt of Netherweave, 2 Knothide Leather, 1 Rune Thread
Bolt of Imbued Netherweave	325	Found	3 Bolt of Netherweave, 2 Arcane Dust
Netherweave Pants	325	Trained	6 Bolt of Netherweave, 1 Rune Thread
Heavy Netherweave Net	325	Found	6 Netherweave Cloth
Netherweave Boots	335	Trained	6 Bolt of Netherweave, 2 Knothide Leather, 1 Rune Thread
Mystic Spellthread	335	Found	1 Rune Thread, 5 Primal Mana
Silver Spellthread	335	Found	1 Rune Thread, 5 Primal Life
Imbued Netherweave Bag	340	Found	4 Bolt of Imbued Netherweave, 2 Netherweb Spider Silk, 1 Greater Planar Essence
Netherweave Robe	340	Found	8 Bolt of Netherweave, 2 Rune Thread
Imbued Netherweave Pants	340	Found	5 Bolt of Imbued Netherweave, 2 Netherweb Spider Silk, 1 Rune Thread
Bag of Jewels	340	Found	6 Bolt of Imbued Netherweave, 4 Knothide Leather
Bolt of Soulcloth	345	Found	1 Bolt of Netherweave, 8 Soul Essence
Netherweave Tunic	345	Found	8 Bolt of Netherweave, 2 Rune Thread

Tailoring

Created Item	Skill Lvl	Source	Reagent(s)
Primal Mooncloth	350	Found	1 Bolt of Imbued Netherweave, 1 Primal Life, 1 Primal Water
Imbued Netherweave Boots	350	Found	4 Bolt of Imbued Netherweave, 6 Knothide Leather, 2 Netherweb Spider Silk, 1 Rune Thread
Arcanoweave Bracers	350	Found	6 Bolt of Netherweave, 12 Arcane Dust, 2 Rune Thread
Unyielding Bracers	350	Found	4 Bolt of Imbued Netherweave, 8 Primal Earth
Bracers of Havok	350	Found	4 Bolt of Imbued Netherweave, 4 Primal Earth, 4 Primal Shadow
Blackstrike Bracers	350	Found	4 Bolt of Imbued Netherweave, 8 Primal Fire
Cloak of the Black Void	350	Found	6 Bolt of Imbued Netherweave, 3 Primal Mana, 3 Primal Shadow
Cloak of Eternity	350	Found	6 Bolt of Imbued Netherweave, 6 Primal Earth
White Remedy Cape	350	Found	6 Bolt of Imbued Netherweave, 6 Primal Life
Spellcloth	350	Found	1 Bolt of Imbued Netherweave, 1 Primal Mana, 1 Primal Fire
Shadowcloth	350	Found	1 Bolt of Imbued Netherweave, 1 Primal Shadow, 1 Primal Fire
Cloak of Arcane Evasion	350	Found	4 Bolt of Imbued Netherweave, 3 Primal Mana, 3 Primal Life, 2 Netherweb Spider Silk
Flameheart Bracers	350	Found	5 Bolt of Netherweave, 5 Primal Fire, 2 Rune Thread
Spellfire Belt	355	Found	4 Spellcloth, 10 Primal Fire, 2 Netherweb Spider Silk
Frozen Shadoweave Shoulders	355	Found	4 Shadowcloth, 10 Primal Water, 2 Netherweb Spider Silk
Primal Mooncloth Belt	355	Found	6 Primal Mooncloth, 2 Netherweb Spider Silk
Soulcloth Gloves	355	Found	5 Bolt of Soulcloth, 6 Knothide Leather, 4 Rune Thread
Lifeblood Belt	355	Found	6 Bolt of Netherweave, 4 Knothide Leather, 3 Primal Water, 3 Primal Life, 2 Netherweb Spider Silk
Lifeblood Bracers	355	Found	4 Bolt of Netherweave, 4 Knothide Leather, 2 Primal Water, 2 Primal Life, 2 Netherweb Spider Silk
Lifeblood Leggings	355	Found	10 Bolt of Netherweave, 5 Primal Water, 5 Primal Life, 2 Netherweb Spider Silk
Netherflame Belt	355	Found	6 Bolt of Netherweave, 4 Knothide Leather, 3 Primal Fire, 4 Primal Shadow, 2 Netherweb Spider Silk
Netherflame Boots	355	Found	6 Bolt of Netherweave, 4 Knothide Leather, 2 Primal Fire, 6 Primal Shadow, 2 Netherweb Spider Silk

Tailoring

Created Item	Skill Lvl	Source	Reagent(s)
Netherflame Robe	355	Found	10 Bolt of Netherweave, 5 Primal Fire, 6 Primal Shadow, 2 Netherweb Spider Silk
Imbued Netherweave Robe	360	Found	6 Bolt of Imbued Netherweave, 2 Netherweb Spider Silk, 1 Rune Thread
Imbued Netherweave Tunic	360	Found	6 Bolt of Imbued Netherweave, 2 Netherweb Spider Silk, 1 Rune Thread
Arcanoweave Boots	360	Found	8 Bolt of Netherweave, 16 Arcane Dust, 2 Rune Thread
Flameheart Gloves	360	Found	7 Bolt of Netherweave, 7 Primal Fire, 2 Rune Thread
Spellfire Gloves	365	Found	8 Spellcloth, 12 Primal Fire, 4 Netherweb Spider Silk
Frozen Shadoweave Boots	365	Found	8 Shadowcloth, 12 Primal Water, 2 Netherweb Spider Silk
Primal Mooncloth Shoulders	365	Found	12 Primal Mooncloth, 2 Netherweb Spider Silk
Soulcloth Shoulders	365	Found	6 Bolt of Soulcloth, 4 Rune Thread
Unyielding Girdle	365	Found	8 Primal Mooncloth, 16 Primal Earth, 1 Primal Nether
Girdle of Ruination	365	Found	10 Shadowcloth, 16 Primal Fire, 1 Primal Nether
Black Belt of Knowledge	365	Found	6 Bolt of Imbued Netherweave, 14 Primal Mana, 1 Primal Nether
Resolute Cape	365	Found	10 Primal Mooncloth, 12 Primal Earth, 1 Primal Nether
Vengeance Wrap	365	Found	10 Shadowcloth, 14 Primal Air, 1 Primal Nether
Manaweave Cloak	365	Found	10 Spellcloth, 12 Primal Mana, 1 Primal Nether
Arcanoweave Robe	370	Found	12 Bolt of Netherweave, 20 Arcane Dust, 2 Rune Thread
Flameheart Vest	370	Found	9 Bolt of Netherweave, 9 Primal Fire, 2 Rune Thread
Spellfire Vest	375	Found	14 Spellcloth, 16 Primal Fire, 4 Netherweb Spider Silk
Spellfire Bag	375	Found	6 Spellcloth, 4 Greater Planar Essence, 4 Netherweb Spider Silk
Frozen Shadoweave Vest	375	Found	14 Shadowcloth, 16 Primal Water, 4 Netherweb Spider Silk
Ebon Shadowbag	375	Found	6 Shadowcloth, 4 Netherweb Spider Silk
Primal Mooncloth Robe	375	Found	20 Primal Mooncloth, 10 Primal Mana, 4 Netherweb Spider Silk
Primal Mooncloth Bag	375	Found	8 Primal Mooncloth, 4 Netherweb Spider Silk
Soulcloth Vest	375	Found	8 Bolt of Soulcloth, 4 Rune Thread
Runic Spellthread	375	Found	1 Rune Thread, 10 Primal Mana, 1 Primal Nether
Golden Spellthread	375	Found	1 Rune Thread, 10 Primal Life, 1 Primal Nether
Whitemend Pants	375	Found	10 Primal Mooncloth, 5 Primal Might, 1 Primal Nether
Spellstrike Pants	375	Found	10 Spellcloth, 5 Primal Might, 1 Primal Nether
Battlecast Pants	375	Found	12 Bolt of Imbued Netherweave, 8 Primal Might, 1 Primal Nether
Whitemend Hood	375	Found	10 Primal Mooncloth, 5 Primal Might, 1 Primal Nether
Spellstrike Hood	375	Found	10 Spellcloth, 5 Primal Might, 1 Primal Nether
Battlecast Hood	375	Found	12 Bolt of Imbued Netherweave, 8 Primal Might, 1 Primal Nether
Belt of Blasting	375	Found	5 Nether Vortex, 4 Bolt of Imbued Netherweave, 2 Primal Fire, 2 Rune Thread
Boots of Blasting	375	Found	2 Primal Nether, 4 Shadowcloth, 4 Spellcloth, 2 Rune Thread
Belt of the Long Road	375	Found	5 Nether Vortex, 4 Bolt of Imbued Netherweave, 2 Primal Life, 2 Rune Thread
Boots of the Long Road	375	Found	2 Primal Nether, 4 Primal Mooncloth, 4 Spellcloth, 2 Rune Thread

STALKING NEW PREY

With new levels to gain and new areas to explore, you can expect there to be new foes to conquer as well. There are not only a huge number of new opponents, but there are entire races in Outland that have never before been seen in the WoW universe. Everything looks better than ever.

ARAKKOA

PRIMARY LOCATIONS:
Hellfire Peninsula, Terokkar Forest, Shattrath City, Blade's Edge Mountains

TAMABLE:
No

The bird-like Skettis are found in several areas of Outland. It may seem at first like all of them are hostile and cruel; many of them are. However, they are pocket groups of these creatures that have renounced combat for the time and are seeking shelter in Shattrath City. Be wary of those you find out in the field, as they are most certainly not of that variety.

Arakkoa like to live both on the ground and higher up in the trees. They are able to create settlements with a fair degree of skill, and they are not shy about patrolling to keep these areas clear of vermin. In Terokkar Forest, home to many different groups of Arakkoa, friendly Arakkoa blessed by the Naaru are interested in fending off the hostile intentions of their former brethren.

Level	Name	Hit Points	Armor	Spells/Abilities
62-63	Shienor Talonite	5341-5527	4304-4599	Dual Wield
62-63	Shienor Sorcerer	3739-3870	2188-2338	Enveloping Winds, Lightning Bolt, Arakkoa Blast, Power of Kran'aish
62-63	Shienor Wing Guard	5341-5527	4304-4599	Shield Bash
63-64	Skithian Dreadhawk	5527-5715	4599-4894	Arakkoa Blast, Wing Clip, Throw
63-64	Skithian Windripper	3870-4002	2338-2489	Windfury, Regrowth, Arakkoa Blast, Power of Kran'aish
63-64	Shalassi Talonguard	5527-5715	4599-4894	Pierce Armor
64-65	Shalassi Oracle	4002-4140	2489-2639	Arakkoa Blast, Lightning Cloud, Chain Lightning, Shock, Power of Kran'aish
65-66	Lashh'an Talonite	5914-6116	5189-5484	Summon Lashh'an Kaliri, Backstab
65-66	Lashh'an Wing Guard	5914-6116	5189-5484	Debilitating Strike
65-66	Lashh'an Windwalker	4554-4709	2639-2789	Lightning Bolt, Lightning Shield
65-66	Vekh'nir Keeneye	5914-6116	5189-5484	Gushing Wound
65-66	Vekh'nir Stormcaller	4731-4892	4178-4416	Lightning Tether, Hurricane
65-66	Vekh'nir Dreadhawk	4731-4892	4178-4416	Heal, Whirlwind
66-67	Ruuan'ok Cloudgazer	4709-4872	2789-2939	Lightning Bolt, Lightning Shield
66-67	Ruuan'ok Skyfury	6116-6326	5484-5780	Lightning Fury
66	Lashh'an Matriarch	6360	4416	Shadow Bolt, Impending Doom, Shadow Mend
66	Vekh'nir Matriarch	6360	4416	Shadow Bolt, Impending Doom, Shadow Mend
67-68	Grishna Falconwing	4428-4579	5780-6075	Throw Scalable
67-68	Grishna Harbinger	4872-5038	2939-3089	Lightning Bolt
67-68	Grishna Scorncrow	6326-6542	5780-6075	Gushing Wound
67	Dark Conclave Talonite	6326	5780	
67	Ruuan'ok Matriarch	6578	4653	Shadow Bolt, Impending Doom, Shadow Mend
67-68	Dark Conclave Shadowmancer	4429-4580	2939-3089	Shadow Bolt, Fear, Dark Mending
68	Dark Conclave Ravenguard	6542	6075	Piercing Howl

The images used herein are concept drawings and in no way suggest final appearance.

Broken (The Broken)

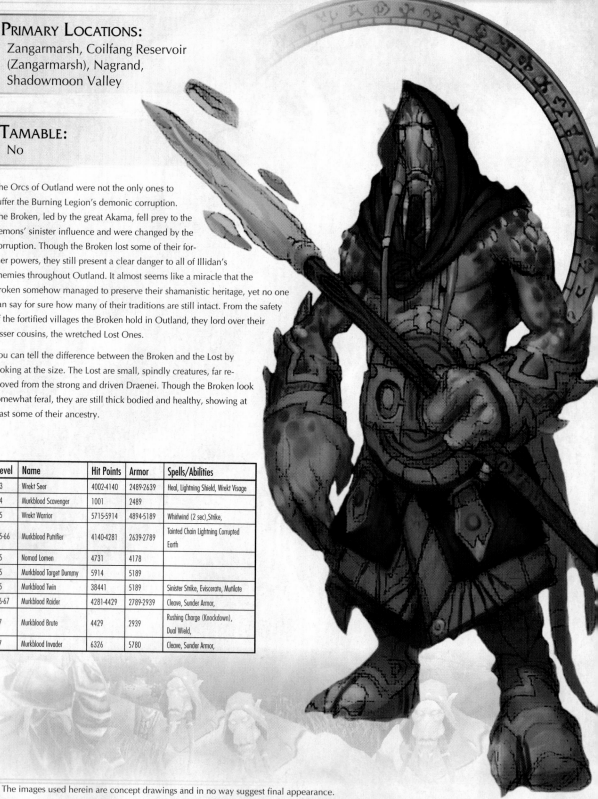

Primary Locations:
Zangarmarsh, Coilfang Reservoir (Zangarmarsh), Nagrand, Shadowmoon Valley

Tamable:
No

The Orcs of Outland were not the only ones to suffer the Burning Legion's demonic corruption. The Broken, led by the great Akama, fell prey to the demons' sinister influence and were changed by the corruption. Though the Broken lost some of their former powers, they still present a clear danger to all of Illidan's enemies throughout Outland. It almost seems like a miracle that the Broken somehow managed to preserve their shamanistic heritage, yet no one can say for sure how many of their traditions are still intact. From the safety of the fortified villages the Broken hold in Outland, they lord over their lesser cousins, the wretched Lost Ones.

You can tell the difference between the Broken and the Lost by looking at the size. The Lost are small, spindly creatures, far removed from the strong and driven Draenei. Though the Broken look somewhat feral, they are still thick bodied and healthy, showing at least some of their ancestry.

Level	Name	Hit Points	Armor	Spells/Abilities
63	Wrekt Seer	4002-4140	2489-2639	Heal, Lightning Shield, Wrekt Visage
64	Murkblood Scavenger	1001	2489	
65	Wrekt Warrior	5715-5914	4894-5189	Whirlwind (2 sec), Strike,
65-66	Murkblood Putrifier	4140-4281	2639-2789	Tainted Chain Lightning Corrupted Earth
65	Nomad Lomen	4731	4178	
65	Murkblood Target Dummy	5914	5189	
65	Murkblood Twin	38441	5189	Sinister Strike, Eviscerate, Mutilate
66-67	Murkblood Raider	4281-4429	2789-2939	Cleave, Sunder Armor,
67	Murkblood Brute	4429	2939	Rushing Charge (Knockdown), Dual Wield,
67	Murkblood Invader	6326	5780	Cleave, Sunder Armor,

The images used herein are concept drawings and in no way suggest final appearance.

Many Demons of the Burning Legion are present in Outland. These evil foes attack settlements directly, but they also construct horrible Fel Cannons, Fel Reavers, and other cruel devices. To disrupt their efforts, adventurers from both factions must do their best to attack the Burning Legion wherever it is found.

There are several new types of Demons in this mix. Siege weapons, machines, various engineers, taskmasters, and so forth are all present. Only in the rarest cases will any of these things be allies in any remote sense; commonly, they are to be killed on sight (and you can expect the same treatment from them if you let your guard down).

The Aldor faction of Shattrath City has the greatest hatred of the Burning Legion. Many of the Demons drop Insignias that can be turned in for Reputation with the Aldor. Use this to your advantage if you wish to court these brave Draenei.

PRIMARY LOCATIONS:

Hellfire Peninsula, Nagrand, Netherstorm, Shadowmoon Valley, Blade's Edge Mountains

TAMABLE:

No

Level	Name	Hit Points	Armor	Spells/Abilities
58	Netherhound	1276	2706	Mana Burn Scalable
58-59	Wrathguard	3191-3313	2706-2749	Flame Wave, Dual Wield
58-59	Fel Handler	3191-3314	3361-3414	Mortal Strike, Cleave, Weapon Chain
62-63	Wrathguard Defender	4274-4422	3465-3703	Flame Wave, Uppercut
69-70	Deathwhisperer	33805-34930	6370-6665	Thrash, Flurry, Mind Flay
70	Dread Tactician	27945	5366	Sleep (20 sec), Carrion Swarm, Inferno
70	Fel Soldier	90818	6665	Cleave, Fel Fire, Cutdown
70	Infernal Siegebreaker	48902	6665	Immolation
71	Wrath Master	143620	6960	

PRIMARY LOCATIONS:
Hellfire Peninsula,
Blade's Edge Mountains

TAMABLE:
No

These worm-like creatures are seen in areas of Outland that have loose soil that allow these burrowing creatures to hide themselves from danger. Then, when prey is close by and ready to pounce upon, they take their opportunity to strike. You know when one of them is near because of the breaking trail of earth that moves about.

Bursters cannot be attacked until they have emerged, thus ruining things like charge or early spellcasting. Then, even during the fight, these worms retreat into the earth and pop up behind your character. Be ready for this by either turning around and moving in (if you are a melee class), or by simply turning and preparing to cast (if you are a ranged class).

Level	Name	Hit Points	Armor	Spells/Abilities
59-60	Crust Buster	4142-4979	3414-3714	Poison Spit, Bore
59-60	Marauding Crust Buster	4142-4979	3414-3714	Crust Borer Inhale, Poison
66-67	Greater Crust Buster	18348-18978	5484-5780	Poison Spit, Bore

Dragonhawks are very rare indeed, and they are most often seen in Eversong Woods, home of the Blood Elves. Beautiful creatures, Dragonhawks are sought after by Hunters from around the world, even though their stats rarely outshine those of more savage beasts.

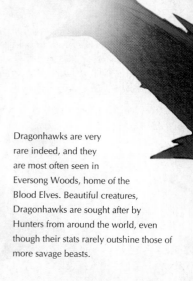

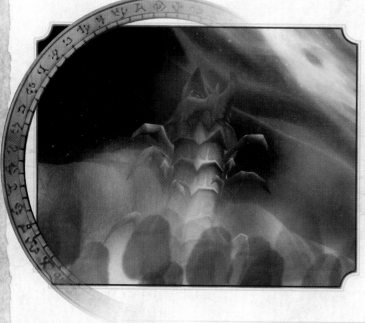

DRAGONHAWKS

PRIMARY LOCATIONS:
Eversong Woods, Tempest Keep
(Netherstorm), Shadowmoon Valley

TAMABLE:
Yes

Level	Name	Hit Points	Armor	Spells/Abilities
5-6	Feral Dragonhawk Hatchling	98-115	83-127	Feather Burst
7-8	Crazed Dragonhawk	131-148	182-244	Feather Burst
67-68	Dragonhawk Protector	6326-6542	5780-6075	
67-68	Eclipsion Dragonhawk	6326-6542	5780-6075	Fire Breath
68-69	Unstable Dragonhawk	6542-6761	6075-6370	
69-69	Bloodfalcon	13522-13522	6370-6370	Swoop, Bloodburn

Elekks are hunted for their great tusks and for the thrill of engaging such powerful creatures. Seen heavily in Nagrand, Elekks are used as mounts by the Draenei and the Kurenai. If you thought that most cavalry was tough to face, imagine a lance of these bearing down on your position!

Elekks take a great deal of damage before collapsing, though they aren't an extremely high DPS foe to defeat. The best place to hunt Elekks in Outland is in southwestern Nagrand, where Wild Elekks are seen in moderate numbers. When trying to befriend the Consortium, this is a wise task because the Wild Elekk drop tusks that the Consortium is interested in acquiring.

PRIMARY LOCATIONS:
Azuremyst Isle, Bloodmyst Isle, Nagrand, Blade's Edge Mountains

TAMABLE:
No

Level	Name	Hit Points	Armor	Spells/Abilities
60-61	Eredar Fel-Lord	4979-5158	3714-4009	
68	Eredar Highlord	31398	4891	Cripple, Dominate Mind, Inferno
68-69	Eredar Tactician	6542-6761	6075-6370	
68-69	Legionlord	6542-6761	6075-6370	
70	Eredar Soul-Eater	33534	5366	Soul Steal, Entropic Aura, Soul Chill
70	Eredar Deathbringer	33534	5366	Unholy Aura, Forceful Cleave, Diminish Soul

TAMABLE:
No

The Eredar are one of the oldest known races in the universe. They comprise the commanders and strategists of the Burning Legion. Exceptionally skilled in magic, their mastery of the arcane arts is renowned throughout the scattered worlds of the Great Dark Beyond. The likes of Archimonde and Kil'jaeden, feared and loathed for their unmatched cruelty and cunning, are among the more infamous members of the Eredar race, the vanguard of an unstoppable, demonic army bent on universal annihilation.

It is rare to face actual Eredar in combat, as they send their minions to do most of the dirty work.

Ethereals

Tamable:
No

Treading the chaotic spaces between worlds, the Ethereals are astral travelers who dwell within the Twisting Nether. They are known to be collectors and traders of arcane items and artifacts. Now drawn to Outland, many Ethereals are seeking to track down treasures and steal them back into the Twisting Nether. They are liars and scoundrels who stop at nothing to pursue their mysterious aims. The Ethereals have no care at all for the Burning Crusade. They would even play both sides of the conflict against each other if doing so would serve to further their own goals.

Members of the Consortium ask you to stop rogue Ethereals all the time. You start to face them in Nagrand, then deal with even more sinister missions in Netherstorm. Elite Ethereals, surrounded by troops armed with some of the finest weapons of the Nether, are camping in that part of Outland and wait for anyone to step against them.

Be ready for Ethereals to use their multi-dimensional abilities against you. Moving oddly through the air, as if they are only part there, these foes sometimes have the ability to Blink, resist damage in various ways, or call strange weapons to aid them in combat. Luckily, they aren't high in Health most of the time, and burst DPS can take care of their threats without too much risk.

Level	Name	Hit Points	Armor	Spells/Abilities
64-65	Ethereal Plunderer	5715-5914	4894-5189	Arcane Missiles, Force Blast, Der'izu Focus
64-65	Ethereal Nethermancer	5715-5914	4894-5189	Backstab, Warp, Dual Wield
64-65	Ethereal Arcanist	5715-5914	4894-5189	Shadow Bolt, Drain Life
65-66	Vir'aani Raider	4731-4892	4178-4416	Gouge, Sinister Strike, Eviscerate, Dual Wield
66-67	Vir'aani Arcanist	4281-4429	2789-2939	Blink, Arcane Bolt, Arcane Explosion, Vir'aani Concentration
67-68	Razaani Raider	6326-6542	5780-6075	Dual Wield, Warp, Energy Flare
67-68	Razaani Nexus Stalker	5060-5233	4653-4891	Arcane Explosion, Intangible Presence
67-68	Razaani Spell-Thief	5060-5233	4653-4891	Energy Surge
68-69	Etherium Assassin	6542-6761	6075-6370	Dual Wield, Backstab, Kick, Warp
68-69	Etherium Shocktrooper	6542-6761	6075-6370	Dual Wield, Glaive, Hamstring, Taunt
69-70	Etherium Researcher	5409-5589	5129-5366	Dual Wield, Energy Charge, Lightning Bolt, Energy Surge
69-70	Etherium Disruptor	6761-6986	6370-6665	Dual Wield, Glaive, Hamstring, Taunt
69-70	Etherium Archon	6761-6986	6370-6665	Dual Wield, Energy Flux, Intangible Presence
69-70	Etherium Overlord	6761-6986	6370-6665	Dual Wield, Battle Shout, Charge, Enchanted Weapons
69-70	Etherium Mace	6761-6986	6370-6665	Dual Wield
70	Etherium Nexus-Stalker	6986	6665	Dual Wield, Shadowsurge
70	Etherium Gladiator	13972	6665	Mortal Strike, Hamstring, Cleave

FEL ORCS

PRIMARY LOCATIONS:
Hellfire Peninsula, Terokkar Forest,
Nagrand, Blade's Edge Mountains

TAMABLE:
Hardly

Mystery and speculation surround the corrupted Fel Orcs who recently appeared in Outland. Though little is known about these savage warriors, the most disturbing revelation to come to light is that their numbers appear to be steadily increasing. Even more perplexing is the fact that the Orcs have discovered some alternate source of Fel energies to feed upon, despite the slaying of Mannoroth and the Horde's subsequent release from demonic corruption. Regardless of their connection to Fel energies, however, it is believed that this new breed is not working with the Burning Legion. What authority they do answer to remains a mystery.

Level	Name	Hit Points	Armor	Spells/Abilities
58-59	Bonechewer Mutant	3989-4142	3361-3414	Bonechewer Bite
58-59	Bonechewer Raider	3989-4142	3361-3414	Throw Net (5 sec), Ghost Visual
58-59	Bonechewer Evoker	2792-2899	1708-1735	Fireball, Immolation
60	Bleeding Hollow Worg	2490	3714	
60	Bleeding Hollow Skeleton	996	3714	
60	Bleeding Hollow Riding Worg	2490	3714	
60-61	Bleeding Hollow Warlock	3984-4126	2990-3228	Incinerate, Curse of Exhaustion
60-61	Bleeding Hollow Dark Shaman	3984-4126	2990-3228	Raise Soul, Shadow Bolt, Lightning Shield, Bloodlust, Fire Nova Totem
60-61	Bonechewer Cannibal	4979-5158	3714-4009	Bloodthirst, Dual Wield, Bonechewer Bite
60-61	Bleeding Hollow Vizier	3984-4126	2990-3228	Shadow Bolt, Death Coil, Shadow Nova
60-61	Bleeding Hollow Necrolyte	3484-3611	1888-2038	Fireball, Summon Skeletons, Raise Dead, Curse of the Bleeding Hollow
60-61	Bleeding Hollow Tormentor	3984-4126	2990-3228	Mend Friend
61	Shattered Hand Grenadier	5158	4009	Throw Dynamite
61-62	Bleeding Hollow Shadowcaster	4126-4274	3228-3465	Shadow Bolt, Death Coil, Shadow Nova
61-62	Shattered Hand Berserker	5158-5341	4009-4304	Dual Wield, Charge
61-62	Hellfire Lieutenant	5158-5341	4009-4304	
61-62	Laughing Skull Berserker	5158-5341	4009-4304	Cleave, Mortal Strike
61-62	Shattered Hand Mage	3611-3739	2038-2188	Fireball, Frost Nova
61-62	Shattered Hand Guard	5158-5341	4009-4304	Strike, Counterstrike
61-62	Shattered Hand Acolyte	4126-4274	3228-3465	Heal, Mind Flay, Power Word: Fortitude
62-63	Shattered Hand Grunt	5341-5527	4304-4599	Strike, Kick
62-63	Shattered Hand Captain	5341-5527	4304-4599	Cleave, Mortal Strike
62-63	Shattered Hand Neophyte	4274-4422	3465-3703	Renew, Shadow Word: Pain, Bloodlust
62-63	Shattered Hand Warlock	4113-4257	2188-2338	Shadow Bolt, Immolate, Demon Armor

The greatest concentration of Fel Orcs is in the area of Hellfire Citadel. There, divisions of the vicious Orcs are led by intelligent commanders who keep them busy with training and patrols. It is said that within Hellfire Citadel are several dungeons of the most powerful Fel Orcs, and what they are building, guarding, or using there is still unknown. What strange cries reverberate from beneath the fortress, and are they friend or foe?

Fleshbeasts

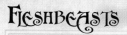

PRIMARY LOCATIONS:
Netherstorm, Karazhan

TAMABLE:
No

It is said that the sleep of reason produces monsters; that fantasy abandoned by sanity brings forth creatures of nightmare. For most, the horrors of their sleeping hours cannot follow them into the waking world; yet some are haunted by them even long after the veils of sleep have parted. The mindless Fleshbeasts were brought into this world by Medivh, summoned from some unspeakable place beyond. Once, the wizard used the Fleshbeasts in his clandestine experiments within the laboratories of Karazhan. Medivh is gone, but the slavering, hungering creatures of his twisted nightmares still remain, forever stalking the gloomy shadows of Karazhan.

A mine in eastern Netherstorm has become infested with Fleshbeasts as well. Consortium representatives are still baffled by this, and they nearly lost two of their soldiers while doing reconnaissance there; one of the agents is missing in action currently, though he is thought to be alive.

Level	Name	Hit Points	Armor	Spells/Abilities
1-2	Volatile Mutation	42-55	0	
61-65	Subservient Flesh Beast	5158-5914	4009-5189	Shadowform
67	Fiendling Flesh Beast	6326	5780	Rapid Pummel
67-68	Mutant Horror	6326-6542	5780-6075	Mutated Blood
69	Parasitic Fleshbeast	6761	6370	Rend, Parasite

Level	Name	Hit Points	Armor	Spells/Abilities
69	Parasitic Fleshling	676	6370	
69-70	Fleshfiend	6761-6986	6370-6665	Rapid Pummel
70	Mutated Fleshfiend	6986	6665	Dual Wield, Glaive, Hamstring, Taunt
72	Fleshbeast	73800	7255	Thrash, Gaping Maw, Infectious Poison
72	Greater Fleshbeast	118080	7255	Thrash, Gaping Maw, Infectious Poison

The images used herein are concept drawings and in no way suggest final appearance.

Floating Eye

PRIMARY LOCATIONS:
Blood Furnace (Hellfire Peninsula), Netherstorm, Auchenai Crypts

TAMABLE:
No

Floating Eyes are only seen in specific locations, and that is probably a good thing; many adventurers are struck with fear at the sight of such odd and malevolent beings. One of the bosses inside the Blood Furnace, a wing of Hellfire Citadel, is said to be such a being. Other than that, only a few lesser Eyes have been located in Netherstorm. Whatever created these abominations is still unknown.

Level	Name	Hit Points	Armor	Spells/Abilities
69	Floating Eye	5409	5129	Tongue Lash, Mind Flay
69-70	Eye of Culuthas	5409-5589	5129-5366	Tongue Lash, Focused Bursts
70	Death Watcher	41916	6665	Tentacle Cleave, Drain Life
70	Entropic Eye	33534	5366	Chaos Breath, Tentacle Cleave

PRIMARY LOCATIONS:
Eversong Woods, Ghostlands

TAMABLE:
No

Long before the rise and fall of humanity's kingdoms, the Amani Trolls of Lordaeron had built an enormous Troll empire. After centuries of war and hate, an alliance of elves and humans finally dealt a crushing blow to the Amani when they defeated a great Troll army at the foot of the Alterac Mountains. The empire did not recover from the defeat, and the Trolls never rose as one nation again. Yet some Forest Trolls survived, each generation nurturing their hatred of the elves in the dark forests of the north for thousands of years.

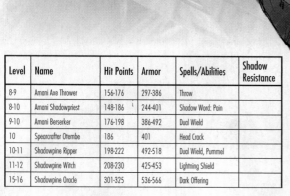

Level	Name	Hit Points	Armor	Spells/Abilities	Shadow Resistance
8-9	Amani Axe Thrower	156-176	297-386	Throw	
8-10	Amani Shadowpriest	148-186	244-401	Shadow Word: Pain	
9-10	Amani Berserker	176-198	386-492	Dual Wield	
10	Spearcrafter Otembe	186	401	Head Crack	
10-11	Shadowpine Ripper	198-222	492-518	Dual Wield, Pummel	
11-12	Shadowpine Witch	208-230	425-453	Lightning Shield	
15-16	Shadowpine Oracle	301-325	536-566	Dark Offering	

Level	Name	Hit Points	Armor	Spells/Abilities	Shadow Resistance
16-17	Mummified Headhunter	356-386	688-722		40
17-18	Shadowpine Headhunter	386-417	722-755	Throw	
17-19	Shadowpine Hexxer	350-404	594-651	Hex (Chicken, 3 sec.), Dispel Magic	
18-19	Shadowpine Catlord	377-404	620-651	Bloodlust (10 sec), Summon Ghostclaw Lynx	

The images used herein are concept drawings and in no way suggest final appearance.

Fungal Giants

PRIMARY LOCATIONS:
Zangarmarsh, Coilfang Reservoir
(Zangarmarsh)

TAMABLE:
No

Level	Name	Hit Points	Armor	Spells/Abilities
61-62	Withered Giant	5158-5341	4009-4304	Osmosis, Absorb Vitality
61-62	Marsh Lurker	4126-4274	3228-3465	Wild Regeneration
61-62	Marsh Dredger	4126-4274	3228-3465	Strangling Roots
61-62	Lagoon Walker	5158-5341	4009-4304	Wild Regeneration, Moss Covered Feet
63-64	Starving Fungal Giant	5527-5715	4599-4894	Choking Vines, War Stomp, Consume
63-64	Fungal Giant	5527-5715	4599-4894	Fungal Decay, Boglord Bash, Unstable Mushroom
64	Bog Lord	5715	4894	Fungal Decay, Boglord Bash, Unstable Mushroom
64	Starving Bog Lord	5715	4894	Choking Vines, War Stomp, Consume

The unique gases and nutrient-enriched soil of Zangarmarsh have given rise to a wondrous, diverse wetland ecology. The marsh's Fungal Giants stand as a prime example of the habitat's remarkable fauna. These lumbering behemoths are savagely efficient at dispatching their adversaries when provoked, though their low perception and only moderate speed prevent them from going after travelers with any frequency. Fungal Giants feed on other native swamp creatures as well as any Lost Ones unlucky enough to stray too close to the Giants' beloved hideaways.

The friendly creatures of Sporeggar are natural enemies of the Fungal Giants. In southwestern Zangarmarsh there is a constant feud between the two sides, and you can raise your Reputation with the Sporeggar considerably by slaying many of the Giants.

Be careful to avoid any fungus that is dropped by the Giants during combat. The reports of exploding fungal blooms are worrisome, but the Hunters involved stated that they were able to pull the Giants away from their deadly mushrooms before they detonated.

Giant Moths

Gronn

PRIMARY LOCATIONS:
Terokkar Forest, Blade's Edge Mountain

TAMABLE:
No

Giant Moths are usually peaceful, unless there is a major irritant in the area to provoke them. Though large in size, some of these Moths are kept safe more by their ability to emit some type of chemical that pacifies aggressors. Even under direct attack, enemies of the Moths are unable to strike for a modest time while these chemicals are emitted. During such occurrences, it is best to use non-damaging abilities to heal, avoid damage, or otherwise retreat from direct fighting until the effect wears off.

Level	Name	Hit Points	Armor	Spells/Abilities
1	Vale Moth	42	0	
9-11	Blue Flutterer	176-222	386-518	Rake, Screech
14-16	Royal Blue Flutterer	345-409	619-688	Rake, Screech
62-63	Vicious Teromoth	5341-5527	4304-4599	Dazzling Dust, Wing Buffet
62-63	Teromoth	5341-5527	4304-4599	Pacifying Dust
63-64	Royal Teromoth	5527-5715	4599-4894	Pacifying Dust, Wing Buffet
66-67	Grand Silkwing	6116-6326	5484-5780	

PRIMARY LOCATIONS:
Nagrand, Blade's Edge Mountains, Gruul's Lair (Blade's Edge Mountains)

TAMABLE:
There Isn't a Net Big Enough

Monstrous. Terror incarnate. Words cannot begin to describe the terrible Gronn of Outland, the immortal demigods of the Ogre race. Some say the Gronn gave rise to the lesser Ogres, yet if so, the Gronn show little love for their offspring, lording over the Ogre clans with an iron fist. There are said to be only seven Gronn in all of existence. Nonetheless, such rumors are cold comfort in light of the undeniable fact that the Gronn wield devastating power.

Two of the known Gronn are in Nagrand. One of these is powerful but still is likely to be felled by a smart assault for two or three heroes. The other, nicknamed The Hungerer, is an amazingly potent foe; many think that it would take five of the finest champions of Nagrand to stop such a monstrosity.

Farther north, in the Blade's Edge Mountains, more Gronn have been seen. Legends tell of a lair in that area where the greatest of these Gronn may be located. Whether this is true or not has yet to be confirmed…

Eversong Woods, Ghostlands, Terokkar Forest, Blade's Edge Mountains, Netherstorm

Tamable:

No

Level	Name	Hit Points	Armor	Spells/Abilities
1	Springpaw Cub	42	0	
2-3	Springpaw Lynx	55-71	0-25	
6-7	Springpaw Stalker	120-137	156-221	
8-9	Elder Springpaw	156-176	297-386	
9-10	Springpaw Matriarch	194-218	386-492	
9-10	Starving Ghostclaw	176-198	386-492	
13-14	Ghostclaw Lynx	273-300	585-619	
16-17	Ghostclaw Ravager	356-386	688-722	Exploit Weakness
65-66	Grovestalker Lynx	5914-6116	5189-5484	
68-69	Darkmaw Cub	6542-6761	6075-6370	
68-69	Ripfang Lynx	6542-6761	6075-6370	Swipe

Lynxes are a new species of cats that have not been seen in quite some time. They exist in both Azeroth and Outland, but have been at the periphery.

They are consistently aggressive creatures, except in very unusual cases. Being territorial, they have a wide range of attack, so it is best to keep away from them while you are mounted and trying to pass through an area quickly.

Mana Wyrm

Primary Locations:

Eversong Woods, Zangarmarsh, Netherstorm

Tamable:

No

Level	Name	Hit Points	Armor	Spells/Abilities
1	Mana Wyrm	41	0	Faerie Fire
9-10	Mana Serpent	166-186	318-401	Faerie Fire
67-68	Phase Hunter	6326-6542	5780-6075	Phase Slip, Mana Burn
67-68	Mana Snapper	6326-6542	5780-6075	Phase Slip, Mana Burn
67-68	Mana Invader	5060-5233	4653-4891	

With Mana Wyrms, there can be no doubt at all that they are drawn to Mana-rich areas. Found in Blood Elven territory and in sections of Outland that are heavy in Mana, these flying beasts are eager to drink from whatever source of power they find.

NAARU

PRIMARY LOCATIONS:
Shattrath City

TAMABLE:
No

When Sargeras descended on the Eredar's homeworld, a race of sentient energy beings (the Naaru) helped some Eredar escape the corruption. Soon the Eredar refugees began calling themselves the Draenei, or "exiled ones." Moved by the Draenei's courage, the Naaru blessed them with Light-given knowledge and power. Ultimately, the benevolent Naaru hoped to unite all who opposed the Burning Legion and forge these heroes into a single unstoppable army of the Light.

In pursuit of that goal, the Naaru have recently traveled to Outland in a dimensional fortress known as Tempest Keep. Most of the Naaru disembarked to reconnoiter the ravaged land. In their absence, an army of Blood Elves led by Prince Kael'thas Sunstrider overran the keep and took its sole remaining guardian hostage. With Tempest Keep in Blood Elf hands, the Naaru find themselves stranded in Outland, facing a precarious future.

Anyone meeting the Naaru in Shattrath City will find that they are a benevolent race, clearly interested in helping those in need. These are not blind crusaders, struck on a path of violence. Indeed, whether man or woman, Human or Orc, you will be accepted and encouraged by the Naaru.

Disturbing scouting reports from Nagrand state that one of the Naaru may be captured there as well. The demons in Oshu'gun have displayed strange behavior, and the rituals performed in that place draw spirits from far and wide.

Level	Name	Hit Points	Armor	Spells/Abilities
66-67	Lesser Nether Drake	6116-6326	5484-5780	Intangible Presence
67	Adolescent Nether Drake	6326	5780	
67	Mature Nether Drake	6326	5780	
68-69	Nether Drake	6542-6761	6075-6370	Intangible Presence (Ethereal)
69	Netherwing Drake	6761	6370	Rapid Pummel
69	Mature Netherwing Drake	6761	6370	Intangible Presence (Ethereal), Netherbreath
69	Enslaved Netherdrake	6761	6370	

PRIMARY LOCATIONS:
Blade's Edge Mountains, Netherstorm, Shadowmoon Valley

TAMABLE:
No

It is said that Nether Drakes can be broken of their aggressive tendencies and trained to become Flying Mounts. Though likely true, those who meet the Drakes will soon understand that only the bravest or luckiest explorers earn this right! Nether Drakes are naturally aggressive and are quite capable of defending themselves.

Nether Rays

PRIMARY LOCATIONS:
Zangarmarsh, Netherstorm

TAMABLE:
Yes

Nether Rays are a flying species of predator that are often hunted by settlements that wish to keep the region safe. Left to their own devices, these attackers are quick to aggro on anything that passes through their territory. Moving slowly through the air, it is possible to mistake a Nether Ray for a Spore Bat if you aren't looking closely at the shape of the creature, and that mistake might mean getting knocked off of your mount by passing too close to such a foe.

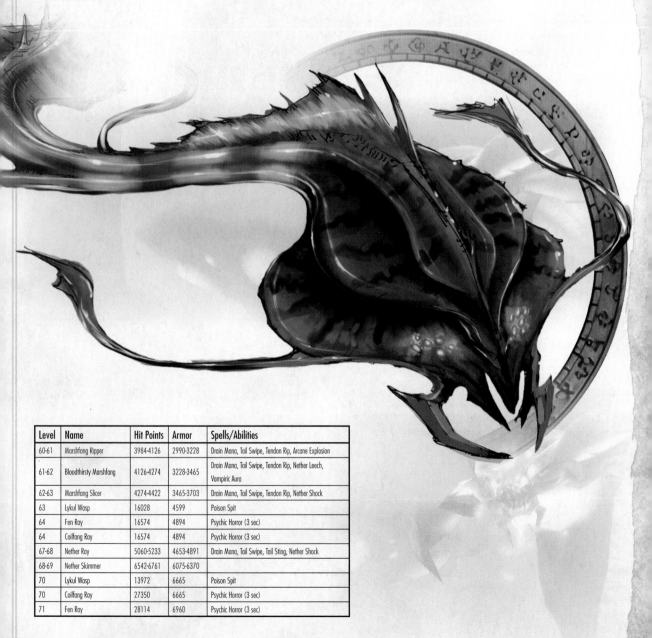

Level	Name	Hit Points	Armor	Spells/Abilities
60-61	Marshfang Ripper	3984-4126	2990-3228	Drain Mana, Tail Swipe, Tendon Rip, Arcane Explosion
61-62	Bloodthirsty Marshfang	4126-4274	3228-3465	Drain Mana, Tail Swipe, Tendon Rip, Nether Leech, Vampiric Aura
62-63	Marshfang Slicer	4274-4422	3465-3703	Drain Mana, Tail Swipe, Tendon Rip, Nether Shock
63	Lykul Wasp	16028	4599	Poison Spit
64	Fen Ray	16574	4894	Psychic Horror (3 sec)
64	Coilfang Ray	16574	4894	Psychic Horror (3 sec)
67-68	Nether Ray	5060-5233	4653-4891	Drain Mana, Tail Swipe, Tail Sting, Nether Shock
68-69	Nether Skimmer	6542-6761	6075-6370	
70	Lykul Wasp	13972	6665	Poison Spit
70	Coilfang Ray	27350	6665	Psychic Horror (3 sec)
71	Fen Ray	28114	6960	Psychic Horror (3 sec)

Ogre Lords

Primary Locations:
Nagrand, Blade's Edge Mountains

Tamable:
No

The Ogre Lords of Outland are the only Ogres known to retain some of the physical traits of their Gronn progenitors, such as the bony, calcified protrusions on their head and back, as well as a portion of the Gronn's immense size and strength. Other unique characteristics possessed by the Ogre Lords are their intelligence and reasoning abilities, which are more acute than those of their Ogre cousins. This combination of brute strength and increased intellect make the Ogre Lords worthy of both respect and fear.

For better and for worse, you won't see many of the Ogre Lords, even in Outland. It is rumored that one of the Lords leads some of the Ogres in northwestern Nagrand, perhaps ruling from the top of the rocky caves there. Perhaps there are even more in Blade's Edge Mountains, where the Ogres are some of the fiercest and strongest in either Azeroth or Outland!

Ravagers

PRIMARY LOCATIONS:
Azuremyst Isle, Bloodmyst Isle, Hellfire Peninsula, Blade's Edge Mountains

TAMABLE:
Yes

These predatory beasts are found all across Outland, often lurking behind rocky clusters and towering escarpments, waiting to pounce on any prey foolhardy enough to wander within striking range of their blindingly fast, razor-sharp claws. Whether or not these creatures were mutated by the volatile energies unleashed when Ner'zhul's multiple portals ripped Outland apart is still a source of speculation. One thing, however, is for certain: these vicious carnivores are not to be trifled with. Interestingly, Ravagers are also found in Azeroth (accidentally brought here by the Draenei). Azuremyst and Bloodmyst Isles both have these alien foes.

Ravagers attack directly and go for the throat. Though rarely gifted with named leaders or Elite forms, Ravagers get their respect through sheer tenacity; they also like to group pretty closely together, making areas with Ravagers very dangerous!

Level	Name	Hit Points	Armor	Spells/Abilities
7-8	Ravager Hatchling	137-156	221-297	
8-9	Ravager Ambusher	156-176	297-386	
9-10	Ravager Specimen	176-198	386-492	Rend
10	Death Ravager	495	492	Enraging Bite, Intimidating Shout, Rend
13-14	Bloodmyst Ravager	273-300	585-619	Ravage
16-17	Enraged Ravager	356-386	688-722	Ravage
59-60	Razorfang Hatchling	4142-4979	3414-3714	Ravage
61	Razorfang Ravager	5158	4009	Ravage
61-62	Quillfang Skitterer	5158-5341	4009-4304	Ravage, Corrosive Mist
62-63	Quillfang Ravager	5341-5527	4304-4599	Ravage, Corrosive Mist
62-63	Thornfang Ravager	5341-5527	4304-4599	Ravage, Thorns
62-63	Thornfang Venomspitter	5341-5527	4304-4599	Ravage, Venom Spit, Thorns

PRIMARY LOCATIONS:

Blade's Edge Mountains, Netherstorm, Hellfire Peninsula

TAMABLE:

No

Rock flayers are one of Outland's indigenous species. Many careless wanderers have been killed by the primitive humanoids who roam the slopes and peaks of the Blade's Edge Mountains in murderous packs. Though they primarily hunt smaller mountain animals, they are not afraid of stalking potential prey that is much bigger than they are. There are accounts of packs of rock flayers taking down even mighty Elekk that had wandered into the Rock Flayers' territory. Their vicious blade scythes and climbing claws are so sharp they can even cut through sheer rock, enabling the rock flayers to climb the most difficult overhangs with ease. Even for a predatory species, they are extremely fast and very aggressive.

Rock Flayers are an awful target for experience grinding. High Health, considerable damage potential, and decent special abilities keep these from being even remotely soft targets. However, the Flayers look so cool that it's fun to fight them occasionally whether it is productive or not. The model is quite awesome to watch in battle, and it feels somewhat thrilling just to trash one even when they are non-Elite.

Level	Name	Hit Points	Armor	Spells/Abilities
60-61	Stonescythe Whelp	4979-5158	3714-4009	
60-61	Stonescythe Flayer	4979-5158	3714-4009	Flay, Rend, Charge, Rock Shell
60-61	Stonescythe Ripper	4979-5158	3714-4009	Rip, Tear Armor

Level	Name	Hit Points	Armor	Spells/Abilities
61	Stonescythe Ambusher	5158	4009	Flay, Cheap Shot, Sneak
61-62	Stonescythe Alpha	5158-5341	4009-4304	Flay, Tear Armor
68-69	Shaleskin Ripper	6542-6761	6075-6370	Rip, Shaleskin

The images used herein are concept drawings and in no way suggest final appearance.

Sporelings are the nicer residents of Zangarmarsh; these indigenous people are a fungal race that try to carve out a niche for themselves between the vicious Naga and Fungal Giants of the region. Living off of Glowcaps and hard work, they stay moderately safe.

Sporelings are often in need of assistance, despite their best efforts! If you want to help them, kill off many of the Fungal Giants in the southwest, then collect Glowcaps to turn in to the Sporelings as payments for their Reputation rewards.

TAMABLE:
No, But They Like You

Level	Name	Hit Points	Armor	Spells/Abilities
60	Sporeggar Spawn	4979	3714	Sporeskin, Rend, Salvation
60	Sporeling Refugee	3662	3714	
63	Sporeggar Betrayer	5527	4599	
63-64	Sporeggar Preserver	4422-4572	3703-3941	Sporeskin, Healing Touch, Faerie Fire
63-64	Sporeggar Harvester	5527-5715	4599-4894	Sporeskin, Rend

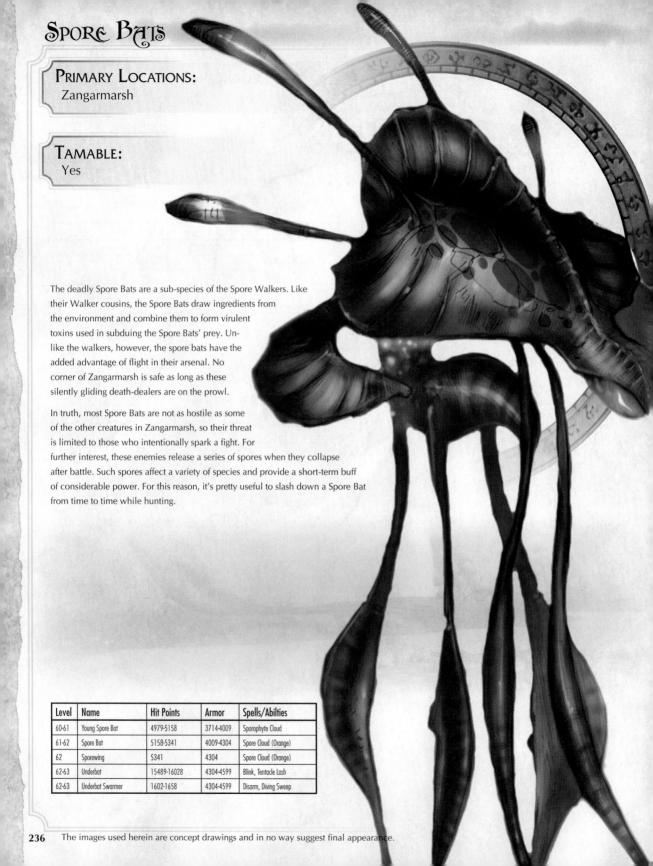

SPORE BATS

PRIMARY LOCATIONS:
Zangarmarsh

TAMABLE:
Yes

The deadly Spore Bats are a sub-species of the Spore Walkers. Like their Walker cousins, the Spore Bats draw ingredients from the environment and combine them to form virulent toxins used in subduing the Spore Bats' prey. Unlike the walkers, however, the spore bats have the added advantage of flight in their arsenal. No corner of Zangarmarsh is safe as long as these silently gliding death-dealers are on the prowl.

In truth, most Spore Bats are not as hostile as some of the other creatures in Zangarmarsh, so their threat is limited to those who intentionally spark a fight. For further interest, these enemies release a series of spores when they collapse after battle. Such spores affect a variety of species and provide a short-term buff of considerable power. For this reason, it's pretty useful to slash down a Spore Bat from time to time while hunting.

Level	Name	Hit Points	Armor	Spells/Abilties
60-61	Young Spore Bat	4979-5158	3714-4009	Sporophyte Cloud
61-62	Spore Bat	5158-5341	4009-4304	Spore Cloud (Orange)
62	Sporewing	5341	4304	Spore Cloud (Orange)
62-63	Underbat	15489-16028	4304-4599	Blink, Tentacle Lash
62-63	Underbat Swarmer	1602-1658	4304-4599	Disarm, Diving Sweep

TAMABLE:
No

It is believed that the Spore Walkers evolved over time from the simple organisms that dwell within the depths of Zangarmarsh into the more efficient hunting, killing, and eating machines that they are today. Utilizing their environment, the Spore Walkers are able to derive toxins from the spores and fungi of the marsh, which they in turn use to stun or immobilize their prey. When traveling through the marsh, adventurers would be wise to steer clear of these highly accomplished predators.

Though majestic to gaze upon, Spore Walkers can be quite a pain to fight. Many of these monsters have channeling abilities that are nasty if you let them get away with the spell. Health or Mana draining is certainly on the menu here, and anything that your character can do to disrupt those activities is worth the effort.

Level	Name	Hit Points	Armor	Spells/Abilities
61	Boglash	15474	4009	Corruption Cloud, Forked Lightning Tether, Thrash
61-62	Fen Strider	5158-5341	4009-4304	Lightning Tether, Thrash
63-64	Marsh Walker	5527-5715	4599-4894	Lightning Tether, Thrash

TALBUKS

PRIMARY LOCATIONS:
Nagrand, Netherstorm

TAMABLE:
No

You might not expect the Talbuks to be aggressive creatures, as they greatly resemble the types of prey animals that many see out in the Barrens and other such areas. However, there are indeed some stronger and more aggressive varieties of these beasts in Outland. Some are passive, but the males of the species are often wary and willing to fight at a moment's notice.

Many Talbuks have a Knockback ability, making it fairly dangerous to fight them near the edges of sudden drops. Keep your back to a wall or open space when engaging these beasts. Don't let their size fool you either; Talbuks can do damage with fair speed if you let them, so it is better to hurry and out-DPS them before this becomes a problem.

Talbuks are used as Mounts by some of the Nagrand factions. Reach Exalted with them to be able to purchase these Epic-speed Mounts.

Level	Name	Hit Points	Armor	Spells/Abilities
64	Injured Talbuk	3715	4894	
64-65	Talbuk Stag	5715-5914	4894-5189	Gore
65-66	Talbuk Thorngrazer	5914-6116	5189-5484	Gore, Talbuk Strike
66-67	Talbuk Patriarch	6116-6326	5484-5780	Gore, Talbuk Strike
68-69	Talbuk Doe	6542-6761	6075-6370	Gore
68-69	Talbuk Sire	6542-6761	6075-6370	Hoof Stomp

WARP STALKERS

PRIMARY LOCATIONS:
Terokkar Forest, Netherstorm

TAMABLE:
Yes

Warp Stalkers are crafty, predatory hunters indigenous to Draenor that have been corrupted by the Burning Legion. Some reports even suggest that Legion officers employ the stalkers as mounts, utilizing the creatures' uncanny abilities to phase in and out of the physical and astral dimensions at will. Unbound by the constraints of physical reality, these powerful, mystical creatures often range far and wide, so that almost no realm is out of reach.

Warp Stalkers are the bane of travelers, for they possess keen senses. Don't expect to move near a Warp Stalker without catching their attention and aggression. Because some of the Warp Stalkers have the ability of Sprint and port about as well, it isn't easy to pass them even on a good mount.

Level	Name	Hit Points	Armor	Spells/Abilities
63-64	Warp Stalker	4422-4572	3703-3941	Phasing Invisibility (30 sec Pulse), Slow, Warp, Phase Burst
64-65	Warp Hunter	5715-5914	4894-5189	Phasing Invisibility (30 sec Pulse), Swipe, Warp, Phase Burst
67-68	Warp Beast	6326-6542	5780-6075	
67-68	Warp Chaser	6326-6542	5780-6075	Phasing Invisibility (30 sec Pulse), Warp Charge, Warp, Venomous Bite
68-69	Ravening Snap Dragon	6542-6761	6075-6370	
68-69	Greater Snap Dragon	6542-6761	6075-6370	

The images used herein are concept drawings and in no way suggest final appearance.

There are many new skins for the models that you have already seen in WoW. The new starting areas, dungeons, and outdoor zones of Outland are filled with creatures that look slightly different in color or style than they did before.

What adds to this greatly is that the use of equipment has been enabled for quite a few monster types. It is really exciting to see Voidwalkers that are draped in old, rotting cloth, or to face Ogres with a variety of armor types, or marvel at the wooly cousins of Kodo of Nagrand. This improvement is a great visual step.

BATTLE CHEST

Updated through patch 2.0.12

ISBN: 0-7440-0860-3

Printing Code: The rightmost double-digit number is the year of the book's printing; the rightmost single-digit number is the number of the book's printing. For example, 07-1 shows that the first printing of the book occurred in 2007.

14 13 12 11 10 09   16 15 14 13

Manufactured in the United States of America.

BRADYGAMES STAFF

Publisher
David Waybright

Editor-In-Chief
H. Leigh Davis

Creative Director
Robin Lasek

Licensing Manager
Mike Degler

CREDITS

Development Editors
Brian Shotton
Ken Schmidt
& the entire editorial staff

Screenshot Editor
Michael Owen

Lead Designer
Brent Gann

Layout Designer
Areva

Cover Artist
Glenn Rane

BLIZZARD ACKNOWLEDGEMENTS

Creative Development Manager
Shawn Carnes

Director of Global Licensing
Cory Jones

Producer
Gloria Soto

Licensing Manager
Brian Hsieh

Art Approvals
Joanna Cleland-Jolly

QA Approvals
Meghan Dawson, Drew Dobernecker, Joseph Magdalena, Andrew Rowe, Shawn Su, Rodney Tsing, Don Vu

Development Team Support
Luis Barriga, J. Allen Brack, Alexander Brazie, Tom Chilton, Jeff Kaplan, Jonathan LeCraft

Blizzard Special Thanks
Ben "But the minis…" Brode, Shane Cargilo, Tim Daniels, Mei Francis, Evelyn Fredericksen, Michael Gilmartin, Carlos Guerrero, John Hsieh, Chris Metzen, Glenn Rane